The Family of
KING GEORGE III

RINCESS CHARLOTTE SOPHIA
of Mecklenburg-Strelitz
1744-1818

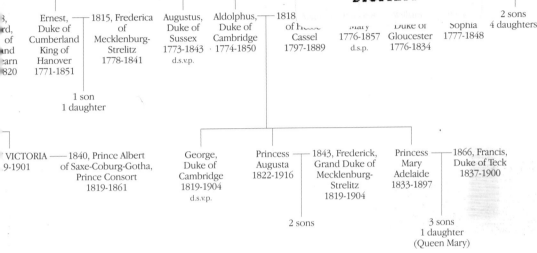

3, rd, of nd earn 820

Ernest, Duke of Cumberland King of Hanover 1771-1851 — 1815, Frederica of Mecklenburg-Strelitz 1778-1841

1 son
1 daughter

Augustus, Duke of Sussex 1773-1843 d.s.v.p.

Aldolphus, Duke of Cambridge 1774-1850 — 1818, ... of Hesse Cassel 1797-1889

Mary 1776-1857 d.s.p.

... Duke of Gloucester 1776-1834

Sophia 1777-1848

2 sons
4 daughters

VICTORIA 9-1901 — 1840, Prince Albert of Saxe-Coburg-Gotha, Prince Consort 1819-1861

George, Duke of Cambridge 1819-1904 d.s.v.p.

Princess Augusta 1822-1916 — 1843, Frederick, Grand Duke of Mecklenburg-Strelitz 1819-1904

2 sons

Princess Mary Adelaide 1833-1897 — 1866, Francis, Duke of Teck 1837-1900

3 sons
1 daughter
(Queen Mary)

The Family of
SAXE-COBURG-SAALFELD

GUSTA REUSS
orf
31

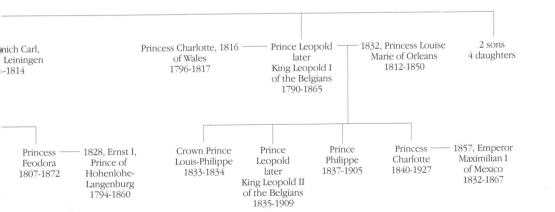

nich Carl, Leiningen -1814

Princess Charlotte, of Wales 1796-1817 — 1816 — Prince Leopold later King Leopold I of the Belgians 1790-1865 — 1832, Princess Louise Marie of Orleans 1812-1850

2 sons
4 daughters

Princess Feodora 1807-1872 — 1828, Ernst I, Prince of Hohenlohe-Langenburg 1794-1860

Crown Prince Louis-Philippe 1833-1834

Prince Leopold later King Leopold II of the Belgians 1835-1909

Prince Philippe 1837-1905

Princess Charlotte 1840-1927 — 1857, Emperor Maximilian I of Mexico 1832-1867

A Royal Christmas

JEREMY ARCHER

First published 2012 by Elliott and Thompson Limited
27 John Street, London WC1N 2BX
www.eandtbooks.com

ISBN: 978-1-908739-22-3

The author and publisher would like to thank all those who have generously given permission to reproduce images in this book. The majority of the photographs are taken from private collections, with the following exceptions:

- The Prince and Princess of Wales with their children at Sandringham, 1871 © Sandringham House
- Queen Victoria's New Year's gift 1900 and Princess Mary's Christmas gift 1914 © the Keep Military Museum

The three jacket images are reproduced by kind permission of the Royal Collection Trust/ © Her Majesty Queen Elizabeth II 2012:

- Queen Victoria's Christmas Tree, 1850 by William Corden the Younger, after James Roberts (front cover)
- King George V delivers the first Christmas broadcast, 1932 (back cover, right)
- Queen Elizabeth II delivers her first Christmas broadcast, 1952 (back cover, left)

9 8 7 6 5 4 3 2 1

A CIP catalogue record for this book is available from the British Library.

Printed and bound in the UK by TJ International

Typeset by Marie Doherty
Jacket designed by Antigone Konstantinidou

Acknowledgements

Through the good offices of Sir Tom Shebbeare, Director, The Prince's Charities, I was very fortunate to be granted privileged access to The Royal Archives. Pamela Clark, Registrar, and Jill Kelsey, Assistant Registrar, soon identified a wealth of hitherto-unused original material, answered my questions and recharged my research trolley. David Ryan, Director of Records, The Royal Household, offered me a great deal of helpful advice, while Leslie Ferrar, Treasurer to Their Royal Highnesses The Prince of Wales and The Duchess of Cornwall, and Nicola Brentnall, Project Director, The Prince's Charities, both assisted me with procedural matters. Meanwhile, Karen Lawson of The Picture Library, The Royal Collection, guided my search for illustrative material.

Beyond The Royal Archives, I am extremely grateful to Celia, Lady Webb-Carter for introducing me to her father, Lord Wigram; to Lord Wigram himself for sharing his experiences of Christmas at Sandringham in 1926 with me; to the distinguished Royal biographers, Hugo Vickers and Sarah Bradford, for their advice and guidance; to Michael Hunter, English Heritage Curator at Osborne House, for sharing his own research with me; to Lord Fellowes and Marcus O'Lone, the Agent at Sandringham, for their helpful suggestions; to Francis Fulford for lending me his father's war-time diaries from Windsor Castle; to Adrian Woodhouse, Archivist at Renishaw Hall, for identifying a number of relevant items in the Sitwell Papers; and to Chip Stidolph, Charlotte Zeepvat, Sophie Dupré and Ian Shapiro for kindly digging deep into their own private collections on my behalf.

In terms of the finished product, I would like to thank my old friend, Ashe Windham, for checking the typescript; Chey Palacios for carrying out the initial proof-reading exercise; Russell Harris for allowing me to borrow so many books from his library; and Christina Murray of The Castle of Mey Trust for sharing her own publishing experiences.

A Royal Christmas would never have been brought to fruition without the support of the team from Elliott & Thompson: chairman Lorne Forsyth; publisher Olivia Bays; reader Carol Anderson; designers Antigone Konstantinidou and Marie Doherty; and publicist Alison Menzies. Once again, I must thank my agent, Roger Field, without whom it is most unlikely that I would ever have been a published author.

It was always my wish to use *A Royal Christmas* – in Diamond Jubilee Year – to raise funds for charity. To that end I would like to thank Major-General Evelyn Webb-Carter, Major-General Martin Rutledge, Sean Bonnington, Rowena Finch and Elizabeth Crawford of ABF The Soldiers' Charity, who have supported the book, thereby raising money for the ABF.

Last – but not least – I would like to thank my ever-tolerant wife, Amanda, for permitting me to write five books in as many years, stealing time from the family in the process.

Contents

Introduction

As well as describing the many and varied ways in which the Royal Family has celebrated Christmas through the ages, *A Royal Christmas* explores the influence that they have had on the way in which Christmas is celebrated today in Great Britain and the Commonwealth.

Since the evolution of Royal Christmases mirrored the changes that were taking place in the Royal Family – and the country – I felt that it was necessary to provide a measure of historical background, not only to the Royal Family, but also to contemporary developments and the prevailing mood that inevitably influenced their Christmas celebrations. The cast of characters is a long and very varied one, with family nicknames often disguising those who appear in diaries and journals. I have done my best to open such doors, without endless repetition.

On the basis that descriptions of chronologically-arranged Christmases might become rather dull, the subject matter has therefore been broken down into a series of themed chapters, some of which are inevitably rather longer than others. An attraction of this approach is that *A Royal Christmas* can be read in 'bite-sized' portions. My intention was always to produce a Christmas pudding that enfolds as many silver threepenny pieces as I could unearth.

What comes over most strongly from Queen Victoria's Journals is the importance of family: the joys they shared, the trials they endured and the carefully-selected gifts that Victoria and Albert exchanged. While the thread of *A Royal Christmas* is that of a family celebrating Christmas, tragedy is a common bed-fellow, particularly in earlier times, when oppressively cold and damp weather was so much more difficult to avoid, while medical treatment was far more primitive than it is today. On 26 April 1948, in his Royal Silver Wedding sermon in St. Paul's Cathedral, the Archbishop of Canterbury said: 'The Royal Family has borne with all other families its own share of domestic griefs and burdens.'[1] In the interests of a rather broader narrative, I have therefore extended my 'catchment area' to the whole of December and a month after Christmas Day.

[1] Hugo Vickers, *Elizabeth The Queen Mother*, London: Arrow Books, 2006, p. 272.

Conflict is seldom very far away, even during the Victorian period, despite the general perception that the Empire was at peace. During the twentieth century, of course, two world wars had a severely dampening effect on Christmas celebrations. It is worth remembering that, during wartime, King George V felt that 'his most useful function . . . was not to inflict upon Ministers or commanders his own views of policy or strategy, but, with constant vigilance, to "advise, to encourage and to warn"'.[2] His second son was of like mind.

While researching at the Royal Archives, in the Round Tower at Windsor Castle, I had the enormous privilege of being allowed to handle, read and transcribe original diaries, journals, letters, cards and manuscripts written by members of the Royal Family and the Royal Household. I had the strongest sensation, when holding Queen Victoria's first hand-written journal or King George V's final diary, that I was cradling history in my hands.

[2] Harold Nicolson, *King George the Fifth: His Life and Reign*, London: Constable & Co., 1952, pp. 255–6.

Medieval and Tudor Christmases

Although Christmas had been widely celebrated before the Norman invasion of these islands, 'the Anglo-Norman kings introduced increased splendour at this festival, as they did on all other occasions; the king wearing his crown and robes of state, and the prelates and nobles attending, with great pomp and ceremony, to partake of the feast provided by their monarch, and to receive from him presents, as marks of his royal favour; returning, probably, more than an equivalent'.[1] The cynic might suggest that this was merely a subtle way for the sovereign to bestow favour, while accepting homage from his loyal servants, under the guise of a religious festival.

Having triumphed at the Battle of Hastings on 14 October that year, King William I, the Conqueror, was crowned in Westminster Abbey on Christmas Day 1066. The occasion was recorded in verse in 'The Kentishmen with Long Tayles', also known as 'the Kentish Ballad', sung 'to the tune of Rogero':[2]

> When as the Duke of Normandie,
> with glistring Speare and Shield,
> Had entred into faire England,
> and told his foes in fielde;
> On Christmas day in solemne sort,
> then was he crowned heere
> By Albert Archbishop of Yorke,
> with many a noble Peere.

It was a memorable occasion, during which his knights, who had cordoned off the Abbey precincts, overreacted to the loud acclamations of 'Vivat Rex'. The Norman chronicler, Orderic Vitalis, explained:

> The armed guard outside, hearing the tumult of the joyful crowd in the church and the harsh accents of a foreign tongue, imagined that some

[1] William Sandys, *Christmastide, its History, Festivities and Carols, with their Music*, London: John Russell Smith, 1852, p. 23.

[2] Thomas Deloney, *Strange Histories or, Songs and Sonnets, of Kinges, Princes, Dukes, Lords, Ladyes, Knights, and Gentlemen*, London: R. B. for William Barley, 1612, p. 3.

> treachery was afoot, and rashly set fire to some of the buildings. The fire spread rapidly from house to house; the crowd who had been rejoicing in the church took fright and throngs of men and women of every rank and condition rushed out of the church in frantic haste. Only the bishops and a few clergy and monks remained, terrified, in the sanctuary, and with difficulty completed the consecration of the king who was trembling from head to foot. Almost all the rest made for the scene of the conflagration, some to fight the flames and many others hoping to find loot for themselves in the general confusion. The English, after hearing of the perpetration of such misdeeds, never again trusted the Normans who seemed to have betrayed them, but nursed their anger and bided their time to take revenge. So King William received the crown and reigned well and justly in prosperity and adversity for twenty years, eight months, and sixteen days.[3]

Nevertheless, the festive traditions continued down the generations, with boar's head assuming prominence at the Christmas feast. William Sandys, the music writer and antiquary, wrote: 'At the coronation feast of Henry the Sixth there were boars' heads in "castellys of golde and enamel." By Henry the Eighth's time it had become an established Christmas dish, and we find it ushered in at this season to his daughter the Princess Mary, with all the usual ceremonies, and no doubt to the table of the monarch himself, who was not likely to dispense with so royal a dish; and so to the time of Queen Elizabeth, and the revels in the Inns of Court in her time, when at the Inner Temple a fair and large boar's head was served on a silver platter, with minstrelsy.'[4] The procession accompanying the boar's head sang an ancient carol:[5]

> The Boar's Head in hand bring I
> With garlands gay and rosemary,
> I pray you all sing merrily.

As the world became more stable and the Royal Family more established on the throne, there was a noticeable acceleration in the scale of the celebrations during the festive season, particularly during the reign of King Henry VIII: 'Henry the Eighth kept up the festivities of Christmas with the

[3] Marjorie Chibnall, ed. and trans., *The Ecclesiastical History of Orderic Vitalis*, Vol. II, Oxford: Clarendon Press, 1968, p. 185.
[4] Sandys, *Christmastide, its History, Festivities and Carols*, p. 31.
[5] Elizabeth Craig, *Court Favourites*, London: Andre Deutsch, 1953, p. 154.

same jovial spirit with which he promoted every other species of hilarity. It was his custom to keep his Christmas at his different country palaces in the vicinity of London, sometimes at Eltham, at Greenwich, or Richmond; and afterwards at Hampton Court, when that stately edifice came into his possession.'[6] Katherine Thomson provided greater detail of the revelries that took place in 1510:

> On the night of the Epiphany, a pageant was introduced into the hall at Richmond, representing a hill studded with gold and precious stones; and having on its summit a tree of gold, from which hung roses and pomegranates. From the declivity of the hill descended a lady richly attired, who, with the gentlemen, or, as they were then called, children, of honour, danced a morris before the king.
>
> On another occasion, in the presence of the court, an artificial forest was drawn in by a lion and an antelope, the hides of which were richly embroidered with golden ornaments; the animals were harnessed with chains of gold, and on each sat a fair damsel in gay apparel. In the midst of the forest, which was thus introduced, appeared a gilded tower, at the gates of which stood a youth, holding in his hands a garland of roses, as the prize of valour in a tournament which succeeded the pageant.[7]

William Sandys wrote that King Henry VIII kept Christmas 'with great splendour'. He then explained that

> Queen Elizabeth, who, to powerful intellect, joined much of the arbitrary temper of her father, possessed also great vanity and fondness of display. In her time, therefore, the festivities were renewed with great pomp and show; and theatrical entertainments were also particularly encouraged, and were frequently performed before the queen, especially at Christmas time. To restrain somewhat the great expenses of these entertainments, she directed, in her second year, estimates to be made of them previously; but this wholesome practice, judging from the cost of after years, did not exist very long.
>
> In 1559, which may be called her first Christmas, the play before her, on Christmas Night, unluckily contained some offensive or indecent matter,

[6] Katherine Thomson, *Memoirs of the Court of Henry the Eighth*, London: Longman & Co., 1826, Vol. I, p. 176.

[7] Ibid., pp. 60–1.

> as the players were commanded to leave off, and the mask came in dancing. On the Twelfth Night following there was a play, and then a goodly mask, and afterwards a great banquet . . . The play performed on Twelfth Night, 1571, was called *Narcissus*, in which a live fox was let loose and chased by dogs; so that the introduction of live animals on the stage is not a modern invention.[8]

In 1600–01 Queen Elizabeth commissioned William Shakespeare to write the comedy *Twelfth Night* in order to entertain her guest, Virginio Orsini, Duke of Bracciano. In keeping with the occasion, which used to be a Catholic holiday but which had now become an evening of revelry, the brief was that the production 'shall be best furnished with rich apparel, have greate variety and change of Musicke and daunces, and of a Subject that may be most pleasing to her Maiestie'.

Queen Elizabeth I died at Richmond Palace on 24 March 1603. She was succeeded by King James VI of Scotland, who became King James I of England. He was the son of her old rival, Mary, Queen of Scots. William Sandys described an episode of 'excessive conviviality', which took place

> during the visit of the Danish king, Christian the Fourth, in 1606, when, on one occasion, during the personation of the mask of "Solomon, and the Queen of Sheba" – the King of Denmark being the Solomon of the night – the representative of the Queen of Sheba had imprudently imbibed too much of the nectar that she was to have offered to Solomon, and stumbling, distributed her classic offerings of wine, jelly, and cakes, over his dress. He in his turn, attempting to dance, found it necessary to fall, and cling to the floor, until taken off to bed.
>
> Cassio. *Is your Englishman so exquisite in his drinking?*
>
> Iago. *Why, he drinks you with facility, your Dane dead drunk.*
>
> Some ladies, representing Faith, Hope, Charity, Victory, and Peace, who were assumed to have been the attendants of the Queen of Sheba, on her celebrated visit, sympathised with their mistress, and were obliged, with proper assistance to guide their tottering limbs, to retire for a time in a state of maudlin sensibility.[9]

[8] Sandys, *Christmastide, its History, Festivities and Carols*, pp. 91–5.
[9] Ibid., pp. 102–3.

The iconography – but not the behaviour – re-emerged almost three hundred years later, during the *tableaux vivants* at Osborne House. The aspirations and admirable intentions represented by the attire of the five attendants have guided members of the British Royal Family to the present day.

Christmas and the Commonwealth

King James I died at Theobalds House, Hertfordshire, on 27 March 1625 and was succeeded by King Charles I. For the first fifteen years of King Charles's reign, 'Christmas was frequently observed with great splendour, and a variety of plays, masks, and pageants, in which the king and queen, with some of the courtiers, occasionally took part . . . the king had his mask on Twelfth Day, and the queen hers on the Shrovetide following, and considerable sums were granted for the expenses, often exceeding £2000.'[1]

On 19 December 1644, during the English Civil War, Parliament proclaimed that the last Wednesday of every month should be kept as a day of fasting. Since Christmas fell on the last Wednesday of December that year, there was an appeal to Parliament for clarification on whether the traditional Christmas festivities might take place. The response came in the form of an 'Ordinance for the Better Observation of the Feast of the Nativity of Christ':

> Whereas some doubts have been raised whether the next Fast shall be celebrated, because it falleth on the day which, heretofore, was usually called the Feast of the Nativity of our Saviour; the Lords and Commons do order and ordain that public notice be given, that the Fast appointed to be kept on the last Wednesday in every month, ought to be observed until it be otherwise ordered by both houses; and that this day particularly is to be kept with the more solemn humiliation because it may call to remembrance our sins and the sins of our forefathers, who have turned this Feast, pretending the memory of Christ, into an extreme forgetfulness of him, by giving liberty to carnal and sensual delights; being contrary to the life which Christ himself led here upon earth, and to the spiritual life of Christ in our souls; for the sanctifying and saying whereof Christ was pleased both to take a human life, and to lay it down again.[2]

On 3 June 1647, Parliament formally banned Christmas and many other holidays, laying down a series of punishments for those who ignored the

[1] William Sandys, *Christmastide, its History, Festivities and Carols, with their Music*, London: John Russell Smith, 1852, p. 117.

[2] John Ashton, *A righte Merrie Christmasse!!!*, London: Leadenhall Press Ltd., 1894, p. 26.

ban: 'Instead of them, all scholars, apprentices, and servants should, with leave of their masters, have a holiday on the second Tuesday in every month. On this being proclaimed at Canterbury, just prior to the ensuing Christmas, and the mayor directing a market to be kept on that day, a serious disturbance took place, wherein many were severely hurt.'[3] Five years later, this policy was enshrined in the following statement: 'Resolved by the Parliament: That no observation shall be had of the five and twentieth day of December commonly called Christmas-Day; nor any solemnity used or exercised in churches upon the day in respect thereof.'

The writer, gardener and diarist John Evelyn, who lived at Sayes Court, Deptford, wrote:

> 25th December, 1657. I went to London with my wife, to celebrate Christmas-day, Mr Gunning preaching in Exeter chapel [of Exeter house in the Strand], on *Micah* vii. 2. Sermon ended, as he was giving us the Holy Sacrament, the chapel was surrounded with soldiers, and all the communicants and assembly surprised and kept prisoners by them, some in the house, others carried away. It fell to my share to be confined to a room in the house, where yet I was permitted to dine with the master of it, the Countess of Dorset, Lady Hatton, and some others of quality who invited me. In the afternoon came Colonel Whaley, Goffe, and others, from Whitehall, to examine us one by one; some they committed to the marshal, some to prison.
>
> When I came before them they took my name and abode, examined me why, contrary to the ordinance made, that none should any longer observe the superstitious time of the nativity (so esteemed by them), I durst offend, and particularly be at common prayers, which they told me was but the mass in English, and particularly pray for Charles Stuart, for which we had no Scripture. I told them we did not pray for Charles Stuart, but for all Christian kings, princes, and governors. They replied, in so doing we prayed for the King of Spain too, who was their enemy and a papist, with other frivolous and ensnaring questions and much threatening; and finding no color to detain me, they dismissed me with much pity of my ignorance. These were men of high flight and above ordinances, and spoke spiteful things of our Lord's nativity. As we went up to receive the Sacrament, the miscreants held their muskets against us, as if they would have shot us at

[3] Ibid., pp. 118–19.

> the altar; but yet suffering us to finish the office of Communion, as perhaps not having instructions what to do, in case they found us in that action. So I got home late the next day; blessed be God.[4]

The restoration of King Charles II was proclaimed on 8 May 1660 and Christmas was once again celebrated, in a democratic, if sometimes disappointing, manner, as Samuel Pepys, a close friend of John Evelyn, described in his diary on 24 December 1667:

> Up, and all the morning in the office; and at noon with my clerks to dinner and then to the office again, busy at the office till 6 at night; and then by coach to St. James's, it being now about 6 at night, my design being to see the Ceremonys, this night being the Eve of Christmas, at the Queen's Chapel, But it being not begun, I to Westminster hall and there stayed and walked; and then to the *Swan* and there drank and talked, and did besar a little Frank; and so to Whitehall and sent my coach round, and I through the park to chapel, where I got in almost up to the rail and with a great deal of patience, stayed from 9 at night to 2 in the morning in a very great Crowd; and there expected, but found nothing extraordinary, there being nothing but a high Masse.
>
> The Queen [the Catholic Catherine of Braganza] was there and some ladies. But Lord, what an odd thing it was for me to be in a crowd of people, here a footman, there a beggar, there a fine lady, there a zealous poor papist, and here a Protestant, two or three together, come to see the show. I was afeared of my pocket being picked very much. Their music very good endeed, but their service I confess too frivolous, that there can be no zeal go along with it; and I do find by them themselfs, that they do run over their beads with one hand, and point and play and talk and make signs with the other, in the midst of their Messe. But all things very rich and beautiful. And I see the papists had the wit, most of them, to bring cushions to kneel on; which I wanted, and was mightily troubled to kneel. All being done, and I sorry for my coming, missing of what I expected; which was to have a child borne and dressed there and a great deal of do, but we broke up and nothing like it done; and there I left people receiving the sacrament, and the Queen gone, and ladies; only my [Lady] Castlemayne, who looks prettily in her night-clothes.

[4] William Bray, ed., *The Diary of John Evelyn*, New York and London: M. Walter Dunne, New York & London, 1901, p. 319.

And so took my coach, which waited, and away through Covent garden to set down two gentlemen and a lady, who came thither to see also and did make mighty mirth in their talk of the folly of this religion; and so I stopped, having set them down, and drank some burnt wine at the *Rose* tavern door, while the constables came and two or three Bell-men went by, it being a fine light moonshine morning; and so home round the City and stopped and dropped money at five or six places, which I was the willinger to do, it being Christmas day; and so home and there find wife in bed, and Jane and the maids making pyes, and so I to bed and slept well.[5]

[5] Robert Latham, ed., *The Shorter Pepys*, Berkeley: University of California Press, 1985, pp. 855–6.

Queen Charlotte's Christmas: The Hanoverian Influence

With Queen Anne's death on 1 August 1714, the ruling Stuart line came to an end. Some years earlier, it was recognised that a way had to be found to prevent the Catholic 'Old Pretender', the son of King James II (of England) and VII (of Scotland), from succeeding to the throne and re-establishing Papal supremacy, which had lapsed after King Henry VIII's 'break with Rome' in 1538. Fortunately, Salic law did not apply in Britain; thus female heirs were not excluded from the succession. After Queen Anne's only surviving child, William, Duke of Gloucester, died at the age of eleven on 29 July 1700, the Act of Settlement 1701 determined that the Crown should go to 'the most excellent princess Sophia, electress and duchess-dowager of Hanover and the heirs of her body, being Protestant'. She was the closest living Protestant descendant of her grandfather, King James I.

Princess Sophia died on 8 June 1714, with the result that Queen Anne was succeeded by Sophia's son and her own second cousin, Georg Louis, Elector of Hanover, who ascended the throne as King George I. Charles Abbey and John Overton wrote of the Hanoverian succession that 'England was freed from superstition and tyranny, but it was at the cost of many a noble life and the loss of many a noble sentiment. The success of the Georges delivered the English Church from all danger from the side of Rome, a danger which, humanly speaking, could not have been averted if the Stuart line had been restored.'[1]

The Reverend A. H. Hore wrote:

> Equally undistinguished as his father, both in body and mind, was his son and successor, George II; scarcely more conspicuous for good qualities, and not less addicted to vice; equally with his father a stranger to this country in feelings and taste, speaking its language only a little better . . . and caring only for his money and for Hanover. Of the land of his adoption the second George was wont to speak in language far from complimentary: 'I

[1] Charles J. Abbey and John H. Overton, *The English Church in the Eighteenth Century*, London: Longmans, Green and Co., 1878, pp. 104–5.

> wish with all my heart,' he said to his wife, 'that the Devil may take your Bishops, and the Devil may take your Ministers, and the Devil take the Parliament, and the Devil take the whole Island, providing I can get out of it and go to Hanover.'
>
> No wonder the feeling was reciprocated in England. 'If,' said Lord Chesterfield in the House of Lords, 'we have a mind effectually to prevent the Pretender from ever obtaining the Crown, we should make him Elector of Hanover, for the people of England will never fetch another king from thence.'[2]

Of the religious festivals during the eighteenth century, Abbey and Overton wrote:

> In the Olney Hymns, published 1779, Christmas Day only is referred to among all the Christian seasons. This was somewhat characteristic of the English Church in general during the greater part of the Georgian period. Other Christian seasons were often all but unheeded; Christmas was always kept much as it is now. It may be inferred, from a passage in one of Horsley's Charges, that in some country churches, towards the end of the century, there was no religious observance of the day. But such neglect was altogether exceptional. The custom of carol singing was continued only in a few places, more generally in Yorkshire than elsewhere. There is some mention of it in the 'Vicar of Wakefield;' and one well-known carol, 'Christians, awake! Salute the happy morn!' was produced about the middle of the century by John Byrom.
>
> In George Herbert's time it had been a frequent custom on all great festivals to deck the church with boughs. This usage became almost, if not quite, obsolete except at Christmastide. We most of us remember with what sort of decorative skill the clerk was wont, at this season, to 'stick' the pews and pulpit with sprays of holly. In the time of the 'Spectator' and of Gay, and later still, rosemary was also used, doubtless by old tradition, as referring in its name to the mother of the Lord. Nor was mistletoe excluded. In connection with this plant, Stanley says a curious custom was kept up at York, which in 1754 had not long been discontinued. 'On the eve of Christmas Day they carried mistletoe to the high altar of the cathedral and proclaimed a public universal liberty, pardon, and freedom to all sorts

2 A.H. Hore, *The Church in England from William III to Victoria*, Oxford: Parker and Co., 1886, pp. 275–6.

> of inferior and even wicked people, at the gates of the city, toward the four quarters of heaven.'[3]

On 25 October 1760 Prince George William Frederick, eldest son of the late Frederick, Prince of Wales, succeeded his grandfather as King George III. On 8 September 1761 at the Chapel Royal, St James's Palace, he was married to Charlotte, youngest daughter of Duke Charles Louis Frederick of Mecklenburg-Strelitz, Prince of Mirow. Charlotte Louise Henrietta Albert was born on 2 July 1765, the daughter of Frederick Albert, who 'began life in the service of the reigning Duke of Mecklenburg-Strelitz' and was 'chosen to accompany [Charlotte] to England' in 1761.[4] On 16 January 1783 she was married to Christopher Papendiek, page to the Princess Royal. In her autobiography, she wrote of December 1786: 'Before Christmas the Royal Family removed to town agreeably to their usual custom, but after the New Year's Day drawing-room they returned to Windsor, which they continued to do weekly through the season as before, on account of the pleasure of the hunt to the King. The two elder Princesses, being both now introduced, always accompanied their Majesties.'[5]

At the end of the parliamentary session in the summer of 1788, King George III went to Cheltenham, the furthest that he had ever been from London, in order to recover his strength. That November his health took a dramatic turn for the worse and stories started to circulate in society, including one that he had shaken hands with a tree in the belief that it was the King of Prussia. A more reliable witness is Charlotte Papendiek, who recounted the story of what happened the following month:

> A pitiable and painful event occurred on Christmas Day. The King found out that it was the 25th, and asked why he had not been told that the Archbishop of Canterbury had arrived to administer the sacrament to him. No particular answer was given, when, upon his becoming impatient, his Majesty was reminded that all those things rested with the doctors, as well as others of moment, and that they, the pages, were acting solely upon their orders.

[3] Abbey and Overton, *The English Church in the Eighteenth Century*, pp. 451–2.
[4] Mrs Vernon Delves Broughton, ed., *Court and Private Life in the Time of Queen Charlotte: Being the Journals of Mrs. Papendiek, Assistant Keeper of the Wardrobe and Reader to Her Majesty*, 2 vols., London: Richard Bentley & Son, 1887, Vol. I, p. 42.
[5] Ibid., Vol. I, p. 264.

> The fever ran high, yet the King appeared calm, and tasted his dinner but could not eat. Suddenly, in an instant he got under the sofa, saying that as on that day everything had been denied him, he would there converse with his Saviour, and no one could interrupt them. How touching, and how truly sad! When he was a little calmer, Mr. Papendiek got under to him, having previously given orders to the attendants that the sofa should be lifted straight up from over them. He remained a moment lying with his Majesty, then by pure strength lifted him in his arms and laid him on his couch, where in a short time he fell asleep.[6]

In February 1789 the Regency Bill, which would enable the Prince of Wales to act as Regent in his father's place, was introduced to, and then voted through by, the House of Commons. However, before it could also pass through the House of Lords, the King had recovered. Mrs Papendiek recalled that, 'on March 1 a prayer of thanksgiving for the King's recovery was given to each member of the household by her Majesty, which was also to be read in all the churches of the Metropolis and the suburbs on that day. By the following Sunday, there was not a private family or a church in the whole of England where it had not been offered up. It was truly a heartfelt thanksgiving, shared by all his Majesty's subjects.'[7]

Although the King's recovery was maintained, he was advised to go further afield for his health. During the dramatic summer of 1789, he therefore ventured as far as Weymouth, both in order to bathe in the sea and also to enjoy the other diversions on offer in that sophisticated resort. Mrs Papendiek later wrote that 'the King and Royal Family attended the theatre several times, when Quick and Mrs. Wells performed in comedy admirably, but there were no other actors of any note till Mrs. Siddons, who was staying at Weymouth for her health, was prevailed upon to play "Lady Townly," and afterwards the part of "Mrs. Oakley," as neither the King nor Queen were fond of tragedy. The performance was not equal to her usual acting, as comedy was not her line, though it is needless to add that Mrs. Siddons could do nothing *badly*.'[8]

King George III and Queen Charlotte were a popular and well-respected couple, as Miss Fanny Burney described to her father that summer:

[6] Ibid., Vol. II, p. 21.
[7] Ibid., Vol. II, p. 68.
[8] Ibid., Vol. II, p. 113.

> His Majesty is in delightful health and much improved spirits. All agree he never looked better. The loyalty of this place is excessive: they have dressed out every street with labels of 'God save the King;' all the shops have it over their doors; all the children wear it in their caps, all the labourers in their hats, and all the sailors *in their voices*, for they never approach the house without shouting it aloud, nor see the King, or his shadow, without beginning to huzza, and going on to three cheers.
>
> The bathing machines make it their motto over all their windows; and those bathers that belong to the Royal dippers wear it in bandeaux on their bonnets, to go into the sea; and have it again in large letters round their waists, to encounter the waves. Flannel dresses tucked up, and no shoes nor stockings, with bandeaux and girdles, have a most singular appearance, and when I first surveyed these loyal nymphs it was with some difficulty I kept my features in order. Nor is this all. Think but of the surprise of his Majesty, when, for the first time of his bathing, he had no sooner popped his Royal head under water than a band of music, concealed in a neighbouring machine, struck up 'God save Great George our King'.[9]

In her memoirs, Charlotte Papendiek wrote of the same summer: 'After the time [one month] specified for this stay at Saltram they returned to Weymouth, and then immediately began their homeward journey. On their way back to Windsor they stopped at Longleat, in Wiltshire, the beautiful seat of the Marquis of Bath, and then at Tottenham Park, in Wiltshire, the seat of Lord Ailesbury, whence, after remaining a couple of days to rest, they proceeded direct to Windsor, which was reached about the middle of September – I do not recollect the exact date – after an enjoyable and successful tour.'[10] However brief it might have been, the visit to Tottenham Park established a tradition that has been maintained into modern times.

The Hon. Amelia Matilda Murray, Maid of Honour 1837–53 and Woman of the Bedchamber to Queen Victoria 1853–5, was the daughter of the Rt Hon. and Rt Rev. Lord George Murray, Bishop of St David's 1801–3, whose wife was appointed Lady-in-waiting to King George III's two eldest unmarried daughters, the Princesses Augusta and Elizabeth, in 1808. Sixty years later she published her memoirs, in which she explained that Queen Charlotte told 'anecdotes of her early years': 'The English people did not like me much, because I was not pretty; but the King was fond of driving a

9 Ibid., Vol. II, pp. 114–15.
10 Ibid., Vol. II, p. 116.

phaeton in those days, and once he overturned me in a turnip-field, and that fall broke my nose. I think I was not quite so ugly after dat [sic].'[11]

For Christmas 1789, 'Mr. Papendiek proposed an illuminated tree, according to the German fashion, but the Blagroves being at home for their fortnight, and the party at Mrs. Roach's for the holidays, I objected to it. Our eldest girl, Charlotte, being only six the 30th of this November, I thought our children too young to be amused at so much expense and trouble. Mr. Papendiek was vexed – yet I hope and trust the children were made happy.'[12]

The first original account of a Royal Christmas appears in Queen Charlotte's diary that same year, as she describes the Christmas festivities at Windsor Castle:

> 24 December – At 9 we breakfasted, & at 10 the King went into His library, the Younger Princesses home, & we went into Our rooms. I read & wrote till 12, then went to Lady Cremorne, staid [sic] till ½ past one, went to Dress saw de Lue till 4, then went to Dinner, staid below till six, then went up Stairs read with the Princesses, P & A till the King came, then Music began which was the *Messiah* at 8 the Y.P. & Lady Courtown came, we drank Tea. The Bishop of Salisbury came, we did not play at cards, but workd. Parted ½ past 10. Suppd & retired at 11. Lady Caroline Waldegrave was taken suddenly ill in the afternoon of an Inflammation in Her Bowels. Very Whet [sic] all day.
>
> 25 December – We breakfasted at 9 & at 10 we went to our rooms. I read to the Princesses a Sermon for the Day, & prayers for the Sacrament. At 12 we went to Church. The Reverend Dr Fisher read Prayers & the Bishop of Salisbury Preachd & gave the Sacrament. We returned ½ hour after 2, then Dressd, at 9 the Younger Princesses came & dined with us. We staid below till six then went up Stairs & read Proper Service for the Day, till the King came had again Sacred Music, did not play. Lady Courtown came at 7. We parted of it suppd & retired at 11. Lady Caroline Waldegrave continues very Ill. I send an express for Sir Lucas Pepys at 10. Very Whet & Windy all day.[13]

[11] Amelia Murray, *Recollections from 1803–37: With a Conclusion in 1868*, London: Longmans, Green and Co., 1868, p. 16.

[12] Broughton, *Court and Private Life in the Time of Queen Charlotte: Being the Journals of Mrs. Papendiek, Assistant Keeper of the Wardrobe and Reader to Her Majesty*, Vol. II, p. 158.

[13] Lady Caroline Waldegrave was the younger daughter of John, 3rd Earl Waldegrave and sister of Lady Elizabeth Waldegrave, Lady of the Bedchamber to Queen Charlotte 1793–1809. By 27 December she was 'out of Danger'.

There were other plans afoot for entertaining the Royal Family during the festive season, as Mrs Papendiek explained:

> The Christmas week was taken up in preparing for a juvenile ball at the Lodge, which it was thought would amuse the King without the trouble of ceremony to him. His Majesty was always particularly fond of children, and this idea, which was a novelty, was to be carried out upon a scale calculated to give great pleasure to them and to the King also, in watching the delight of the little ones. The Queen planned that the party should take place on January 1, as the New Year's Day drawing-room was, for the first time since the accession of the King, to be dispensed with, as well as the Odes and other formal observances of congratulation on the beginning of another year.
>
> The King was apprised of the Queen's proposal and approved, but when the time drew near he altogether objected to it. He said that the rooms in which it was proposed to hold the entertainment, four rooms upstairs and two below, which were well suited to the purpose, were too near to his own apartments, and that the noise over his head would disturb him. This objection was only raised the very day before this joyous party was to take place; and at supper on the last day of the old year his Majesty said unless it were held at the Castle, it should not be held at all. Mr. Garton, the controller, was sent for. He was gone home. Then Mr. Papendiek volunteered to go down to him, which he did, and found him in his dressing-room. At first he would not hear of the change, said it would not be possible &c., but Mr. Papendiek encouraged him by saying that it never would be forgotten, that at a command from him, all would fly to obey, and that he thought it might be done.
>
> It ended in Mr. Garton putting on his coat again, and then, returning to the Lodge together, Mr. Papendiek entered the supper-room with a smiling countenance, and in answer to the interrogatory 'Well?' from both King and Queen, he said that Mr. Garton was at the door. He was summoned immediately, and when admitted simply bowed and said that his Majesty's commands should be obeyed, and that by six o'clock the next evening (the hour originally fixed upon) all should be ready at the Castle. Princess Amelia was at that time only six years old, Princesses Mary and Sophia, fourteen and twelve. The elder Princesses had planned very pretty decorations, and the Princess Royal had painted two scenes, behind which were to have been placed the choristers and the regimental bands, so that

all was to be fairy-land to surprise the very young. Our little girls were to be placed so as to see and hear the whole, and the Princess Royal had given them each a pink satin sash to wear on the occasion. She had for many days had the children with her to cut paper for bows, so as to pretend that they were assisting her in the preparations. Our dear Princess had such a kind heart, and was always so good to the little ones!

The equerries had the altered invitations to send out. Garton sent messengers as far as Maidenhead to the two principal inns there, to Salt Hill, and to Staines, for new decorations and assistance in this emergency, and also to the King's confectioners in London. All responded with alacrity, but of course there was much bustle and hurry. And so closed this eventful year, begun in so much sadness, but ended, thank God, in joy and thankfulness for the restoration of our gracious monarch to his loving subjects, a feeling shared by all, from the highest to the lowest in the land. My heart was lifted up in thankfulness, too, to the Great Giver of all things for the continued blessings and happiness of my own dear home.

All was ready in good time on this 1st of January, 1790, and the juvenile ball went off well. Yet a little disappointment at the change was felt, as many of the arrangements and surprises that were planned for the Lodge had to be dispensed with at the Castle, which was too public for children, at any rate for infant children. The King's band were ordered, but many of them were absent on a holiday. Their places were filled, by Mr. Papendiek's contrivance, from the regimental band, and it was not discovered. Mr. Garton was immortalised for his successful exertions, and did not withhold his thanks to Mr. Papendiek for his encouragement.[14]

On 28 December 1901 Miss Ella Taylor, formerly a Lady-in-waiting to the Duchess of Cambridge, explored the issue of the Christmas tree in a letter to the Duchess's granddaughter, Princess Mary of Teck, who had recently become the Princess of Wales:

Two brace of fine pheasants arrived just now from Sandringham & I beg Your Royal Highness to accept my best thanks for your kind remembrance of me. My thoughts were much with you over Christmas Eve. I regret that the festivities were marred by the absence of the Queen. My sisters Rose, Alice & myself spent Xmas Eve with my sister Minnie & her

[14] Broughton, *Court and Private Life in the Time of Queen Charlotte: Being the Journals of Mrs. Papendiek, Assistant Keeper of the Wardrobe and Reader to Her Majesty*, Vol. II, pp. 158–62.

> husband in true old German fashion . . . I have lately been making many enquiries among my friends in Germany as to the origin of the custom of Christmas trees and invariably got the answer 'Nobody knows but it is a very ancient custom.' However Frau von Wengersheim sends me a pretty book entitled 'Weihnacht' by Professor Bietschol, here I find the answer to all my questions.
>
> The custom only dates from the beginning of the last century. Xmas trees were sold for the first time at the Dresdener 'Christmarkt' in 1807. The custom before that time was to decorate the interior of houses with fir branches as we still do in England. The bringing of the entire tree into the house was impossible on account of the strict Forestry Laws forbidding the uprooting of young trees. This year 84,000 trees were sold at the 'Christmarkt' in Berlin! Surely this must lead to fresh Forestry Laws. The pictures of Luther and his family gathered round a Christmas tree are all modern.[15]

The key phrase here would appear to be 'true old German fashion', even if Miss Taylor acknowledges that the emphasis should really be on 'German', rather than on 'old'.

However, the traditional Christmas trees may have been imported from Germany slightly earlier than Miss Taylor thought. In her memoirs, Amelia Murray explained that 'Christmas-trees are now common. In the early part of this century they were seldom seen, but Queen Charlotte always had one dressed up in the room of Madame Berkendorff, her German attendant; it was hung with presents for the children, who were invited to see it, and I well remember the pleasure it was to hunt for one's own name, which was sure to be attached to one or more of the pretty gifts.'[16]

According to John Watkins, Queen Charlotte placed a tree centre-stage at a party that she hosted on Christmas Day 1800:

> At the beginning of October the royal family left the coast for Windsor, where Her Majesty kept the Christmas-day following in a very pleasing manner. Sixty poor families had a substantial dinner given them; and in the evening the children of the principal families in the neighbourhood were invited to an entertainment at the Lodge. Here, among other amusing objects for the gratification of the juvenile visitors, in the middle of the

[15] Royal Archives: QM/PRIV/CC47/79.
[16] Murray, *Recollections from 1803–37: With a Conclusion in 1868*, pp. 61–2.

> room stood an immense tub with a yew-tree placed in it, from the branches of which hung bunches of sweetmeats, almonds, and raisins, in papers, fruits, and toys, most tastefully arranged, and the whole illuminated by small wax candles. After the company had walked round and admired the tree, each child obtained a portion of the sweets which it bore, together with a toy, and then all returned home quite delighted.[17]

Queen Charlotte was German, as were the spouses of most members of the Royal Family from the Hanoverian succession until recent times. Between the marriage on 3 September 1660 of Lady Anne Hyde with James, Duke of York, later King James II, and that on 29 July 1981 of Lady Diana Spencer with Charles, Prince of Wales, no Englishwoman married the heir apparent, or heir presumptive, to the British throne, excepting some morganatic examples. Sir Sidney Lee wrote that 'Christmas, again, was for the children and their elders a season of well-organised festivity on the German pattern. Each member of the family had his or her Christmas tree decorated with candles and gifts.'[18]

From the time of King George III and Queen Charlotte, 'festivity on the German pattern' provided the foundation for Royal Christmases, as the Hon. Eleanor Stanley, Maid of Honour to Queen Victoria 1842–62, described in a letter to her mother on Christmas Day 1847: 'A merry Xmas, and many happy returns of the day to you and all the family at the dear old Castle. Yesterday evening we were desired, at a quarter to seven, to come down to the Corridor, to get our Gifts; we found all the gentlemen and Mrs. Anson already assembled, and presently the page desired us to go to the Oak-room, where the Queen and Prince already were, standing by a large table with a white cloth, in the middle of which was a little fir-tree, in the German fashion, covered with bonbons, gilt walnuts, and little coloured tapers.'[19]

The same Christmas, Prince Albert wrote: 'I must now seek in the children an echo of what Ernest and I were in the old time, of what we felt and thought; and their delight in the Christmas-trees is not less than ours used to be.' Meanwhile, Queen Victoria wrote in her Journal that Christmas Eve: 'This festive day, the eve of such blessings & the day when ever since our

[17] John Watkins, *Memoirs of Her Most Excellent Majesty Sophia-Charlotte, Queen of Great Britain, from Authentic Documents*, London: Henry Colburn, 1819, pp. 462–3.

[18] Sidney Lee, *King Edward VII: A Biography: From Birth to Accession*, London: Macmillan & Co., 1925, p. 18.

[19] Beatrice Erskine, ed., *Twenty Years at Court: From the Correspondence of the Hon. Eleanor Stanley*, London: Nisbet & Co., 1916, pp. 155–7.

childhood we have been happy & joyous, in giving & receiving, – I hail with gratitude & joy, I know no day, or rather more anniversary which we celebrate with more feelings of mutual joy & goodwill. The bustle of all the preparations is a great delight.'[20]

In her letter, Eleanor Stanley provides contemporary acknowledgement of Christmas trees 'in the German fashion'. However, perhaps the defining moment for the popularisation of Christmas trees in Britain came with the publication the following year, in the Christmas supplement of *The Illustrated London News*, of an engraving, based on a drawing by J. L. Williams, of the Royal Family gathered around a Christmas tree at Windsor Castle. As early as 1852, William Sandys wrote:

> In recent times the Christmas tree has been introduced from the continent, and is productive of much amusement to old and young, and much taste can be displayed and expense also incurred in preparing its glittering and attractive fruit. It is delightful to watch the animated expectation and enjoyment of the children as the treasures are displayed and distributed; the parents equally participating in the pleasure, and enjoying the sports of their childhood over again. And where can the weary world-worn man find greater relief from his anxious toil and many cares, and haply his many sorrows, than in contemplating the amusements of artless children, and assisting as far as he is able; for it is not every one has tact for this purpose, and our young friends soon detect this, and discover the right 'Simon Pure'.[21]

On Christmas Eve 1818, Augusta, Dowager Duchess of Saxe-Coburg-Saalfeld, Queen Victoria's maternal grandmother, wrote in her diary: 'In beautiful weather I lunched at Ketschendorf and went in the evening to Sophie [her eldest daughter, Countess Mensdorff-Pouilly] for her Christmas tree and "Bescherung" for her children, which was most successful and they were very delighted with their gifts. Julie, Leopold [husband of the late Princess Charlotte of Wales], and everyone from the Schloss were also there. Christmas always reminds me of former happy days.'[22]

20 Royal Archives: VIC/MAIN/QVJ/1847.
21 Sandys, *Christmastide, its History, Festivities and Carols*, p. 151.
22 HRH Princess Beatrice, ed., *In Napoleonic Days: Extracts from the Private Diary of Augusta, Duchess of Saxe-Coburg-Saalfeld, Queen Victoria's Maternal Grandmother 1806–21*, London: John Murray, 1941, p. 202.

On 16 January 1865, Queen Victoria wrote to Major Howard Elphinstone, tutor to Prince Arthur (later Duke of Connaught), her third son and seventh child, who was born on 1 May 1850, the eighty-first birthday of the Duke of Wellington, and named after the 'beloved hero': 'The Christmas trees for the Artillery soldiers' children pleased her much also, and she rejoices to think that the Prince & herself are the cause of Christmas trees being so generally adopted in this country.'[23] Thus, although conclusive evidence is hard to find, Queen Victoria gracefully acknowledged appreciation for the contribution that she and her husband had made to the way in which Christmas is celebrated in Britain. In *The Kissing Bough*, a greetings card printed in 1953, Lawrence Whistler wrote that 'the Kissing Bough, the ancient symbol of Christmas in England, was largely replaced by the German Christmas Tree in Victorian times'.

Early Victorian Christmases were summarised by Elizabeth Longford, who wrote:

> December came with the present tables, and Christmas trees ordered by Prince Albert from Coburg. Queen Victoria was ecstatic about dearest Albert's innovation. Actually Queen Charlotte had set up a Christmas tree of yew at Windsor before the beginning of the century, but the country acclaimed the idea as Prince Albert's and enthusiastically followed his lead. At Claremont he made Victoria a snowman twelve feet high, played Blind Man's Buff with the ladies and taught them a delightful new round game, *Naine Jaune*. There was also *Loto Dauphine*, *Maccoo*, *Speculation* and *Vingt-et-Un*, on which a gentleman once won a guinea. *Maccoo*, his brother Ernest's introduction, was too much of a wild gamble to please the Queen.
>
> Prince Albert was the dextrous coachman of the family sledge jingling across the snow with grey ponies and scarlet grooms, the knight of Victoria's ice-chair, the champion skater on Frogmore pond. How she admired the elegant swan's head at the tip of each skate. When he slipped down playing ice-hockey she was amazed at the agility with which he sprang to his feet again . . . Christmas entertainments held for Queen Victoria all the happiness in the world.[24]

[23] Royal Archives: Vic. Add. MSS. A/25.

[24] Elizabeth Longford, *Victoria R.I.*, London: Weidenfeld & Nicolson, 1964, p. 169.

In *The Victorians*, Jeremy Paxman wrote: 'The developing German national consciousness through the course of the century had led to a greater awareness of German culture, in particular the rich tradition of the folktale with its hinterland of dark forests, uplands and other worldly creatures.'[25] In this context, there was another Royal Christmas innovation on Christmas Eve 1856, as Queen Victoria described in her Journal:

> Albert arranged a surprise for the Children. In Germany the old saying that St. Nicholas appears with a rod for naughty children, & gingerbread for good ones, is constantly represented, & Arthur hearing of this begged for one. Accordingly Albert got up a St. Nicholas, most formidable looking, in black, covered with snow, a long white beard, & red nose, of a gigantic stature! He came in asking the Children, who were somewhat awed & alarmed, – 'are you a good child,' & giving them gingerbread & apples. I since heard that it was Cowley (the Jäger) whom Albert had taught his part beautifully, but the Children went on guessing every kind of person, & even now have not been told for certain.[26]

Gingerbread remains a traditional feature of German Christmases and is widely offered for sale at Christmas markets. The hard version – as opposed to *Lebkuchen* – is baked in a variety of different shapes, before the addition of icing and decorations.

Princess Mary of Teck spent Christmas 1873 at Strelitz, the home of her aunt, Augusta, Grand Duchess of Mecklenburg-Strelitz, granddaughter of King George III and elder sister of the Duchess of Teck. On Christmas Day the Grand Duchess wrote to the Duke of Cambridge: 'It was a serious Christmas this time, dearest Mamma not being able to join our Circle in the Saal but she was able to have a Tree in her anteroom, where she gave us presents and received ours . . . There was a beautiful "Etalage" of presents and the darling chicks were delighted and brightened up the scene with their happy faces and by their childlike prattle and screams of joy.'[27]

[25] Jeremy Paxman, *The Victorians*, London: BBC Books, 2009, pp. 250–51.
[26] Royal Archives: VIC/MAIN/QVJ/1856.
[27] Royal Archives, Grand Duchess of Mecklenburg-Strelitz to Duke of Cambridge, 25 December 1873, quoted in James Pope-Hennessy, *Queen Mary, 1867–1953*, London: George Allen and Unwin, 1959, pp. 95–6.

James Pope-Hennessy described another German Christmas custom:

> At Strelitz the Christmas Eve dinner and distribution of presents round the tall, sparkling Christmas tree was enlivened by the North German custom of *Juhl-Klaps*. These consisted of little jokes in verse, with bon-bons and chocolates or comic prints attached to them, which the servants would hurl into the great *Saal* at unexpected intervals. The verses or tags would refer somewhat crudely to a peculiarity of the royal personage at whom it was flung: a box of chocolates addressed, for example, to Princess Mary Adelaide once bore the label: 'For the private picking of Queen Gourmandiza.' Dressed up with comic noses and wigs, the children would impersonate imaginary characters. The proceedings were jolly, and became noisy. Princess May and her brothers would sleep a part of the day, so as to be able to sit up and join in the fun until ten p.m.'[28]

Princess Mary Adelaide herself wrote: 'The best joke of all was this, I was dressed up as Lady Augusta de Noiman, with a long black gown, a Turkish shawl trailing on the ground, a pink bonnet, black curls, and a long nose; in my hand there was a paper, with "Souvenir from Augusta de Noiman" on it, which I was to bring to Gussy, and in it was a quantity of black hair. William Norman, son of one of the *Dames d'Honneur*, was dressed as Baron Noiman, and brought Mama a letter of funny nonsense. The whole evening was excessively amusing.'[29] As we shall see, Queen Victoria would adapt elements of *Juhl-Klaps*.

There is another tradition, also of German origin, to which the Royal Family still adheres – *Heiligabend Bescherung* – or the giving of gifts on Holy Evening, or Christmas Eve. On Christmas Eve 1843, Queen Victoria wrote in her Journal: 'After luncheon we all walked out, & on coming in, had the excitement & agitation of finishing arranging the "Bescheerung" [sic] & presents, which to me is such a pleasure.'[30] The following day Eleanor Stanley wrote from Windsor Castle to her mother: 'All the world got Royal Christmas gifts yesterday, studs, hunting-whips, pins, pencil-cases, and bracelets; they were all very pretty, and the Equerries got two apiece, one from the Queen and one from the Prince.'[31]

[28] Ibid., p. 96.

[29] Clement Kinloch Cooke, *A Memoir of Her Royal Highness Princess Mary Adelaide, Duchess of Teck*, London: John Murray, 1900, p. 61.

[30] Royal Archives: VIC/MAIN/QVJ/1843.

[31] Erskine, *Twenty Years at Court: From the Correspondence of the Hon. Eleanor Stanley*, pp. 77–8.

In this context it is helpful to be reminded that, under the instruction of her governess, Louise Lehzen, Princess Victoria spoke only German until the age of three. The Royal Family was multilingual, which involved fluency – or near-fluency – in German and also French, the language of diplomacy. Philip Ziegler wrote that, during the Duke of Windsor's controversial visit to Germany in October 1937, 'Hitler was conspicuously affable, though he mildly irritated the Duke by insisting on using an interpreter rather than speaking directly to him in German'.[32]

At the end of each year, Queen Victoria invariably looked both backwards and forwards. New Year's wishes were part of this process. On the last day of 1837, Queen Victoria wrote in her Journal: 'Found a little note, 2 New Year's Cards and the Christmas Keepsake on my table, from Mama.' The last entry for 1838 and the first of the following year were: 'I can only be most grateful to Providence in having brought me so safely through this year, and, with the exception of the loss of poor dear Louis [Princess Charlotte's dresser and later the housekeeper at Claremont], who is ever present to my memory, favoured me so highly . . . Most fervently do I beseech Almighty God to preserve me and all those most dear to me safely through this year, and to grant that all may go on as it has hitherto done, and to make me daily more fit for my station.'[33]

On New Year's Day 1839, the Queen continued: 'Read in *Oliver Twist* while I was lacing. Got from M^{a} 2 Vases, 2 Almanacks, some New Year's wishes, and some artificial flowers, as also a Diamond Pin, 2 paper weights, and a little basket. Gave her 2 vases, 2 pins, a book, and a New Year's wish. Dearest Daisy gave me the evening before a dear little Vinegrette [sic] and 3 pretty New Year's Wishes. I gave her a bracelet – signed.'[34]

In 1840, Prince Albert's friend and supporter, Henry Cole, had been involved, as a civil servant, in the introduction of the penny post. Recognising its potential, Cole introduced the first commercial Christmas card, using artwork by John Callcott Horsley, three years later. At his behest a total of 2,050 cards were produced, in two batches, and sold at a shilling apiece. On 24 November 2001, one of those cards, which Henry Cole had sent to his grandmother, was sold at auction for an astonishing £22,500.

The Royal Family soon recognised the importance of this new, seasonal greetings card. Queen Mary was an enthusiastic devotee and her extensive

[32] Philip Ziegler, *King Edward VIII*, Philip Ziegler, London: Collins, 1990, p. 392.
[33] Royal Archives: VIC/MAIN/QVJ/1838.
[34] Royal Archives: VIC/MAIN/QVJ/1839.

collection is now in the British Museum. The official recipients of Christmas cards from Queen Mary in 1952, the last Christmas of her life, included, among many others, the Maharajah of Gwalior, India, and the Nawab of Bahawalpur, Pakistan, together with many British and Empire regiments and other military services.

In the Royal Archives there is a brown leather-bound volume of New Year's wishes from Queen Victoria to her loyal, if somewhat rough and controversial, Highland manservant, John Brown. On 24 February 1865, the Queen wrote to her uncle Leopold: 'I continue to ride daily (I fear to-day I shall not be able) on my pony, and have *now* appointed that *excellent* Highland servant of mine to attend me ALWAYS and everywhere out of doors, whether riding or driving or on foot; and it is a *real* comfort, for he is so devoted to me – so simple, so intelligent, *so unlike* an *ordinary* servant, and so cheerful and attentive'.[35] Though frowned upon by most of her family and also by many courtiers, it was a very important relationship to the widowed Queen. On 1 January 1877, she sent John Brown these verses, printed beneath the picture of 'a dashing parlour-maid':[36]

I send my serving maiden
With New Year letter laden,
Its words will prove
My faith and love
To you my heart's best treasure,
Then smile on her and smile on me
And let your answer loving be,
And give me pleasure.

In her own hand, the Queen wrote: 'To my best friend J.B. From his best friend, V.R.I.' After John Brown's death, Sir Henry Ponsonby wrote in a private letter: 'He was the only person who could fight and make the Queen do what she did not wish. He did not always succeed nor was his advice always the best. But I believe he was honest, and with all his want of

[35] George Earle Buckle, ed., *The Letters of Queen Victoria, Second Series: A Selection from Her Majesty's Correspondence between the years 1862 and 1885*, 3 vols., London: John Murray in 1926-8 (LQV II), Vol. 1, p. 255.
[36] Royal Archives: c3/57-8, quoted in Longford, *Victoria R.I.*, pp. 456–7.

education, his roughness, his prejudices and other faults he was undoubtedly a most excellent servant to her.'[37]

The following year, the Queen chose a Scottish 'Guid New Year' card, with this verse:

> Yon heather Theekit Hames were blythe
> When Winter Nights were lang,
> Wi' spinning wheels and jonkin lads
> An' ilka lassies sang.

On the back of the card she wrote: 'A happy New Year to my kind friend from his true & devoted one, V.R.I. Osborne, January 1st, 1878.'[38]

Members of the Royal Family also exchanged New Year's wishes. From Tsarskoe Selo on the last day of 1894 the Tsar and Tsarina of Russia sent to Queen Victoria, their 'tenderest wishes for the New Year to you and all relations at Osborne – Nicky, Alix'.[39] The Tsarina Alexandra was the second daughter of Princess Alice, Grand Duchess of Hesse, and was therefore a granddaughter of Queen Victoria.

[37] Arthur Ponsonby, *Henry Ponsonby, Queen Victoria's Private Secretary: His Life from his Letters*, London: Macmillan & Co., 1942, p. 128.

[38] Royal Archives: c3/57-8, quoted in Longford, *Victoria R.I.*, p. 457.

[39] George Earle Buckle, ed., *The Letters of Queen Victoria, Third Series: a Selection from Her Majesty's Correspondence between the years 1886 and 1901*, 3 vols., London: John Murray, in 1930–32 (LQV III), Vol. II, p. 459.

Young Victoria's Christmases

In his memoir of his mother-in-law, the Marquis of Lorne described the marriage of the Duke of Sussex to Lady Augusta Murray in Rome in 1793 as being 'contrary to the provisions of the Royal Marriage Act of 12th George III [1772], which enacted that no descendant of George II, other than the issue of princes married into foreign countries, was capable of contracting matrimony without the previous consent of the King, signified under the Great Seal'.[1] Against that background, Amelia Murray wrote:

> As usual with the gossiping world, many unkind things were said of the daughters of George III. As young Princesses, whose marriages in their own rank of life were almost out of the question (the Continent being sealed up, as far as England was concerned, by the will of the first Napoleon), they were unceasingly thrown into attractive and agreeable society, and, of course, were exposed to the risk of forming attachments which could not (after the Marriage Act) be legalised. It is supposed that, had the poor Princess Amelia lived, she would have confessed to a private marriage with General Fitzroy, and she certainly left him all the property she could call her own.'[2]

Despite having thirteen children who lived into adulthood, it is estimated that King George III and Queen Charlotte had more than fifty illegitimate grandchildren – but just six legitimate ones. On 29 January 1820, the day that King George III died, his eldest surviving granddaughter, eight-month-old Princess Alexandrina Victoria, daughter of the late King's recently deceased fourth son, the Duke of Kent, and his wife, Princess Victoria of Saxe-Coburg-Saafeld, was fourth in line to succeed to the British throne, after the King's three eldest sons, none of whom had legitimate offspring, within the terms of the Royal Marriage Act 1772.

Queen Victoria had a difficult childhood, despite her undoubtedly privileged background. She was born and brought up at Kensington Palace,

[1] The Marquis of Lorne (now His Grace The Duke of Argyll), *VRI: Queen Victoria: Her Life and Empire*, London: Harper & Brothers, 1901, p. 157.

[2] Murray, Amelia, *Recollections from 1803–37: With a Conclusion in 1868*, London: Longmans, Green and Co., 1868, p. 71.

described by James Pope-Hennessy as 'for many years, the home of exiles; William III, Prince George of Denmark, George I, George II, Caroline, Augusta Princess of Wales, none of these could ever feel for England as they did for their native country. Germany in particular, which for so long supplied rulers for the chief countries of Europe, maintains a hold on the hearts of her children which neither power not wealth nor popularity in a foreign country can ever quite shake off.'[3]

At Kensington Palace, household politics were a constant backdrop, with the devious John Conroy using 'interest' in an attempt to fashion a position of great influence when Victoria ascended the throne. An officer in the Royal Artillery, John Conroy was appointed equerry to the Duke of Kent in 1817, three years before his death. He was also one of the Duke's two executors, served as Comptroller of the widowed Duchess of Kent's household and was appointed a Knight Commander of the Hanoverian Guelphic Order in August 1827. Between them, the Duchess of Kent and Sir John Conroy devised the so-called 'Kensington System', a notably strict and controlled upbringing that the Princess deeply resented. It must be more than a coincidence that Sir John Conroy's youngest daughter, who was born on 12 August 1819, less than three months after Princess Victoria, was named Victoria Maria Louisa, and was known to Princess Victoria as Victoire.

In the rather trying atmosphere of Kensington Palace, Princess Victoria was supported against the intrigues of Sir John Conroy by her governess, Fräulein Louise Lehzen, daughter of a Lutheran pastor in Coburg, who served as nurse to Princess Feodora, child of the Duchess of Kent's first marriage to Emich Carl, Prince of Leiningen. In the Journals, Louise Lehzen, who was created a German baroness in 1827, was often referred to as 'Daisy'.

At Windsor Castle on New Year's Eve 1837, the first of her reign, Queen Victoria wrote of St George's Chapel: 'It was dreadfully cold at church. Felt very low and triste but my beloved Lehzen cheered me.' In troubled times, Baroness Lehzen was a thoroughly dependable ally. From the point of view of historians, Elizabeth Longford explained that 'the best thing Lehzen ever did for Princess Victoria was to teach her to keep a diary every day of her life'.[4] On 27 June 1837, exactly a week after the death of King William IV, the new Queen dismissed Sir John Conroy from her household and banned him from her apartments in Kensington Palace. On the advice of the prime

[3] James Pope-Hennessy, *London Fabric*, London: B. T. Batsford, 1939.

[4] Elizabeth Longford, *Victoria R.I.*, London: Weidenfeld & Nicolson, 1964, p. 30.

minister, Lord Melbourne, he was given a baronetcy and granted a pension of £3,000 per annum.

Princess Victoria spent Christmas 1832 at Kensington Palace. This is the first Christmas that the future Queen Victoria described in a Journal that survives, in this instance in the original form. Princess Victoria wrote on the flyleaf of this unassuming, leather-backed notebook: 'This book, Mamma gave me, that I might write the journal of my journey to Wales in it. Victoria, Kensington Palace, July 31st.' The essential format of that early Christmas was retained for the following sixty-eight Christmases:

> Monday 24th December – I awoke at 7 & got up at 8. At 9 we breakfasted. At ½ past 9 came the Dean; & I gave him Mama's & my Christmas box. He stayed till ½ past 11. In the course of the morning I gave Mrs. Brock a Christmas box & all our people. At ½ past 1 we lunched. At ½ past 2 came Mr. Westall till ½ past 3. At 4 came Mr. Sale till 5. At ¼ to 7 we dined with the whole Conroy family and Mr. Hore downstairs, as our Christmas tables were arranged in our dining-room. After dinner we went upstairs. I then saw *Flora* the dog which Sir John was going to give Mama. Aunt Sophia came also. We then went into the drawing-room near the dining-room.
>
> After Mama had rung a bell 3 times we went in. There were two large round tables on which were placed two trees hung with lights & sugar ornaments. All the presents being placed round the tree. I had one table for myself & the Conroy family had the other together. Lehzen had likewise a little table. Mama gave me a lovely little pink bag which she had worked with a little sachet likewise done by her; a beautiful little opal brooch & earrings, books, some lovely prints, a pink satin dress & a cloak lined with fur. Aunt Sophia gave me a dress which she worked herself, & Aunt Mary a pair of amethyst earrings, Lehzen a lovely music-book, Victoire a very pretty white bag worked by herself, and Sir John a silver brush. I gave Lehzen some little things & Mama gave her a writing-table.
>
> We then went to my room where I had arranged Mama's table. I gave Mama a white bag which I had worked, a collar & a steel chain for *Flora*, and an annual; Aunt Sophia a pair of Turquoise earrings; Lehzen a little white and gold pincushion and a pin with two little gold hearts hanging to it; Sir John, *Flora*, a book-holder and an annual. Mama then took me up into my bedroom with all the ladies. There was my new toilet table with a white muslin cover over pink, and all my silver things standing on it with a fine new looking-glass. I stayed up till ½ past 9. The dog went away again

to the doctor for her leg. I saw good Louis for an instant & she gave me a lovely little wooden box with bottles. I was soon in bed & asleep.

Tuesday 25th December – I awoke at 8 & got up at ½ past 8. At ½ past 9 we breakfasted. At 10 we went down to prayers with Jane, Victoire, Mr. Hore & Henry. At ½ past 1 we lunched. At 3 came Victoire till 6. In the course of the afternoon Lady Conroy came with her two little nephews George & Augustus Conroy, very pretty little boys. At 7 we dined. At 8 came Aunt Sophia & went with Mama to Lady Conroy. I stayed up till ½ past 8. I was soon in bed & asleep.

Monday 31st December – I awoke at ½ past 7 & got up at 8. At 9 we breakfasted. At ½ past 9 came the Dean till 10 minutes to 11. At a ¼ to 1 I went out in the carriage. At ½ past 1 we lunched. At ½ past 2 came Mr. Westall till ½ past 3. At 4 came Mr. Sale till 5. At 7 we dined. I stayed up till ½ past 8. Just as I got in bed I found a letter on my pillow. It was a letter from Mama, with some beautiful new-year's wishes in it. I was soon asleep.

Tuesday 1st January 1833 – Today is the first day of the new year. I awoke at ½ past 6. Mama gave me a lovely pink pincushion done by herself, with a chrysoprase *ferronière* on it, two annuals, & a new-year wish from Spèth & a fine nosegay. I gave her a picture painted by me, an annual, two new-year's wishes, a nosegay, and two new-year's wishes from Spèth. My little nephew & niece, Charles & Eliza Hohenlohe, sent me a new-year's wish. Lehzen gave me a lovely china figure & a beautiful new-year's wish. Mama gave her a silver candlestick, & a phosphorus box; & I gave her a pair of scissors, a memorandum book, a German almanac, a new-year's wish from Spèth, & one from me. I got up at 8. At 9 we breakfasted. Mama gave me two fine hyacinths in pots & some lovely prints. At ½ past 1 we lunched. Poor Victoire was unable to come. At ¼ to 7 we went to dinner to Lady Conroy's. Mr. Bing [Byng] was there. After dinner Mama sung & we sung. Mr. Bing danced the Tirolienne & afterwards walsed [sic] with Victoire. I stayed till 10 minutes to 10. I was soon in bed & asleep.[5]

[5] Royal Archives: VIC/MAIN/QVJ/1832, quoted in Alison Plowden, *The Young Victoria*, Weidenfeld & Nicolson, 1981, p. 113.

Queen Victoria and Her First Prime Minister

Much has been written about the relationship between Queen Victoria and her first Prime Minister, William Lamb, 2nd Viscount Melbourne. Elizabeth Longford wrote that 'the three-year partnership' was 'one of the romances of history'. She explains that 'the list of Melbourne's gifts to the Queen are a tribute to the generosity of his nature. He gave her self-confidence through affection and praise; sophistication through inimitable table-talk; enthusiasm for her work through the delight with which he invested it.'[1] A contemporary commentator, Charles Greville, Clerk of the Council in Ordinary 1821–60, observed that Lord Melbourne 'treats her with unbounded consideration and respect, he consults her tastes and her wishes and he puts her at her ease by his frank and natural manners, while he amuses her by the quaint, queer, epigrammatic turn of his mind, and his varied knowledge upon all subjects.'[2] Charles Greville's diaries were edited and published, after his death, by his friend, Henry Reeve. Queen Victoria wrote that she was 'horrified and indignant at this dreadful and really scandalous book. Mr. Greville's indiscretion, indelicacy, ingratitude, betrayal of confidence and shameful disloyalty towards his Sovereign make it very important that the book should be severely censored and discredited.' She also wrote that 'the tone in which he speaks of royalty is unlike anything which one sees in history, even of people hundreds of years ago, and is most reprehensible'.[3]

In his second book about Queen Victoria, which focused on the story of her early years, told through her Journals, Viscount Esher wrote:

> Lord Melbourne's life had been chequered by curious experiences, and his mind had been thoroughly well trained, for a man of his station, according to the lights of those days. A classical education, the privilege from youth upwards of free intercourse with every one worth knowing, the best Whig connection, and an inherited capacity for governing men under oligarchic

[1] Elizabeth Longford, *Victoria R.I.*, London: Weidenfeld & Nicolson, 1964, pp. 66–8.
[2] Henry Reeve, ed., *The Greville Memoirs: A Journal of the Reign of Queen Victoria from 1837 to 1852*, Vol. IV, London: Longmans, Green & Co., 1885, pp. 22–3.
[3] Christopher Hibbert, *Oxford Dictionary of National Biography*, Vol. 23, Oxford: OUP, 2004, p. 781.

> institutions, had equipped his intellect and judgment with everything that was necessary to enable him carefully to watch and safeguard the blossoming of the character of the girl who was both his pupil and his Sovereign.
>
> He was no longer young, but he was not old. His person was attractive. According to Leslie, no mean judge, his head was a truly noble one, and he was a fine specimen of manly beauty in the meridian of life. Not only were his features handsome, but the expression was in the highest degree intellectual. His laugh was frequent and the most joyous possible, his voice so deep and musical that to hear him say the most ordinary thing was a pleasure; and his frankness, his freedom from affectation, and his peculiar humour rendered almost everything he said, however easy and natural, quite original . . .
>
> He treated the Queen with unbounded consideration and respect, yet he did not hesitate to administer reproof. He consulted her tastes and her wishes, but he checked her inclination to be headstrong and arbitrary. He knew well how to chide with parental firmness, but he did so with a deference that could not fail to fascinate any young girl in a man of his age and attainments. The Queen was completely under his charm. The ease of his frank and natural manners, his quaint epigrams and humorous paradox, his romantic bias and worldly shrewdness, were magnified by her into the noblest manly virtues.
>
> He saw her every day, but never appeared to weary of her society. She certainly never tired of his. Yet he was fifty-eight years old, a time-worn politician, and she was a girl of eighteen. He was her confidential servant and at the same time her guardian. She was his ward and at the same time his Sovereign. The situation was full of the possibilities of drama, yet nothing can be more delightful than the high comedy revealed in the passages of the Journals that refer to Lord Melbourne. That he should have happened to be First Minister of the Crown when King William died was a rare piece of good fortune for the new Sovereign and for the country.[4]

During the early years of her reign, Queen Victoria and Lord Melbourne spent a great deal of time in one another's company, including long periods over Christmas. Since the Journals that cover this period have suffered rather less severely from over-enthusiastic editing than those which followed, it is

[4] Reginald Baliol Brett, ed., *The Girlhood of Queen Victoria: A Selection from Her Majesty's Diaries between the Years 1832 and 1840*, London: 1912 (GQV), pp. 33–4.

possible to enjoy lively descriptions of the interaction between the teenage monarch and her first Prime Minister.

Christmas 1837

At Buckingham Palace on 23 December 1837, only six months after King William IV had died, the Prime Minister was already weaving his magic spell:

> Lord Melbourne was in excellent spirits and looked quite well and blooming, I was happy to see. He was full of fun at dinner about Christmas Parties and New Year, and made me die with laughing. The Duchess of Sutherland was looking very handsome. After dinner I sat on the sofa with the Duchess of Sutherland and Lady Mulgrave; Lord Melbourne sitting near me the whole evening. The Duke of Sutherland sat near him. Lord Melbourne talked to me about Miss Dillon and I moralised about her, and we perfectly agreed. He is so sensible and so reasonable upon every point and has such right feelings about everything . . .
>
> Lord Melbourne is so kind and good to me about everything. He has, I must repeat, such a kind, mild and gentle manner which must endear him to every one who knows him very well, as I do; and with all that, is so manly, firm and decided. He was very cheerful this evening. Stayed up till 10 m. p. 11. It was a very pleasant evening. What renders Lord Melbourne still more perfect in my eyes, is that he knows how to appreciate my beloved Lehzen. Having experienced in my life so much ingratitude and dishonesty, with the exception of my adored Lehzen to whom I owe everything, who has, I may say, saved me from perdition and misery, and who has been much more than a mother to me, I value the kindness, honesty and disinterestedness of Lord Melbourne still more than I would otherwise almost, as I know what a rare thing and what a treasure an honest, straightforward and fearless person, and a kind heart, is. Looked at an Annual with Lord Melbourne who was very funny about it.

Two days after her first Christmas as Queen, it would appear that Victoria simply could not get enough information about Lord Melbourne. Now at Windsor Castle, she wrote:

> I sat between the Duke of Sutherland and Mr. Cowper. I talked a great deal with the latter, and a great deal about Lord Melbourne. He says that all

the people who have never seen Lord Melbourne and come to have interviews with him, and those Members of the H. of Commons who dine with him and have not seen or known him before and expect to find the Prime Minister a very proud, stiff person, are quite delighted with his very kind, unaffected, merry and open, frank manner, which I think everybody must and ought to be. He told me some amusing anecdotes about him, &c., &c., and many other funny things. Lord Melbourne is very absent when in company, often, and talks to himself every now and then, loud enough to be heard but never loud enough to be understood. I am now, from habit, quite accustomed to it, but at first I turned round sometimes, thinking he was talking to me. Mr. Cowper says he does not think his uncle is aware of it; he says he is much less absent than he used to be.

She returns to the same subject on New Year's Day:

The Duke of Sutherland told me the other night, that Lord Melbourne's mother (whom he knew) was a very agreeable, sensible, clever woman, and that Lord Melbourne was very like her as to features; Lady Melbourne was very large latterly. Lord Melbourne's father, on the contrary, the Duke said, was very far from agreeable or clever; he was a short fat man and not like any of his children. He died at the age of 80. The Duchess of Sutherland spoke to me last night about Lady Caroline Lamb, Lord Melbourne's wife; she was Lord Duncannon's only sister, and the strangest person that ever lived, really half crazy, and quite so when she died; she was not good-looking, but very clever and could be amusing. She teazed [sic] that excellent Lord Melbourne in every way, dreadfully, and quite embittered his life, which it ought to have been her pride to study to render a happy one; he was the kindest of husbands to her, and bore it most admirably; any other man but him would have separated from such a Wife. He has now the greatest horror of any woman who is not as she should be and who is extravagant, which shows how he must have suffered from such a Wife. The Duchess told me the strangest stories about her.[5]

[5] Royal Archives: VIC/MAIN/QVJ/1837.

Christmas 1838

The following Christmas was spent at King George IV's marvellous confection, Brighton Pavilion, with which Queen Victoria had not been particularly impressed during her first visit in October 1837. On that occasion she wrote that 'the Pavilion is a strange, odd, Chinese looking place, both outside & inside. Most of the rooms are low, & I can only see a morsel of the sea, from one of my sitting room windows, which is strange, considering how close one is to the sea.' However, when she returned to Brighton on 18 December 1838, she wrote in her Journal: 'The Pavilion lighted up, looked cheerful . . . & my impression of it, was not so cheerless as last year.'[6]

Five days later, she reverted to the subject of Lord Melbourne, and his most unfortunate absence from the party:

> Got before breakfast such a very kind letter from Lord Melbourne, that I felt quite contrite at having pressed him so indiscreetly to come down. It is too long to copy down the whole, which would indeed be useless, and I, of course, keep with the greatest care all his letters, but I cannot refrain from transcribing parts of it, and in the 1st instance, the beginning: 'Lord Melbourne presents his humble duty to Your Majesty, and cannot express how deeply concerned he is to find himself restrained from at once obeying Your Majesty's commands, and repairing without delay to Brighton. Both his duty and his inclination would prompt him to do this without a moment's delay, if he did not feel it incumbent upon him to represent to Your Majesty the very important circumstances which require his presence for two or three days longer in London.' He then states that the approach of the Session of Parliament, and 'the questions to be considered and proposed are of the most appalling magnitude and of the greatest difficulty'; that many of the Ministers in the highest places were absent on account of family calamities, and that consequently it was necessary someone should superintend what was going on. This is most true. 'Lord Melbourne assured Your Majesty that he would not delay in London, if he did not feel it to be absolutely necessary for Your Majesty's service.' This is very kind.

On Christmas Eve she wrote – with almost girlish regret – of what was missing in her life: 'Had a very bad sick-headache. Wrote a few lines to Lord

[6] Jessica Rutherford, *A Prince's Passion: The Life of the Royal Pavilion*, Brighton: The Royal Pavilion, 2003, pp. 156–7.

Melbourne. Signed. Oh! what a pity Lord Melbourne cannot spend Xmas with me. It is this day week I had my last charming delightful ride at Windsor, and this day fortnight I had that charming walk to the Farm, both of which I will always remember with delight.' Later the same day came the letter that she really wanted: 'Received a very kind letter from Lord Melbourne, the beginning part of which is as follows: "Lord Melbourne presents his humble duty to Your Majesty and acknowledges with great gratitude Your Majesty's most gracious letter. Your Majesty may feel assured that nothing but zeal for Your Majesty's service and the well-being of the country could prevent him from being near Your Majesty's Person, where he feels it to be his duty to attend. Lord Melbourne will certainly come down on Wednesday and hopes to be able to remain till the following Monday and perhaps longer." This is delightful news.'

Lord Melbourne finally arrived on Boxing Day and the Queen's relief and joy are almost palpable:

> Talked of the gentlemen having been leaping in the School on the side saddle in the day, &c.; of horses, Quentin's admirable temper with horses, which Lord M. said all the Germans had, never flogging them. 'Nothing so bad for animals as striking them,' said Lord M., 'flogging is good for men, women, and boys, as they know what it's for, but not for animals', which made me laugh, but which is very true . . .
>
> After dinner before we sat down, Lord Melbourne admired the Pavilion, which has been regilt and cleaned up; and talked of what it was in 1805, when the Prince of Wales, Lord M. said, lent it to his father, after his eldest brother Peniston died. Talked of the Prince of Wales walking up and down every evening in the summer on the Steyne with numbers of people; very gay here then, said Lord M., but too much drinking, &c., &c. We were seated much as generally, Lord Melbourne being in his old place by my side. I told him what a great happiness it was to have him here again, and I expressed my regret at having written to him so often and pressed him so, which he would not allow.

On 28 December, though, there was an altogether more serious aspect to their conversations, when

> Lord M. said, that he had seen Mr. Rice, and had had a long conversation with him; about the state of the country; about the failure of this Belgian

> Bank, which he said would affect a good many English who were in it; 'It's a bad thing for them (the Belgians) at this moment,' said Lord M. Asked Lord M. how the Revenue here was. 'The Revenue is going on very well,' he replied; 'it's better this quarter.' Talked of our having had some money difficulties; 'There were one or two crashes,' said Lord M., 'in 26 and in 36, when those American houses failed.' Lord M. said Brown's house at Liverpool failed, and two others, and Baring was near failing by Bates drawing him into it.

Two days later, the joyful badinage returned, when

> Lord M. said he had never had his hair dressed, or worn powder, but that he had great difficulty to persuade his father to let him crop his hair. Lord Normanby reminded Lord M. how very black his hair was when he first knew him; Lord M. said it was beginning to turn then; 'I began to be seriously alarmed about it,' said Lord M., 'when I was at Paris; I had all the grey hairs pulled out; I had three women at it, and in a week's time there were just as many; and you have no idea how painful it is, when you go on doing it for an hour together.' He said this so funnily.

It showed no signs of fading on New Year's Eve:

> Talked of George IV's saying that the women now weren't as handsome as they used to be. 'Oh! he used to say,' Lord M. said, 'the women are now fit to be spit upon .' But I observed they were <u>much better</u>; 'A little,' said Lord M., 'rather more correct; when he (George IV) came into the world, it was a time of great license [sic]'; and he agreed they were much better; 'hardly any then that were not very improper, or who were proper, not one of them,' he added . . . Talked of my feeling cross and low, and Lord M. said: 'That's because you are not well'; that he had been so very low these last few days for no reason; 'I am at this moment,' he said, 'in very low spirits', which grieved me deeply. Talked of my feeling often shy and saying stupid things, which he said, I did not, and of plaguing him with questions, &c. . . .

The repartee continued on New Year's Day:

> Talked of my getting on in *Oliver Twist*; of the descriptions of 'squalid vice' in it; of the accounts of starvation in the Workhouses and Schools, Mr. Dickens gives in all his books. Lord M. says, in many schools they give children the worst things to eat, and bad beer, to save expense; told him Mama admonished me for reading light books. Lord M. took 2 apples (*Newtown pippins*), put one on his plate, and wrapped up the 2nd in his napkin, and hid it in his lap; he did this in such a playful manner as made me and himself laugh very much. When the one was eaten, the 2nd was produced from its hiding place. He then mentioned Mrs. Jordan as such a charming actress, though a little vulgar; 'there was nothing like her,' he said, her spirits and all.[7] Talked of Mme. Vestris, her being half Italian; Garrick's mother being Italian, which Lord M. told us and which I never knew. 'It's very rare to see a good actress,' said Lord M., 'it's very rare to see a good anything, that's the fact.'[8]

Christmas 1839

By the following Christmas, which was spent at Windsor Castle, the idyll was beginning to come to an end, with the approaching marriage – engineered by her uncle Leopold – of Queen Victoria to her first cousin, Prince Albert of Saxe-Coburg and Gotha. The conversations that took place between the bride-to-be and her father-figure are gently reminiscent of those that typically take place six weeks before weddings. Who was to be invited? Where was the ceremony to take place? Would the two families get on? Who would have precedence over whom? On Christmas Eve, the Queen recorded the following:

> Wrote to Lord Melbourne and Uncle Leopold. Wrote my journal. Sat to Ross. At 12 m. to 1 Lord Melbourne came to see me and stayed with me till 20 m. to 2. He was quite well. 'Lord Seaford will do this,' he said, giving me a letter from Lord S. saying he would second the Address. 'Here's a letter from Lord Holland about the Duke of Sussex,' he said, no doubt the

[7] For twenty years, until 1811, Mrs Dorothea Jordan was the mistress of the Duke of Clarence, later King William IV, with whom she had ten illegitimate children, who all bore the surname FitzClarence.
[8] Royal Archives: VIC/MAIN/QVJ/1838.

D. of S. thought he had got 'a capital pint', which Lord M. says is a joke amongst them all, for the Duke always says pint instead of point.[9]

Lord Holland states all the reasons why the Duke ought to give way; but Lord M. says it will never do to argue it with him. Lord H. also says, perhaps if the Duke were told he were to give me away, it would soften him; but Lord M. said that wouldn't do, as I declare if he does not consent, he shall not give me away. Lord Holland states that when George III's brother, the Duke of York, was made a Privy Councillor, the Duke of Cumberland, the Duke's Uncle, said his rank must be settled, upon which the Statute says: 'The King's sons, brothers, uncles', – upon which the Duke of Cumberland said, 'then I go after the Duke of York', and others present agreed in this. Talked of the King giving his Wife rank by marriage, and likewise that she didn't require being naturalised; now the Queen's husband is quite in another position, and derives no rank from his wife, &c. I said I thought some rank ought to be settled. Lord M. then said he had seen Mr. Musgrave again, and talked to me about how it was settled.

I showed him a letter from the Duchess of Bedford (Lady T.) wishing I should be married in St. Paul's!! which we agreed would be worse than the Coronation, &c. Told Lord M. I had been writing to Uncle Leopold about Albert's Household. 'We shall have great difficulty with those Appointments about the Prince,' said Lord M., in which I agreed, and said I thought Albert didn't quite understand it. 'It won't do at all to give a Tory character to it,' said Lord M. in which I quite agreed; 'for else he would be in opposition to you; he must stand by your Government; for else if the Tories see the least clue, they'll take hold of him, and make use of him even without his knowing'; which would, God knows! put us in opposition to one another which would be too dreadful!! Talked of my knowing so few of my own people before I took them.

Talked of the Germans having all a little Tory feeling; 'All foreigners have,' said Lord M., 'and very naturally, they think our liberal opinions very rough and disagreeable' (these are not the exact words he used, I think, but very nearly). Lord M. is so very fair. Talked of foreigners not understanding England, and vice versa, as Lord M. said; of Uncle Leopold liking the Whigs; of the Kinnairds; the mild weather for Xmas, &c. I then

[9] Prince Augustus Frederick, Duke of Sussex, was the sixth son of King George III and Queen Charlotte. Dismayed by what he regarded as the disorderly interment of his brother, King William IV, in the royal vault at St George's Chapel, Windsor in 1837, he insisted on being buried in the Cemetery of All Souls at Kensal Green, the first member of the British Royal Family to be buried outdoors in a public cemetery.

> took out of my apron pocket a Seal like this (in large), [illustration], on which I had had engraved at one end, Lord M.'s arms, at the other his crest; and I said I hoped he would accept it as a Xmas box, and that it would make me very happy, if he would use it sometimes. 'Thank you, Ma'm,' he said, 'I'm sure I shall always use it', and I pressed his hand in mine; I said he would know now why I had asked for the impression of his seals!

On Christmas Day the Queen went to church with her family and Christmas guests:

> They sang a beautiful anthem by Handel, 'There were shepherds'; I never heard anything so beautiful as the boy's voice. We stayed upstairs during all the prayers in the Communion Service, and then went down, and we all knelt before the Altar; that is I, Mama, Lady Normanby, my 3 ladies, Lord Melbourne, Lord Normanby, Lord and Lady Albemarle, Lady Fanny, and Lord Byron. It was a fine and solemn scene in this fine old Chapel. I felt for one, my dear Albert, – & wished he could be by my side, – also dear Lehzen, – but was very glad Lord Melbourne was there, the one whom I look up to as a father, and I was glad he took it with me.
>
> When we had all received (that is our party) we went upstairs again and remained there till it was all over, which it was at 5 m. to 2. I thought Lord M. seemed affected. It was a beautiful bright day, and I walked away from the Chapel, all the people running after me, – and when I reached the courtyard they all cheered, – which filled good Lord Melbourne's eyes with tears. We then walked on the Terrace, and Lord M. said to me with tears in his eyes, 'It did very well', in which I quite agreed; and he said you could always do everything when you went to the right person, but that if you sent another person and didn't do it yourself, it never would do; for they always said I never could take the Sacrament here. Talked of the Chapel being a fine thing; 'Very fine,' said Lord M. quite touched, good kind man.[10]

After their marriage, Queen Victoria and the Prince Consort took Holy Communion together twice a year, at Christmas and at Easter.[11]

[10] Royal Archives: VIC/MAIN/QVJ/1839.

[11] Sidney Lee, *King Edward VII: A Biography: From Birth to Accession*, London: Macmillan & Co., 1925, p. 47.

During the next three days conversation remained focused on traditional pre-wedding subjects:

> Talked of my having so much money. 'Good thing,' said Lord M., 'good thing to be able by and by to lay by a little, so as to be able to have some in case of an emergency; if ever you wished, sometimes in case of a general election, it's astonishing what £2,000 does; I understand George III gave a great deal in elections.' I said our people never gave enough money; 'We haven't enough,' he said . . . After dinner we were seated as usual; Lord Melbourne sitting near me. He said he was pretty well, but I thought seemed tired; talked of Lady Kinnaird; of church next day; Lord M. would go; I said he never stayed the Communion now; 'Yes, I do,' he said. He ought, I added. He as usual played with *Islay*; the poor little dog is so fond of him, and he so fond of the dog. I observed he was tired, and that I knew when he was bored, which he wouldn't at all allow, but which made him laugh very much, &c.
>
> I observed they were all wanting Lord M. to marry; 'Yes, when people get married, they want everybody else to marry,' said Lord M. I thought his sister wished him to marry; 'Women are always wanting people to marry,' he replied. I said Albert wrote to me that he was glad when he heard of anybody's marrying, as he thought they must be happy; some people thought just the contrary, said Lord M., and he said that a Mr. White once said at Cambridge: 'Take heed, my young Collegers, my friends are all married, and all miserable.'[12]

The Marriage of HM Queen Victoria with Prince Albert of Saxe-Coburg and Gotha, Duke of Saxony

Queen Victoria had no such uncertainty. On 10 February 1840 in the Chapel Royal, St James's Palace, she married Prince Albert of Saxe-Coburg and Gotha, Duke of Saxony. The happy day – in which Lord Melbourne played a full part – is described in detail in her Journal:

> The last time I slept alone. Got up at a ¼ to 9, – well, and having slept well; and breakfasted at ½ p. 9. Mama came before and brought me a Nosegay of orange flowers. My dearest kindest Lehzen gave me a dear little ring.

[12] Royal Archives: VIC/MAIN/QVJ/1839.

Wrote my journal, and to Lord M. Had my hair dressed and the wreath of orange flowers put on. Saw my precious Albert for the last time alone, as my Bridegroom. Dressed. Saw Uncle, and Ernest who dearest Albert brought up. At ½ p. 12 I set off; dearest Albert having gone before. I wore a white satin gown, with a very deep flounce of Honiton lace, imitation of old. I wore my Turkish diamond necklace and earrings, and my Angel's beautiful sapphire broach [sic]. Mama and the Duchess of Sutherland went in the carriage with me; I subjoin an account of the whole, which is pretty correct, only that they put in that I cried, and I did not shed one tear the whole time, and some other foolish things about Albert which they have said. To return to my going to St. James's, I never saw such crowds of people as there were in the Park, and they cheered most enthusiastically . . .

The Ceremony was very imposing, and fine and simple, and I think ought to make an everlasting impression on every one who promises at the Altar to keep what he or she promises. Dearest Albert repeated everything very distinctly. I felt so happy when the ring was put on, and by my precious Albert. As soon as the Service was over, the Procession returned as it came, with the exception that my beloved Albert led me out. The applause was very great, in the Colour Court, as we came through; Lord Melbourne, good man, was very much affected during the Ceremony and at the applause . . .

At 20 m. to 4 Lord Melbourne came to me and stayed with me till 10 m. to 4. I shook hands with him and he kissed and pressed my hand. Talked of how well everything went off. 'Nothing could have gone off better,' he said, and of the people being in such good humour and having also received him well; of my receiving the Addresses from the House of Lords and Commons; of his coming down to Windsor in time for dinner. I begged him not to go to the party; he was a little tired; I would let him know when we arrived; I pressed his hand once more, and he said: 'God bless you, Ma'm,' most kindly, and with such a kind look.

Dearest Albert came up and fetched me downstairs, where we took leave of Mama and drove off at near 4; I and Albert alone, which was so delightful. There was an immense crowd of people outside the Palace, and which I must say never ceased till we reached Windsor Castle. Our reception was most enthusiastic and hearty and gratifying in every way; the people quite deafening us; and horsemen and gigs &c. driving along with us. We came through Eton where all the Boys received us most kindly, – and cheered and shouted. Really I was quite touched . . .

> At ½ p. 10 I went and undressed and was very sick, and at 20 m. p. 10 we both went to bed; (<u>of course</u> in <u>one</u> bed), to lie by his side, and in his arms, and on his dear bosom, and be called by names of tenderness, I have never yet heard used to me before – was bliss beyond belief! Oh! this was the happiest day of my life! – May God help me to do my duty as I ought and be worthy of such blessings![13]

Christmas 1840

Ten months later the relationship between the Queen and her Prime Minister was noticeably more formal and much less flirtatious. At Christmas dinner, Queen Victoria 'sat between Albert & Lord Melbourne, & talked with the latter about various things, also after dinner, amongst which that something might be done to prevent the poaching here'. On Boxing Day, 'our dear little girl came down again, very prettily dressed. I called Lord Melbourne in to look at her & he found her much grown & thought her features very pronounced for so young a child. He then stayed with me for ½ an hour & we had much conversation. He gave me a letter from the Ld Chancellor with reference to the subject of my making a Will. I have, of course, the power to dispose of all my <u>personal</u> property, & that is <u>all</u> I have done. Talked of this; & of making Albert Ranger of the Park, & of something being done to improve the sport, & increasing the game.'[14]

Christmas 1841

Lord Melbourne resigned on 30 August 1841, to be succeeded by Sir Robert Peel, Leader of the Tory Party. There had been discomfort in many circles about the influence wielded by Lord Melbourne over the young Queen.

Christian Friedrich, Baron Stockmar, formerly personal physician to Prince Leopold of Saxe-Coburg-Saalfeld, widower of Princess Charlotte of Wales, later became his private secretary, comptroller of his household and political adviser. The Baron, as he was known, was a close confidant of the Royal Family: for example, his advice was sought on whether Prince Albert was a suitable match for Queen Victoria while, after their marriage, he advised on a number of crises, including the relationship between the Queen and her Prime Minister and the education of her children.

[13] Royal Archives: VIC/MAIN/QVJ/1840.

[14] Royal Archives: VIC/MAIN/QVJ/1840.

Queen Victoria wrote that 'no one gave us better and wiser advice on the education of our Children'.[15]

During the early years of Queen Victoria's reign, George Edward Anson was a courtier of considerable influence: Keeper of Her Majesty's Privy Purse and Treasurer of the Household to Prince Albert. On 6 October 1841, Baron Stockmar wrote a 'severe memorandum' to Queen Victoria, which was read to Lord Melbourne by George Anson. 'Melbourne's face began to work: "God eternally damn it!" he suddenly exploded, leaping from the sofa and striding up and down the room, "flesh and blood cannot stand this."'[16] That Boxing Day, George Anson wrote a memorandum – a formal record of the situation. He explained:

> The Melbourne correspondence still is carried on, but I think is not in its pristine vigour by any means. He has taken no notice of the Baron's remonstrance to him, and we are in the dark in what manner, if at all, he means to deal with it . . . In the evening, instead of her usual conversation with her old Prime Minister, some round game at cards is substituted, which always terminates at eleven. The Prince, to amuse the Queen at this, has nearly left off his chess; his amusements – shooting or hunting – always commence and terminate between eleven and two, not to interfere with Her Majesty's arrangements, in which he is included as her companion.[17]

Three days later a letter was sent from Melbourne Hall, the Lamb family seat in Derbyshire: 'Lord Melbourne presents his humble duty to your Majesty. He received here yesterday your Majesty's letter of the 25th inst., upon a paper adorned with many quaint and humorous Christmas devices, and Lord Melbourne begs to offer to your Majesty, most sincerely and most fervently, the good wishes of the Season. Lord Melbourne will be in town on Friday evening next, and after that day will wait upon your Majesty, whenever your Majesty is pleased to command.'[18]

In early 1842 the Royal Family visited the Brighton Pavilion, for the last time: 'A month was spent there, but public demonstrations of goodwill proved so obtrusive that the Pavilion was abandoned as a royal residence

[15] Harold Nicolson, *King George the Fifth: His Life and Reign*, London: Constable and Co., 1952, p. 14.
[16] Longford, *Victoria R.I.*, p. 157.
[17] Arthur Christopher Benson and Reginald Baliol Brett, eds., *The Letters of Queen Victoria: A Selection from Her Majesty's Correspondence between the Years 1837 and 1861*, 3 vols., London: John Murray, 1908, (LQV I), Vol. I, p. 463.
[18] Ibid.

at the end of the stay.'[19] Lord Melbourne was to suffer a similar fate, fading slowly out of Queen Victoria's life, just as her love for Prince Albert blossomed. As Viscount Esher observed, that Lord Melbourne was Prime Minister in 1837 was 'a rare piece of good fortune'. Queen Victoria visited Lord Melbourne at Brocket Hall that year. It was another thirty-six years before she made a similar, public declaration of friendship, lunching with Benjamin Disraeli at Hughenden.

Christmas 1847

On 30 December 1847, Lord Melbourne wrote to Queen Victoria from Brocket Hall, his Hertfordshire home:

> Lord Melbourne presents his humble duty to your Majesty. He has received with great pleasure your Majesty's letter of this morning, and reciprocates with the most cordial heartiness your Majesty's good wishes of the season, both for your Majesty and His Royal Highness. Lord Melbourne is pretty well in health, perhaps rather better than he has been, but low and depressed in spirits for a cause which has long pressed upon his mind, but which he has never before communicated to your Majesty.
>
> Lord Melbourne has for a long time found himself much straitened in his pecuniary circumstances, and these embarrassments are growing now every day more and more urgent, so that he dreads before long that he shall be obliged to add another to the list of failures and bankruptcies of which there have lately been so many. This is the true reason why Lord Melbourne has always avoided the honour of the Garter, when pressed upon him by his late Majesty and also by your Majesty. Lord Melbourne knows that the expense of accepting the blue ribbon amounts to £1000, and there has been of late years no period at which it would not have been seriously inconvenient to Lord Melbourne to lay down such a sum.[20]

This is slightly at odds with the well-known story concerning Lord Melbourne's views on the Most Noble Order of the Garter, which is that what he liked about it was 'there was no damned merit in it'. As Leader of the Whigs, the party of the aristocracy, Lord Melbourne rather liked the fact that the Order of the Garter was in the gift of the monarch and was awarded

[19] Lee, *King Edward VII: A Biography: From Birth to Accession*, p. 21.
[20] LQV I, Vol. II, p. 165.

at least partly on the basis of breeding. On his twenty-first birthday, Prince Albert, later King George VI, was appointed to the Order by his father, to whom he wrote: 'I cannot thank you enough for having made me a Knight of the Garter. I feel very proud to have it, and will always try to live up to it.' King George V replied: 'I am glad you say you will try & live up to the Garter. Remember it is the oldest Order of Chivalry in the world.'[21] On 11 December 1945 Lord Louis Mountbatten was offered a barony, which he felt slightly demeaned his position, saying to his wife: 'I would gladly have the Garter *instead* if deemed worthy of it. For God's sake be tactful about that. The Order of Merit would be next best.'[22] Lord Melbourne died at Brocket Hall, from the effects of a stroke, on 24 November 1848.

[21] John W. Wheeler-Bennett, *King George VI: His Life and Reign*, London: Macmillan & Co., 1958, p. 100.
[22] Philip Ziegler, *Mountbatten*, London: Collins, 1990, p. 310.

Home for Christmas

Until the death of the Prince Consort – which title Prince Albert was formally granted by his wife on 25 June 1857 – Queen Victoria invariably spent Christmas with her rapidly expanding family at Windsor Castle. After the Prince Consort's death on 14 December 1861, she spent every Christmas – with the exceptions of 1871, 1877, 1886 and 1899 – at Osborne House on the Isle of Wight, which they had bought for just £26,000 in 1844, before embarking on an extensive rebuilding programme. On Christmas Eve 1886, she wrote in her Journal: 'Very busy, arranging the things for Christmas, which it seems quite strange to be spending at Windsor.'[1] The Court normally arrived at Osborne House in mid-December and remained there for two months.

In her Journals, Queen Victoria expresses disbelief – bordering on wonderment – that Prince Albert had willingly left Coburg, where he was very happy, in order to marry the Queen of England. In fact Prince Albert's upbringing was far from uncomplicated: fed up with her husband's behaviour, his mother left the family home when he was only five, and Albert never saw her again. Nevertheless, he later came to understand her decision and what drove her to take such drastic action. On Christmas Day 1840, Queen Victoria wrote: '<u>This</u> day, last year, I was an unmarried girl, & <u>this</u> year I have an angelic husband, & a dear little girl 5 weeks old! As soon as we had finished breakfast we went to see the Baby.' That New Year's Eve she wrote: 'We talked of my great gratitude for the <u>immense</u> blessings vouchsafed to me this year in the union to my precious & beloved Albert, the gift of our healthy little girl, & in my being so strong & well & having been so mercifully preserved in my hour of danger. But in the midst of all my happiness, I feel for my dearest Albert, having left his dear happy home, where he had so many pretty peaceful abodes & recollections, & this, all for <u>my</u> sake! We lovingly wished each other a happy New Year, as the clock struck 12.'[2]

[1] Royal Archives: VIC/MAIN/QVJ/1886.
[2] Royal Archives: VIC/MAIN/QVJ/1840.

Five days earlier, King Leopold I of the Belgians, who had done much to ensure this happy outcome, wrote encouragingly to his niece:

> I can well understand that you feel quite astonished at finding yourself within a year of your marriage a very respectable mother of a nice little girl, but let us thank Heaven that it is so. Any illness to which, unfortunately, we poor human creatures are very subject, would almost have kept you longer in bed, and make you longer weak and uncomfortable, than an event which in your position as Sovereign is of a very great importance.
>
> Because there is no doubt that a Sovereign without heirs direct, or brothers and sisters, which by their attachment may stand in lieu of them, is much to be pitied, viz. Queen Anne's later years. Moreover, children of our own, besides the affection which one feels for them, have also for their parents sentiments which one rarely obtains from strangers. I flatter myself therefore that you will be a delighted and delightful *Maman au milieu d'une belle et nombreuse famille* . . .[3]

Queen Victoria replied: 'I think, dearest Uncle, you cannot really wish me to be the "Mama d'une nombreuse famille," for I think you will see with me the great inconvenience a large family would be to us all, and particularly to the country, independent of the hardship and inconvenience to myself; men never think, at least seldom think, what a hard task it is for us women to go through this very often.'[4] Notwithstanding her initial reservations, Queen Victoria undertook this 'hard task' at regular intervals, giving birth to nine children between November 1840 and April 1857. Jeremy Paxman wrote: 'Victoria may have been celebrated as the ideal mother figure of the age, for example, but she was not terribly keen on child bearing. She called the whole business the "shadow side" of marriage, and resented the fact that it interrupted her sex life. Nor did the Queen much care for small children, especially when they were incapable of anything other than what she called "that terrible frog-like action".'[5] Sarah Bradford wrote: 'Victoria was a passionate and demanding wife – she must, one Royal Historian told Harold Nicolson, "have been great fun in bed".'[6]

[3] Arthur Christopher Benson and Reginald Baliol Brett, eds., *The Letters of Queen Victoria: A Selection from Her Majesty's Correspondence between the Years 1837 and 1861*, 3 vols., London: John Murray, 1908 (LQV I), Vol. I, p. 318.
[4] Ibid., p. 321.
[5] Jeremy Paxman, *The Victorians*, London: BBC Books, 2009, p. 111.
[6] Sarah Bradford, *Elizabeth: A Biography of Her Majesty the Queen*, London: Heinemann, 1996, pp. 4–5.

On 8 May 1872, Queen Victoria wrote from Buckingham Palace to her first-born, Princess Vicky, now Crown Princess Frederick of Prussia:

> I am most thankful to hear you are going on so satisfactorily. I never thought you cared (having 3 of each) whether it was a son or a daughter; indeed I think many Princes are a great misfortune – for they are in one another's and almost everybody's way. I am sure it is the case here – and dear Papa felt this so much that he was always talking of establishing if possible one or two of your brothers and eventual grandchildren (of which I fear there is the prospect of a legion with but little money) in the colonies. I don't dislike babies, though I think very young ones rather disgusting, and I take interest in those of my children when there are two or three – and of people who are dear to me and whom I am fond of – but when they come at a rate of three a year it becomes a cause of mere anxiety for my own children and of no great interest. What name is this fourth daughter to have?[7]

On Christmas Eve 1841, with the future King Edward VII just over six weeks old, Queen Victoria wrote: 'Christmas, I always look upon as a most dear happy time, also for Albert, who enjoyed it naturally still more in his happy home, which mine, certainly as a child, was not. It is a pleasure to have this blessed festival associated with one's happiest days. The very smell of the Christmas Trees of pleasant memories. To think, we have already 2 Children now, & one who already enjoys the sight, – it seems like a dream.'

On Christmas Day, '"Pussy" [Princess Vicky] came down to our breakfast, & was very well, & in the highest spirits. At 12 we had Service, performed by Lord Wriothesley Russell. This day is one we must ever hail with joy & gratitude, as the day on which our Blessed Saviour was born, Who has so mercifully redeemed us, poor sinners. We visited the Nursery & Albert drove me out. After luncheon showed "Pussy" to the Ladies, in the Corridor, & she remained in my room till near 5. The little Boy also came down for a little while; he really is a fine, large, fat Baby.'[8]

On 16 January 1842, Prince Albert described Louise Lehzen in a letter to Baron Stockmar as 'a crazy, common, stupid intriguer, obsessed with lust of power, who regards herself as a demi-god, and anyone who refuses

[7] Roger Fulford, ed., *Darling Child: Private Correspondence of Queen Victoria and the Crown Princess of Prussia 1871–1878*, London: Evans Brothers, 1976, p. 40.
[8] Royal Archives: VIC/MAIN/QVJ/1841.

to acknowledge her as such, as a criminal.'[9] Despite her having shielded the young Princess from the worst excesses of Sir John Conroy and her mother, there was now no place for Baroness Lehzen. Little more than eight months later, 'dearest Lehzen' departed, 'without saying goodbye to Queen Victoria, in order to spare her a scene,' and went to live at Bückeberg in Hanover, on a pension of £800 per annum.[10]

The Queen's Journal entry for New Year's Eve 1841 gives a very clear indication of how – and also of why – she and Prince Albert worked so well together:

> Went to St. George's Hall to look at more old pictures, & the more I see them the more thunderstruck & shocked I am at the way in which the pictures, many fine ones amongst them, & of interesting value, have been thrown about & kept in lumber rooms at Hampton Court, whilst this Castle, & Buckingham Palace are literally without pictures. George III took great care of all of them, George IV grew too ill to settle many things, except in the Corridor, & William IV, who was not famed for his good taste, sent all the pictures away.
>
> My care, as rather more my dearest Albert's, for he delights in these things, will be to have them restored, to find places for them, & to prevent, as much as it is in our power, pictures of the Family, & others of interest & value, from being thrown about again. Attended Evening Service in our Chapel. The Children were downstairs a little while with us, & we went up to the Nursery. There I read to Albert out of *Adolphus*. We dined alone together, read & spent a delightful quiet evening. But when one is as happy as we are, the parting from a year, which began so joyfully, is always sad. However, I must also, & indeed do feel unbounded gratitude to Him Who has ever been so merciful to us. I pray to Him, through His blessed Son, for the long continuation of our happiness.[11]

On 1 January 1844, Queen Victoria wrote in her Journal: 'A new year. May God bless & protect us, & may He grant that our dear Children may grow up to be a blessing & comfort to us! We wished each other tenderly a happy New Year, & I gave my dearest Albert some trifles, including the slippers I had been working, all of which seemed to give him pleasure. Got

[9] Elizabeth Longford, *Victoria R.I.*, London: Weidenfeld & Nicolson, 1964, p. 160.
[10] Ibid., p. 162.
[11] Royal Archives: VIC/MAIN/QVJ/1841.

up rather late, so went to Prayers before breakfast. As we passed through the Breakfast Room, there stood Vicky in her costume which delighted her dear Father & was a great surprise to him. It became her so well & is taken exactly from a print of my aunt, the P[ss] Royal, with Queen Charlotte, after West.'[12]

In a letter to her father, Eleanor Stanley described the Windsor Christmas festivities that year:

> I have not written to you for a perfect age, chiefly, I think, because it struck me the descriptions of Christmas trees and bonbons were more naturally addressed to Mama and dear Granny than to you. On Thursday night, Christmas, the dessert consisted almost entirely of the most lovely bonbons, dogs, men, steam-boats, &c., and the table was abandoned to pillage, everyone coming away loaded with spoils. The younger Royal infants were there during all dinner-time, the elder ones only came in to dessert, Princess Royal and Princess Alice looking very nice in wreaths of holly; the little ones went to bed directly after dinner, but the Princess Royal and Prince of Wales sat up till ten; you can't think how simple and happy all the Royalty looked, just like any other family, of the most united and domestic tastes.

That letter was swiftly followed by an account of how the New Year was welcomed in:

> We got all these joy-wishings and congratulations among ourselves over last night, having literally danced out the old year in a very merry country dance, though as the striking of the clock, midnight, was the signal for the dancing music to stop, and a flourish of trumpets to begin instead, during which the Queen walked round and shook hands with each of us, I can hardly say we danced in the New Year . . . Directly after twelve we broke up and the Queen retired, when the household began vigorously to shake hands, the ladies being most affecting in their salutes to one another, a proceeding which Lord Ormonde and some of the other gentlemen complained of, unless it was general among us all; but to this we of course

[12] Royal Archives: VIC/MAIN/QVJ/1844.

> turned a deaf ear, though there were elegant bits of mistletoe stuck about all the lamps and chandeliers in every direction.[13]

After her own rather dismal experience, the Queen took a great interest in the education of her children. In a commentary with which contemporary parents might well identify strongly – with respect to the excessive use of the word 'like' or the expression 'd'ya know what I mean?' – Queen Victoria wrote to her third son's tutor on 16 January 1865 that she 'must call Major Elphinstone's attention to a habit which Prince Arthur has got into, which ought to be checked: viz. constantly to say 'what' before a person has finished their sentence almost. This is in the first place, not civil, and is besides especially to be guarded against as being a defect in the old Royal Family; the Prince of Wales was very bad about it for some years & Prince Leopold has already begun adopting it. The Queen is glad to hear the lessons are so very good.'[14] Elizabeth Longford noted that 'Ponsonby reported that the devoted Elphinstone was not always pleased by HM's "crisp incessant" orders'.[15]

Neither was Queen Victoria afraid to offer advice on the education of her grandchildren. On 8 January 1868, she wrote to Crown Princess Frederick from Osborne: 'All you tell me about dear Willy interests me very much. That poor arm is a sad thing, but we must take it as a cross sent us and must be thankful if he is so dear, good and clever. But you begin too early with Latin. Our boys only began at 10 – and Willy is not 9.'[16] In many areas, Queen Victoria was notably progressive: having been the first member of the Royal Family to be vaccinated, against smallpox in her youth, she was also the first to use chloroform, administered by her anaesthetist, John Snow MD, during the birth of Prince Leopold on 7 April 1853.

On Christmas Day 1856, Queen Victoria wrote in her Journal: 'Poor Vicky gets low on these anniversaries, of which she feels, poor dear Child, that she will spend so few more with us & her merry brothers & sisters. It is very sad to think of leaving one's happy home to bid adieu to one's

[13] Beatrice Erskine, *Twenty Years at Court: From the Correspondence of the Hon. Eleanor Stanley*, London: Nisbet and Co., 1916, pp. 202–206.

[14] Royal Archives: Vic. Add. MSS. A/25. In writing of the old Royal Family, Queen Victoria was referring to King George III and Queen Charlotte and their children.

[15] Longford, *Victoria R.I.*, pp. 367 and 447. Prince Leopold was created Duke of Albany by letters patent dated 24 May 1881. The day before Queen Victoria wrote to the Princess Royal: 'I always say no one can be a Prince, but anyone can be a duke.'

[16] Roger Fulford, ed., *Your Dear Letter: Private Correspondence of Queen Victoria and the Crown Princess of Prussia 1865–1871*, London: Evans Brothers, 1971, p. 167.

happy childhood.'[17] Although she had turned sixteen just five weeks earlier, Queen Victoria and Prince Albert were already planning the most important of their dynastic intermarriages, that of their eldest daughter with Crown Prince Frederick of Prussia. Exactly two years later, the Queen wrote from Windsor to the Crown Princess:

> How can I sufficiently thank you for your dear gifts? That beautiful quilt – your own dear work – which shall go about with me everywhere, and the lovely bracelet from you both which is set on my arm – so liked, so pretty, so nicely set and gives me immense pleasure. Dearest child, I missed your dear, warm, affectionate hearty greeting – your busy anxious endeavours to help and please us all! No-one showed this more than you, my dearest child! – You are constantly in our thoughts – but your dear letter and your gifts – the kind and touching way in which you thought of us all (for which God bless your warm, loving heart) brought you very near to us, and our spirits joined at least!
>
> I had your picture on my arm (a little photograph in the wedding dress) and Affie's [Alfred, Duke of Edinburgh, the Queen's second son] in a locket, and your pretty little locket given me the last evening at dear Babelsberg round my neck – and while I gazed on the happy merry faces – amongst whom you used to be – I thought of the inroad time had made in the "children"! But then I thought also with pleasure, with thankfulness and with security that our dear child was and is surrounded by tender love and affection, is prized and cherished as her loving parents' anxious hearts could wish – by the most devoted of husbands and the kindest of parents-in-law. This is a blessed assurance.[18]

As time went on, Queen Victoria exercised a less rigid control over her younger children's choice of spouse. At Osborne House on 23 December 1884, she wrote in her Journal: 'After tea Louis Battenberg brought his brother Liko, who has come from Berlin to spend Xmas with him and Victoria, and they three dined with us and Helen.' Six days later, the Queen

> received a letter from Liko Battenberg saying that my kind reception of him encouraged him to ask my consent to speaking to Beatrice, for whom,

[17] Royal Archives: VIC/MAIN/QVJ/1856.

[18] Roger Fulford, ed., *Dearest Child: Private Correspondence of Queen Victoria and the Crown Princess of Prussia 1858–1861*, London: Evans Brothers Limited, 1964, pp. 152–3.

> since they met in Darmstadt 8 months ago, he had felt the greatest affection! I had known for some time that she had had the same feelings towards him. They seem sincerely attached to each other, of that there can be no doubt. I let Liko know, to come up after tea, and I saw him in dear Albert's room. Then I called the dear child, and gave them my blessing. Lenchen [Princess Helena] was so delighted that all was satisfactorily settled, and poor Helen so pleased too, though it must be very trying for her.
>
> Ludwig, Victoria, and of course Liko, dined with us, and were all very happy. Besides the family, J. Ely, Mrs. Moreton, Miss Loch, Mr. White (my Minister at Bucharest), Sir J. Cowell, and Adm. de Horsey, dined. Beatrice looked very happy, but very quiet, and sat near her dear Liko, who is certainly very charming. Mr. White is an oldish man, clever and agreeable, with a very loud voice. He spoke in high terms of Sandro, and a good deal of the King and Queen of Roumania.'[19]

The following day, she wrote to Crown Princess Frederick: 'Lenchen & Beatrice have both written to you & the former has told you of the pain it has caused me that my darling Beatrice shld. wish to marry – wh. she never did till she lost her dear Brother – as I hate marriages specially of my daughters; but as I like Liko very much & as they are both so vy. much devoted to each other, I cannot refuse my consent. Nothing was settled till yesterday – & I cld. have said nothing before, as all was uncertain.'[20]

On 6 January 1885 Princess Beatrice wrote to Lady Waterpark: 'If good wishes could make me happy, I am sure I ought to be so, but I think I have every reason to look with confidence to the future. It is a great comfort to me that Mama is now thoroughly reconciled to the thought of my marrying, & that my future husband has already endeared himself to Her. Please God this event may brighten her life, & our one wish both of us, is to devote our lives to Her.'[21]

Princess Beatrice and Prince Henry of Battenberg, who was always known as Liko within the family, were married at St Mildred's, Whippingham, the parish church closest to Osborne House, on 23 July 1885. Queen Victoria's only stipulation was that Beatrice and Liko should live with her at Osborne,

[19] George Earle Buckle, ed., *The Letters of Queen Victoria, Second Series: A Selection from Her Majesty's Correspondence between the Years 1862 and 1885*, London: John Murray, 1926–8 (LQV II), Vol. III, p. 586.
[20] Roger Fulford, ed., *Beloved Mama: Private Correspondence of Queen Victoria and the Crown Princess of Prussia 1878–1885*, London: Evans Brothers, 1981, p. 176.
[21] *The Diary of Lady Waterpark, Lady-in-Waiting to Queen Victoria 1865–91*, British Library ref. Add. 60750, p. 290.

in order to keep her company. On New Year's Eve 1887, her Golden Jubilee Year, the Queen wrote:

> The last day of this eventful year. – Very dull all day. – After breakfast out with Beatrice I (alas! as always now) in my pony chair, & Beatrice walking. Called at Kent House, which I have lent Mrs. Bigge for her & her 3 children. The youngest, a boy, is just 10 days older than our little Scotch Baby, & a large fine child.[22] – In the afternoon, drove with Helen, & Marie A. Dull, dark & dreary. – The Maharajah of Kuch Behar, who had been staying for the few days at Quarr Abbey for a Ball at Ryde, & came over from there, Jane C., Marie A., Sir H. Ponsonby, Sir J. Cowell, &c. dined with us, & afterwards, the other Ladies & Gentlemen came into the Drawingroom. The Maharajah took leave, on his return to India. The Marine string Band played in the Hall. Went upstairs, & Jane C. read to me, & I remained quietly writing. After 12, Beatrice & Liko, came in, & wished me a happy New Year.[23]

Just three days earlier her eldest daughter, Vicky, had written, full of foreboding, to her mother:

> So many affectionate thanks for your dear letter written on Christmas Eve. This will be my last letter in the Old Year, your Jubilee Year, never to be forgotten, which has brought much happiness, also much anxiety. It is not without the usual uncertainty that the New Year begins – but still I am full of hope, as Sir Morell Mackenzie is even more satisfied this time than he was before, and more reassured about the appearance of Fritz's throat than a week ago . . . [William] must buy his own experience, as he does not listen to us. The people who for almost 30 years have been nasty to Fritz and especially to me, are the very same who run after William, who have him quite in their pocket and Dona also, the same people or clique as used to persecute my parents-in-law, as long as they were Prince and Princess of Prussia, and who only became such devoted admirers of the Emperor since he dropped all his old principles and all his old friends, and took

[22] Princess Victoria Eugenie of Battenburg, later Queen Ena of Spain, was born at Balmoral on 24 October 1887, the only royal princess to be born at Balmoral.
[23] Royal Archives: VIC/MAIN/QVJ/1887.

> Bismarck in 1863, and the retrograde era began . . . But I must not bore you with these things, which can only be of secondary interest to you.[24]

On Christmas Day 1890, Queen Victoria's eldest grandson, now the German Emperor, wrote to her from Berlin:

> Dearest Grandmama,
> Let me thank you from all my heart for your kind letter sent through General v. Wittich and the presents, which I brought to Dona at Christmas Eve. I am deeply touched by the kindness you so graciously showed to my envoy, and he himself cannot enough express his gratitude for all you did for him. It must have been a fine and imposing ceremony, the more so [as] the much lamented sculptor was so suddenly called away. What a great loss he will be to you all! Wittich thinks the statue the very best likeness he has ever seen of dear Papa, and was quite full of its beauty.
>
> As there are only a few days left before the New Year arrives, I beg you to kindly accept my most hearty and best wishes for the New Year, which may bring you happiness and success in every way. My prayers are that the Lord may keep His watchful hands over you night and day. The end of '90 is indeed on the whole the most peaceful we have had for a long time. Especially in England, the sudden fall of Parnell and the exposure of the plans of Gladstone are [such] a piece of good fortune, as seldom falls to a statesman, and right glad am I for Lord Salisbury and you! Here we are getting on very well with Caprivi, who is already adored by friends and revered by his Opposition.[25] I think he is one of the finest characters Germany ever produced, and am sure you would immediately like him as soon as you saw him . . .
>
> I end my letter with my sincerest wishes for a happy New Year and a Merry Christmas, and kiss your hands, remaining your most devoted and affectionate grandson, William I. R.[26]

[24] Frederick Ponsonby, ed., *Letters of the Empress Frederick*, London: Macmillan & Co., 1930, pp. 270–71.
[25] Leo von Caprivi succeeded Bismarck as Chancellor and served from 1890 to 1894. He gave his name to the Caprivi Strip, a 280-mile eastward extension of Namibia, which borders Angola, Zambia and Botswana and had been exchanged with the United Kingdom in order provide German South-West Africa (now Namibia) with access to the Zambezi, and thus to German East Africa (now Burundi, Rwanda and the mainland part of Tanzania).
[26] George Earle Buckle, ed., *The Letters of Queen Victoria, Third Series: a Selection from Her Majesty's Correspondence between the years 1886 and 1901*, 3 vols., London: John Murray, 1930–32 (LQV III), Vol. 1, pp. 665–6.

On 30 December 1893, Queen Victoria wrote in her Journal: 'A good deal troubled with pain in my legs, which makes it so difficult for me to get about. After breakfast and my Indian lesson, which I do very regularly, went out with Louise, Beatrice, and Victoria, and went to the churchyard at Whippingham, where I placed some flowers on good Mrs. Prothero's grave. In the afternoon drove with Victoria and Lorne through Newport. He always makes himself so pleasant.'[27] On 7 August the previous year, Queen Victoria had written: 'Tea out with Lenchen & Thora [Princess Helena Victoria of Schleswig-Holstein, Lenchen's elder daughter], & later, drove to Whippingham to enquire after poor Mrs. Prothero, who was going away next day. She came up to the carriage, looking very bad, crying, & speaking as if she would never see us again. We tried to cheer her up.'

Bernard Mallet, the husband of the Hon. Marie Adeane, one of Queen Victoria's Ladies-in-waiting, had been invited by the Queen to stay at Osborne for Christmas during the Diamond Jubilee Year.[28] He wrote in his diary on 23 December 1897: 'Xmas Eve at ¼ to 6 I was present at the household Xmas Tree at which the Queen gave her presents to the household. The Princesses were there, and the most handsome presents were given all round, Marie getting a case of large silver gilt spoons, the usual pocket book and some odds and ends, including a man of gingerbread, a German custom. When the Princesses left they fell on the tree and divided the spoils, filling waste paper baskets! I forgot that she gave me a Jubilee pin at the tree which Princess Beatrice presented. I hope my son will always keep it! I wrote, as is the custom, to thank her Majesty.'[29]

On Christmas Day 1897, he wrote:

> A most lovely warm sunny day, with frost at night. Chapel in house – a long low ugly room, the building and ugly decoration of which cost between 5 and 6 thousand. The Rector of Whippingham preached a good simple sermon. Short service, with carol and hymn. Afterwards Lord Lorne and I had a second game of golf in the lovely grounds towards the sea and he won today! Called with Marie on Bigges and Edwards in afternoon, and after tea was summoned with the household to the Durbar Room to see the Royal presents set out on long tables round the room. The Queen in

[27] LQV III, Vol. II, p. 334.

[28] Sir Bernard Mallet KCB (1859–1932), Registrar General and President of the Royal Statistical Society 1916–18.

[29] Victor Mallet, ed., *Life with Queen Victoria: Marie Mallet's Letters from Court 1887–1901*, London: John Murray, 1968, pp. 125–6.

her chair was wheeled round to see her presents and examined everything with the most evident and lively interest and pleasure – a touching sight. N.B. This happened on Xmas Eve after our own presents had been given. The whole household, including myself, dined with the Queen, but not unluckily in the Indian room, which was full of presents. Baron of beef, woodcock pie from the Lord Lieut. of Ireland, boar's head displayed on sideboard. I was placed as on the evening before. A very pleasant evening. At night played as before with Lord Lorne at billiards and had a great deal of pleasant talk.[30]

On Boxing Day, Bernard Mallet wrote: 'A great day for Christmas cards all round, the Queen sending one to Marie and one to Victor [their son] with their names written by herself on the back.'[31]

Of Christmas Day 1899, which she spent at Windsor, Queen Victoria wrote:

A very beautiful bright Xmas day. – Breakfasted all together in the Oak Room. – Service at 11, at which the Dean preached a particularly nice sermon. – Went out afterwards with Louise & Lorne. – Again a very large luncheon. – Drove with Beatrice & Helen, getting out at the Mausoleum, to place some sprigs of holly round the sarcophagus, & stopped at the Shaw Farm & Gardens to give my Xmas presents to Mr. Tait & Mr. Thomas. – We had our tree lit up again, after tea, & the Ladies & Gentlemen came in to see our presents – Had a big dinner in the large Diningroom, all the family including Louis & Victoria B., Affie & Thora & Drino, as well as all the Household. We were 31 & 19 family! One could not help feeling sad in the midst of it all, thinking of this anxious war.[32]

In 1862 the Sandringham Estate, which then comprised some 7,000 acres and was owned by Spencer Cowper, an absentee landlord, was purchased by Queen Victoria for £220,000 for her eldest son and his new wife.[33] After his death on 6 May 1910, King Edward VII's widow, Queen Alexandra, continued to live at Sandringham House, while King George V and his family used York Cottage, which had been given to him as a wedding present by

[30] Ibid., p. 125.
[31] Ibid., p. 126.
[32] Royal Archives: VIC/MAIN/QVJ/1899.
[33] Sidney Lee, *King Edward VII: A Biography: From Birth to Accession*, London: Macmillan & Co., 1925, p. 143.

his father. Harold Nicolson described it as 'a glum little villa, encompassed by thickets of laurel and rhododendron, shadowed by huge Wellingtonias and separated by an abrupt rim of lawn from a pond, at the edge of which a leaden pelican gazes in dejection upon the water lilies and bamboos'.[34] York Cottage is now the Sandringham Estate Office. Both Sandringham and Balmoral are private residences which belong to the Royal Family, although the contents, for the most part, belong to the Royal Collection. A peculiarity of Sandringham – and indeed of King George V – was that during his reign all the clocks on the estate were set half an hour fast, which was known as 'Sandringham time'.

Osborne House was given to the nation by King Edward VII, according to the terms of the 1902 Osborne Estate Act. Since that time, the Royal Family has traditionally spent Christmas at Sandringham. On Saturday, 22 December 1901, the Prince of Wales wrote in his diary: 'May & I left with Lady Mary & Cust by 12.5 train, we reached Wolferton 40 mins late. Saw Mother dear & Toria at the house. Lady Knollys, Baba & Edge also arrived. Found the children flourishing. After tea we sorted out all the presents. After dinner played snooker & piquet with Cust.' The following day, with ' 9½° of frost, a nice bright morning', he 'went to church at 11.30. Papa & I paid Probyn a long visit, the first time I have seen him since his accident.[35] In the afternoon took all our Xmas presents up to the house & had them put on the tables.'[36]

King George V's leisure preoccupations can reasonably be called 'the three Ss': stamps, sailing and shooting. His biographer wrote: 'As a stamp collector, he was the equal of any of the world's philatelists. As a yachtsman, he knew as much about sailing as the most veteran of the Cowes specialists. And he was recognised as one of the best shots in England, with whom only Lord Ripon and Henry Stonor could compete.'[37] As if to emphasise his structured work/life balance of people, politics and pleasure, his diary entry for Wednesday 22 February 1933 reads, in its entirety: '4° of frost. Very cold NE wind. Held an investiture at 11.0 in uniform when I gave 115 decorations & 25 Police medals. I also receiv[d] the new Haytian [sic]

[34] Nicolson, *King George the Fifth: His Life and Reign*, p. 51.

[35] General Sir Dighton Probyn VC (1833-1924), Comptroller and Treasurer to the Prince of Wales's Household 1877–1901, Keeper of the Privy Purse 1901–10 and Comptroller of the Household to Queen Alexandra 1910–24.

[36] Royal Archives: GV/PRIV/GVD/1901.

[37] Nicolson, *King George the Fifth: His Life and Reign*, p. 142.

Minister. Chose stamps with Bacon in afternoon. Usual work with Wigram & Alec.'[38]

In 1904 a world record price of £1,450 was paid at auction for a mint, two-pence 'Post Office' Mauritius stamp. A member of his Household asked the Prince of Wales if he had seen that 'some damned fool had paid as much as 1400 pounds for one stamp'. 'Yes,' came the reply. 'I was that damned fool!'[39] The King was an equally obsessive 'bagger' of birds. On 18 December 1913 at Hall Barn, Beaconsfield, King George V was one of seven guns to have enjoyed perhaps the greatest-ever day of pheasant shooting, with a bag of 3,937 birds. The King shot 1,760 cartridges. The other six guns were the Prince of Wales, Lord Charles Fitzmaurice, Lord Ilchester, Lord Dalhousie, Lord Herbert Vane-Tempest and the Hon. Henry Stonor. It was a veritable *fin de siècle* occasion, at the end of the last shooting season before the outbreak of the First World War.

With his sense of duty and discipline, King George V insisted that his sons should describe each day's sport accurately in their game books. At Buckingham Palace on 22 December 1912, the Prince of Wales wrote in his diary: 'I changed at 7.00 & finished packing before dinner at 8.30. Afterwards I copied out some bits for Papa for Xmas & showed my game book which was not aproved [sic] of quite.' There was a mutually satisfactory solution, though. A week later, he wrote: 'In the evening I worked at history till 7.00 & then Mr. Jones helped Bertie & self with our game books.'[40]

King Edward VII had taken a great deal of trouble to develop his Norfolk estate: 'The sandy soil of the Sandringham estate well rewarded the Prince's strenuous efforts to perfect its shooting facilities by developing the coverts and adding to the stock of game. Grouse hardly flourished there, but partridges and pheasants multiplied, and marshy ground and good pools were attractive homes for snipe, woodcock, and wild duck.'[41]

It would not be completely unfair to describe King George V's personal diary as an expanded game book. On 9 November 1901 he was created Prince of Wales and Earl of Chester. His diary that Christmas is representative of the predominance of field sports during the festive season.

[38] Royal Archives: GV/PRIV/GVD/1933.

[39] www.royal.gov.uk.

[40] Royal Archives: EDW/PRIV/DIARY/1912.

[41] Lee, *King Edward VII: A Biography: From Birth to Accession*, p. 577.

On Christmas Eve 1901,

> Cust & I went to Castle Rising to shoot with Horace, we shot Wootton Carr, 6 guns, H. Stonor, Horace, W. Pack & Marsham, it was frosty & foggy, which prevented the birds flying well, we got about 280 cocks & 10 woodcock. Lady Farquharson came out to lunch. Home by 4.15. Alge came to stay with us. We all went up to tea at the house at 5.0, the children too. Aunt Louise & Lorne, Louise & Macduff, Frank, the Little Admiral & Harry Stephenson & Harry Stonor arrived. At 6.0 we went into the hall room & had the Xmas tree & saw all our lovely presents, the room quite looks like a shop, with all the tables covered with beautiful things. The children enjoyed themselves very much, poor baby [Prince Henry, later the Duke of Gloucester] couldn't come as he wasn't well, cutting his teeth. Only got home at 7.30.

Christmas Day was 'very mild, dull but fine with South wind. We all went to church at 11.30 & we received the Holy Communion together. In afternoon went to the house with Alge [Prince Alexander of Teck, 1st Earl of Athlone] & we brought Aunt Louise back & showed her the Cottage. At 4.30 May & I gave our presents to all the servants & people. Sweet Baby is much better today. Wrote letters all the evening. We all dined at the house, gave the Clergy their presents afterwards. Played billiards with Harry Stonor against Forty & Holzmann. Bed at 12.45.' For the traditional Boxing Day shoot, 'Papa, Frank, Alge & I went down to Wolferton & we shot the Marsh warren, the rabbits ran well, it was a lovely bright day & we got 636. Lunched in reading room, then had 4 drives over the halts & whins below Wolferton wood & got 30 pheasants, 18 partridges, 22 hares & 5 snipe.'[42]

In her diary on New Year's Day, the Duchess of York wrote: 'Bridget & I joined the shooters at lunch at Hillington & walked with them afterwards. At 5.30 we went up to the house with the children & were given our Xmas presents in the Ball room where a large Xmas tree stood. We received lovely things. We only got back at 7.30. After dinner we sent off cards. Good bye to 1901!'[43]

During the first ten days of his Sandringham sojourn, the Prince of Wales went shooting on six days, missing only Christmas Day, both Sundays and a 'quite impossible' Monday. According to a recent BBC 2 documentary,

[42] Royal Archives: GV/PRIV/GVD/1901.

[43] Royal Archives: QM/PRIV/QMD/1901.

King George and Queen Mary: The Royals who Rescued the Monarchy, 'Her husband's passions left his wife decidedly cold. After one particularly dull shooting party, she confided: "It was so stiff, I could have turned cartwheels for sixpence."'[44]

Until the First World War there was very little variation in the Christmas and New Year routine, as the Prince of Wales, the future King Edward VIII, described in his diary on New Year's Eve 1912:

> I wrote several letters before going out shooting with Papa at 10.15. The beat was Congham & I was not shooting as only 6 guns were wanted. They were Papa, Uncle Charles, Bertie, Lord Farquhar, Harry Stonor, Sir F. Ponsonby. I went out to watch & was with Papa most of the day. First they had 2 partridge drives & then shot the osier bed. Then they went in the Wood & had 2 rises & after that moved on over a field to another long covert where we had rises. Lunch was had in a tent beyond the wood & Mama & Mary came out.
>
> In the afternoon they first had a partridge drive & then shot the coverts they did in the morning the reverse way. There were a lot of woodcock about & Papa got 4. We got back at 4.15 & had tea at 5.00. In the evening I did some history & worked at my game book with Mr. Jones, & alone. Dinner was at 8.30 & we went up to the House before 10.00 to help distribute presents at the servants' Xmas tree which was all over in ¾ hour. There were a lot of people there. We got back at 11.15. Here ends another year, & we must take leave of 1912. For me, it has been a pleasant one taking it all round, & all I wish is that the New Year may be as pleasant to all I know & myself.'[45]

Over Christmas and New Year 1913, the two elder Princes were initially separated, with Prince Albert, the future King George VI, on duty in Gibraltar until late December.

On New Year's Eve, which began for him at Buckingham Palace, Prince Albert wrote in his diary: 'I got up at 8.0 and after breakfast I saw Davis about my new clothes. I arranged some things and wrote letters. At 12 I left the Palace and arrived at St. Pancras at 12.15. Captain Bremner met me and I had a good talk with him. I left by the 12.20 train arriving at Wolferton at 3.45. I motored here with Sir Charles Cust. I saw Mama and Mary on my

[44] BBC 2, *King George and Queen Mary: The Royals who Rescued the Monarchy*, 4 January 2012.
[45] Royal Archives: EDW/PRIV/DIARY/1912.

arrival, and the others when they returned from shooting. After tea I was given my presents by Papa and Mama. Dinner was at 8.30 and after that we went to the House for servants' Xmas tree. Bed at 11.30 p.m.'[46]

On 2 January 1914, Queen Mary wrote to her Aunt Augusta: 'Last night we all dined with Mama & even danced afterwards much to the enjoyment of the young people. God grant that this year may be a peaceful one & that the clouds over these dear Islands may disperse!!'[47] Despite this nervousness, none of the party can really have had the slightest idea how that dreadful year would end.

During the twenty-five years that King George V was on the throne, there was very little change in the Christmas routine, except that his immediate family moved from York Cottage to Sandringham House after Queen Alexandra had died. On 20 December 1927, which the King recorded as 'George's birthday (25)' and which was spent at Buckingham Palace, 'we dined early & took George & Paynter to the New Theatre to see 'The Wrecker' which was quite exciting.'[48] The following day, his sisters, 'Toria & Maud [Princess Victoria, King George V's unmarried middle sister, and his youngest sister, Queen Maud of Norway] came to tea, the latter starts for Norway tomorrow'.

On 22 December, 'May & I left for Sandringham by special train at 12.55, dear little Elizabeth (granddaughter), Lady Minto, Lady Katherine Hamilton (May's new Lady), Wigram & Paynter came with us. We arrived at 3.20, raining hard. Read all the evening.' The next day, the sport began, while there was also a worrying incident involving Prince George, later the Duke of Kent: 'Dark & raw with rain off & on. Paynter, Wigram, H. Betts & I shot Whin Hill wood & after lunching in reading room, we shot the belts, but the pheasants did not fly well on account of the wet. Home by 4.0. Our bag was over 260 pheasants; 22 hares; 7 rabb; 11 woodcock; & 3 var: Worked in the evening. George arrived at 8.45, having motored from London, just before reaching Hillington, his car skidded & turned over, but thank God neither he or his people were hurt, but all the glass was smashed.' 'Dear little Elizabeth', the future Queen Elizabeth II, was born in London on 21 April 1926 and was therefore just twenty months old that Christmas.

On Christmas Eve 1927, the King 'worked at my boxes all the morning & arranged Xmas presents with May. In afternoon we went to the stables

[46] Royal Archives: GVI/PRIV. DIARY/1913.
[47] James Pope-Hennessy, *Queen Mary, 1867–1953*, London: George Allen and Unwin, 1959, p. 482.
[48] Royal Archives: GV/PRIV/GVD/1927.

to see the meat given away to all the people on the estate. David, Harry, Derek, Bridget & Victoria Keppel, Colin & Etta Keppel, Bertie & Elizabeth, Campbell & Dick Molyneux arrived in the afternoon. After tea we went to the ball room for the Xmas tree & gave everybody their presents. Little Elizabeth was delighted with her toys.' On Christmas Day, 'we went to church at 11.30 & received the Holy Communion. It began to snow as we came out of church with strong bitterly cold N.E. wind, which became a regular blizzard & continued all day. After luncheon May & I gave all the servants their presents.'

On 30 December, 'May & I showed Elizabeth the kitchen &c. & we then had a short walk in the grounds.' On the last day of 1927, 'Bertie & Elizabeth & all our guests left this morning, but our grandchild remains. Went for a walk with May, freezing with sun & no wind, quite pleasant.' On New Year's Day 1928, the King 'gave Wigram the K.C.V.O. & knighted him. In afternoon we walked to the gardens & stud & saw the mares & yearlings. Claudie Hamilton & Alec Hardinge relieved Wigram & George Paynter.'[49] The year that they had just ushered in proved to be a difficult one for the Royal Family, with the King's illness and prolonged recuperation.

By the end of 1930 the King was fully recovered from his debilitating illness of 1928–9. On Christmas Eve, after 'a capital day's sport round Shernbourne' the previous day, he was 'busy all the morning arranging all the Xmas things & working. After luncheon went up to the stables to see the meat given away to all the people. At 3.30 Bertie & Elizabeth, George & Dorothy Cambridge & their daughter Mary, the Colin Keppels, Walter Lawrence, Harry Stonor, Dick Molyneux, Campbell & Harry Verney arrived. David & George got here in time for tea. We gave them their presents in the hall room at 5.45, the children were delighted.' On Boxing Day, 'David & George left after luncheon for Melton to hunt tomorrow.'[50]

[49] Royal Archives: GV/PRIV/GVD/1927.
[50] Royal Archives: GV/PRIV/GVD/1930.

Away at Christmas

Queen Victoria adopted a regular pattern for Christmas after her marriage; although different, the Royal Household's Christmas regime was equally predictable after the death of the Prince Consort. Notwithstanding the fact that travel was a rather more complicated affair, Queen Victoria took her responsibilities extremely seriously and probably did not contemplate an extended absence from her despatch boxes. Apart from frequent visits to her family in Germany, the Queen seldom ventured far during the early years of her widowhood. In the summer of 1868, though, she visited Switzerland with her four youngest children, bringing back a selection of sketches and watercolours. The family unit was also beginning to break up as, one by one, her children married. In 1869 the Prince and Princess of Wales and their young family spent six weeks over the Christmas period with the King and Queen of Denmark, at Fredensborg Castle. More than a decade later, Queen Victoria was so enamoured with her first visit to the French Riviera that she returned there on nine occasions.

In January 1873, Queen Victoria summoned her Private Secretary: 'I am an Empress & in common conversation am sometimes called Empress of India. Why have I never officially assumed this title? I feel I ought to do so & wish to have preliminary enquiries made.'[1] Despite having her wish granted on 1 May 1876, Queen Victoria never visited India, preferring instead to bring the country to her, both through the employment of Indian servants within her household, and also through the construction of the Durbar Room at Osborne House in 1890–91. Queen Victoria was never 'away at Christmas'.

The Duke of Edinburgh in India, 1869–70

On the other hand, her children, grandchildren and great-grandchildren were encouraged to travel widely, both in order to understand the nature of their responsibilities and also to assist in binding the Empire together. Until 8 January 1864, when the first child of his elder brother, Albert Edward, the Prince of Wales, was born, Prince Alfred was second in line to the throne. An

[1] Elizabeth Longford, *Victoria R.I.*, London: Weidenfeld & Nicolson, 1964, p. 404.

officer in the Royal Navy, he was promoted captain on 23 February 1866 and appointed to the command of the frigate HMS *Galatea*. On 24 May 1866, in the Queen's Birthday Honours, he was created Duke of Edinburgh, and he visited Australia in 1867–8, narrowly surviving an assassination attempt in Sydney on 12 March 1868. In late 1869 he embarked on another lengthy tour, once again in HMS *Galatea*, during which he was the first British Prince to visit India and Ceylon.

Writing from Calcutta to Queen Victoria on 27 December 1869, the Earl of Mayo described the welcome that the Duke received:

> The Viceroy and Governor-General of India presents his most humble duty to your Majesty, and begs to inform your Majesty, that his Royal Highness the Duke of Edinburgh arrived at Calcutta on Wednesday the 22nd. Owing to a fortunate state of the tide, the *Galatea* was enabled to come right up the Hooghly at once, and his Royal Highness landed at Prinseps Ghat, within a few yards of Fort William. The hour appointed was four o'clock in the afternoon; and the ship would have arrived at the proper time had it not been that, when she met the fresh water in the river, it had such an effect upon her boilers that she was obliged to reduce her speed by one-half.
>
> There was an immense concourse of people on the Maidan, and a line of two miles and a quarter was formed on the plain, by three Regiments of Europeans, and seven Regiments of Native Infantry. The form of procession described in the enclosed programme was followed, but unfortunately the night closed in before the long line of horsemen and carriages reached the middle of the Course, and it was quite dark when his Royal Highness reached Government House. The Duke looked remarkably well, he sat his Arab with great steadiness throughout though he was rather fidgety, for, though an Eastern charger is well used to troops and to firing, he is quite unaccustomed to the cheering and clapping of hands which accompany popular demonstrations.
>
> The whole scene, while light lasted, was very remarkable. Nothing like it was ever witnessed before at Calcutta. The natives turned out in immense numbers, and it is believed that every European resident in Calcutta and the neighbourhood was present. The side of the line reserved for carriages was lined with every description of conveyance, while the left side, which was kept wholly for Government people, was a great sea of heads. The natives appeared in all their finery, and the variety of colour, complexion

> and costume, made it a most picturesque assemblage. The troops comprised specimens of nearly all the races in the military service of your Majesty, while a semi-circle of seventy elephants in front of Government House made a most effective close to the pageant . . .
>
> On Thursday a Levée was held which was the largest which ever took place in India, being attended by seven Native Princes, and 1,500 European and Native gentlemen. In the evening the whole party witnessed a very fair display of fireworks on the Maidan, and afterwards drove for nearly four miles through the City to see the general illuminations, though for the most part they were conducted in the native fashion and consisted of an innumerable quantity of small lamps. The effect was excellent. The crowds in the streets of the native part of the city were enormous, and it is said that, of the 400,000 inhabitants of Calcutta, few were absent. The native police managed this immense concourse of people with great success, and with the exception of a few broken carriage panels no accident has been reported.
>
> The Viceroy has great satisfaction in informing your Majesty that his Royal Highness has already won golden opinions from everyone here. He is most courteous and considerate, and appears sincerely desirous to please. He willingly adopts every suggestion made either by the Viceroy or [Major-General, later Field Marshal] Sir Neville Chamberlain, and the Viceroy has little doubt that his Royal Highness will during his visit comport himself in a way worthy of his position, and in a manner which will be satisfactory to your Majesty.[2]

The Prince of Wales in India, 1875–6

Six years later, the Prince of Wales, later King Edward VII, also visited Ceylon and India, the first time that the heir to the throne had done so. On 1 December 1875 Queen Victoria wrote to Crown Princess Frederick: 'The accounts of dear Bertie are good and satisfactory but he does too much! – and in that heat.'[3] As if to emphasise the point, he sent a telegram from Ceylon to his mother six days later: 'Shot one elephant and wounded severely two

[2] George Earle Buckle, ed., *The Letters of Queen Victoria, Second Series: A Selection from Her Majesty's Correspondence between the Years 1862 and 1885*, 3 vols., London: John Murray, 1926–8 (LQV II), Vol. I, pp. 635–6.

[3] Roger Fulford, ed., *Darling Child: Private Correspondence of Queen Victoria and the Crown Princess of Prussia 1871–1878*, London: Evans Brothers, 1976, p. 200.

others.'[4] William Howard Russell of *The Times*, who had been sent by his editor, John Delane, to report on the conduct of the Crimean War in 1854 – thereby exposing a great deal of incompetence and lack of preparation and care – acted as the Prince's Honorary Private Secretary during the eight-month visit. He wrote 'a Journal or Diary kept from day to day', of which these are brief extracts:

> Calcutta, December 24th – The reception of the great Chiefs by the Prince at Government House to day, although accounted 'private,' was a very stately ceremonial, conducted with much official pomp and care . . . The receptions finished, a Levee was held in the Throne-room. The Prince, in full uniform, stood before the throne for more than two hours, bowing to the stream passing before him . . . After a grand banquet at Government House the Prince went to the entertainment prepared by a committee of Native gentlemen, at Belgatchia, a villa five miles away, from which the company did not get away till past midnight. What pleases Native gentlemen is not quite to English taste. There was a little too much smoke – too great a luxury of fireworks and illuminations to be agreeable to those who are so used to them by this time as to be very exacting and fastidious, but there were many pretty things. Above all, there was the intense wish to please. The dancing girls were so laden with clothes that only their faces and toes were visible, and dancing was lost in drapery.
>
> December 25th – Christmas Day. The Prince and the Viceroy attended Divine service in the Cathedral. It was a full choral service. Every seat was filled. The Communion-table was decorated with flowers, and the choir began the service by singing the Christmas Hymn, advancing in procession to the altar from the porch . . . The Prince, after his return from the Cathedral, drove to Prinsep's Ghaut, where thousands of natives and hundreds of Europeans, attracted by the *Serapis* dressed out with flags, had assembled. Two lines of sailors (Commander Bedford) and marines (Major Snow) were drawn up on the gangway, which was covered with scarlet cloth, and on pontoons extending from the shore to the ship. Outside, the officers of the *Serapis* and of the *Osborne*. Most of the blue-jackets had flowers in their breast. The deck was artfully transformed into a winter scene by means of shrubs and branches covered with cotton-wool

[4] Sidney Lee, *King Edward VII: A Biography: From Birth to Accession*, London: Macmillan & Co., 1925, p. 385.

to represent snow, which, with the aid of some glistening white powder, it did most successfully. Holly and ivy wreaths, fabricated on board, were suspended on the bunting-walls alongside inscriptions of 'Welcome, merry Christmas!' 'Happy new year!' 'God bless the Prince of Wales!' '*Cead mille failthe.*' 'Welcome.' Old Father Christmas was duly represented.

December 26th – After church the Prince made an excursion by water to Chandernagore. The visit delighted the residents in that pretty settlement. Some time ago it was supposed that France might be disposed to exchange it for an equal or larger slice of land in extension of Pondicherry. But times have changed, and any proposal of the kind now would be, it is said, embarrassing . . . By the time the Prince returned to the Ghaut all Chandernagore was there to cheer him, and cry, 'Vive le Prince de *Galles*'.[5]

December 31st – Tent-pegging – feats of horsemanship by troopers of the 10th Bengal Cavalry at 9 A.M. . . . The Prince was so much pleased that he gave a hunting-knife to the best man. A British trooper would have probably received the unexpected gift with much delight and *mauvaise honte.* The Towanna man was able to express a wish that he might be allowed to wear the knife when in uniform, and the wish was acceded to.

January 1st, 1876 – All fashionable Calcutta was awake early . . . The spectacle of the processions leaving was by far the most picturesque part of the pageant. The Viceroy, the Grand Crosses, and the Grand Knight Commanders and Companions following in reverse order of their entry. The pomp of elephants, the noisy cavalcade of Eastern ceremonial were wanting, and there was no token of the public interest such a grand spectacle would arouse on the part of the inhabitants in any European capital . . . In the afternoon the Prince, accompanied by the Viceroy, unveiled an equestrian statue of Lord Mayo on the Maidan, near Government House . . . After this ceremony, the Prince put on plain clothes, and drove to the Racecourse with the Viceroy, to witness a polo-match, an exciting contest between the Calcutta and Munipuri players; the former big men, on well-fed, well-groomed ponies; the latter light men, on ragged, poor-looking tats. The contest was rendered equal by the skill of the Munipuri men. The Prince went next to the display of fireworks on the Racecourse, which were not quite equal to expectation; but the spectacle of tens of

[5] Chandernagore was governed as part of French India until 1950, under the political control of the French Governor-General in Pondicherry. It was officially transferred to India on 6 June 1952, almost five years after the end of British rule in India.

> thousands of faces lighted up by mortars, rockets, and coloured fires, was worth seeing.[6]

On 2 February 1876, Queen Victoria wrote that 'Bertie's progresses lose a little interest and are very wearing – as there is such a constant repetition of elephants – trappings – jewels – illumination and fireworks.'[7] In her speech at the Opening of Parliament six days later, however, the Queen said: 'I am deeply thankful for the uninterrupted health which my dear son, the Prince of Wales, has enjoyed during his voyage through India. The hearty affection with which he has been received by my Indian subjects of all classes and races assures me that they are happy under my rule and loyal to my throne.'[8]

The Duchess of Teck in Florence, 1883–5

Princess Mary Adelaide of Cambridge, younger daughter of Prince Adolphus, Duke of Cambridge, youngest son of King George III, was married to Prince Francis of Teck, who was created Duke of Teck in 1871 and granted the title His Highness in Queen Victoria's Golden Jubilee year. Their eldest child was Princess Victoria Mary of Teck, who married the Duke of York, later King George V. In answer to a question posed at Sandringham in August 1951, Queen Mary explained that 'my parents were always in *short street* so they had to go abroad to economise. In September 1883 we went out to Florence and stayed in Paoli's Hotel on the Lungarno; then we stayed with cousins in Austria and so on; and then for the winter of 1884 we were lent (which suited my mother's finances) by a Miss Light, the Villa I Cedri, about two and a half miles outside the Porta San Niccolò.'

On 22 December 1884, the Princess of Wales wrote to the Duchess of Teck: 'It seems a perfect age since we parted & heard anything from each other – & now I can stand it no longer & send you these small offerings [diamond brooches, a photo frame, an 'egg pencil, owl & monkey'] as a *reminder* of me – & hope they will cheer you up as little Christmas messages from home . . . How are you all getting on – We all miss you terribly here & I most of all as you know . . . I saw dear Aunt Cambridge today – she is

[6] William Howard Russell, *The Prince of Wales' Tour: A Diary in India*, London: Sampson Low, Marston, Searle & Rivington, 1877, pp. 352–77.

[7] Fulford, *Darling Child: Private Correspondence of Queen Victoria and the Crown Princess of Prussia 1871–1978*, p. 204.

[8] Lee, *King Edward VII: A Biography: From Birth to Accession*, p. 393.

looking much about the same – but complains bitterly at never hearing from you!!'[9] The Tecks returned to London in May 1885.

Prince George with the Royal Navy at Malta, 1886

When the Prince of Wales's second son was born on 3 June 1865 at Marlborough House, Queen Victoria remarked: 'George only came over with the Hanoverian family. However, if the dear child grows up good and wise I shall not mind what his name is.'[10] In 1877, at the tender age of twelve, Prince George joined the Royal Navy. In a memorandum dated 15 February 1877, Queen Victoria wrote that 'the very rough sort of life to which boys are exposed on board ship is the very thing not calculated to make a refined and amiable Prince'.[11] In reality, though, it may well have been the making of Prince George. After spending two years in the naval training ship *Britannia*, between 1880 and 1883 he sailed round the world in the *Bacchante* in the company of his elder brother Prince Eddy, Duke of Clarence.

By then serving in HMS *Thunderer*, one of just two Devastation-class battleships, Prince George spent Christmas 1886 with his aunt and uncle, the Duke and Duchess of Edinburgh, on Malta. Queen Victoria's second son, Prince Alfred, the Duke of Edinburgh, was Commander-in-Chief of the Mediterranean Fleet and was married to Grand Duchess Marie Alexandrovna of Russia, daughter of Tsar Alexander II.

At San Antonio Palace, Prince George wrote in his diary on Christmas Eve:

> Got up at 8.0. Breakfasted at 8.30 all together. Finished arranging the Xmas tree. Lunched at 1.0. Choosing presents to give for Xmas till 3.0 when I went for a short walk by myself. Got a letter from darling little Julie. At 5.0 the Chair of the 'Alex' came & sang some carrols [sic] with Carlf. At 5.30 the dear little Admiral arrived from England & brought all my presents from Papa & Mama. At 6.45 we went & saw our tables & the Xmas tree, uncle Alfred & aunt Marie gave me some lovely presents. Gimlette goes home tomorrow, (made a mess of everything & behaved very badly, did not suit at all), Colin Keppel is now Flag Lieutenant, the dear little

[9] James Pope-Hennessy, *Queen Mary, 1867–1953*, London: George Allen and Unwin, 1959, pp. 112 and 137.

[10] Lee, *King Edward VII: A Biography: From Birth to Accession*, pp. 180–81.

[11] Harold Nicolson, *King George the Fifth: His Life and Reign*, London: Constable and Co., 1952, p. 14.

Admiral delighted. Dined at 7.0. Lestrange came to dinner. Played whist with aunt Marie, uncle Alfred & Lady Harriot [sic]. Bed at 11.15.

On Christmas Day he 'drove down to Custom House & went on board the old "Dreadnought". Divisions & church. Went on board "Thunderer" & wished them all a merry Xmas. At 12.0 walked round mess deck, messes beautifully decorated.' Into his diary he pasted a label, presumably saved from a Christmas present:

Xmas 1886
For my darling Georgie from
Old Motherdear

However, there was also work to be done, as he described on 29 December:

Breakfast at 7.30 in my room. At 7.45 drove down to the Custom House, got on board just in time to start off with my company at 8.30. We had 8 companies in each battalion (3), I was No. 8 of 1st batt., we marched out to the Marsa, then marched past 3 times or rather waded past as there was a fearful lot of mud, & it rained most of the time, Bourke commanded our batt. We also did the new plan of attack, there was also a battery of 12 guns, there were about 1500 men, it was only a rehearsal for tomorrow. Got on board at 12.30. Lunched at 1.0. Had a nap. Rained off & on all day. Wrote letters all the afternoon. Dined at 7.30 with Capt. Stephenson, the dear little Admiral, Capt. Drummond, Bourke & Donner dined. At 9.30 we all went to a danse [sic] given by Admiral Ward, a fearful crush. Bed at 1.45. It has rained all day, a horrible night.[12]

On New Year's Eve 1886, the Princess of Wales wrote to her second son:

I must write these few lines the last night of the dear old year – just to tell you how sorry I am that you are not here with us & also how dreadfully I missed you for Xmas. There were all the tables excepting yrs. & there were all their cheery voices excepting the cheeriest of all & yr. bright little face with its turned up snout oh I did miss it so & really shed a little secret

[12] Royal Archives: GV/PRIV/GVD/1886.

> tear for my Georgie dear! Yr very nice letter reached me on Xmas Eve with the pretty card which touched me so much & I liked the one coming straight from you . . . Thank God everything went off well Xmas & I was all right this time & not knocked up. Do you remember last year & when I was ill just now with that horrid diphtheria & the night of the tree & squirts when we two fought, I with the hunting whip & you with the squirt? It hardly seems like a year ago does it?
>
> . . . A thousand thanks first of all for all your blessed letters. I am so glad you spent such a happy Xmas with Alfred and Aunt Marie who I am sure were most kind to you but I regretted sincerely & do so still that somehow it was not managed that you went to Athens for their Christmas when poor Uncle Willy was so anxious for it. It may have been just as you say about ships &c. difficult to manage! . . . And I think Alfred might have done something towards it. I see Aunt Marie went in 'the Surprise' to fetch Aunt Louise at Naples & it strikes me that there must be plenty of ships at the 'Commander in Chief's' wish & orders. And so Papa is going to Cannes again when he will be joined by my Georgie dear & I need hardly say how much I would have liked to have gone too just to have had a peep of you my dear boy! – but it could not be managed this time but all the same I am dreadfully jealous that Papa should see you but not poor Ma.[13]

Prince George spent the following Christmas on Malta, before returning to Sandringham for Christmas 1888. On New Year's Eve in the latter year, he wrote in his diary: 'We all went to the bowling alley & at 12 o'clock drank the old year out & the new one in. Bed at 1.0. Another poor old year finished. Here endeth 1888!!!!!! Good-bye dear old Diary & never let anyone read you. You are full now so I shan't write in you any more. Tut! Ta-a-a!!!'[14]

Prince George with the Royal Navy at Bermuda, 1890

Two years later, Prince George had his own command, HMS *Thrush*, a first-class gunboat based at Bermuda. On Christmas Eve, he wrote in his diary: 'A lovely day. Read Articles of War & Court Martial returns. At 11.0 went over to stay with the Admiral & Mrs. Watson. Lunched at 1.15. Played tennis in afternoon, some capital sets with Mrs. Alison & Kilcoursie. Played whist. Dined at 7.30. Charades & singing.' He spent Christmas Day at Admiralty

[13] Michèle Brown, *Royal Christmas Book*, London: Windward, 1985, p. 94.
[14] Nicolson, *King George the Fifth: His Life and Reign*, p. 79.

House, Clarence Cove: 'Went over with Capt. Drury Divisions. Church in dockyard. Went round lower deck at 12.0. Came back with Admiral to Clarence Cove. Lunch at 1.0. Played tennis. Sang songs with choruses. Played whist. Dined at 7.30. Sat between Mrs. Watson & Miss Daisy. Played games & sang.' On New Year's Eve he wrote: 'Bed at 11.30. Good bye old 1890. Wish I was at home, thought of all those darlings I love best.'[15] Little more than a year later, his life was to change for ever, after the death of his elder brother, Prince Eddy, Duke of Clarence.

Princess Beatrice in Egypt, 1903–4

While Queen Victoria was still alive, it was impossible for Princess Beatrice, as her mother's chief support and confidante, to lead a life of her own. Three years after Queen Victoria's death, however, Princess Beatrice embarked on 'the most adventurous holiday she would take':

> Accompanied by two of her children, Ena [later the Queen of Spain] and the invalid Leopold, along with the children's cousin and Beatrice's goddaughter, nineteen-year-old Beatrice of Coburg, Beatrice arrived in Cairo for Christmas. The depleted family – Drino and Maurice remained at home, Drino having begun training with the Royal Navy the previous year, and Maurice still at school – spent Christmas as guests of the Khedive at the Jhezireh Palace. Warmed by the African sun and released by distance and the strangeness of all around her from the anxieties that had oppressed her since her mother's death, Beatrice rode camels, visited the bazaar, ancient temples and the Sphinx. The Khedive loaned the royal party his yacht, the *Ferouz*, in which they travelled up the Nile, stopping to visit recent excavations. They viewed the digs at the Plain of Thebes and there met Howard Carter, who with Lord Caernarvon would later discover Tutankhamen's tomb . . . Both Beatrice and Ena took photographs by the dozen. It was not a trip Beatrice could have made while the Queen was alive.[16]

[15] Royal Archives: GV/PRIV/GVD/1890.
[16] Matthew Dennison, *The Last Princess: The Devoted Life of Queen Victoria's Youngest Daughter*, London: Weidenfeld & Nicolson, 2007, pp. 229–30.

The Prince and Princess of Wales in India, 1905–6

In 1905–6 the Prince and Princess of Wales visited India and Burma, where 'the Prince met many of the more favoured among the Indian Rajahs and had long discussions with the British officials, both military and civilian'.[17] At Agra he also met Abdul Karim, CIE, CVO, who had been Queen Victoria's personal Indian Secretary. In the company of Mohammed Buksh, Karim had been chosen to join the Royal Household in the Golden Jubilee year. Having met them both at Frogmore House, the Queen described Abdul Karim in her Journal on 23 June 1887: 'The other, much younger, is much lighter, tall, and with a fine serious countenance. His father is a native doctor at Agra. They both kissed my feet.' Known as 'the Munshi', from the Urdu for 'clerk' or 'teacher', he exercised an uncomfortable – to the rest of the Royal Household – influence over Queen Victoria during the last few years of her reign. In eyes of his critics, he had replaced the Highlander, John Brown, who had died in 1883. The Prince of Wales was able to report back to his father that 'he has not grown more beautiful & is getting fat. He wore his C.V.O. which I had no idea he had got. I must say he was most civil & humble & really pleased to see us.'[18]

On 19 December 1905, the Princess of Wales wrote from Agra to her old governess, Mademoiselle Hélène Bricka: 'Thanks to the amount of Indian reading which I have done I really am not so ignorant about India as most of the English women here are. In fact Sir W. Lawrence told me one day "I consider you have a very good grasp on Indian affairs, quite remarkable in a woman". I felt much flattered & repeat this for yr ears only as you know what trouble I took to get the right books. The religions too I know something of, Hindu, Mohammedan, & Buddhism. All this knowledge, however small, helps one to take a keen interest in all one sees & I therefore enjoy to the utmost every detail of the wonderful sights.'[19]

Eight days later, she wrote from Lucknow to her second son, Bertie:

> We are very glad to hear that you have quite got over yr tiresome colds. The new photos by Ralph reached us safely, they are very good & we are very glad to have them. Please tell Lalla that we think Baby looks rather like a prize pig, he has grown so terribly fat! We thought so much of you

[17] Nicolson, *King George the Fifth: His Life and Reign*, p. 85.
[18] Ibid., p. 86.
[19] Pope-Hennessy, *Queen Mary, 1867–1953*, pp. 395–6.

> all on Xmas Eve & Xmas day which we spent at Gwalior where we had a delightful visit of 6 days & thoroughly enjoyed ourselves. Papa was lucky enough to get 3 tigers, I went out the first day & it was most exciting watching the shoot. On Xmas day I gave a Xmas Tree to the Gwalior children who were delighted with the presents I gave them, especially with the crackers which I pulled with them. They had never seen a Tree before so you can imagine their delight. One of the gentlemen dressed up as Father Xmas. We left Gwalior that evening & arrived here yesterday. I am sending you all Postcards of the famous Residency here which no doubt Mr. Hansell has told you all about. We spent 2 hours going over it yesterday & a Col. Banham who was shut up in the Residency in 1857 described to us the various scenes.[20]

Although his grandfather, father and elder brother all visited India, George VI, the last King Emperor, was unable to do so, as politics and the Second World War intervened. The Siege of the Residency at Lucknow during the Indian Mutiny was an extraordinary epic, to the extent that the former Residency Compound is preserved today, in memory of both sides. Henry Hansell – known to the two Princes as 'Mider', a corruption of 'Mister' – who commended himself to the Prince of Wales as a Norfolk man, a keen sailor and an excellent shot, had been appointed tutor to Prince Edward and Prince Albert in 1902. He served in that capacity until December 1912, as the Prince of Wales described that Boxing Day: 'I spent the evening clearing up Mider's drawers.' The following day, 'Mider left in the morning for Cromer & Mr. Zernon arrived in the evening.' He studied history at Magdalen College, Oxford, so it seems highly unlikely that 'Mider' would have neglected to mention the Siege of Lucknow Residency to his charges. When India became independent in 1947, King George VI 'had but one personal request and one which reflected his strong sense of historical tradition. On receiving Lord Listowel, his last Secretary of State for India, at Balmoral on 15 August, he asked that the last of the Union Jacks which had flown night and day above the Residency at Lucknow since the memorable siege of 1857, might be presented to him so that it might hang at Windsor with other historical flags already there, and this wish was fulfilled six weeks later.'[21]

[20] Royal Archives: GVI/PRIV/RF/11/014.

[21] John W. Wheeler-Bennett, *King George VI: His Life and Reign*, London: Macmillan & Co., 1958, p. 716.

King George V and Queen Mary attend the Delhi Durbar, 1911

On 11 November 1911, King George V and Queen Mary left England, bound for Bombay. The Coronation Durbar, at which he was proclaimed Emperor of India, took place at Delhi on 12 December. There had been two previous Durbars – on New Year's Day in 1877 and 1903 – but this was the first time that the 'to-be-proclaimed' Emperor had attended in person. King George V wrote to his mother: 'The Durbar yesterday was the most wonderful & beautiful sight I have ever seen & one I shall remember all my days.' Three days later, he laid the foundation stone for New Delhi, in an unsuitable place, as it later transpired. From Jaipur on 20 December, Queen Mary explained to her Aunt Augusta: 'I parted from George on Sat. 16th after our wonderful 10 days at Delhi, he went to Nepaul to shoot while I left for Agra which I wanted to see again and for a tour of Rajputana. I had a delightful 2 days at Agra seeing the beautiful Taj again & the fine old Fort built in the Moghul Emperors' time as well as various other smaller places I wished to revisit.'[22]

These are the entries from the King's diary, beginning on Christmas Eve, written at Kasra Camp, Nepal Terai, India:

> We got the English mail early this morning, got a great many letters. At 11.0 we attended Divine Service in a tent, the service was conducted by Mr. Godber, chaplain to the Bishop of Calcutta. I spent the whole day reading my letters & boxes. Lady & Miss McMahon, & Mrs. Manners Smith lunched with us, also their husbands, they have a separate camp near ours. At 4.0 the Maharaja came & presented a wonderful collection of animals to me most of them from Nepal, such as a baby elephant & rhino, leopards, bears, snow leopards, deer, goats, & birds. I shall probably give them to the Zoo. He also gave me some beautiful things all made in Nepal, brass work, wood carvings, stuffs, beads, skins &c. which were all laid out in a tent. I then gave him the G.C.V.O., my miniature, the gold coronation medal & a silver box with diamond monogram, & presents to all his sons & his leading people here, shikaris & mahouts. Read before & after dinner. Mr. Godber dined. Bed at 11.0.
>
> Monday Xmas Day – Breakfast with Bigge [later 1st Baron Stamfordham] at 8.45. Mr. Godber read the Service at 9.30 to which the

[22] Pope-Hennessy, *Queen Mary*, pp. 459–60.

> Ladies came. We started at 10.45 in motors & mounted our elephants after going about three miles. We made a ring & I shot a very fine tiger of 9 ft. 10 ins. with one shot through the heart while he was charging through the long grass & he never moved again. I then went after rhino & saw one asleep which I missed, she made off with her calf, some of the elephants headed her & she turned & charged me as hard as she could come. I shot her through the chest & she fell dead. We then tried to catch the calf, at first he remained with his dead mother for half an hour quite quietly, all of a sudden he began rushing round the ring, which he soon broke & disappeared. The Ladies lunched with us, also the 3 Manners Smith little girls, at 1.30 in the jungle. In afternoon I shot another rhino cow stone dead, one shot through the heart while in line, also a hag deer. Got back to camp soon after 5.0. The other party got 3 tigers & a rhino. Saw people & read. Today is the first Xmas day on which I have been parted from darling May since we married 18 years ago which is sad. Dined at 8.0 we were 16 at dinner, turkey, plum pudding & mince pies. Bed at 11.15.[23]

By now reunited, the King and Queen spent New Year's Eve at Government House, Calcutta, with the King reflecting in his diary: 'This has been a heavy & anxious year for me, I am thankful to God for the way he has watched over me & given me health to carry out all my numerous duties & responsibilities. Good bye dear old 1911 the most eventful year of my life.'

Prince Albert with the Royal Navy at Gibraltar, 1913

Cadet HRH Prince Albert of Wales, later King George VI, passed out of the Royal Naval College, Osborne in last place out of 68 cadets in December 1910. The prospect of spending Christmas at home was evidently a distraction, as his tutor, James Watt, described in a letter to Henry Hansell: 'I am afraid that there is no disguising to you the fact that P. A. has gone a mucker. He has been quite off his head, with the excitement of getting home, for the last few days, and unfortunately as these were the days of the examination he has quite come to grief.' John Wheeler-Bennett added that 'there is no record of Prince Albert's reception on his return to Sandringham for Christmas'.[24] He later managed a small improvement – to sixty-first out

[23] Royal Archives: GV/PRIV/GVD/1911.
[24] Wheeler-Bennett, *King George VI: His Life and Reign*, p. 47.

of sixty-seven at the Royal Naval College, Dartmouth. Nevertheless, on 15 September 1913 Midshipman Prince Albert joined HMS *Collingwood*, a St Vincent-class battleship with a main armament of 10 12-inch Mark XI guns. That Christmas was spent in port, at Gibraltar.

On 23 December, Prince Albert wrote, in the diary that he kept only intermittently: 'I got up at 6.30 and watched the 1st cutter being cleaned out. After divisions I did navigation and in the afternoon torpedo. At 4.30 I went to tea with Sir Herbert Miles at Government House. Dinner was at 6.45 and then I went to a concert given on board.' On Christmas Eve, he 'kept the morning watch from 5.30 to 7.30. At 9.15 I left the ship with Mr. Napier, Bovell and Woodall to go out hunting. We rode along the beach for about 5 miles to the meet, which was at the duke of Kent's farm.[25] We had two short runs but did not kill. The rain came down in torrents most of the day, and the going was very heavy and difficult. We returned at 5.15. After dinner I turned in.'

On Christmas Day, he 'got up at 5.30 and went in the cutter to land the postman. After breakfast I went to divisions and church on the upper deck. After that I went into the wardroom with all the members of the gunroom and then they came into the gunroom to return the visit. At 11.30 we all went the rounds of the mess deck. All the messes were beautifully decorated, and we were offered pieces of cake etc. After our own lunch I wrote letters. At 8.45 the Admiral gave all the Wardroom, Gunroom and Warrant Officers dinner in his cabin. After that we had a concert in the wardroom.'[26]

The Duke and Duchess of York on Safari in Kenya, 1924–5

On 26 April 1923 in Westminster Abbey, Prince Albert, on whom his father had conferred the title Duke of York on 3 June 1920, was married to Lady Elizabeth Bowes-Lyon, the first wedding of a prince of the Royal House in the Abbey for 530 years. As his biographer wrote, 'both the Duke and Duchess of York desired to travel and see something of the Commonwealth before settling down to the regular routine of married life'.[27] In the event, though, the opportunity did not present itself for more than eighteen months:

[25] Officially, HRH The Duke of Kent, Queen Victoria's father, was Governor of Gibraltar from 24 May 1802 until his death on 23 January 1820. However, following a mutiny by two British regiments, he was recalled by the Duke of York after little more than a year, was forbidden to return and was represented thereafter by the Acting Governor.

[26] Royal Archives: GVI/PRIV/DIARY/1913.

[27] Wheeler-Bennett, *King George VI: His Life and Reign*, p. 191.

'In the winter of 1924 the long cherished desire of the Duke of York to see something of the British Empire at first hand was at last gratified', in the shape of a visit to East Africa and the Sudan.[28] Having landed at Mombasa on 22 December, the Duke of York re-adopted the habit of writing a daily diary, something that he had ceased to do during the second year of the First World War. The Duke and Duchess spent Christmas Eve at Government House, Nairobi, as guests of Sir Robert Coryndon.

The Duke of York wrote in his diary: 'Some of us had a ride before breakfast between 7.0 & 8.30. We rode through the town to the race course & back. There is no real gallop you can get unfortunately. I got some things in the town in the morning to complete my Safari kit. Did nothing in the afternoon till 4.30 when we went to open the new City Park. It is 5 miles out of the town & is a lovely place. It was a dense forest a short time ago, but now paths have been cut, & the undergrowth cleared. Then I went to the Nairobi Club & met some of the business people. The Governor gave a dinner & afterwards we went to the Muthaiga Club & danced.'

On Christmas Day,

> we went to church in the English Church at 10.30 when the bishop of Mombasa preached. After our service we went to the C of E church built by the natives themselves, to hear them sing a hymn & the National Anthem in Swahili. We were busy packing our Safari kit most of the day, with the help of a native boy who looks after each of us. Mine speaks English which is useful, & seems to be fairly intelligent. At 4.30 the Governor gave a garden party where [we] met most of the residents. After dinner we went to see Martin Johnson's Film on Big Game. A very good film & most of it was taken in the part of the country to which we are going tomorrow. It will be very nice to start on our Safari at last.

Three days after Christmas, the promised safari got under way in earnest, based at Siolo Camp:

> Anderson & I left camp at 6.0 on mules & we rode part of the way. We saw plenty of game on the plain. I stalked some Oryx but could not get near enough to shoot as there was so little cover. They were very wild & suspicious & went off. Then we went after some Zebra & I had a shot but

[28] Ibid., p. 198.

missed. This was really for practice as the light & distances have to be got used to. After this we turned back & tried to get up to some Grant Gazelle but they also went off before I could shoot. We saw some more Oryx but the ground was too open to stalk them. We found one Oryx alone shortly afterwards & we got up to him within 200 yds by keeping a tree between us & him. I took a rest off the tree & fired & hit him. He was facing me. He went off & we followed & I hit him 3 more times when he lay down.

I was going to finish him off when we saw a Rhino on the edge of a thick patch of bush. We forgot about the Oryx and went after the Rhino. We followed him into the bush & suddenly came upon not one but 2 Rhinos lying down in the thickest part of the bush 8 yards away. One got up towards us & Anderson fired & killed it. I did not fire as I could not see him properly. It was most exciting. The other one ran away. After this we went back & finished off the Oryx. It was very hot by now at 11.30 & we were glad of the mules to ride home on. Elizabeth came out with us in the afternoon after tea to have a look at the Rhino.[29]

On 3 January 1925, the Duke of York wrote to Queen Mary: 'We are both so impressed with this wonderful country & it has certainly come up to & passed our expectations. I am certain people at home have no idea what its possibilities are & what its future one day is going to be.'[30] Letters crossed and, the same day, Queen Mary wrote from York Cottage, Sandringham to her second son:

Thank you very much for yr letter of Dec: 10th posted at Port Said, & will you please thank Elizabeth for her letter posted at Aden of Dec 16th. We were so glad to get news of you both & to know that you are enjoying yr first glimpse of the East. I envy you the sunshine & warmth tho' perhaps in some parts it wld have been too hot for me. I am sorry to hear poor Capt: Brooke has had bronchitis. We miss you & E. most dreadfully here, luckily Christmas & New Year have passed off well & smoothly as far as poor Grannie was concerned as we feared the excitement for her, but she seemed to enjoy it all & at the Xmas tree giving for our people here she herself gave presents off the Tree.

'We go up to tea <u>very</u> often, as she likes this & we are able to see more of A^t Maud in this way. They stay till Jan: 10th which is nice. I must say that

[29] Royal Archives: GVI/PRIV/DIARY/1924/25.
[30] Wheeler-Bennett, *King George VI: His Life and Reign*, p. 202.

> Cousin Minny is a great help to Grannie in the absence of A[t] Toria, the latter writes happily from Lugano in Switzerland which she likes. David & Harry have left us but Georgie stays till 6th when he must go to London to see the dentist tho' we hope he will return here later on, he leaves for China on Feb: 5th so I think we shall go to London Feb: 4th. We have had the most awful gales the last week tho' we have been luckier than in some parts where the rain has been torrential & the consequent flooding very bad indeed. It has not been at all cold so far. I will not write to E. this mail as you can show her this letter. My thoughts are much with you both & all best wishes for New Year. [P.S.] How ungrateful I am, I never thanked you both for yr share in charming presents, namely some small Chinese plants in pots.[31]

On 6 January 1925, the Duchess of York wrote to her brother, David: 'The birds are simply marvellous. Thousands of partridges – a little bigger than ours, and flocks of guinea fowl, & quail & pigeons & anything you like. It is exactly like a warm summer evening at Glamis here – nice & cool & Scotch.'[32]

Sadly, an extremely successful visit had to be curtailed, after the unexpected death of Sir Robert Coryndon on 10 February 1925. However, the party also managed to visit both Uganda and the Sudan, before boarding a train at Khartoum for Port Sudan on 9 April 1925 and sailing home, with the English cricket team, in the *Maloja*. In conversation with Sir Eric Anderson, former Headmaster and Provost of Eton College, in 1994, Queen Elizabeth described the safari as 'wonderful. Best bit of one's life.'[33]

Queen Mary at Badminton House, 1939–45

The morning after the declaration of war on 3 September 1939, Queen Mary drove from Sandringham to stay at Badminton House in Gloucestershire, the home of her niece's husband, the 10th Duke of Beaufort. 'My servants & luggage followed my cars – quite a fleet,' she noted.[34] She was not exaggerating, since she took with her most of her Marlborough House staff of 63, together with many of their dependants.

[31] Royal Archives: GVI/PRIV/RF/11/342.
[32] Sarah Bradford, *Elizabeth: A Biography of Her Majesty the Queen*, London: Heinemann, 1996, p. 226. Glamis Castle in Angus is the ancestral home of the Earls of Strathmore, the Duchess of York's family.
[33] Ibid., p. 241.
[34] Pope-Hennessy, *Queen Mary*, p. 596.

Over Christmas 1940 Queen Mary visited the Canteen Hut to give 'small presents in a bran tub to the Detachment here after which some of the men regaled us with a "Sing Song" which was great fun'.[35] While at Badminton, for the duration of the war, Queen Mary busied herself by coordinating the activities of the 'Ivy Squad', later renamed the 'Wooding Squad'. On New Year's Day 1941, she wrote in her diary that the 'Wooding Squad' 'worked in Stride's Coppice in the afternoon, many of the children coming with us – we liked the new place which is well worth clearing out'.[36] In this respect, her reputation spread far and wide, as Sir Osbert Sitwell explains: 'In November 1944 I received a letter from Queen Mary asking me to spend from December 22nd to 28th at Badminton. I wrote to Her Majesty at once to accept, at the same time declaring immediately, so that there could be no mistake about it, that my doctor absolutely forbade me to clear or cut timber.'[37]

Sir Osbert Sitwell described that Christmas in considerable – and rather amusing – detail. First of all, he set the scene: 'The Christmas house-party consisted of Queen Mary, the Princess Royal and Lord Harewood, the Beauforts, Lady Constance Milnes-Gaskell, who was in waiting, Lord Claud Hamilton and Sir Richard Molyneux.'[38] He then described the staffing arrangements:

> There were seven men waiting in the small dining-room on Christmas night. During the daytime, they seemed always to be in the process of carrying in larger and larger tables, because Queen Mary insisted always on a two-foot space each side of her at meals. By this time the royal pages had been obliged to abandon their scarlet coats, and were wearing blue battle dress, with the royal cypher on the breast, that had been designed for them recently by King George. Some of them much resented the change, and one of Queen Mary's pages had actually left when obliged to discard the scarlet livery which he had worn for thirty years. Queen Mary sent for him and told him that it was an act of direct rebellion against the King's commands.[39]

35 Ibid., p. 606.
36 Ibid., p. 606.
37 Osbert Sitwell, *Queen Mary and Others*, London: Michael Joseph, 1974, p. 51.
38 Lord Claud Hamilton, Deputy Master of the Household 1921–36 and Treasurer and Extra Equerry to Queen Mary 1936–53; Major the Hon. Richard Molyneux, Groom-in-waiting to King George V 1919–36 and Extra Equerry to Queen Mary 1936–52.
39 Sitwell, *Queen Mary and Others*, pp. 56–7.

Sitwell's account continued:

> On Christmas evening as I was going upstairs to change for dinner, I met old Dick Molyneux, who roared at me, 'You and I have had all the hard work to do in this party. Would you like a glass of champagne before dinner? I don't expect we'll get any at dinner. Claud's too mean! I think we deserve it, and I've brought a bottle down with me in my luggage.'
>
> I said I should like nothing better. His room was near mine, and I arrived there at 8.15 – dinner was due at 8.30. His servant was just leaving, having put out on the table, and having opened, a bottle of *Perier Jouet* 1928, and placed near it a plate of biscuits. The old gentleman himself was sitting by the table in a chair by the fire; he poured me out a glass, and said 'I think it's wiser to have half a biscuit.' Just then he tasted the champagne, and a look of complete tragedy came into his eye. 'It's corked,' he shouted 'and the only bottle!' So we went downstairs, to find that we were being given champagne. Dick Molyneux sat opposite me, and as he tasted it, I saw a look in his eye that I had seen before. 'It's corked,' it stated as plainly as possible. A second bottle was produced, but proved to be similarly afflicted. Dick Molyneux was by now in a courtier's rage, though outwardly calm; he took me into corners after dinner to complain, 'I don't mind about the champagne, but I'm so *thirsty*,' he kept on saying. 'It's all Claud Hamilton's fault. Queen Mary never drinks champagne herself, and so doesn't know. It's left to Claud, and he's too mean to give us the best. I shall speak to him about it this time.' But when he remonstrated, he received an answer which made him still more angry. 'The champagne was getting old, and I wanted to see if it was still fit to be drunk – and we're all old friends, so it doesn't matter. And I knew you'd tell me.'
>
> Several people from the neighbourhood dined with Queen Mary that night, including an officer with the imposing title of Captain of the Garrison, but I could not help feeling that she must be thinking of other Christmases in the past. Now, with her, she had only the Princess Royal. The Duke of Windsor had abdicated, and lived abroad; the King was fully occupied; the Duke of Gloucester was away; and her favourite son, the Duke of Kent, who so much resembled her in her tastes, and who could do anything with her he liked, had been killed in an aeroplane accident. Certainly she looked superb, wearing enormous sapphires, a pearl collar, and huge diamond and pearl brooches and pendants. With her clear skin, she could wear white and such colours as usually only girls can wear,

> and look well in them, even by daylight. Tonight she wore silver. As this magnificent figure, blazing and sparkling, led the way from the room, Dick Molyneux turned to me and said in his loud, deaf voice, like that of a man shouting from a cave into a strong wind, 'I wonder if you realise it, but after that old lady has gone, you'll never see anything like this, or like her, again!'[40]

On 18 May 1945, ten days after VE-Day, the Duchess of Beaufort wrote to Sir Osbert Sitwell: 'The Queen is here until 11th June. I expect it is Marlborough House that is in a state of eruption, revolt and tumult. Vans of boxes and hampers and trunks all marked with the royal cypher continually leaving the house. Today I saw such a van leaving with royal crowns and M.R.s bursting from every side, but at the very back and perched on the top of these dignified boxes sat, very cheerily and cheekily a common enamel slop-pail – very plebeian, and showing no sign of its royal ownership.'[41]

[40] Ibid., pp. 59–61.
[41] Ibid., p. 61.

The Time of Gifts

For now the time of gifts is gone –
O boys that grow, O snows that melt,
O bathos that the years must fill –
Here is dull earth to build upon
Undecorated; we have reached
Twelfth Night or what you will . . . you will.

'Twelfth Night' by Louis MacNeice

Bescherung, or the ritual of the Christmas tree, revolved around the exchange of presents. Queen Victoria gave due weight to this solemn and serious process, taking great care to describe who had received what, and from whom. Just a few months before acceding to the throne, she spent the festive season with her mother and the Conroy family at Claremont House, near Esher in Surrey. In 1816 an Act of Parliament was passed to enable the purchase of Claremont House as a wedding present from the nation to Princess Charlotte of Wales and her husband, Prince Leopold. Although he retained ownership of the estate until his death in 1855, he often lent it to his sister, the Duchess of Kent.

On Christmas Eve 1836, Princess Victoria wrote in her Journal:

> At a little after 10 we left Kensington with dearest Lehzen, Lady Conroy, and – Dashy! and reached Claremont at a ¼ to 12 . . . Received from dearest Lehzen as a Christmas box: 2 lovely little Dresden china figures, 2 pairs of lovely little chased gold buttons, a small lovely button with an angel's head which she used to wear herself, and a pretty music book; from good Louis a beautiful piece of Persian stuff for an album; and from Victoire and Emily Gardiner a small box worked by themselves. Wrote my journal. Went down to arrange Mama's table for her. At 6 we dined . . .
>
> Very soon after dinner Mama sent for us into the Gallery, where all the things were arranged on different tables. From my dear Mama I received a beautiful massive gold buccle [sic] in the shape of two serpents; a lovely delicate little gold chain with a turquoise clasp; a fine album of brown moroccow [sic] with a silver clasp; a lovely coloured sketch of dearest

▲
'Day turned into night': Queen Victoria seated by a bust of Prince Albert, with the Prince of Wales and Crown Princess Frederick of Prussia standing behind her and Princess Alice kneeling next to her, Windsor Castle, March 1862.

◄ The Prince and Princess of Wales with their children on the frozen lake at Sandringham by Karl Bauerle, January 1871.

The kitchen, Windsor Castle, 1878.

Duke Karl Borwin of Mecklenburg-Strelitz, cousin of Queen Mary, dressed as a star, Christmas 1891. Defending his sister's honour, he was killed in a duel with his brother-in-law, Count George Jametel, in August 1908.

▲ 'The Idlers' 1894/5: (left to right) Lady Elizabeth Meade, Miss Minnie Cochrane, The Hon. Bertha Lambart, Miss Heseltine, Miss Percival, Mrs. Trower.

'Christmas' 1894/5: (left to right) Princess Alice of Albany, Mr. Müther, Prince Charles Edward of Albany, Prince Leopold of Battenberg (kneeling), Princess Ena of Battenberg, Prince Alexander of Battenberg, Miss Trower, Miss Blake. ▼

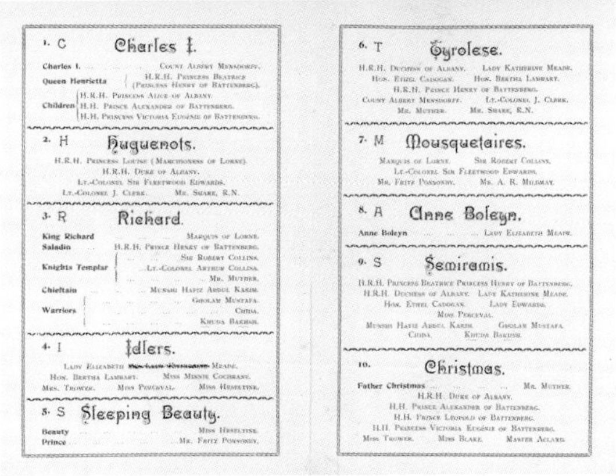

1. C **Charles I.**

Charles I. … Count Albert Mensdorff.
Queen Henrietta … H.R.H. Princess Beatrice (Princess Henry of Battenberg).
Children: H.R.H. Princess Alice of Albany. H.H. Prince Alexander of Battenberg. H.H. Princess Victoria Eugénie of Battenberg.

2. H **Huguenots.**

H.R.H. Princess Louise (Marchioness of Lorne).
H.R.H. Duke of Albany.
Lt.-Colonel Sir Fleetwood Edwards.
Lt.-Colonel J. Clerk. Mr. Shake, R.N.

3. R **Richard.**

King Richard … Marquis of Lorne.
Saladin … H.R.H. Prince Henry of Battenberg.
Knights Templar … Sir Robert Collins. Lt.-Colonel Arthur Collins. Mr. Muther.
Chieftain … Munshi Hafiz Abdul Karim.
Warriors … Gholam Mustafa. Chida. Khuda Bakhsh.

4. I **Idlers.**

Lady Elizabeth [illegible] Meade.
Hon. Bertha Lambart. Miss Minnie Cochrane.
Mrs. Trower. Miss Percival. Miss Heseltine.

5. S **Sleeping Beauty.**

Beauty … Miss Heseltine.
Prince … Mr. Fritz Ponsonby.

6. T **Tyrolese.**

H.R.H. Duchess of Albany. Lady Katherine Meade.
Hon. Ethel Cadogan. Hon. Bertha Lambart.
H.R.H. Prince Henry of Battenberg.
Count Albert Mensdorff. Lt.-Colonel J. Clerk.
Mr. Muther. Mr. Shake, R.N.

7. M **Mousquetaires.**

Marquis of Lorne. Sir Robert Collins.
Lt.-Colonel Sir Fleetwood Edwards.
Mr. Fritz Ponsonby. Mr. A. R. Mildmay.

8. A **Anne Boleyn.**

Anne Boleyn … Lady Elizabeth Meade.

9. S **Semiramis.**

H.R.H. Princess Beatrice Princess Henry of Battenberg.
H.R.H. Duchess of Albany. Lady Katherine Meade.
Hon. Ethel Cadogan. Lady Edwards.
Miss Percival.
Munshi Hafiz Abdul Karim. Gholam Mustafa.
Chida. Khuda Bakhsh.

10. **Christmas.**

Father Christmas … Mr. Muther.
H.R.H. Duke of Albany.
H.H. Prince Alexander of Battenberg.
H.H. Prince Leopold of Battenberg.
H.H. Princess Victoria Eugénie of Battenberg.
Miss Trower. Miss Blake. Master Acland.

▲ Programme for the *tableaux vivants*, Osborne 1894/5.

▲
Queen Victoria's New Year's gift, 1899/1900.

▲
Prince Georg of Saxony dressed as one of St. Nicholas's helpers for a *Weihnachtspiel*, Christmas 1903.

Prince Friedrich Christian of Saxony dressed as a Christmas tree for a *Weihnachtspiel*, Christmas 1903.
▼

Christmas card, 1904: a watercolour by A. Van Haddenham, signed by two future Kings, David (King Edward VIII) and Bertie (King George VI).

Emperor William II's grandsons, Princes Wilhelm (right) and Louis Ferdinand of Prussia, in a composite Christmas card, 1908. On 26 May 1940 at Nivelles, Prince Wilhelm died of wounds received during the German invasion of France.

▲ Emperor William II's grandsons, Princes Wilhelm (right) and Louis Ferdinand of Prussia, 1912/13.

◀ The Prince of Wales in uniform, 1914.

Princess Mary's Christmas gift, 1914. ▼

Prince Bertil and Princess Ingrid of Sweden (on the sledge), 1914.

Prince Ludwig of Bavaria as Father Christmas, Christmas 1919.

▲ The children of Charles I, the last Emperor of Austria, circa 1925: Archduchess Adelheid, Archdukes Felix, Robert, Karl Ludwig, Rudolf and Crown Prince Otto. Their father had died in Madeira on 1 April 1922, while Otto and Felix both died in 2011.

◀ Emperor William II's stepdaughter, Princess Henriette of Schönaich-Carolath, in front of the Christmas tree at Doorn in the Netherlands, 1927.

Aunt Louise by Partridge, copied from the picture he brought, and so like her; 3 beautiful drawings by Munn, one lovely sea view by Purser, and one beautiful cattle piece by Cooper (all coloured), 3 prints, a book called 'Finden's Tableaux'; 'Heath's picturesq [sic] Annual for 1837, Ireland'; both these are very pretty; 'Friendship's Offering', and 'The English Annual for 1837'; 'The Holy Land', illustrated beautifully; two handkerchiefs, a very pretty black satin apron trimmed with red velvet; and two almanacks. I am very thankful to my dear Mama for all these very pretty things.

From dear Uncle Leopold, a beautiful turquoise ring; from the Queen a fine piece of Indian gold tissue; and from Sir J. Conroy a print. I gave my dear Lehzen a green moroccow jewel case, and the Picturesq Annual; Mama gave her a shawl, a dress, a pair of turquoise earrings, an annual, and handkerchiefs. I then took Mama to the Library where my humble table was arranged. I gave her a bracelet made of my hair, the clasp of which contains Charles', Feodore's, and my hair; and the 'Keepsake' and 'Oriental Annual'. Lehzen gave her two pairs of little buttons just like mine. I danced a little with Victoire. Stayed up till 11.'[1]

Queen Victoria's first Christmas as Sovereign was spent at Buckingham Palace, before the Royal Household moved to Windsor Castle for the New Year's celebrations. That Christmas Eve, the Queen wrote in her Journal:

Gave a little Christmas box to Lady Mulgrave, who gave me a pair of pretty worked slippers. At ½ p. 11 I went to Chapel with all my ladies and gentlemen. The Dean read and the Bishop of London preached. The text was from the 13th chap: of *St. Paul's Epistle to the Romans*, 12th verse. It was a very severe, harsh sermon . . . Got from my dearest beloved Lehzen two very pretty boxes to hold covers and paper; and a very pretty stand for pens. Gave her a dressing-case. At 6 I went into the former Closet, where Mama had arranged a table for me. From her I received her picture (in a bracelet), painted by Ross, and excessively like; a beautiful sable muff; a very pretty silver lamp; two Annuals, and a number of very fine prints. From Queen Adelaide I got, a very pretty little bracelet, *féronière*, and two pins. I then gave Mama her table; I gave her my bust in marble by Weekes; a little bracelet; 2 Annuals, a dress and two Turquish [sic] handkerchiefs.[2]

[1] Royal Archives: VIC/MAIN/QVJ/1836.
[2] Royal Archives: VIC/MAIN/QVJ/1837.

The following year, Christmas was spent at the Brighton Pavilion. *Bescherung* once again dominated Christmas Eve, as Queen Victoria described:

> Got before breakfast a very kind letter from dearest Louise (with better news from poor Marie, who had borne her journey as far as Pietro Santo wonderfully), accompanied by a very pretty little *féronière* like one Clementine gave her, and which I admired so much when she was in England; and also a very kind letter from Uncle Leopold; and one from the Duchess of Gloucester with a little box from her and Aunt Sophia . . . Dressed for riding. But before I rode I went to look at the picture of herself and little Leopold which Louise has been so kind as to send me; and which is quite lovely, so like her, and beautifully painted (in oils) by a German painter called Winterhalter; it is the size of life, but only goes to the knees; Leopold is the loveliest child I ever saw, quite his father's eyes, but the lower part very like Louis Philippe . . .[3]
>
> Dearest Daisy gave me a very pretty little smelling bottle and seal; the latter I put to my bunch of keys instantly. I had given her 2 pins in the morning. Arranged Mama's table and then sent for her. I gave her an enamel after Hayter's picture of me (without the crown) in a bracelet, with which she was quite enchanted; a chain with an ornament which she wished very much to have; two pieces of stuff for dresses, and an Annual. Spèth sent her two beautiful artificial white roses, and she sent me two beautiful pink ones. Soon after this I went over to Mama's room, where she had arranged a table for me; she gave me an exceedingly pretty whip; the top being Dash's head, made in enamel, and so ridiculously like; the collar round his throat of precious stones, spelling Dash; a pair of gold pins in a little Tunbridge Ware box, 3 cravats, a little Scotch carpet, 2 Annuals, 2 Almanacks, 3 Prints, and some gingerbread.[4]

In 1839 Christmas was spent at Windsor Castle, marking the fourth different location for the Royal Household in four years. In her Journal entry for Christmas Eve, the Queen wrote: 'Received a very pretty box and 2 pretty pins from the Queen Dowager with a kind note. Mama gave me my table; the presents consisted of, a very pretty set of turquoises (broach and

[3] Leopold I, King of the Belgians, was married to Princess Louise, eldest daughter of King Louis Philippe of France, who reigned from 1830 to 1848. Their eldest son died in infancy, while their second son became King Leopold II.

[4] Royal Archives: VIC/MAIN/QVJ/1838.

earrings, in the shape of doves); books, and prints. I then gave her a table; I gave her a curious pair of enamel and pearl earrings, and 2 pieces of stuff for gowns, scarfs, &c. and Albert, his picture in a bracelet set just like the one I gave her last year with my picture. Dearest Daisy gave me a pretty silver candlestick, and I gave her a turquoise buckle.'[5]

By 1840 the pattern for the next twenty-one Christmases was established. That Christmas Eve, the Queen wrote in her Journal at Windsor Castle: 'I then arranged the present tables for Albert & Mama, with 2 fine Christmas trees, in my large room, after which I went into the little middle blue room, where dearest Albert had arranged my table, with a beautiful tree. From him I received a lovely sketch of our dear little girl by Ross, also ornaments for my table, & other pretty & useful things. Mama gave me a bracelet with her portrait, books &c. I gave Albert a curious picture by Lucas Cranach, a walkingstick, & pictures, with all of which he was delighted. We gave all our people presents.'[6]

Prince Albert's many practical talents, admirable attention to detail and great love for his wife shine forth from the pages of Queen Victoria's Journals. On Christmas Eve 1841, the Queen wrote:

> Arranged Albert's table with Xmas presents, in my former bedroom, & there we, together, arranged Mama's. At about 6, we had our trees, & we first gave Mama her presents, then I gave Albert his, & he gave me mine. Amongst my presents to him was a large lifesize picture of 'Eos', by Landseer, with which he was quite delighted, & it came as a complete surprise. I received such lovely gifts, all arranged in the small middle blue room.
>
> One of the things I value the most is an enamel of 'Pussy' after Ross, mounted as a brooch, with diamond wings, & the little cross hanging from the hands, in 2 rubies & 4 diamonds. The workmanship & design are quite exquisite, & dear Albert was so pleased at my delight over it, it having been entirely his own idea & taste. 'Pussy' was brought down for a moment & she was in such ecstasies at the trees.[7]

[5] Royal Archives: VIC/MAIN/QVJ/1839.
[6] Royal Archives: VIC/MAIN/QVJ/1840.
[7] Royal Archives: VIC/MAIN/QVJ/1841.

Eos was Prince Albert's favourite greyhound while 'Pussy' was Princess Vicky, later the Empress Frederick. The image that the Queen conveys of well-chosen presents, joyously received, is memorable.

On Christmas Eve 1846, 'Albert's gifts were quite beautiful, amongst them that lovely full length picture of Bertie, in his sailor's dress, by Winterhalter. It is such a perfect likeness & such a charming composition . . . I gave my beloved one a small picture by Stanfield, of St. Michael's Mount with our yacht, another pretty picture of a woman with 2 Children, by Gallois, a Belgian artist, & various other things.'[8] The Prime Minister, Sir Robert Peel, described the Winterhalter as 'the prettiest picture I have ever seen'.[9]

The following Christmas, the Queen already had a family of five children and was heavily pregnant with her sixth, Princess Louise, who was born on 18 March 1848.

Queen Victoria's Maid of Honour, the Hon. Eleanor Stanley, sent her mother a description of the Christmas scene:

> Round [the tree] were all our presents, with the name of each person, written by the Queen on a slip of paper lying by the present; Caroline's and mine were two very pretty little chains for round the neck, with a hand in front, which holds the ring, to which is fastened a heart or locket; mine is in carbuncles and little diamonds, and Caroline's in *Pavé de Vienne*, of the same pattern.
>
> We also got, in common with all the others, a new print of the Prince of Wales and Prince Alfred in Highland costume, from a sketch by Sir William Ross, and one of the Queen, from a water-colour by Winterhalter; both very pretty, but the latter the best; the children are hardly done justice to in Ross's. They are both lithographed by Thomas Fairland, Lord Rosebery's friend. We also each got an almanac and some gingerbread. Some of the presents were very pretty; Col. Grey got a set of carbuncle waistcoat buttons; Genl. Bowles a lovely set of pearl studs, and a gold pocket book; Lord Waterpark a very handsome seal, and Lady Canning a blue enamel bracelet with ruby and diamond clasp. After we had got ours, we followed the Queen and Prince to see their own presents, and the children's and the Duchess of Kent's. The latter's were, little statues of the

[8] Royal Archives: VIC/MAIN/QVJ/1846.
[9] www.royalcollection.org.uk.

> Princess Royal and Princess Alice, the size of life, from the Queen and Prince, and some other little trifles.
>
> The Queen's were the handsomest; some of the things very pretty, particularly a large drawing from Overbeck's cartoons, and several bronze copies of old statues, the Hercules, &c. There were also some blue and diamond brooches, the Duchess of Kent gave her, very pretty. The Prince's were also very nice; the Queen's gifts were a small picture by Landseer, of herself and the two eldest children, standing by the Lake at Ardverikie, with a Highland man and pony near them – a beautiful picture;[10] also a sketch of a Magdalen by Winterhalter, very pretty. The children had each a little table with their new toys, and were running about in great glee showing them off; Prince Alfred, in a glorious tinsel helmet that almost covered his face, was shooting us all with a new gun, and Princess Alice was making us admire her dolls, etc. They had one Christmas tree among them, like us, but the Queen, Prince, and Duchess had each one, and altogether I never saw anything prettier than the whole arrangement.[11]

On Christmas Eve three years later, Prince Albert's creative skills were once again to the fore, as Queen Victoria described in her Journal:

> The frost gone, & a raw dull morning. Albert out shooting, & I, walking with the Children. We walked out in the afternoon, & found it raw and damp. We began, by giving our presents to poor Lady Lyttelton, a bracelet containing the portraits of our 5 younger Children, & 2 prints of the Children. Then gave presents to our personal servants &c. & were busy arranging the tables. A little after 6 we all assembled & my beloved Albert first took me to my tree & table, covered by such numberless gifts, really too much, too magnificent. I am delighted with the really splendid picture in watercolours by Corbauld, representing the famous scene at the Coronation in 'Le Prophète' – & a very pretty oil painting of 'Faith' represented by a female figure & 2 angels, by Mrs. Richards, also a fine oil painting of 'l'Allegro' & 'Il Penseroso', by Hurseley.
>
> The one present from dearest Albert, which is of infinite value to me is a miniature of my beloved Louise in a clasp to a bracelet in dull, deepish

[10] Ardverikie, which belonged to the Earl of Abercorn, was the first choice as a Scottish home for Queen Victoria and Prince Albert, since it 'reminded us much of Thuringen'.

[11] Beatrice Erskine, *Twenty Years at Court: From the Correspondence of the Hon. Eleanor Stanley*, London: Nisbet & Co., 1916, pp. 156–7.

blue enamel, with a black cross, the cipher & stars in diamonds, all dear Albert's own design & very lovely. I annex a sketch of it. I also received charming gifts from dear Mama. The 3 girls, all worked me something. The 7 Children were then taken to their tree, jumping & shouting with joy over their toys & other presents; the Boys could think of nothing but the swords we had given them & Bertie of some armour, which however he complained, pinched him! Mama had her tree & table in the same room, & Albert his, in the 3rd last room.

Amongst my gifts was a painting by Landseer, as a present to his 'Lassie', – a Highlander in a snowstorm 'on the Hull', with a dead eagle in one hand, & a dog near him. The colouring is beautiful, & the whole thing is a 'chef d'oeuvre'. Dear Albert was kindly pleased with everything, but I felt it was so poor in comparison with what he had given me. At 7, we gave the Ladies & Gentlemen their tree & gifts, & then showed them our things.

The Journal for 1850 ends: 'The last day of this very eventful sad year. It has been one of great mourning & sorrow for so many, & God knows! greatly so to us! Still we must be full of gratitude to Him for our little Arthur's birth, & for many other blessings. We must never forget all we owe to God, for his ever merciful protection! . . . Our last good night in the old year. Oh! if only time did not fly so fast!'[12]

On the last day of 1852, Princess Mary Adelaide of Cambridge wrote from Cambridge Cottage, Kew (now part of the Royal Botanic Gardens) to her former governess, Miss Draper:

'Pray accept my best wishes for the year 1853, and my most affectionate thanks for the beautiful Portuguese matting, which is *du meilleur goût*, and will ornament my new sitting-room at St. James's, where I intend to place it under my writing-table. I long to give you a *hug* and a *kiss* for it. I hope you will tell Mr. Barry how much I admire it, and his taste in ordering it. We spent Christmas Eve very happily, but very quietly, as we had no tree, on the plea of being too old for such juvenile pastimes. So Mama and I consoled ourselves by dressing a large tree up for the servants and schoolchildren, which succeeded remarkably well, and gave general satisfaction. In the course of the evening we interchanged our presents, making

[12] Royal Archives: VIC/MAIN/QVJ/1850.

> the most of them by packing them up and sending them in directed, but without the name of the donor being attached. On Christmas Day we dined at my brother's, and afterwards adjourned to Aunt Mary's, who had asked a few people, and had very kindly provided a tree covered with loveliest bonbons for the occasion. I received beautiful presents from Mama and all the family, principally *des objets de toilette*. To-night we dine at Gloucester House.[13]

On Christmas Eve the following year, the only real changes in the Queen's Journal were that the children were much more fun and active, while the presents that the Royal couple exchanged had slipped into the background:

> 'Were very much busied after seeing Lord Aberdeen, with arranging the Xmas trees & gifts & giving ours to our personal servants &c. At length at ½ p. 6 we went with Mama in the room where the Children's tree was, the 7 Children jumping & shouting with delight. Toys, without end, for the little ones, books, prints, articles for work, games for Boys &c. were given to them all & an undress uniform of the Grenadier Guards, to little Arthur.'[14]

The death of the Prince Consort changed everything, as Queen Victoria makes very clear in her Journal on Christmas Eve 1864:

> Again this festive time has returned, which we used to celebrate so gladly & brightly. The 3d Xmas since my beloved one left us! Out with Lenchen, & we kept in the shelter of the wood, where the sun was warm & pleasant. Directly after luncheon took a short turn in the pony chair, Katharine B. going with me, & at 4 went with the Children, including Louise, to the Servant's Hall, where, as last year, there was a tree with cake, books, toys, & clothes for the schoolchildren on the estate. I also gave each of the labourers' wives a flannel petticoat. At 6 we had our tree & presents in the Dining Room. Ernest L. joined us. The 3 dear girls did so much for me & sweet Baby worked a large blotting book, Arthur's drawings very nice, & Lenchen's & Louise's charming. But how unlike Xmas it is, & how sad!

[13] Clement Kinloch Cooke, *A Memoir of Her Royal Highness Princess Mary Adelaide, Duchess of Teck*, London: John Murray, 1900, p. 133.
[14] Royal Archives: VIC/MAIN/QVJ/1853.

> Felt tired & depressed. What a happy, gay, bustling it used to be in former blessed times, with dear Albert.[15]

Eliza Jane, Lady Waterpark, one of Queen Victoria's Ladies-in-waiting, was at Osborne when she wrote in her diary on Christmas Eve 1870, at the height of the Franco-Prussian War: 'Very cold, there was some skating. I drove with the Queen – after tea we went to receive our Christmas Presents. The Queen gave me a gold & turquoise bracelet, a nice edition of Adams's allegories & a pocket book, velvet. We went to see the Queen's & the Princesses' Table. All the Household dines with the Queen.'[16]

As she grew older Queen Victoria took great care to maintain the long-established Christmas traditions, which she delightedly shared with her younger children and also with her grandchildren. These included thank-you letters.

On 28 December 1877, using writing paper, embossed with a green frog under a tree, playing a banjo, with the words, 'NO PLACE LIKE HOME', Prince George wrote to Queen Victoria: 'I thank you very much for the engraving of yourself and for the story book which you so kindly sent me this Christmas. We are enjoying our holidays very much here; the snow has all melted this morning and it is quite warm. We go to the station this afternoon to meet Captain Fairfax who is coming to stay till Monday. Please give my love to aunt Beatrice and with much to yourself.'[17]

Exactly a year later, Prince George wrote from Sandringham to his grandmother: 'I thank you very much for the pretty writing case and the stories from Shakespere [sic] which I like very much. All our presents were put out yesterday evening in one of the rooms here. It is thawing here now but while the frost lasted we had a little skating. I hope dear uncle Arthur and uncle Leopold are both quite well. Please give my love to dear auntie Beatrice who I hope is also well. Have you much snow now in the Isle of Wight? The ground here is covered with it still. Now with very much love and many kisses to you and auntie Beatrice, I remain your affectionate and dutiful grandson, George.'[18]

In the volumes of Queen Victoria's grandchildren's letters is one, written from Potsdam on 21 December 1879 by Prince William of Germany,

[15] Royal Archives: VIC/MAIN/QVJ/1864.

[16] *The Diary of Lady Waterpark, Lady-in-Waiting to Queen Victoria 1865-91*, British Library ref. Add. 60750, p. 34.

[17] Royal Archives: *Letters from the Queen's Grandchildren, Volume II* – Z 79, folio 94.

[18] Royal Archives: *Letters from the Queen's Grandchildren, Volume III* – Z 80, folio 4.

her eldest grandchild, that is subtly indicative of the future Kaiser's belligerent inclinations:

> Please forgive a patient confined to his bed the uncivillity [sic] in writing with pencil to you, but the good wishes for you shall not be the less warm, than if they had been written down in in [sic] ink on parchment. I wish you a merry Xmas & a happy New Year. May the New Year bring good news of success to your arms & of victory over all the dangerous foes. May also the Lord's hand ward off all disease & sorrow from you & your family & spare you so hard trials, as visited you a year ago.
>
> I have, with your kind permission, taken the liberty to venture to send you a little gift for Xmas. It is a painted photograph of myself in the Windsor uniform, which I had the honour to wear for the first time last year. It is also to be a sign of thankful remembrance of the lovely days & happy hours I was allowed to spend with you & my dear uncles & aunts at Windsor Castle last year. I am again forced to lie in bed for 2 to 3 weeks which I do not like in the least, but one must put on one's best face to the matter & hope that the leg will soon be all right again. With your kind permission I end here & kissing your hand, I remain, Ever your most devoted & respectful Nephew [sic], William Prince of Prussia.[19]

Almost half a century later, Prince William's uncle's biographer wrote: 'The insolence of the Kaiser's young manhood grew in his middle years into a rarely paralleled egotism which made short work of family affection. Only in the case of his grandmother, Queen Victoria, among his English kinfolk, did he show in his maturity a domestic sentiment which could be credited with sincerity.'[20] His charm did not always work on Queen Victoria either. On 22 January 1895, six years to the day before she died, the Queen described her thirty-seven-year-old grandson as 'this impetuous and conceited youth'.[21]

On Christmas Eve 1887, the Empress Frederick wrote to Queen Victoria: 'Let me hasten to thank you a thousand times for all the beautiful and charming things with which you made our Christmas table and Christmas Eve bright, so many tokens of your love and care . . . Fritz was

[19] Royal Archives: *Letters from the Queen's Grandchildren, Volume III* – Z 80, folio 48.

[20] Sidney Lee, *King Edward VII: A Biography: From Birth to Accession*, London: Macmillan & Co., 1925, p. 644.

[21] Ibid., p. 670.

charmed with his stick, with the watch, and with the beautiful book and Landseer etchings, and I with my beautiful silver candlesticks. I have often wished for a pair and admired them in other people's houses in England.'[22]

On Christmas Day 1894, Queen Victoria wrote to the Empress Frederick: 'Thank you so much for the lovely painting by Professor Lutteroth. It is so like the lovely scene of the Riviera which D.V. [*Deo volente*; God willing] I hope to see again early next spring. Christmas was rather sad this year from the many who are gone since then and whose families are mourning. The heads of the House and I myself feel [it]. And it is rather sad to be rolled about in the *Bescherung* and with glasses to look at everything near and far. It is sad. I have suffered a good deal since our return to Windsor, which I am sure was most unwelcome, with my legs.'[23]

The following Christmas Eve, the Queen wrote in her Journal: 'A very wet morning. – Very busy getting all the Christmas presents ready, & did not go out . . . It did not rain but was very dark & dull. Had to have candles all day in my room. Gave my own personal servants & maids their presents. At a little after 6 went down to our Christmas tree. The children were in a great state of excitement, but it was somewhat sad to miss Liko & to think of his being so far away & exposed to such a bad climate. The present tables were arranged much the same as usual. I received many pretty things. Bertie gave me a stained glass window, with a design of flowers, to be placed over the fireplace in the Chapel, Lenchen a small tryptic of watercolour paintings by Meacci of St. George, St. Andrew & St. Patrick. All my other children & grandchildren gave me charming things. Dined in the Durbar Room, where we also lunched.'[24]

On Boxing Day, Queen Victoria wrote to the Empress Frederick: 'Many loving thanks for your lovely presents. The little vase is lovely and the large collection of views of your beautiful house are delightful to have and beautifully done. Many, many thanks for them. Our Christmas *Bescherung* was rather sad but still went off cheerfully enough. The children are so grown that only two could play with toys.'[25]

Unfortunately, the 'bad climate' was too much for Liko, who died of malaria on Africa's Gold Coast during the Ashanti War on 20 January 1896.

[22] Agatha Ramm, ed., *Beloved and Darling Child: Last Letters between Queen Victoria and her Eldest Daughter 1886–1901*, Stroud: Sutton, 1990, p. 61.
[23] Ibid., p. 174.
[24] Royal Archives: VIC/MAIN/QVJ/1895.
[25] Ramm, *Beloved and Darling Child: Last Letters between Queen Victoria and Her Eldest Daughter 1886–1901*, p. 185.

On 21 December that year Princess Beatrice wrote to Lady Martin: 'Christmas could not fail to be very trying, the terrible blank my husband has left in the home circle seems to make itself more keenly felt. It seems so hard to begin a new year without him or at least the cheering hope of a happy meeting before very long.'[26]

On Christmas Day 1896, the Empress Frederick wrote from Kiel to Queen Victoria: 'So many wishes and blessings for today. I well know what a sad Christmas it must be for you, and I feel so much for you and Beatrice for her sorrow must naturally be yours. Let me thank you now most tenderly for all the beautiful gifts you have so kindly sent and which I found on the table under the Christmas tree: the pretty views of dear Osborne terrace with the bright geraniums, the lustre of staghorn with the ancient figure I was so anxious to have and which will look so well in the old Schloss at Kronberg.'[27]

On 28 December 1907, Prince Edward wrote, on behalf of the three elder Princes, from York Cottage to Canon Edgar Sheppard, Sub-Dean of the Chapels Royal, who was known to them all as 'Sub': 'We all thank you very much for the chocolates. They are not at all bad, but you must send some better ones next time, please. We all wish you and Mrs. Sub a happy New Year. Mind you are at Windsor in January. Beware!!! Take great Care!!'[28] On Christmas Day five years later their sister, Princess Mary, wrote to 'Sub': 'I thank you so much for the charming tray, the chocolates and the calendar. It is most kind of you to have sent me so many things. I am delighted to have all the brothers here again and we are enjoying ourselves very much.'[29]

Nor were the servants neglected, as James Pope-Hennessy described:

> On another occasion a young footman from Mar Lodge, who had accompanied Princess Louise to Sandringham for Christmas, was found by Queen Alexandra gazing dreamily out over the snow-covered garden. 'You look lonely', she said, 'and I cannot bear anyone to be lonely in my house at Christmas time.' She asked him his name, and after a long talk with him she disappeared, enjoining him to remain where he was. A few minutes later the Queen returned, holding in her hand a little leather case

[26] Matthew Dennison, *The Last Princess: The Devoted Life of Queen Victoria's Youngest Daughter*, London: Weidenfeld & Nicolson, 2007, p. 196.
[27] Ibid., pp. 197–8.
[28] Royal Archives: Canon Edgar Sheppard's Papers 1905–13: AEC/GG/13/folio 56.
[29] Royal Archives: Canon Edgar Sheppard's Papers 1905-13: AEC/GG/13/folio 104.

> containing some gold links. 'Now these are my personal present to you,' she said, 'you will get your ordinary presents at the Tree tonight.'[30]

The most unusual Royal Christmas present that I have unearthed was that from the Maharajah of Gwalior to King George V in 1914. An undated and unsigned letter from 92 Onslow Gardens, London, explains that 'I have been commissioned by his Highness the Maharaja Sindhia of Gwalior to offer – on his behalf – to Your Majesty as a Christmas present a Fleet of 41 Motor Ambulance cars, 4 Officers' Cars, 5 Lorries, and 10 Motor Cycles, in service with the Navy and the Army. His Highness hopes that this gift may be accepted as a mark of his loyalty and devotion to Your Majesty and of his earnest desire to provide aid to the Sailors and Soldiers who are wounded in action while fighting for the honour of England, against Your Majesty's enemies.'[31]

On 11 December 1914, Lieutenant-Colonel Sir James Dunlop Smith wrote to the King's Assistant Private Secretary:

> I have spoken to David Barr about the presentation of Scindia's gift. It is supposed to be a Xmas gift so we would suggest the day before Their Majesties go to Sandringham for Xmas at any hour convenient to the King. I would suggest that the fleet – about 50 vehicles in all be parked to the south of the Palace inside the gates & file past His Majesty in front of the entrance to the courtyard leaving the Palace by the gate to the north. The persons present would be Sir David Barr whom the Maharaja has commissioned to represent him & Mr. G. Hooper who is H.H.'s Agent in England & who has got the fleet together and myself. The whole thing would be over very quickly. It would give the Maharaja great pleasure if a cinema film could be taken of the ceremony. It could be sent out to India & shown in Gwalior & would have an excellent effect.[32]

The presentation of this remarkably generous and unusual – but entirely appropriate – gift took place at 11.30 a.m. on Monday 21 December 1914. The Williamson Kinematograph Co. sent a representative to take a 'cinema film'.

[30] Pope-Hennessy, *Queen Mary*, p. 362.
[31] Royal Archives: MRH/MRH/GV/FUNC/014/03.
[32] Royal Archives: MRH/MRH/GV/FUNC/014/04.

Collecting items made by the House of Fabergé was a passion of members of the Royal Family, most particularly Queen Mary. On 27 December 1939, Queen Elizabeth wrote to Queen Mary from Sandringham: 'I send my grateful and loving thanks for the exquisite Fabergé fan, which the family have so kindly joined in giving me. It really is quite lovely, and I am enchanted to have it. I do thank you from my heart for your share in such a delightful present.'[33] Five years later, she wrote to her mother-in-law: 'I write to thank you with all my heart for your share in the charming Fabergé clock – it is so delightfully pretty, & so useful as well! I am enchanted to have it, and send a million thanks.'[34]

Sir Osbert Sitwell was just a little nervous about '*Bescherung*' at Badminton in 1944, as he explained:

> Christmas grew nearer. Presents had been my great worry, for I had been warned that the traditional Sandringham ritual still continued. An enormous table was placed in the hall. It was divided up into sections by ribbons, themselves relics of thirty or forty years. Each section was labelled, beginning next to the window with Queen Mary's; then came that of the Princess Royal, and the series ended with mine, on the extreme right. To find gifts for so many people in shops that had been depleted by war, was no easy matter. Moreover, at a moment when taxes were unprecedentedly high, it could be most costly. I had written to grumble about this to Mary Beaufort, who wrote back to me, saying, yes, it was very ruinous, but I need not buy presents for her or Master; would I, instead, bring down something I already possessed or would have to buy soon, for them to give me, and she would choose two objects from the lumber-room, or perhaps take two books from the library, for me to give them. In this fashion we should get what we wanted, and not be put to extra expense. Accordingly, I brought to Badminton a hundred Turkish cigarettes, made by Sullivan Powell (which I always smoked) for Master's present to me, and a recent book on Sickert, which I needed for reference for an essay I was writing, for Mary to give me. In return Mary found a green-shagreen *étui*, circa 1780, for me to give her, and a book on hunting for me to give Master.
>
> On the afternoon of Christmas Eve, which fell on a Sunday, the tree which had been placed in the middle of the hall was lighted up, and the purple cloth which had covered the table was removed to show the presents.

[33] Royal Archives: QM/PRIV/CC12/116.

[34] Royal Archives QM/PRIV/CC13/114.

Queen Mary examined them all in detail, and evinced some curiosity concerning the *étui* I had given her niece; she asked where I had discovered it; you do not often find such things nowadays. I was obliged to improvise in reply as best I could: but I think Her Majesty had no inkling of the deceit we practised. To Queen Mary, I presented a copy describing Lord Castlemain's special embassy to the Pope – the last sent to a pontiff by an English monarch, James II: it is a fine baroque book, profusely illustrated with large folding plates of the coaches and horses and liveries employed, and of the presents offered and bestowed, the banquets and the galas that took place. For the Princess Royal I had found a book on the theatrical performances organised at Windsor Castle for Queen Victoria. Each chapter was given a programme for its heading. Her Majesty gave me the Phaidon Press book of the Holbein drawings in the library of Windsor Castle, and four volumes she had bought in Bath one day, with delightful mid-nineteenth century French engravings. In the evening I moved the presents I had been given up to my room, remembering Queen Mary's passion for tidiness, but I believe I thereby committed a solecism, for Harewood told me later that members of the Royal Family were very fond of coming down in any spare moment to gloat over the presents, other people's as much as their own.[35]

On 27 December 1960, Queen Elizabeth the Queen Mother wrote from Sandringham House to Sir Osbert Sitwell:

'I am so enchanted with the 'Royal Dramatic Record' and send you a thousand thanks for giving me such a charming Christmas present. It is delightfully written, and gives such a vivid picture of those evenings at Windsor. One can see Queen Victoria in the Rubens Room, sitting on a small dais, and it makes one think of the stupendous and extraordinary changes that have happened in the world since she saw the 'Merchant of Venice' in 1848 . . . It has been very nice to be here with my children and grandchildren, and my new son-in-law Tony Armstrong-Jones has had his first plunge into an enormous family party [Princess Margaret and Antony Armstrong-Jones were married in Westminster Abbey on 6 May 1960]. He is a most charming person, very kind, with a creative and lively mind, and great fun too. They are blissfully happy, so one is deeply grateful.'[36]

[35] Osbert Sitwell, *Queen Mary and Others*, London: Michael Joseph, 1974, pp. 57–8.
[36] Renishaw Hall Archives: RHA/1/4.11.

Festive Feasts

According to Elizabeth Craig: 'Plum pudding, which is now queen of the feast, is a Royal descendant of Plum Broth, by way of Plum Pottage and Plum Porridge. It was not until the days of William and Mary that the original Plum Broth, which was served as soup in the days of Charles the First, and was composed of mutton stock, currants, prunes, raisins, sack and sherry, and later on was stiffened with brown bread, became known as Plum Pudding.'[1]

Christmas 1815

For Christmas 1815, the year of Waterloo and the conclusive end of the Napoleonic Wars, the recipe for Royal 'Plum Broth' demanded an extensive list of ingredients:[2]

90 lbs Beef
38 ½ lbs Veal
78 lbs Currants
78 lbs Raisins
12 oz Mace
8 oz Cinnamon
8 oz Cloves
12 oz Nutmeg
8 oz Ginger
4 oz Cochinile [sic]
72 oz Prunes
8 oz Lisbon Sugar
50 oz Butter
½ hundred Eggs

[1] Elizabeth Craig, *Court Favourites*, London: Andre Deutsch, 1953, p. 154.
[2] Royal Archives: Ledger, Windsor Castle 1815: MRH/MRHF/MENUS/MAIN/WC/1815. Apart from numbers, the quantities of the first four items were not specified, but pounds seems a reasonable assumption, when set against the other quantities.

Christmas 1844 – Windsor Castle

On Christmas Day 1844, Queen Victoria and Prince Albert entertained the following guests to dinner at Windsor Castle:[3]

Duchess of Kent
Lord Hawarden [Lord-in-waiting]
Lady Charlemont [Lady of the Bedchamber]
Lord Aberdeen [the Prime Minister]
Lady F. Howard
Lady C. Cocks [Maid of Honour]
Countess Wratisham
Miss Devereux [Maid of Honour]
Lord C. Wellesley [Chief Equerry and Clerk Marshal to Her Majesty]
Mr. and Mrs. Anson [Keeper of Her Majesty's Privy Purse and Woman of the Bedchamber]
Sir G. & Lady Cowper
Lady & Miss Lyttelton [Lady-in-waiting to Her Majesty and her daughter]
Capt[n] Seymour [Groom-in-waiting to Prince Albert]
Sir E. Bowater [Groom-in-waiting in Ordinary to Her Majesty]
Sir R. Otway [Groom of the Bedchamber to Her Majesty]
M[r.] Courtney
D[r.] Boetorius

The menu for 'Her Majesty's Dinner' was lavish and included soups, fish, turkey, beef, rabbit, pheasant, cabinet pudding and mince pies. There was also a side table with further meat dishes.

Rather charmingly, there was also a separate 'menu' for the 'Prince of Wales & Princesses', though children of the age of four or below might just struggle with some of the following fare:

Chicken Broth
Roast Fowl
Loin of Mutton
Mutton Broth
Roast Pheasant
Veal Broth

[3] Royal Archives: Ledger, Windsor Castle 1844: MRH/MRHF/MENUS/MAIN/WC/1844.

Christmas 1896 – Osborne House

On Christmas Day 1896, Queen Victoria wrote in her Journal: 'Went down again to the Durbar Room after tea, where the Children played about very happily, the 2 little boys, delighted with their bearskins, which they had particularly wished for.'[4] This was the Christmas Day dinner menu at Osborne House:

Potages
La Tête de Veau en tortue, aux trois racines
Poissons
Le Turbot bouilli sauce hollandaise
Les Filets de soles frits

Entrée
Les Kromeskys à la Toulouse

Releves
Les Dindes rôties à la Chipolata
Chine of Pork
Roast Sirloin of Beef
Plum Pudding

Entremets
Les Asperges sauce mousseline
Mince Pies
Le Pain de riz à la cintra

Side Table
Baron of Beef
Woodcock Pie
Brawn
Wild Boar's Head
Game Pie

[4] Royal Archives: VIC/MAIN/QVJ/1896.

The Lord Lieutenant's Woodcock Pie

Towards the end of 1915, the Master of the Royal Household sent a memorandum to Queen Mary: 'A Woodcock Pie was sent every year at Xmas to King Edward, by the Lord Lieutenant of Ireland, until 1909, since when none has been sent.'[5] On 20 December that year, the Comptroller, Vice-Regal Lodge, Dublin wrote to Lord Stamfordham, the King's Private Secretary: 'In accordance with what the Lord Lieutenant understands is an ancient custom associated with this season of the year His Excellency is today forwarding a woodcock pie to Buckingham Palace for His Majesty's gracious acceptance.'[6] According to the files, this custom continued at least until Christmas 1931.

Empire Christmas Pudding, 1927–8

On 11 February 1927 the Secretary of State for the Colonies, the Rt Hon. Leo Amery, wrote to Sir Derek Keppel, the Master of the Royal Household:

> You were very kind last December in helping to forward the suggestion that the King and Queen might confine their dinner on Christmas evening to foods produced within the Empire. Might I ask your advice again upon a somewhat similar project for next Christmas? Last autumn at short notice the Empire Marketing Board published a recipe for an Empire Christmas pudding. The recipe was, in fact, provided by our advertising agents, and we should like to prepare for publication next autumn, about the time when people are making their Christmas puddings, a fuller recipe with a note of the various parts of the Empire from which each particular ingredient can be obtained. We want to give a full share of the ingredients to the home country, but we also want to include as many of the overseas parts of the Empire as we can possibly find room for.
>
> It has been suggested that possibly Their Majesties would permit their own chef to provide us for this purpose with a recipe for an Empire Christmas pudding, and to permit us to make known the source from which the recipe had been obtained. Given the recipe, and such brief instructions for the making of the pudding as might seem necessary, we would be responsible for allotting the different ingredients among the different

[5] Royal Archives: MRH/MRH/GV/MAIN/072/02.
[6] Royal Archives: MRH/MRH/GV/MAIN/072/03.

> parts of the Empire. I write, therefore, to ask whether you would feel this suggestion to be suitable for submission to the King. There is no doubt that the idea of an Empire Christmas pudding, which was improvised last autumn, could be used to greater advantage next October or November, and the Empire Marketing Board would feel much honoured, as their work would be notably reinforced, if Their Majesties felt able to assist their purpose in the manner described.[7]

He received the following reply: 'With reference to your letter to me of the 11th February last and my answer of the 14th February, I have submitted to The King and Queen your request for permission of Their Majesties' Chef to provide you with a recipe for the above, and authority to make known the source from which the recipe has been obtained. The King and Queen are entirely in sympathy with your object and have been graciously pleased to grant the necessary permission. I therefore enclose the recipe which I have obtained from Mr. Cédard, and trust that it may prove useful to you (and to the Empire Marketing Board).'[8]

PLUM PUDDING

(Prepared only with British Empire Products).

5 lbs. Currants	Australia
5 lbs. Sultanas	Australia
5 lbs. Stoned Raisins	Australia
2 lbs. Cut Candied Peel	South Africa
5 lbs. Bread-Crumbs	Great Britain
5 lbs. Beef Suet	Great Britain
2½ lbs. Flour	Canada
2½ lbs. Demerara Sugar	West Indies
20 Eggs	Great Britain
1½ ozs. Ground Nutmeg	Straits Settlements
1½ ozs. Ground Cloves	Straits Settlements
2 ozs. Ground Cinnamon	Ceylon
1 gill Brandy	South Africa
2 gills Rum	Jamaica
2 quarts Old Beer	Great Britain

7 Royal Archives: MRH/MRH/GV/MAIN/580/10.

8 Royal Archives: MRH/MRH/GV/MAIN/580/11.

Sauce Sabayon

a) Place into whipping bowl, the yolks of 6 eggs, 1 oz. Caster Sugar, 1 gill Sherry, 1 gill Water. Set bowl over a slow gas, and whip continuously until quite frothy, as whipped cream. Serve immediately.

or b) Place into whipping bowl, the yolks of 6 eggs, 1 oz. Caster Sugar, 1 gill Sauterne, 1 gill Water. Set bowl over a slow gas, and whip continuously until quite frothy, as whipped cream. Serve immediately. Just before serving sprinkle a few drops of Brandy and Rum.

Brandy Butter

Beat to a cream, 8 ozs. Butter and 8 ozs. Fine Sugar, add 2 gills Brandy, beating continuously. This can be served in Sauce-boat or placed on the ice to set and cut into fancy shapes, and served on a napkin.

On 12 March 1927, Leo Amery wrote back to Sir Derek Keppel: 'The Empire Marketing Board would, I know, wish me to express their respectful gratitude to the King and Queen for the kindness with which they have permitted Mr. Cédard to assist them in this matter. The material which you have obtained from him will be of the greatest value to us. There are one or two minor adjustments in the allocation of the ingredients to the various parts of the Empire which may prove expedient, in view of the jealous eagerness with which a recipe from so high a quarter will be received in His Majesty's Dominions. I daresay Mr. Cédard will allow one of the officers of the Board to talk over these small problems with him when we come to put his recipe into final shape for the press.'[9] The result was the following text, printed on a poster, which reflects a number of small, but significant, changes from the original:[10]

The King's Chef, Mr. Cédard, with Their Majesties' gracious consent, has supplied to the Empire Marketing Board the following recipe for

An Empire Christmas Pudding

5 lbs. of currants	Australia
5 lbs. of sultanas	Australia
5 lbs. of stoned raisins	South Africa
1½ lbs. of minced apple	Canada

[9] Royal Archives: MRH/MRH/GV/MAIN/580/13.

[10] Royal Archives: MRH/MRH/GV/MAIN/580/21.

5 lbs. of bread crumbs	United Kingdom
5 lbs. beef suet	New Zealand
2 lbs. cut candied peel	South Africa
2½ lbs. flour	United Kingdom
2½ lbs. demerara sugar	West Indies
20 eggs	Irish Free State
2 ozs. ground cinnamon	Ceylon
1½ ozs. ground cloves	Zanzibar
1½ ozs. ground nutmeg	Straits Settlements
1 teaspoonful pudding spice	India
1 gill brandy	Cyprus
2 gills rum	Jamaica
2 quarts old beer	England

Recipes for a sauce and for brandy butter, also made exclusively from Empire ingredients, to accompany the pudding have been supplied by His Majesty's Chef. Copies can be obtained free on application to the Empire Marketing Board, 2 Queen Anne's Gate Bldgs., London, S.W.1

Christmas Pastimes

During the Georgian period, gambling was a fashionable pastime and there was nothing incongruous about the way King George II celebrated the end of the festive season in the fourth year of his reign, as reported in *The Monthly Intelligencer*:

> Wednesday 6 Jan. 1731. This being the Twelfth Day his Majesty, the Prince of Wales, and the Kts Companions of the Garter, Thistle, and Bath, appear'd in the Collars of their respective Orders. Their Majesties, the Prince of Wales, and the 3 eldest Princesses, preceded by the Heralds etc., went to the Chapel-Royal, and heard divine Service. The D[uke] of *Manchester* carried the Sword of State. The King and Prince made the Offerings at the altar, of Gold, Frankincense and Myrrh, according to Custom. At night, their Majesties etc., play'd at *Hazard*, for the Benefit of the *Groomporter*, and 'twas said the King won 600 Guineas, and the Queen 360, Princess *Amelia* 20, Princess *Caroline* 10, the Earl of *Portmore* and the Duke of *Grafton*, several thousands.[1]

Society slowly changed and propriety insisted that, for later generations, the pastimes enjoyed by the Royal Family during the Christmas period were not so very different from those enjoyed by any enthusiastic, outdoor family. Of course, both money and opportunity enter the equation. For example, not many families will have had access to the facilities enjoyed by Queen Victoria in 1838, while spending Christmas at the Brighton Pavilion.

On Christmas Eve, Queen Victoria and her guests made good use of her late uncle's splendid Riding House – now Brighton Corn Exchange – as she described in her Journal:

> Drove over with Daisy, Mrs. Brand and Miss Murray at a little after ½ p. 1 to the riding house. The gentlemen and Sir George and Miss Quentin were there, and all rode. I first rode *De Vere*, whose canter is very pleasant; after him I got on *Snowdrop*, who is raw at present, but I don't think I shall ever like; the bar was put up, and I was much amused by seeing Lord

[1] Hugh Douglas, comp., *A Right Royal Christmas: An Anthology*, Stroud: Sutton Publishing, 2001, pp. 87–8.

> Torrington and Major Keppel go over a good height. Then I got on dear *Tartar*, who was very fresh and plunged a little, but was soon conquered; but it is quite extraordinary how fanciful he is about other horses and how fond he is of *Edmond*; he couldn't stand *Uxbridge*, which Sir George was riding; and Col: Buckley sent for *Edmond* and rode him next to me; and *Tartar* went like a lamb, though *Edmond* pranced about a good deal; I rode *Tartar* the longest of any.
>
> After him I got on *Midnight* whom I like very much; his trot is charming, and I like his gallop very much too; we had the bar put up again, and Sir George proposed I should go over, which I did readily – 6 times; it was not very high and *Midnight* did it very easily, but I was told I sat it remarkably well; Sir G. led him over as I couldn't make him go, but next time I shall go alone, and higher. The gentlemen then went over. Afterwards I got on *Comus*, who went stupidly in the School. Daisy and Mrs. Brand remained in the School the whole time. We came home at ½ p. 3, much amused.'[2]

On Christmas Eve 1840, just five weeks after the birth of her first child, Queen Victoria wrote in her Journal: 'Just before 12 we walked out for ½ an hour. It was cold, but bright & fine. We walked to the old oak & back, & I walked very well. Albert then went down to Frogmore & skated.' That evening, 'we had a Band playing during dinner, & my Band (stringed instruments) afterwards – a great pleasure. We stayed up till shortly after ½ past 10.' On 30 December, 'we drove down to Frogmore & Albert pushed me in a sledge chair on the ice, which was delightful & it went with such rapidity. I had never been on the ice before. I then walked up & down, whilst Albert & the others skated; & I watched them playing hockey. He had a fall but got up directly again.' The next day's entry commences: 'Alas! it thawed in the night, & our pleasure on the ice has come to an end for the moment, but I hope only for the moment. I am so sorry for dear Albert, who did so enjoy the skating, & it did him so much good & was such a nice change for him.'[3]

On New Year's Eve the following year, the Queen wrote in her Journal: 'We played & sang some of dear Albert's songs.'[4] Among his many talents, Prince Albert was a composer of sacred music, with a particular emphasis on choral music. He composed a Christmas Hymn, while his *Jubilate Deo* was

[2] Royal Archives: VIC/MAIN/QVJ/1838.
[3] Royal Archives: VIC/MAIN/QVJ/1840.
[4] Royal Archives: VIC/MAIN/QVJ/1841.

sung in Westminster Abbey as recently as the 1980s. In the German tradition, he also wrote lieder, or songs, reminiscent of those written by Mendelssohn and Schubert. The *Collected Compositions of His Royal Highness The Prince Consort*, edited by W. G. Cusins, comprises forty works, of which thirty are songs.

On Christmas Day 1843, 'Albert was occupied the whole evening in composing a *Te Deum*, which is a very difficult thing & it gave him great trouble. As far as it has gone, more than ½, it is beautiful.' On Boxing Day, after the Queen had 'sat with Albert, whilst he went on, composing his beautiful *Te Deum* . . . Haydn's 'Toy Symphony' was played, which is extremely funny & original, & which we had on Christmas Eve last year. Lady Douro, I forgot to mention, played 2 pieces on the harp quite beautifully, yesterday evening after dinner. She looked so very handsome as she played, & is so unconscious of her marvellous beauty.'[5]

Eleanor Stanley described the Boxing Day entertainment in a letter to her mother:

> The Duke of Wellington and Lady Rivers are here; and yesterday evening we had a curious piece of music executed by the Queen's hand, to imitate the various sounds of penny trumpets, rattles, drums, and all sorts of toys, supposed to be Christmas gifts to the children of the family; it was composed by Haydn for the Esterhazy children. We were all much amused by it; but still more, when it was all over and we got up to go away, and the Duke, who was sitting by the Duchess of Kent, remained seated on his chair, fast asleep, and poor Lady Douro was desired to wake him, which she was very shy of doing before so many people, but could not help herself, so she did it with the assistance of the Duchess of Kent, who kept repeating in a gentle voice, 'It is all over, Duke.'[6]

Elizabeth Longford wrote that 'One Christmas a group of Red Indians came to Windsor.'[7] A group of Ojibbeway Indians from the northern shore of Lake Huron in Upper Canada was a great success when they appeared at the Egyptian Hall in Piccadilly. A party of nine – comprising two aged

[5] Royal Archives: VIC/MAIN/QVJ/1843.
[6] Beatrice Erskine, *Twenty Years at Court: From the Correspondence of the Hon. Eleanor Stanley*, London: Nisbet and Co., 1916, p. 78.
[7] Elizabeth Longford, *Victoria R.I.*, London: Weidenfeld & Nicolson, 1964, p. 169.

chiefs, four young warriors, two women and a ten-year-old girl – was therefore invited to perform before Queen Victoria, Prince Albert, the Duchess of Kent and the Royal Household on 20 December 1843.

A lively description of the visit was published in *Punch*:

> These illustrious foreigners have had an audience of the Queen, but the report that has appeared in the papers is not so correct as, by our peculiar resources, we are able to render it. On their arriving at Windsor, the porter, in his red and gold livery, was hailed with a most unanimous whoop of delight from the whole party. They declared that they had come expecting to see the great Mother, as they called the Queen, but that they had found the great grandfather Sykes, the porter, who was instantly converted into a sort of Maypole, round which the party went through one of their national war dances – occasionally illustrating some Indian manoeuvres by pokes with their tomahawks, and evolutions with the scalping-knives. Sykes, who was glad enough to get rid of them, handed them over to one of the pages, who ran up the great staircase with the whole tribe at his heels, indulging in one of their national yells . . .
>
> The War-chief was understood to say that he was glad to see the faces of the English all wearing pleasant looks; upon which her Majesty observed, that 'the gentleman in beads and feathers could not have seen a Tax-collector, or he would not have described all the English faces as pleasant'. The War-chief alluded to the size of her Majesty's wig-wam – the name he was pleased to bestow on Windsor Castle. When the Queen good naturedly suggested that 'if it was any wam, it was a Tory and not a Whig wam, since the change in the ministry', the War-chief then gave a very broad hint which was not taken. He remarked that presents had often been sent them from this country – but her Majesty having no loose cash about her, did not act upon the suggestion of *Pattona-quotta-weebe*, for such was the name of the unfathomable and venerable rasper who had been addressing her. The Party then went through several of their dances, in which *Weenish-ka-weebe* – the 'Flying Gull' – greatly distinguished himself.[8]

[8] 'The Ojibbeway Indians', *Punch*, Vol. 6, No. 130, 6 January 1844, p. 14.

The Queen herself wrote:

> After luncheon we went with all the Court over to the Waterloo Gallery, where we saw some very extraordinary Red Indians (American Savages) & they fully justify their appearance & name of savages . . . They were wrapped in buffalo hides, with leggings & sleeves of the same & wore various kinds of beads & ornaments, & a head dress of feathers; the beads & chains gave a clanking sound when they walked; their faces are so thickly painted with black & red stripes, that no features are discernible. The old man had a necklace of fur, with the claws of the grizzly bear round his neck. The squaws were somewhat like gipsy women, very high-shouldered and high cheek-boned with black long fine hair & black eyes, & a spot of red paint on each cheek. They also were wrapped in hides when they arrived, but they took them off & spread them on the floor, to sit down upon. The old man did the same. The women's & child's dress underneath were also composed of hide, giving quite a comic appearance.
>
> They all shook hands with Albert, & the only one who came up close to where I sat, was the little girl whom I shook hands with. The old Chief addressed us in his language, saying he was ill, & could not make a speech; he therefore pointed to the 2nd Chief, a very fine looking one, who spoke in a singular loud voice, making impetuous gesticulations. A ½ cast acted as interpreter, whose father had been a French Canadian. The Indian was very eloquent about England & their having come to see 'their Great Mother', as they called me. The men then went out to prepare themselves for dancing, the women & old Chief seating themselves on either side of the throne. When the men returned, the spokesman carried a little drum, upon which he beat with a little stick, singing, or rather more yelling a very extraordinary kind of song, the others, dancing round & screaming, & whenever they stopped, giving a most horrid whoop, which quite startled one. They were naked down to the waist, having only retained their lower garments, but owing to their whole bodies being painted, & being naturally dark, one scarcely noticed their naked skins. All the dances ended with a war whoop, & it was a very curious, though somewhat alarming sight.[9]

9 Royal Archives: VIC/MAIN/QVJ/1843.

Queen Victoria's life was centred on her family, who gave her constant pleasure. On Christmas Day 1847, she wrote in her Journal: 'After luncheon the 5 Children were in the greatest delight over a little miniature Barouche, with a box for a coachman, & place for a footman, which the Queen Dow^{r} has given them. The 3 girls seated themselves inside, while the 2 Boys sat, the one on the box, & the other standing up behind, the Gentlemen dragging the carriage up & down the Corridor to their intense joy. They were much occupied with their different presents.'[10] The youngest child, Princess Helena, was then just nineteen months old.

The Queen delighted in performances of any description: singing, dancing, musical recitals, poetry readings, plays and variations on the theme of charades. Her particular favourites were *tableaux vivants*, for which the participants were dressed in costume, before acting out scenes from the *Bible*, myth, history or literature. On Boxing Day 1850, the Queen wrote:

> A dull & raw morning. Albert, out hunting, & I, walking with the Children. The little McDonalds & little Flemmings (to whom I had also given something) were much delighted with their Xmas presents, when we went in to see them. Rode afterwards in the Riding School on 'Hammon' & 'Ronald'. A rainy afternoon, but got out for a short walk.
>
> At ½ p. 6 the Children performed their Charade, the same as last year, but without the dancing & the last scene. Some of the scenery from our Theatre was made use of, & the whole looked very nice. The Children were particularly well got up, but did not act as well, being rather absent. Bertie spoke the best. They each recited a piece of poetry & Bertie, the *7 Ages*, by Shakespeare, which he did remarkably well. The performance ended with a little dance with the Phipps Children, who had come to see the Charade.[11]

On New Year's Eve 1853, 'Albert & the Gentlemen went out shooting, & I went with the Children down to the Skating Pond, where we went in chairs, & tried to push ourselves along, with spiked poles. The Children all got on very well.' However, the best had been saved till last: 'At 3 we all went down to the ice, where were assembled all the Gentlemen & at least 7 or 8 Officers. The Band was playing on a small island in the centre of the pond. The games were extremely animated. Before they began all the Children, &

[10] Royal Archives: VIC/MAIN/QVJ/1847.
[11] Royal Archives: VIC/MAIN/QVJ/1850.

we Ladies, were driven about in chairs, which is always delightful. The Boys always join in the game & are most active, never minding how many falls they get. Miss Knollys (staying with the Phipps's) skated very gracefully.[12] We remained till ½ p. 4, & it was a most gay & pretty scene. Mulled wine is always served afterwards in the Orangery.'

That evening, 'our 4 eldest Children, the Greys, Col: Phipps, & his daughter Minnie, Lady E. De Ros, Lady Caroline & Mary Barrington, the Coopers, Lord J. Murray, James Farquharson, & Lord Mount Charles, came after a dinner, & we had a nice & merry dance, Quadrilles, Valses & a Reel, & ending up with a Country Dance, which stopped as the clock struck 12. A flourish of trumpets, accompanied by drums, ushered in the New Year, & a general wishing of a happy new year took place. Vicky was the only one of the Children, allowed to stay up for this, which greatly delighted her.'[13]

On 6 January 1855, Princess Mary Adelaide wrote in her diary: 'A rainy day! We breakfasted punctually at a quarter to nine, and then I wrote letters . . . After luncheon, at two, we drove down to Frogmore, and on our return I read 'Corinne' to Mama. At six o'clock the children's Christmas-tree was lighted, and we joined their little party. Some people arrived for dinner, and I sat next to Albert. Very agreeable! In the evening the Twelfth Cake appeared, and we ended up with snapdragon, which was great fun.'[14]

In *Dictionary of the English Language*, first published in 1755, Samuel Johnson described the parlour game snapdragon as 'a play in which they catch raisins out of burning brandy and, extinguishing them by closing the mouth, eat them'. In Victorian times, snapdragon was a typical Twelfth Night entertainment.

Although the Queen went into full mourning for three years after the death of the Prince Consort, and played little part in public life for rather longer, her family life had to continue. After all, Princess Beatrice was only four years old when her father died. From Osborne House on 16 January 1865, she wrote to Major Elphinstone that she was 'much pleased to hear of the success of the Charades, but would like to have an account how each Vegetable was represented'.[15]

[12] Colonel the Hon. Sir Charles Phipps (1801–66), brother of Lord Normanby, British Ambassador in Paris, was Private Secretary to Prince Albert 1847–49 and Keeper of the Privy Purse 1859–66.

[13] Royal Archives: VIC/MAIN/QVJ/1853.

[14] Clement Kinloch Cooke, *A Memoir of Her Royal Highness Princess Mary Adelaide, Duchess of Teck*, London: John Murray, 1900, p. 152.

[15] Royal Archives: Vic. Add. MSS. A/25.

On 27 December 1867, fourteen-year-old Prince Leopold wrote to his elder sister, Alice, in Darmstadt: 'We are spending a very merry Christmas here, last night the tree was stripped . . . and after the tree had been stripped we played at "Blind man's buff". We are going to act charades next week so we are very busy preparing for them.' 'Homely' and 'Final' were the words chosen for the charades, the former tactful given the store set by the Queen on a full, obedient and uncomplaining participation in the family life of her peripatetic home by all her unmarried children. Three weeks later the children acted in closer accord with their natural tastes, offering 'Banditti' on 21 January. Far from objecting, the Queen mustered commendations even for Leopold's performances.[16]

In a letter to her mother, Lady Elizabeth Biddulph, dated 3 January 1888, the Hon. Marie Adeane, one of Queen Victoria's Maids of Honour, described an evening of music and merriment at Osborne: 'I was summoned to warble duets with Prince Henry, fearfully difficult sections from Gounod's operas, which *he* knew *perfectly well* and which I was expected to sing at sight. I enacted the role of Juliet, Mireille, and I do not know what else while he shouted violent sentiments such as "ange adorable!" at me and at one moment it was so comic that I nearly laughed outright; he has a good voice but cannot manage it and sings with very little expression. Princess Beatrice accompanied us and smiled benignly.'

Three days later, she described the preparations for the *tableaux vivants*:

> We are very busy getting up the 'tableau' which comes off tonight and will I hope be very successful. We had a full dress-rehearsal yesterday after tea and it all went well. The Princess looks so handsome as Queen Elizabeth and quite like a Holbein. You shall have a programme tomorrow which will give you all the details. I figure first as a Spanish Dancing Girl in 'Carmen' with very short petticoats and then as an Attendant Lady on Queen Elizabeth in flowing robes of a bright sky-blue, well bedizened with pearls! We are all to be photographed tomorrow by Byrne of Richmond so I shall have an interesting record of the Royal Revels on Twelfth Day, 1888.[17]

[16] Matthew Dennison, *The Last Princess: The Devoted Life of Queen Victoria's Youngest Daughter*, London: Weidenfeld & Nicolson, 2007, pp. 52–3.
[17] Victor Mallet, ed., *Life with Queen Victoria: Marie Mallet's Letters from Court 1887–1901*, London: John Murray, 1968, pp. 15–16.

In her Journal, Queen Victoria wrote:

> I dined with Jane C., Mary Ponsonby, her daughter Maggy, & Mary Biddulph. Waited afterwards, for some little time in the Drawingroom, as the Band of the Marines had not arrived. At length, at ¼ to 10, we were summoned to the Council Room, where all the ladies & Gentlemen, not taking part in the performance, a few neighbours, & some of the servants were assembled. The stage was arranged just as last year for the Kendalls, with a new drop scene. The *Tableaux* were quite beautiful & so well arranged. After the Band playing a short overture, the curtains rose slowly, & brought the Queen of Sheba before Solomon, to view. Beatrice looked very well in this, in real Eastern draperies, Indian shawls, & jewels. Sir H. Ponsonby was admirable as Solomon. The curtain rose 3 times, & the poses were slightly altered.
>
> The Band played again for ¼ of an hour, & the curtain rose on a new scene in 'Carmen', the music of the charming Opera being played to it. Liko as Torreador (looking very handsome), Minnie Cochrane as Carmen, and Major Bigge as the jealous Don José, were admirable. The 3rd *Tableau*, & in some ways perhaps, the finest, was the statue scene from Shakespeare's 'Winter's Tale'. Marcia Dalrymple as 'Hermione' was simply beautiful & just like a statue. In the 2nd pose she had come down from the pedestal & was in her Husband's arms. Capt. Dalrymple looked so handsome. The 4th *Tableau* represented Queen Elizabeth & Sir Walter Raleigh. Beatrice was wonderfully well got up like the pictures of Queen Elizabeth. Liko took the part of Sir W. Raleigh, & Mrs. Yorke that of Ld Leicester.
>
> When this was over, Beatrice, Liko, & the others sat with us to see the last *Tableau* 'Homage', which was a very unexpected surprise. My bust, being wreathed with flowers, stood in the centre, & ladies were grouped round below it. The Band played 'Home, sweet Home'. This brought to a close, what really were lovely *Tableaux* & a great treat. We all went into the Drawingroom for a few minutes, & then, those who had taken part, went to supper. All were delighted, that everything went so well.[18]

Dorothy Blake, who was born in November 1886, was a daughter of Queen Victoria's land agent, who lived at Barton Manor, next to Osborne House. In 1965 she gave a radio interview in which she described her

[18] Royal Archives: VIC/MAIN/QVJ/1888.

memories of Christmas spent at Osborne:

> At Christmas time there was much gaiety with theatrical performances. There was a very beautiful newly built room called the Durbar Room, built in Indian style, and in this fine room there were always at Christmas time three evenings of dramatic performances, sometimes plays and sometimes *tableaux vivants* and these were acted by ladies and gentlemen in waiting. A very large audience gathered for three nights. The Queen, of course, was very gracious to everyone and she decided that in 1895 the royal children ought to take part and so the programme was arranged as a series of *tableaux vivants* scenes and the initial of each scene spelt out the word 'Christmas'.
>
> Then the final scene was the Christmas scene itself – bringing in the Yule log – with the German librarian as Father Christmas and the royal children in various pretty attitudes on a snow-strewn stage, some throwing snowballs and some sitting on the log and so on. Princess Louise stage-managed that scene. The Queen was thrilled with this scene, she had the curtain up three times and then the next day she had the scene photographed. They were all very well done, with wigs from Clarksons and costumes from London and special make-up service. And footlights, of course, and in 1895, the year that I took part in the *tableau vivant* scene, electric light was used for the footlights for the first time, which was thought a very exciting thing.

Queen Victoria wrote in her Journal on 29 December 1894: 'Christmas was the concluding tableau. The scene was a wood in snow, Mr. Muther as 'Father Christmas' dragging the yule log assisted by a group of children, who were, Alice & Charlie Albany, Drino, Ena, Leopold, Mrs. Trower's little girl & little Acland girl. All the Tableaux were most successful, but alas! I no longer see well enough to make out any features without opera glasses. The Huguenots, the Tyroleans & Richard with the meeting between the King & Saladin I liked perhaps the best. The last Tableau Christmas, with the Children was charming.' Queen Victoria's poor eyesight apparently meant that she did not see eight year-old Dorothy Blake amongst the group of children. Alternatively, Miss Blake may only have taken part on 2 January 1895, when the Queen 'went to the Durbar Room where there was a 2nd performance of the *Tableaux*, equally, if not more successful than the first, & they went so quickly. There were more guests than last time . . .'[19]

In his biography of his father, Sir Henry Ponsonby, Queen Victoria's Private Secretary, Arthur, 1st Baron Ponsonby of Shulbrede, wrote:

> the Queen inaugurated as well amateur theatricals both at Balmoral and Osborne. In two of her Grooms-in-waiting, the Hon. Alec Yorke and Colonel Arthur Collins, she had two excellent actors and competent stage managers. What she enjoyed most of all was superintending the rehearsals, altering to her liking the script of the plays and criticizing the performances of the Princesses and courtiers who were the actors . . .
>
> Amateur theatricals which superseded *tableaux vivants* became almost an annual event. One more may be mentioned, in January 1893 when *She Stoops to Conquer* was performed, admirably produced by Colonel Collins in the Council Room at Osborne. Sir Henry himself had a small part and three of his children also performed. The chief ladies' parts were taken by Princess Louise and Princess Beatrice. It was rather an ambitious attempt. But any failure of memory on the part of the performers was tactfully concealed by a claque of footmen at the back of the audience.[20]

Supporting Lord Ponsonby's observations in old age, Queen Victoria wrote in her Journal on 24 January 1893:

> Saw the dressed rehearsal of 'She Stoops to Conquer,' which went extremely well. The dresses were very pretty, & both Louise & Beatrice looked very nice. Maggie Ponsonby, dressed up as an old woman, looked too wonderful & acted inimitably. But Col: Collins as the old father, Mr. Hardcastle, & Arthur Ponsonby, who is only 21, as the mischievous, rollicking Tony Lumpkin were incomparably good & could not be surpassed by any professional actors. All the others were very good too, & the whole was very well put on the stage. It is a wonderfully clever, amusing, old fashioned play. Mr. Rutland's amateur band from Cowes played very nicely.[21]

[19] Royal Archives: VIC/MAIN/QVJ/1894/95.

[20] Arthur Ponsonby, *Henry Ponsonby, Queen Victoria's Private Secretary: His Life from his Letters*, London Macmillan & Co., 1942, p. 84.

[21] Royal Archives: VIC/MAIN/QVJ/1893.

Bearing in mind the Queen's acute powers of observation, the cast may have got off lightly, as Arthur Ponsonby explained: 'Princess Louise who could act but couldn't learn her part was Miss Hardcastle; Princess Beatrice who couldn't act but could learn her part was Constantina Neville . . . There was one critical moment when Princess Louise got into her part in the wrong Act.'[22] His brother Frederick told a similar story: 'Both Princess Louise and Princess Beatrice were quite good in their parts, but very sketchy with the words. I therefore learnt their parts as well as my own, so that I could either say their words or prompt them. Everyone else did the same, but there was one small bit when they were both on together and of course they stuck, each one thinking it was the other's fault. After an awkward pause the servants gave a round of applause, which I thought was a very intelligent way of helping them, but although the prompter was able to start them again, they could not get going and the stage carpenter solved the problem by letting the curtain down.'[23]

As far as outdoor pastimes were concerned, Arthur Ponsonby recalled:

> At Christmas-time skating at Osborne on a pond close to the old manor-house at Barton was much enjoyed by some of the royal family and by the Ponsonby children, who joined in the hockey on the ice. Their father was often the life and soul of the game. As one of the Princesses slowly and helplessly revolved with the cork bung between her skates, he would go round her beating the ice with his stick and shouting "Don't let the Princess have it all her own way." The Queen however strongly disapproved of hockey on the ice. So when her outrider was seen coming over the hill, all sticks were quickly thrown on to the bank. The whole company turned innocently to figure skating, or some attempt at it, till the carriage which had stopped to allow the Queen to view the skating had passed on out of sight, when the game was resumed.[24]

Two decades later a more active generation found numerous physical activities with which to amuse themselves, with shooting to the fore. However, the facilities at Buckingham Palace and Sandringham offered a range of options for the younger generation, as Queen Victoria's great-grandson, the eighteen-year-old Prince of Wales, described in his 1912 diary.

22 Michael Turner, *Osborne House*, London: English Heritage, 1989, p. 35.
23 Frederick Ponsonby, *Recollections of Three Reigns*, London: Eyre &Spottiswoode, 1957, p. 51.
24 Ponsonby, *Henry Ponsonby, Queen Victoria's Private Secretary: His Life from his Letters*, p. 389.

On 22 December he 'wrote & worked all the afternoon & in the evening had 2 sets of tennis with Bertie, at 5.30 afterwards we had some footer there with Harry; we got good exercise'. The next day the Royal Family went by train to York Cottage, Sandringham and 'we all went out for a walk at 4.00 to the kennels & West Newton'. On Christmas Eve, 'I sent all my presents to the House & did some writing till 11.30 which kept me busy. Then I went out with the brothers & we went to the village bicycled & rowed about & fooled in the boat.'

The day seems to have ended in a frustratingly subdued manner: 'We walked & talked aimlessly till 7.30 when we came back & I did some more writing.' Christmas Day was equally quiet; however, on Boxing Day, 'at 12.00 I had a round of golf with Bertie & Mary; 3 ball game. Bertie & I were all square on the 9 holes. We had a good game. Lunch was at 1.30 & in the afternoon at 3.00 we changed & played footter [sic] amongst ourselves. E. Knollys came. We had a rugger & soccer ball. We finished up with a run to & from the house.' On 29 December the Prince of Wales 'played a round of golf with Bertie & Harry & the former won'.[25]

[25] Royal Archives: EDW/PRIV/DIARY/1912.

Observers' Royal Christmases

Lord Torrington at Windsor Castle, 1860

George Byng, 7th Viscount Torrington, was a Permanent Lord-in-waiting to the Prince Consort from 1853 to 1859, and then to Queen Victoria from 1859 until he died on 26 April 1884, aged seventy-one. He was a regular correspondent of John Delane, editor of *The Times*, to whom he often signed his letters 'Your Windsor official'.[1] For Delane's benefit he described Christmas at Windsor Castle in a letter, later quoted in the former's biography, which was written by his nephew:[2]

> December 23 – Your biography of Lord Aberdeen was really and truly appreciated, not merely by myself, but by every one in the Castle, including the Prince Consort. Sitting before my fire yesterday at five o'clock, in nothing but my shirt and trousers, in walked the Prince of Wales and Prince Albert to beg I would come and play billiards with them. I apologised for my want of dress, and tumbled into it. They, in the meantime, were much amused with the study of the pictures in the room . . . I have just been to church with Her Majesty and the rest of the Royal family; a wonderfully fine and short sermon from Dr. Goulburn. Her Majesty honoured me with a long chat; but nothing very remarkable, though very kind in her inquiries about my health. I went with Biddulph and the Dean of Windsor's wife, a very pretty woman, to see the baron of beef roasting, 360lb. weight. Four men are constantly on for ten hours turning the spit, when they hope it will be done to a turn. I am sure the men will. Prince Alfred starts on Wednesday for Berlin, and is due to be back at Plymouth to join the *St. George* on January 6.

[1] Sidney Lee, *King Edward VII: A Biography: From Birth to Accession*, London: Macmillan & Co., 1925, p. 126 note.

[2] Royal Archives: Vic. Add. C/24, quoted in Arthur Irwin Dasent, *John Thadeus Delane, Editor of 'The Times'*, Vol. II, London: John Murray, 1908, pp. 14–17.

On Christmas Eve, Queen Victoria wrote in her Journal:

Already this dear Festival returned again, & this year with true Xmas weather, snow on the ground & sharp frost. Albert & the Princes went out shooting, but Louis [the Prince of Hesse] preferred remaining with Alice. Walked down with them to the skating pond, where we found the other girls, &c. All skated again after luncheon, when there was a regular game at Hockey, in which Louis joined with great spirit. We came home after 4, & then began the arranging of the present tables, which was most bewildering, but however at last with dear Albert's great indefatigability, we succeeded. Everything was as usual, only this time we had both our elder Boys home, & Louis' things were placed on the same table as Alice's.

At a little after 6 we all went into the 'Bescheerung', including dear Mama & the Leiningens. Everyone seemed delighted with their presents. I got charming & beautiful things perhaps the one gift most precious to me being a little bracelet in the clasp of which are small coloured photographs of dear Alice & Louis, their united cyphers on the top, & their hair at the back, given by them. All the dear Children worked me something, also Mama. At 7 we gave my gifts to the Ladies & Gentlemen who afterwards came over to see our things. As usual, such a merry happy night with all the Children, & not the least happy, dear Alice & Louis. We remained all together till near 8. No additions to our dinner, but Gen & Mrs. Bruce.[3]

Lord Torrington's account continued:

Christmas Day

I return your Portsmouth correspondent's letter, and I hope before I close to send you the drawing of *La Gloire*, but our friend the P.C. [the Prince Consort] has carried it off to study or copy and only gave me back the letter. I am going to give you a brief account of our proceedings last evening, with which in every way I was most agreeably surprised and pleased.

The Queen's private sitting-rooms, 3 in number, were lighted up with Christmas Trees hung from the ceiling, the chandeliers being taken down. These trees, of immense size, besides others on the tables, were covered with bonbons and coloured wax lights. Some of the trees were made to appear as if partially covered with snow. These rooms contained all the

[3] Royal Archives: VIC/MAIN/QVJ/1860.

presents for the Royal Family the one to the other. Each member gave a present to one another, so that, including our Hesse and the D of Kent, every person had to receive or give 13 presents. The two small rooms contained the presents given to the Queen, the others to the P.C.; and the large room had the appearance of a superb bazaar, filled with everything that was handsome, various, and in good taste.

I have never seen a much more agreeable sight. It was Royalty putting aside its state and becoming in words, acts and deeds one of ourselves – no forms and not a vestige of ceremony. Even as in a public bazaar, where people jostle with one another, so Lords, Grooms, Queen, and Princes laughed and talked, forgot to bow, and freely turned their backs on one another. Little Princesses, who on ordinary occasions dare hardly to look at a Gent-in-waiting, in the happiest manner shewed each person they could lay hands on the Treasures they had received & they might have been taken for little shop women deluding a customer. Prince Arthur (the flower of the flock) speedily got into a volunteer uniform, which, with endless other things, including a little rifle, fell to his lot, took a pot-shot at his Pa, and then presented arms.

Some of the presents were beautiful in taste and suited to the receiver, and even the presents of children to their parents were selected so that even the Queen might find use for them. I saw no jewellery of any sort except those given by the Queen to the Household, and all that was done in another Room. I received a supply of studs, sleeve buttons, and waistcoat ditto, handsome plain gold; a pocket-book, and every one of us a large cake of Nuremberg gingerbread. Whether the Prince Consort had a quiet joke in his mind when he selected presents for Phipps, Biddulph, Grey, and Bruce, I don't know, but Phipps had salt cellars resting on little fish with their mouths open, Biddulph a bread basket, Grey a sugar bason [sic], and Bruce a claret jug; but at any rate the four articles were somewhat true Emblems of the Loaves and Fishes. The parties concerned have not observed the possible joke, nor have I suggested the idea.

I never saw more real happiness than the scene of the mother and all her children: the Prince lost his stiffness, even to his very straps and your Windsor special had much cheerful and friendly conversation with them. Altogether, it was a sight I should have liked you to have seen, and therefore have briefly described it.

I went to see the Roasting in the kitchen of turkeys, geese, and beef – a mighty sight: at least 50 turkeys before one fire. The Lord Lieutenant of

> Ireland, by custom or law, sends over every year a large Woodcock Pie. This one is composed of one hundred birds, and I certainly intend to try whether Carlisle's cook knows how to prepare a worthy dish to set before the Queen.

Prince Louis of Hesse, a minor German princeling who became Grand Duke of Hesse and by Rhine in 1877, had been proposed by Crown Princess Frederick of Prussia as a suitable husband for her younger sister, seventeen-year-old Princess Alice. On 1 July 1862 Louis and Alice were married in the dining room at Osborne House. Only four years later, however, the two sisters found themselves on opposing sides during the Austro-Prussian War, in which Prince Louis led the Hessian cavalry against the Prussian invaders.

A book in the Royal Archives, *Christmas Presents 1841–1861*, provides further detail on the four presents:[4]

> - Sir Charles Phipps – four dolphin salt cellars & spoons – Turner – £22 10s
> - Colonel Thomas Biddulph – pierced silver bread basket – Garrard – £18
> - General Charles Grey – silver butter cooler – £7
> - General Robert Bruce – large crystal claret jug with an ornamental top – £19

Lord Torrington's 'set of buttons & studs & court buttons in gold' also came from Garrard and cost £9. Nor was Baroness Lehzen forgotten: her silver inkstand from Turner cost £17 10s.

On Christmas Day, the Queen wrote:

> An intensely hard frost, 28 degrees! The windows were frozen, the trees all white with frost. Had very satisfactory news from China, except the beheading of 2 poor Prisoners. After breakfast we all went to the Xmas Room to look at our various tables, & then down to the ice. It was so fine, the sun out & the church bells ringing had such a beautiful effect. Service at 12, to which Leopold came for the 1st time. Dear Mama & the Leiningens came to luncheon. Again all skating & there was a great game of Hockey. The Leiningens, Phippses, Greys, Wellesleys, Biddulphs, &c.

[4] Royal Archives: VIC/ADDT/312.

> dined. Louis was introduced to all the Xmas delicacies. The little Boys & precious Baby down to dessert & the other girls after dinner.[5]

Lord Torrington's letter concluded:

> The Dinner yesterday was really wonderful. How I live to tell the tale I don't know but after I thought I had dined I took some of the Baron of Beef, the Boar's Head, and the Lord Lieutenant's pie. Fortunately, I did not go to bed till near 3 o'c, as we finished the evening with some pool and billiards; and Captain Du Plat & self cleared the remainder of the Gents out of every silver coin they possessed. Altogether a jolly day, as I sincerely hope yours was.
>
> P.S. – I will make another attempt to get back *La Gloire.*
>
> December 30 – I return *La Gloire,* which I only got back last night. The Prince of Wales inspected it by the side of the picture of the *Warrior* in *The Illustrated London News.*

The first ironclad battleship, *La Gloire*, developed by the French, had been launched at Toulon on 24 November 1859. She rendered existing warships obsolescent. However, the French only constructed two sister ships for *La Gloire*, while the Royal Navy swiftly countered with the more heavily armoured HMS *Warrior*, which is preserved at Portsmouth.

There was a perceived threat from across the Channel which led to the construction of 'Palmerston's follies', the remains of which forts and gun platforms still survive along England's southern coastline. The rivalry is all the more ironic when one bears in mind that France had been our ally in the Crimean War, which had formally ended in the Treaty of Paris signed on 30 March 1856, less than five years earlier. On 31 December, Queen Victoria expressed her nervousness in her Journal: 'I feel much moved, so anxious for the future, that no war shd. come, & fear for the state of Europe. My precious husband cheered me & held me in his dear arms saying, "We must have trust, & we have trust that God will protect us."'[6] In the event the Franco-Prussian War of 1870–71 put French territorial ambitions on hold for a generation.

[5] Royal Archives: VIC/MAIN/QVJ/1860.
[6] Royal Archives: VIC/MAIN/QVJ/1860.

As Elizabeth Longford noted: 'It was a poignant scene in view of what lay in store.' She continued: 'Fortunately her last Christmas Day with Prince Albert was a glorious one, Windsor at its best. There were twenty-eight degrees of frost, windows frozen over, floods of sunshine, wild games of ice-hockey, Louis and Alice sharing a present table, Mama to luncheon, Leopold and Baby coming down to dessert and the older ones appearing after dinner; Albert telling stories, Albert cracking jokes, Albert swinging Baby in a dinner napkin, Albert, Albert, Albert.'[7]

The Marquis of Lorne at Osborne House, 1890s

On 21 March 1871 Princess Louise married the Marquis of Lorne, eldest son of the 8th Duke of Argyll, the first time an English princess had married a commoner since 13 May 1515, when Princess Mary Tudor, younger sister of King Henry VII and widow of King Louis XII of France, married Charles Brandon, Duke of Suffolk. The Lornes had no children. In the year of the Queen's death, he published a memoir of his mother-in-law, in which he wrote:

> At Osborne she incessantly took the greatest personal trouble, and showed the liveliest interest, in the arrangements for the tableaux, or representations, by the house party, of famous scenes in pictures, Meissonier's 'Quarrel Scene,' as well as some of Gustave Doré's compositions, being very successfully rendered. These little entertainments were at first held in the Council Room, but after the Indian Hall was built large audiences assembled before a wider stage. The children in the house, as well as the ladies and gentlemen of the household, became important actors and actresses, and the Queen always liked them to keep on the dress in which they had appeared until the reception of the guests, which was always concluded with a supper, was over.
>
> All, indeed, was the revival of the old English country life, and especially at Christmas-time, when everybody in the Queen's employment had the old-fashioned good cheer. Every one received something as a memorial of their gracious mistress, and wherever she was she took care, if it was at all possible, to be present at the distribution of gifts. Sometimes it was on Christmas Eve, sometimes on the day itself, but all the aged and

[7] Elizabeth Longford, *Victoria R.I.*, London: Weidenfeld & Nicolson, 1964, pp. 283 and 288.

infirm were assembled that presents might be made to them, and given by her own hands.

Then there were all the servants to consider in the same way, and sometimes to the number of nearly three hundred if the Court was at Windsor. The Queen chose the gifts with careful thought for the wants of each. A lighted tree, with snow-laden branches, appeared as a centre around which the presents were arranged. These, however, were too numerous to be grouped in one place, and had to be spread over long tables. Then in another room another Christmas-tree was placed, where other souvenirs awaited the ladies and gentlemen of the Court. Thus were all thought of and gratified, before the Queen allowed herself to devote time to family affections, about which most people think first and foremost at such times.

At six o'clock in the evening came the hour when the family and immediate guests staying with the Queen were to have their turn. A large room was reserved for them, and they all entered it following her Majesty. There they saw a row of separate tables, each covered with a white cloth, and stretching right and left of the lighted tree, which was full of what used in those days to be called French and German bonbons. It was to the tables that attention was turned, for each member of the family or guest had a separate little table, and on this were laid out the remembrances sent from far and near . . .

On Christmas Day itself there was a beautiful service, with the choristers of St. George's Chapel to sing the lovely carols, of which the Queen was always very fond. Then came the visit to the people who deserved notice, afterwards the lighted tree, and a fresh inspection of the gifts. Following this there was often music, as when Mendelssohn came with his choir to give 'Athalie'. And so the stately cheer went on, work and hospitality mingling with the family happiness. As it was in the early days, so the customs were continued as far as possible; but, alas! how many changes, how many old faces, came to be missing, how many honoured ones could no more be seen! But there was an abundance of young faces, whose merriment cannot be marred by any such thoughts. It was in children that the Queen took delight. Though her own share in joy might be small, yet she watched with sympathy the enjoyment of all others, and in the observance of the festival she kept to what her husband did. This was always good in her eyes. As he ordered things, so she desired that they might be fulfilled. He was no niggard in anything, and his wholesome discipline and the rein

> he gave to pleasure remained the ideal of his widow to the last, and in unselfish thought for others she found her best reward.
>
> One of the best pleasures we can have is to keep a family and its connections together in harmony and well-doing. Christmas festivals give an opportunity to do this, and it was always the Queen's wish, and a wish that found fulfilment in success, to make her family life an example to her countrymen. Her lifetime was, as far as she was able to influence it, that of which the Christmas-tree may be thought to be a symbol – namely, stanch [sic] and strong and bright with lights to gladden the grateful faces of children and children's children forming the family circle around the Christmas-tree at Windsor or at Osborne.[8]

Much later, Lord Ponsonby recalled that 'Christmas-time at Osborne was quite festive. The Queen's presents arrived punctually on Christmas Eve and were an excitement, specially so when the children were in the toy stages. Later the inkstands and blotting-books and improving volumes were less exciting. The boxes of bonbons and *Lebkuchen* from Germany – a sort of gingerbread with almonds on it – were much appreciated. The duty of having to thank the Queen with a curtsey or a bow after the snapdragon on Twelfth Night they performed very indifferently.'[9] The 'less exciting' nature of the proceedings was described by Eleanor Stanley in a letter to her mother from Windsor Castle on Christmas Eve 1851: 'Lady Caroline Barrington has been in a great state, helping the Queen to arrange and select toys and things for the children. I saw some of the things for the elder ones yesterday, but they, of course, are too old for toys; what I saw was books, work, both crochet and cross-stitch, and a quantity of very smart gilt and illuminated notepaper with envelopes to match, which it seems is what pleases the children most, to write to their foreign cousins upon; also a colour box for Princess Louise.'[10]

[8] The Marquis of Lorne (now His Grace The Duke of Argyll), *VRI: Queen Victoria: Her Life and Empire*, London: Harper & Brothers, 1901, pp. 355–7.

[9] Arthur Ponsonby, *Henry Ponsonby, Queen Victoria's Private Secretary: His Life from his Letters*, London: Macmillan & Co., 1942, p. 389.

[10] Beatrice Erskine, *Twenty Years at Court: From the Correspondence of the Hon. Eleanor Stanley*, London: Nisbet & Co., 1916, pp. 201–202.

The Wigram Family at Sandringham, 1926

A former aide-de-camp to Lord Curzon, Viceroy of India, Captain Clive Wigram had been attached to the Prince of Wales as Assistant Chief of Staff during his first Indian tour 1905–6. The following year he was appointed as his Equerry, before becoming Assistant Private Secretary in 1910. On 29 April 1912, King George V wrote to his Private Secretary, Lord Stamfordham: 'Wigram has done quite splendidly: never made a mistake: is simply a glutton for work, besides being a charming fellow. I am indeed lucky in having found a man like him.'[11]

On 10 September 1925 Sir Henry Ponsonby's elder son, Sir Frederick Ponsonby, later 1st Baron Sysonby, known to the Royal Family as Fritz, wrote to Clive Wigram about his elder son, ten-year-old Neville, the King's godson: 'I am glad to tell you that the King has appointed your boy to be a Page. Not an easy choice because there are so many boys ripe with good claims. The King, however, without hesitation, chose your boy.'[12] Such an appointment was one of many rewards for holding a senior position in the Royal Household.

In conversation with Neville, 2nd Baron Wigram, I learned that 'all the Pages were sons of Courtiers and we had to buy our own uniform. I can't remember what we were paid but we didn't see the money.'[13] He also said 'we lived in those days in the Norman Tower at Windsor Castle and the garden surrounding the Round Tower was our garden, with three permanent gardeners. We didn't have to pay rent – it wasn't like it is nowadays.'

Lord Wigram explained:

> My father spent alternate months on duty and, for some reason, December was always his month. As a consequence we never saw him at Christmas. The first thing that I always had to do after Christmas was sit down and write him a thank-you letter. Queen Alexandra died in 1925 and the King was then able to move from York Cottage at Sandringham into the big house. The King realised that we were without a father at Christmas-time so very kindly invited us to spend Christmas with him at Sandringham in 1926. The party comprised my mother, sister and younger brother;

[11] Harold Nicolson, *King George the Fifth: His Life and Reign*, London: Constable & Co., 1952, p. 195.
[12] Neville, 2nd Baron Wigram, *Some Memoirs of my Early Life*, privately published, 2002.
[13] Neville, 2nd Baron Wigram, in conversation with the author, 24 June 2011.

Sawyers, my father's valet; Carrie, my mother's lady's maid; and Nanny Hunt, whom we just called 'Nanny'.

We had a separate carriage on the Royal Train, which stopped at Wolferton, which was the only stop. We got there mid-afternoon. My father, my sister, Sawyers and I then walked a couple of miles with him to Sandringham, while the rest of the party went by car. We stayed in the wing that used to be occupied by Sir Dighton Probyn: there were three bedrooms and a small sitting room for the children, and my brother shared a bedroom with Nanny. We also had a special Page, or perhaps a Footman, rather than a Page. The King and Queen came to see that we were all right in our little suite. They couldn't have been kinder to us.

In his diary for 23 December 1926, King George V recorded: 'Colder even than yesterday, wind N.E. Gave Bigge, Fritz & Derek their presents. We left in special at 12.55 from King's Cross for Sandringham, with Harry, George, Lady Airlie, Lady Joan [Verney], Reggie [Seymour], the Wigrams & their three children [Neville, Anne and Francis]. Unpacked my things. Wrote letters all the evening.'[14]

Lord Wigram's description of a Christmas from almost eighty-five years earlier continued:

On Christmas Eve the King and Queen led a crocodile to the Ball Room, where there was a big Christmas tree and long tables around three sides had been covered with white tablecloths. Strips of red ribbon separated the different groups of presents, with the name of the recipient printed on the edge of the table. I was given a lovely gold watch by the King, one of a number of watches that the Royal Family gave me over the years. The Princes gave me a hunting crop, which, unfortunately, I haven't still got. Somebody gave me a carpentry set, which was my favourite present of the lot really. After opening our presents we walked round, looking at everyone else's. I remember that we also went to see the distribution of the meat. There were at least fifty estate workers and keepers and they were all given great chunks of meat.

On Christmas Day we went for a family walk before my sister and I were invited to dine with the whole party, which included the equerries and the ladies-in-waiting. I wore a dinner jacket, which I had just started

[14] Royal Archives: GV/PRIV/GVD/1926.

> wearing in those days, while the rest of the party wore white tie.[15] As soon as we sat down to dinner, the Royal Princes started to throw bread rolls across the table but the King didn't seem to mind! After dinner I left with the ladies and we went into the Drawing Room, where Queen Mary very kindly said: 'Come and talk to me.' I was amazed to see that the first thing she did was light up a cigarette, with a long holder. My mother was delighted because that meant that she could light up too.[16] She smoked Turkish, of course, *Balkan Sobranie*: you were thought an awful cad if you were caught smoking *Virginian*. That's one below being a s**t, isn't it really?!
>
> On Boxing Day there was a shoot and I went out with the ladies at lunchtime. A marquee had been put up, with a miniature Royal Standard on top, while we were waited on by footmen, in their scarlet livery. I think we ate shepherd's pie, which was brought out in special boxes. After lunch the King very kindly invited me to stand next to him on one of the drives. His valet, Howlett, acted as his loader and he was using two guns, rather than his normal three. I don't remembering him missing anything and he shot more than sixty pheasants on that drive. Some of them were rather low birds, though! I remember playing golf on the private nine-hole course at Sandringham – there was also a private course in the Home Park at Windsor.

In his diary, King George V described the day's shooting, which took place on Monday 27 December, since Boxing Day fell on a Sunday: '8° of frost. Fine day but less cold. We shot Woodcock Beat with keepers & amateur beaters. We saw some woodcock & got 23 but ought to have got more. The Ladies joined us at Fally for luncheon & walked with us afterwards. Bertie, Harry, George & Dick made the 5 guns.[17] We got 380 pheasants, 5 hares, 7 rabbits, 51 duck, & 7 various.'[18]

That April, Neville's mother, Nora Mary, had been given a book by Rosamund Wigram 'that I should write down matters of interest for my

[15] Lord Wigram told me that, from that time on, he had to wear a dinner jacket every evening at home, except on Sundays.

[16] In *Some Memoirs of My Early Life*, Lord Wigram wrote: 'In 1920 Lord Dawson of Penn, the King's doctor, recommended that she should take up smoking, which she continued for the rest of her life!'

[17] The King's three younger sons, together with Dick Molyneux, who was unmarried and often spent Christmas with the Royal Family.

[18] Royal Archives: GV/PRIV/GVD/1926.

family in the hereafter'. Much of the book comprises her recollections of Christmas at Sandringham in 1926, which form a unique description:[19]

St. James's Palace – December 23rd – A great day. We are all leaving London, Anne, Neville, Francis and I to stay with the King & Queen for Christmas.

Sandringham, Norfolk – December 23rd – We left St. James's soon after 12 o'clock and drove in a Royal Bus to St. Pancras. An employee of the Railway tried to stop our entrance to the reserved Royal Platform but on my explaining that the 3 children and myself were passengers by the Royal Train he allowed us to pass with a sniff of extreme suspicion. Later on various pressmen asked Clive who the children were and he replied irascibly that he believed they were some of the children's servants! We marched down with Regie Seymour and Lady Airlie & Lady Joan Verney. Lady Airlie said she had been having fainting fits but seemed quite light-hearted and was her usual delightful, gallant and amusing self. On reaching King's Lynn [actually Wolferton] I advanced with my brood of 3. We all stood in a line and Francis performed his 1st Royal Bow – quite good except that it swerved rather! I went off in the car following the King & Queen with Regie & Joan. Clive walked up with Neville & Anne while Francis was driven up in state with his Nanny in a Royal Landau.

On my arrival at Sandringham House the King & Queen insisted on showing us the children's rooms and my own. One's host & hostess don't usually take so much trouble. The children's apartments were 1st visited – consisting of a large sitting room, out of which opened an even larger bedroom, with 3 beds, and beyond was the bathroom, a truly palatial affair with its 3 basins all with running taps of water and a particularly deep bath into which Francis practically disappeared. The 3 Bears & Goldilocks were the only things missing. Anne's bedroom was upstairs near mine, which proved to be a great big room with a crude blue wallpaper and covered with prints illustrating coronations, marriages and various activities of the Royal Family, beginning with the picture of Queen Victoria receiving Lord Melbourne on her accession. She had autographed the picture. I just managed to hustle into a thin dress in time to go down to tea.

The meal proved to be from 1st to last the most alarming – and dare I say the one boring meal of the visit. A long table placed in the middle of

[19] Lady Wigram's Private Journal – courtesy of Lord Wigram.

the hall, with an orderly row of little chairs in which one's knees nearly touched one's chin and one's neighbour's elbows were a constant menace to one's tea drinking, added to which the King's terrier, Jack, would suddenly leap onto one's lap! Conversation was fairly brisk – but if one was sitting next the King, anything His Majesty said was listened to in silence, which unfortunately prolonged itself to enjoy my platitudinous reply – most trying.

After tea the King said he wished to see the children. They had not had time to change so with the roil & moil of travel on them they entered – Anne & Neville quite unconcerned. Francis, grappling with the situation heroically, getting rather white and holding on firmly to his Daddy. 'What have you done with your tooth, Francis?' said H.M., pointing to an unsightly cavity. 'It came out in an apple,' mumbled the poor man. Roars of applause at this announcement eased the situation, and when the King most kindly suggested that 'Rose Marie' should be played on his really beautiful gramophone, Francis was quite reassured.

December 24th – Sandringham – Sat next the King at dinner, who was charming in his hopes that the family were all happily established. We had an interesting talk on Ludwig's book on the German Emperor, which he said gave a very accurate portrait of the Emperor's personality.[20] . . .

The rest of the guests arrived this afternoon. The Prince of Wales, the Duke and Duchess of York, Prince Henry, Sir Colin & Lady Keppel, Admiral Henry Campbell and Dick Molyneux. Directly after lunch we all attended the first Christmas ceremony, which consisted in the distribution of meat to all the employees on the estate. It took place in a large coach house. The King & Queen with the Duchess of York & Lady Airlie sitting on one side, and the house party, with the Prince of Wales, Duke of York, Prince Henry and Prince George sitting opposite. A large buffet ran round the room, decorated with holly, from behind which peeped out large joints of beef.

The meat was served out by men in butcher blue coats and the recipients all arrived with white towels in which to remove the joints. I think my memory is accurate in saying that 18 bullocks provided the fare. It was a cold performance lasting nearly an hour. Francis sat on my lap, which was comforting, but his comments had to be restrained at times.

[20] Emil Ludwig, *Kaiser Wilhelm II*, trans. E. C. Mayne, London and New York: G. P. Putnam's Sons, 1926.

The Prince of Wales was the one who tried to appear the most interested. Lady Airlie dropped her glasses. He tore across the intervening space to pick them up, all but colliding with a jovial farmhand bearing his round of beef. With mutual apologies they disentangled each other. By that time the glasses had been picked up. However a few moments later an elderly lady, weighed down with her 'portion', got a bit dazed and 'green'. The Prince was the 1st on his feet to lead her and the joint to safety. He certainly has a great charm of manner.

Christmas Day 1926

There is a lot to describe of the happenings of yesterday afternoon. A peaceful day until tea time, when we were told that directly after tea we were all to go into the Ball Room to receive our presents, so we fortified ourselves with a hearty meal and after tea Clive collected the children. The procession was formed, led by the King and Queen, who said that the children must come with them. There was an enormous Christmas tree also lit up, but no presents on it, but round the room. There was, for want of a better word, a buffet, covered with a white material and a strip of pink tape separated the different groups of presents, and the recipient's name was printed on the edge of the long table. The King's presents started the line and the line of pink tape separated the Queen's presents, which came next, followed by the Prince of Wales, the Duke & Duchess of York and so on, & it eventually reached the equerry Major Seymour. The children had a group to themselves, the opposite side of the room. The children were led up to their group and the rest of the company remained in the middle of the room until summoned by the King & Queen to their individual group.

My turn came eventually and I was overcome by the generosity of the King & Queen & these were the things I got: a Kashmir shawl, a rose bowl, antique tea-caddy of tortoiseshell & ivory, grey leather bag, an evening bag of gold tissue, 2 little enamel boxes and an ashtray. Clive's group was next mine: a set of silver cruets, 3 gardening books, a pencil case, etc. It was too amusing looking along the line, everyone in front of their own little group, gloating over and playing with their treasures. Presently we began to pay each other visits and mutually examine our presents, and eventually the King and Queen invited us to go and look at their gifts. The Queen had given the King a Munnings picture of the Royal Procession at Ascot, and she had received from the King a large lozenge-shaped brooch containing all the badges of the Brigade of Guards in diamonds etc.

She explained to me that it was a long-felt want of hers, a brooch of the badges to wear when visiting any of the Regts.

The Prince of Wales had received rather a gruesome present I thought: a dozen ordinary bottle corks, decorated with the Prince of Wales's three feathers in silver. Prince George and I examined the Duke of York's presents, among which was rather a florid tie pin. Prince George eyeing it with disfavour said, 'That pin belonged to Papa. He doesn't like it so passed it onto Bertie. Of course he will never wear it but one day he will give it to his son if he has one'!

December 26th – Anne & Neville were invited to lunch. Prince Henry sat between Anne and myself and was so nice to Anne. He told me he had much enjoyed his trip to Brussels when he had gone to represent the King at the Duke of Brabant's wedding. He was at Eton with the Duke and said he was always most awfully nice, and he was full of praise for the bride, not really good-looking but so 'chic' and charming. Rather curious, she can hardly talk French and is busy learning it.

A most festive dinner, to which the children were again invited. The table decorated with large bowls of Christmas roses and scarlet crackers – and a great fusillade at the end, everybody wearing their caps except the King. The bright Duchess enchanting in a large poke paper bonnet; the Queen with a sort of Pope's mitre on her head; the Prince of Wales with a penguin's head! and Clive most coy with a Glengarry! We all wandered into the Ball Room after dinner to play with our presents again! The Duchess with the 4 Princes stood in one corner, singing the most low class musical hall melodies, in a low tone. Rather charmingly, the King was at the far end of the room, listening vaguely. Turned to one of the Household saying, 'Listen to those children of mine, rather delightful with their Christmas carols'! (if he could but have heard the words which was my privilege!)

The King had a really beautiful gramophone and most nights he turns it on after dinner, supervises the turns himself while we all sit round chatting and smoking. We had been listening to *Traviata*, the *Volga Boating Song* etc when a tune struck us as vaguely familiar. With one accord we all sprang to our feet realizing it was *the National Anthem*. The King in fits of laughter saying, 'I just wondered how long it would be before you all recognised it and got up. You were all talking so hard'!

In 1924, for the Queen's Dolls' House, the Gramophone Company Ltd made a miniature gramophone. According to Lucinda Lambton, 'Queen Mary wrote to Princess Mary Louise "that the gramophone should go in the nursery as G. [George] hates them!"'[21] Over the intervening two years, the King's attitude had clearly changed.

December 30th – The Queen showed us all her private rooms here, which have been done up. I had been in the Sittingroom before, when it was Queen Alexandra's. In those days it was so crowded it would have literally been impossible to find a place for another photograph frame. The rather pathetic tuile hard uncomfortable sofa was still there which Princess Victoria pointed out to me last year as being the one Queen Alexandra was sitting on, when she fell forward in a faint, struck down by her final illness.[22] Queen Mary has made the room all blue, walls, carpets & curtains. To my mind none of the blues quite match and are too hard and cold in tone. The furniture all satinwood, with watercolours on the walls, consisting entirely of flower gardens. There are some individual beautiful things in the room, chiefly in jade and amber, but as a whole it is a room lacking in distinction. The Queen always surprises me in this way. She has very real knowledge of art etc but she lacks taste in arranging and combining things and especially the sense of colour.

This house altogether is curious in that way. The country house of the sovereign, and yet it does not contain a single good picture, or for the matter of that, any good pieces of furniture. The Queen is in great good looks. She has several new evening frocks, the result of being in mourning for a year! And certainly last night in her beautiful rose-coloured brocade, worn with the pearls given to her by the Ladies of England, it would be impossible to see anyone looking more like a Royal Queen than she did.

She is always so interested in everything. Lady Airlie and I were sitting some distance away from her, one would have thought out of earshot. We were having a very interesting talk on the Italian Renaissance. The Queen was knitting and chatting spasmodically to Grace Verney, when she could bear it no longer and shouted across to us, 'Do repeat that story about Beatrice D'Este – I couldn't quite catch it.' One afternoon I discussed Ludwig's life of William II with her.[23] She said that of course all the Royal

[21] Lucinda Lambton, *The Queen's Dolls' House*, London: Royal Collection Enterprises, 2010, p. 84.
[22] Queen Alexandra died at Sandringham House on 20 November 1925.
[23] Emil Ludwig, *Kaiser Wilhelm II.*

Family had been deeply interested by it. They all felt that the Empress Frederick's attitude had been exaggerated but that Princess Beatrice had said there was a never-ending antagonism between the Emperor and his brother, when he was quite a small boy even.

The shooting here has been great fun. Especially on Boxing Day, when everybody turned out to beat, including Anne & Neville, who went floundering through the bracken. Neville was sent in pursuit of a wounded duck. The chase was long and arduous, the duck leaping into the air, Neville leaping still higher in his efforts to whack the enemy on the head! The children were invited to the shooting lunch and made a prodigious meal, Anne sitting next the Duchess of York, who was so charming to her. She certainly is a fascinating little lady and altho' so 'petite' has a great dignity. The Duke of York has improved a lot by matrimony. I found him very forthcoming when sitting next him but none of the Princes strike me as having the ability of the Prince of Wales. He gives one the feeling of really knowing about things, and thinking about them. And there is no doubt that he has got wonderful personal charm but I don't think any of them have the real kindness of the King.

I am always being struck by this. He is so sympathetic. Poor Mrs. Grant came to tea wearing the most deplorable clothes. We all pulled her thoroughly to pieces afterwards. The King laughed heartily at her uncouth appearance – but said, 'Poor soul, she can't dress and is really a good sort.' It has been a wonderful visit. I wish I hadn't felt so seedy all the time but I have been much cheered by my family's excellent and most correct behaviour!

Norman Tower – January 3rd 1927 – The King & Queen were in the Hall to say goodbye to us. The ordeal of writing in the Visitors' Book had first to be faced, the King supervising every detail. He asked Francis if he could write. 'Very well,' answered that gentleman. However there were no blots, and after our final curtseys the Royal *Daimler* tore out of the grounds at their usual, is it 60, miles an hour. And here we are safe and sound and I feel like going to bed for a week. I think I hear the children say, 'What are we going to do now, Mummy'!

That was the last entry Lady Wigram made in her smart, green leather-bound, lockable volume. Her mother, Lady Chamberlain, kept diaries for each of the three grandchildren. In Neville's 'diary', she wrote that 'the boys were delighted to find the same motto inscribed over the bath at Norman Tower "Cleanliness is next to Godliness"'. In Francis's 'diary', she recorded that the King and Queen gave him for Christmas a wooden dog, a Chinese cat, *Stealers of Light* by the Queen of Rumania [*sic*], a set of toy soldier cruets and, slightly surprisingly for a six-year-old, a pouch and pipe and two ashtrays. Rather more appropriately, the four Princes gave him a toy fort. Lady Chamberlain wrote that 'Anne was bidden to tea with their Majesties & guests; she confided to Francis that she was rather alarmed, on which he replied "Poof, you shouldn't be afraid of the King of your Country!"' Captain the Hon. Francis Wigram, 6th Battalion, The Grenadier Guards, was killed in action at Salerno, Italy on 12 September 1943.

Faith, Hope and Charity: *Fides, Spes et Caritas*

According to the King James Bible, 1 Corinthians, Chapter 13, Verse 13: 'And now abideth faith, hope, charity, these three; but the greatest of these *is* charity.' At the beginning of the Second World War, Royal Air Force air-cover of Malta was limited to three slow – but highly manoeuvrable – Gloster Gladiator bi-planes. Called Faith, Hope and Charity, they achieved their first combat victory on 11 June 1940, the day after Italy declared war, by shooting down a Macchi 200 fighter. Faith, the only survivor, is in the National War Museum, Valletta, Malta. The Royal Family's website explains: 'Members of the Royal Family are invited to become patrons by a wide range of charities and organisations. Between them, members of the Royal Family hold approximately 3,000 patronages of charitable organisations.'[1]

Princess Charlotte of Wales at Claremont and Oatlands, 1816

On 8 April 1795, George, Prince of Wales, was married to his cousin, Princess Caroline of Brunswick-Wolfenbüttel. Their only child, Princess Charlotte, was born at Carlton House on 7 January 1796. Three days later, George made a new will, leaving all his property to Mrs Fitzherbert, whom he had secretly married eleven years earlier. Just one shilling was to be left to Caroline, who went to live in Charlton and then Blackheath, while Charlotte was left in the charge of governesses. On 2 May 1816, in the Crimson Drawing Room at Carlton House, Princess Charlotte of Wales married Prince Leopold of Saxe-Coburg-Saalfeld.

On Boxing Day 1816, Princess Charlotte wrote to her trusted friend and confidante, the Hon. Margaret Mercer Elphinstone, daughter of George Elphinstone, 1st Viscount Keith: 'We are doing a great deal to improve the place, which employs a vast many poor labouring people who would otherwise be quite out of work & probably starving for want of it; this I think the best charity of all. I am in great hopes we shall get an augmentation of ground on one side of the Park which very much wants it & which will

[1] www.royal.gov.uk/CharitiesandPatronages/Overview.aspx.

be a great improvement. We are in the middle now of rather an expensive piece of work but one exceedingly necessary, & which could no longer be delayed, namely new paling entirely round the Park, & when you see it again I flatter myself you will see considerable additions.'

She visited Oatlands House, home of the Duke of York, second son of King George III and Commander-in-Chief of the British Army, situated between Weybridge and Walton-on-Thames in Surrey:

> Xmas eve is a great day always at Oatlands: the Dss. has a sort of fête & fair for everybody. We dined there with a large party which is always assembled there at that time, & who keep it up till *the* 6th of next month when she will be once more a quiet & solitary inhabitant of the house. It was the gayest & prettiest sight I ever saw I think, the numbers of children, their parents, & all the happy, merry faces, the noises they make with their toys & things. Everybody has their lot & share, great & small, both in & out of the house, by wh. means the Dss. contrives to please everybody & to do a great deal of good by distributing clothing &c. to the poor & needy of the village &c. All this is at her own expence & is annual. I had often heard a great deal of it, & longed & sighed in vain to be there. It was also a very *very* long promise we mutually made each other, that I should come the first moment I could; she claimed the promise & I most willingly fulfilled it.[2]

Prince Leopold's mother, Augusta, Dowager Duchess of Saxe-Coburg-Saalfeld, wrote in her diary on 13 November 1817: 'I am daily awaiting with anxiety and impatience the arrival of the Courier, bringing news of Charlotte's confinement.' Three days later, she wrote: 'The Courier has come – Charlotte is dead! I am quite overcome by the enormity of this calamity! Poor dear Leopold! I feel quite ill and can hardly think or write! All day I have been thinking in despair of the kind fine woman, of whom we were so proud, and whose going has shattered all the hopes of happiness of poor Leopold's life. The ways of Providence are indeed inscrutable and it is difficult to understand why this beautiful young creature should be cut off, on the very threshold of life. Taking her child with her.'[3]

[2] Arthur Aspinall, ed., *Letters of the Princess Charlotte 1811–17*, London: Home and Van Thal, pp. 245–6.

[3] HRH Princess Beatrice, *In Napoleonic Days: Extracts from the Private Diary of Augusta, Duchess of Saxe-Coburg-Saalfeld, Queen Victoria's Maternal Grandmother 1806–21*, London: John Murray, 1941, p. 185.

On 6 November, Princess Charlotte had died after giving birth to a stillborn son. Prince Leopold himself wrote to Sir Thomas Lawrence: 'Two generations gone. Gone in a moment! I have felt for myself, but I have also felt for the Prince Regent. My Charlotte is gone from the country – it has lost her. She was a good, she was an admirable woman. None could know my Charlotte as I did know her! It was my study, my duty, to know her character, but it was my delight!'[4]

The Gipsies at Claremont, 1836

From her earliest surviving Journals, it is clear that young Princess Victoria was a caring, sensitive and charitable person, deeply conscious of her privileged position. A very early example dates from Christmas Eve 1836, when she wrote in her Journal at Claremont House: 'At 2 dearest Lehzen, Victoire and I went out and came back at 20 minutes p. 3. No one was stirring about the Gipsy encampment except George, which I was sorry for, as I was anxious to know how our poor friends were after this bitterly cold night.'

On Christmas Day, the Princess ventured forth again to what she described as 'the chief ornament of the Portsmouth Road':[5]

> At a little before 2 dearest Lehzen, Victoire, and I went out and came home at 3. As we were approaching <u>the camp</u>, we met Rea coming from it, who had been sent there by Mama to enquire into the story of these poor wanderers. He told us (what I was <u>quite sure</u> of before) that all was <u>quite true</u>, that the poor young woman and baby were doing very well, though very weak and miserable and that what they wanted chiefly was fuel and nourishment. Mama has ordered broth and fuel to be sent tonight, as also 2 blankets; and several of our people have sent old flannel things for them. Mama has ordered that the broth and fuel is to be sent each day till the woman is recovered. Lehzen sent them by our footman a little worsted knit jacket for the poor baby, and when we drove by, Aunt Sarah, the old woman and the Husband all looked out and bowed most gratefully. Rea gave them directly a sovereign.
>
> I cannot say how happy I am, that these poor creatures are assisted, for they are such a nice set of Gipsies, so quiet, so affectionate to one another,

[4] James Chambers, *Charlotte and Leopold*, London: Old Street Publishing, 2007, p. 201.

[5] VIC/MAIN/QVJ/1836, quoted in Elizabeth Longford, *Victoria R.I.*, London: Weidenfeld & Nicolson, 1964, p. 44.

> so discreet, not at all forward or importunate, and <u>so</u> grateful; so unlike the gossiping, fortune-telling race-gipsies; and this is such a peculiar and touching case. Their being assisted makes me quite merry and happy today, for yesterday night when I was safe and happy at home in that cold night and today when it snowed so and everything looked white, I felt quite unhappy and grieved to think that our poor gipsy friends should perish and shiver for want; and now today I shall go to bed happy, knowing they are better off and more comfortable . . . I heard that the poor Gipsies were in ecstasies at what they received, which consisted of broth and wood (which as I before said they are to receive every day till the poor young woman is recovered) and the bundle of things, the blankets not being quite ready. I went to bed with a light heart, knowing these poor good people were better off and would not feel the cold quite so much.[6]

Four days later, Princess Victoria and her party paid the gipsies another visit:

> At 12 we went out with dear Lehzen and came home at 2. Everything still looked very white and the ground rather slippery but not so much as yesterday. It snowed part of the time we were walking. I saw Aunt Sarah and the least pretty of the two sisters-in-law, who has returned, in a shop in Esher. How I do wish I could do something for their <u>spiritual</u> and <u>mental</u> benefit and for the education of their children and in particular for the poor little baby who I have known since its birth, in the admirable manner Mr. Crabbe in his *Gipsies' Advocate* so strongly urges; he beseeches and urges those who have kind hearts and Christian feelings to think of these poor wanderers, who have many good qualities and who have many good people amongst them.
>
> He says, and alas! I <u>too well</u> know its truth, from experience, that whenever any poor Gipsies are encamped anywhere and crimes & robberies, &c. occur, it is invariably laid to their account, which is shocking; and if they are always looked upon as vagabonds, how <u>can</u> they become good people? I trust in Heaven that the day may come when <u>I</u> may do something for these poor people, and for this particular family! I am sure that the little kindness which they have experienced from us will have a good and lasting effect on them!

[6] Royal Archives: VIC/MAIN/QVJ/1836, quoted in Alison Plowden, *The Young Victoria*, London: Weidenfeld & Nicolson, 1981, p. 161.

The following day,

> when we passed the encampment the old woman came out and told Lehzen that she had called twice at the lodge yesterday and today and had got no soup. Poor thing! there have been some misunderstandings and confusions I am sorry to say. But they have got blankets, old clothes and some money and I trust and really think they are as comfortable as poor Gipsies generally are. She further said that the young woman & baby were going on well; that they were all Coopers and the young woman, who was her daughter-in-law, was called Eliza Lee before her marriage; and that her own daughter Sarah had no husband, which she said looking down sadly, and that little George was Sarah's only child. She had a singular clever but withered countenance herself, with not one grey hair, and is very respectful and well bred in her manner.'

On New Year's Day, 'as we passed the camp, the old woman and Aunt Sarah came out dressed in their best, and wished us most heartily and cordially a happy new year . . . I only wish dear Lehzen and I could have seen more and done more for them, but alas! we cannot, and I am very happy that we have been able to give them some comfort and assistance.' Such was the impact of 'our poor friends', that Princess Victoria painted a number of watercolours of the Gipsy women and children.

As she had hoped, the time came when the Queen could do something for the poor and needy, as described in her Journal on 31 December 1853: 'After breakfast we went with George, all the Children, & Ladies & Gentlemen to see the annual New Year's gifts distributed to the Poor, in the Riding School.'[7] According to Elizabeth Longford, 'it was in the Queen's nature to help individuals wherever possible but to misunderstand their frantic efforts to help themselves. When she heard that the deaths of two sailors at a Spithead review had driven the wife of one mad, she sent money to both families; she worried about "the three unfortunate men" in Eddystone lighthouse; she wondered whether a dwarf who acted Napoleon for her on the Palace table was kindly treated.'[8]

[7] Royal Archives: VIC/MAIN/QVJ/1853.
[8] Longford, *Victoria R.I.*, p. 180.

Blankets and Provisions for the Poor People of Windsor, 1844

On New Year's Day, Queen Victoria wrote in her Journal: 'We walked in snow, which had succeeded the rain, down to the Riding School, & went up to the room, where were spread upon tables, the meat, bread, plum pudding & blankets which were to be distributed to the poor people. There were 180 families, who received blankets, & 186, provisions, including children, which in all, came to near upon 1000 persons. It was a pretty sight watching the distribution & the way in which it was carried out, having just the right effect upon the poor people. Hitherto it had been so badly done that they hardly knew the gifts came from us.'[9]

The Irish Potato Famine, 1846–7

Between 1845 and 1847, following the arrival of blight, *Phytophthora infestans*, the Irish potato crop dropped 80 per cent, resulting in a fall in population of around one-quarter, due to a combination of starvation and emigration. On 28 September 1846, Queen Victoria wrote in her Journal: 'Talked of the extreme distress in Ireland & the fear that the Landowners would try & turn the intended employment for the poor into an improvement of their own properties at the public expense.' On 31 December she wrote: 'Received some heartrending accounts of the state of Ireland, – really too terrible to think of. In one district alone, 197 people have died from fever, produced by want, & ½ as many have died in their cabins, & in the lanes & streets, of starvation. To save expense, they are buried without offices, or the services of any Clergy. The scenes of horror, the starving people, shivering with cold, & devouring raw turnips, are they say too dreadful, & in the midst of all this, the Landlords appropriate the people's corn! After all we have done to supply the needy with food! God alone can bring help, for no human means seem to be able!'[10]

[9] Royal Archives: VIC/MAIN/QVJ/1844.

[10] Longford, *Victoria R.I.*, p. 190.

The McDonald family in the Home Park, Windsor, 1850 and 1853

Reading Queen Victoria's Journals, her care for her household staff, whichever rank they held, is very apparent. Prince Albert retained two 'Jägers' to manage the kennels at Windsor: McDonald and Cowley. On Christmas Day 1850, the Queen wrote in her Journal: 'The return of this blessed season must always fill one with gratitude & with the deepest devotion to Our Lord & Saviour! May God grant that we may all see many happy returns of this great Festival. We walked with the Children to the Kennels, where I gave the good little McDonalds toys & stuff for dresses. The day was beautiful but almost too mild for Christmas!'[11] On Boxing Day three years later, 'an extremely hard frost, & very fine. – Albert went out shooting with our Cousin Leopold & I walked with the girls & took some Xmas gifts to Mrs. McDonald, at the Kennels.'[12] On Christmas Eve 1899, the Queen wrote that she had 'heard also that good Flora McDonald, who was so long with me, was alarmingly ill.'[13]

The Patriotic Fund, 1854–5

In 1854 Queen Victoria wrote in her Journal: 'Poor Christmas Eve, that happiest of festivals, comes this year at such a sad troubled time, which is quite distressing. How many, many a home is sad & mourning dear ones, & how cold & dreary are our beloved & noble heroes in the Crimea, – in an enemy's land!' Two days later, she 'read an interesting letter from George Gordon (son of Ld Francis Gordon) formerly my Page, giving an account of the misery of the men from the wet, the total want of clothes & covering, the bad roads, & miserable conditions of the poor wretched half starved horses, & there is constantly lack of food. But all these trials the men bear so nobly. It makes me quite miserable. Gen. Codrington's Diary, which we have again seen gives a most deplorable account of the sufferings caused by the terrible weather. The poor young recruits die very fast after arriving. All this is heartbreaking.' On the last day of the year, she wrote: 'What a trying eventful year 54 has been! Much worry, sorrow, & anxiety, but also much

[11] Royal Archives: VIC/MAIN/QVJ/1850.
[12] Royal Archives: VIC/MAIN/QVJ/1853.
[13] Royal Archives: VIC/MAIN/QVJ/1899.

glory, success & many mercies vouchsafed to us. May God guide & help us in the coming year with its unknown future!'[14]

On 11 December 1854, Princess Mary Adelaide wrote:

> I will not conclude this without proffering a small request. I am endeavouring in a humble way to collect subscriptions amongst my friends, with which to supply the soldiers' widows in the Cambridge Asylum and the girls in the Female Orphan Asylum with the materials for knitting socks and stockings for our brave soldiers. These will then be sent to the Committee of the 'Crimean Army Fund'. It thus becomes a twofold charity, and any subscriptions down to one shilling will be most thankfully received. Perhaps you will kindly interest yourself in my little plan, and mention it to any friends who would be willing to contribute. We have this instant received letters from George, dated Constantinople, where he arrived on the 27th. He is, thank God, much better, and only wants a little rest and relaxation for a few days before returning to his post.[15]

The subject was close to the Princess's heart as her only brother, Lieutenant-General George, 2nd Duke of Cambridge, commanded the 1st Division – which comprised the Guards and Highland Brigades – in the Crimean War. Sadly, this challenging command – and the climate – proved beyond the capabilities of a relatively inexperienced 35 year-old, whose commander-in-chief, General Lord Raglan, was almost twice his age. The Duke wrote: 'We went over the field of battle [of Inkerman] to behold a field of blood and destruction, and misery, which nothing in this world can possibly surpass. After dinner I had to ride with Lord Raglan to consult with him, and on my return I was so overpowered by all that I had gone through, that I felt perfectly broken down.'[16] Although the Duke never did return 'to his post' in the Crimea, he became Commander-in-Chief of the British Army the following year, holding that position until 1895, shielded by Queen Victoria from frequent attempts by more visionary soldiers to unseat him.

Princess Mary Adelaide was referring to the Patriotic Fund, for which a sale was organised in Pall Mall in the spring of 1855. Princess Victoria

[14] Royal Archives: VIC/MAIN/QVJ/1854.

[15] Clement Kinloch Cooke, *A Memoir of Her Royal Highness Princess Mary Adelaide, Duchess of Teck*, London: John Murray, 1900, p. 205.

[16] Algernon Percy, *A Bearskin's Crimea*, Barnsley: Leo Cooper, 2005, p. 78.

contributed a watercolour, *The Field of Battle*, described as 'the most remarkable work in the collection', which raised 250 guineas for the charity. The Prince of Wales submitted a pencil drawing entitled *The Knight*, which sold for 55 guineas. Queen Victoria bought her eldest daughter's painting for the Royal Collection, and lithographs were also produced for the Patriotic Fund.

Leaves from the Journal of our Life in the Highlands, 1868–9

On 21 December 1867, Queen Victoria wrote to Crown Princess Frederick:

> Heintz & Balmoral makes me think of my little book wh. you know I gave you a private Copy of. Well, it was so much liked, that I was begged & asked to allow it to be published – the good Dean of Windsor amongst other wise & kind people – saying it wld., from its simplicity & the kindly feelings expressed to those below us – do so much good. I therefore consented – cutting out some of the more familiar descriptions, & being subjected by Mr. Helps & others to a very severe scrutiny of the style & grammar, the correspondence about wh. wld. have amused you very much – & adding our first Journals & Visits to Scotland – & yachting tours in the Channel Islands & visits to Ireland.
>
> 'I have likewise added a little allusion to your Engagement to dear Fritz, – & what I wrote on the death of the Duke of Wellington. The whole is edited by Mr. Helps who has written a very pretty Preface to it. It has given a gt. deal of trouble for one had so carefully to exclude even the slightest observation wh. might hurt anyone's feelings, – but it has been an interest & an occupation – for no one can conceive the trouble of printing a book; the mistakes wh. are endless &c. It will finally come out on the 10th & you shall have a Copy before that.[17]

The day after publication Queen Victoria explained to the Crown Princess: 'It has been most affectionately, warmly received by the public and you will be gratified and touched by the articles in *The Times* and *Daily Telegraph*. Good Mr. Helps says "It is a new bond of union" between me and my people; that I was "immensely loved before" but "will be still more so now". And many other true friends express the same feeling. There is much

[17] Roger Fulford, *Your Dear Letter: Private Correspondence of Queen Victoria and the Crown Princess of Prussia 1865–1871*, London: Evans Brothers, 1971, p. 166.

about you as a dear little girl which I am sure will recall former happy days to you.'[18]

From Osborne House on New Year's Day 1869, Queen Victoria wrote a letter concerning the profits on her book, *Leaves from the Journal of our Life in the Highlands*, edited by Arthur Helps and published on 10 January the previous year:

> The Queen thanks Mr. Martin very much for his two letters and for the cheque which she has this day sent to Mr. Helps. She quite approves of what he intends doing with the remaining £4,016 6s. Of this the Queen would wish him to send her a cheque for £50, which she wishes to give away. £2,516 she wishes absolutely to devote to a charity such as she spoke of, and the remaining £1,450 she wishes to keep for other gifts of a charitable nature, at least to people who are not rich. Would Mr. Martin just keep an account of the sums he sends her so that we may know how and at what time the money has been disposed of? The Queen will keep a copy with the names which she does not wish others to know.[19]

No less than 103,000 copies of the cheap edition, priced at 2s 6d, were sold in the first year. Magdalen Ponsonby wrote: 'Rather amusing the literary line the Queen has taken up since her book was published.'[20]

Queen Victoria's Tea, Windsor, 1899

On Boxing Day 1899, Queen Victoria gave tea to families of soldiers serving in the Second Anglo-Boer War, writing in her Journal:

> Dull & foggy. – When I went out with Beatrice, it came on to rain, so that I was able to take only quite a short turn. On coming in I went into St. George's Hall to look at the beautiful big Xmas tree, 25ft high, hung with all sorts of little presents, sweets, toys & glittering ornaments, which Beatrice, Helen & the ladies have worked hard in decorating. – Took a short drive in a closed carriage, after luncheon, with Harriet P. & Alice M.

[18] Ibid., p. 169.

[19] George Earle Buckle, ed., *The Letters of Queen Victoria, Second Series: A Selection from Her Majesty's Correspondence between the Years 1862 and 1885*, 3 vols., London: John Murray, 1926–8 (LQV II), Vol. I, p. 575.

[20] Matthew Dennison, *The Last Princess: The Devoted Life of Queen Victoria's Youngest Daughter*. London: Weidenfeld & Nicolson, 2007, pp. 73–4.

> – At ½ p. 4 went to St. George's Hall with all my family, including Lenchen, Victoria B. & her children, where I gave the wives of the soldiers & their children, a tea & the Xmas tree. The Committee who are looking after those who are left here, as well as those of the Reservists, were presented to me, Mary Eliot & Freddy Crutchley being amongst them. The Dean, the Mayor, the Vicar of Eton, &c. were there.
>
> Then all the women & children trooped in, & after looking at the tree they all sat down to tea at 2 very long tables, below the tree. Every one helped to serve them, including my family, old and young, and my ladies and gentlemen. I was rolled up & down the tables, after which I went away for a short while to have my own tea, returning when the tree was beginning to be stripped, handing myself many of the things to the wives and dear little children, many of whom were very pretty, & mostly very young. They were so neatly dressed & very well behaved. There were some babies of a few weeks and months old. The women seemed very nice & respectable. It was a very touching sight, when one thinks of the poor husbands and fathers, who are all away, and some of whom may not return. They seemed all very much pleased.[21]

Queen Victoria, now in her eighties, was astonishingly committed to – and aware of developments in – the war. On 1 March 1900 she wrote in her Journal: 'Before I got up Lizzie Stewart, my wardrobe maid, came in saying the telegraph clerk had just come in with a telegram he was very anxious I should have at once. It was as follows; "Dundonald with Natal Carabineers & composite Reg[t] entered Ladysmith last night. The country between me & there is reported clear of the enemy, I am moving on Nelthorpe," signed Buller. My joy was unbounded & I let everyone in the Castle know, & telegraphed to the relations.'[22]

Queen Victoria's New Year's Gift, 1899–1900

After a torrid start to the Second Anglo-Boer War, Queen Victoria expressed a desire to present gifts to her soldiers and sailors. Elizabeth Longford wrote: 'Parcels of knitting were dispatched to her "dear brave soldiers" and when it transpired that the dear brave officer-class had got them all, she ordered

[21] Royal Archives: VIC/MAIN/QVJ/1899.
[22] Royal Archives: VIC/MAIN/QVJ/1900.

100,000 tins of chocolate for the men.'[23] On 7 February 1900 the Hon. Mrs Marie Mallet, one of Queen Victoria's Ladies-in-waiting, shed more light on the decision-making process in her diary: 'Last night too, we talked of the chocolate, the Queen as usual truthful as the light, said "I did not think of it myself, I said I wished to give something to each of my soldiers but I could not decide what form the present should take; then three alternatives were suggested and I chose the box of chocolates".'[24]

On 4 February 1854, Cadbury Brothers had received a Royal Warrant as 'manufacturers of cocoa and chocolate to Queen Victoria'. The firm was therefore the first point of contact to produce chocolate, packaged in a suitable container. As Quakers and pacifists, however, Richard and George Cadbury were in a dilemma: they neither wished to decline the honour nor to present their competition with commercial advantage. They resolved to invite fellow Quakers, Joseph Storrs Fry and Joseph Rowntree, to join them in partnership to satisfy the prestigious commission.

As mentioned above, this gift was intended for non-commissioned officers and men and not for officers. An initial order was for 90,000 tins; the number was later increased to 120,000. Wooden crates, each containing fifty tins inscribed 'I wish you a happy New Year – Victoria RI', were shipped to South Africa, with most distributed early in the New Year. Three thousand tins from Fry's were set aside for the gallant defenders of both Kimberley, relieved on 15 February 1900, and also of Mafeking, relieved on 17 May 1900. It was soon recognised that many wished to send their chocolate gift home. This was arranged for 5 shillings, plus 4d to register and 1d per ounce.

These gifts from Queen Victoria were treasured by the recipients. In December 1899, Private Charles Ernest Edward Jackson, 2nd (Special Service) Battalion, Royal Canadian Regiment of Infantry, wrote to his family: 'I have just received a box of chocolate, Her Majesty's present to the South African soldiers, which arrived just today. It is very nice, in fact almost too good to keep here, there is such a demand for them by the officers and everybody else, as mementos. In fact I have been offered £5 for mine, and at the Cape as much as £10 is being paid, so you will readily understand why I am sending mine home. Somebody might take a fancy to it as they did to my match safe. Take good care of it until I return, which I expect will be

[23] Longford, *Victoria R.I.*, p. 554.

[24] Victor Mallet, ed., *Life with Queen Victoria: Marie Mallet's Letters from Court 1887–1901*, London: John Murray, 1968, p. 181.

in a few months.' Very sadly, Charles Jackson never returned home: he was killed in action at Paardeberg on 18 February 1900.

Marie Mallet's account stressed the impact of the Queen's initiative: 'The gift has been appreciated beyond the wildest expectations and the invalids at Netley talk more of the chocolate than of their wounds. They have not yet received it but they will do so in time. I feel more than ever what a splendid sense of proportion the Queen has, but it can only be realised by those who come in direct contact with her, even those just outside the inner circle get such distorted views of her opinions and prejudices.'[25]

Unfortunately, Queen Victoria was not accompanied by Marie Mallet on 16 May 1900 when she

> reached Netley at ¼ to 4. The line has been extended now & the train brings one right up to the door of the Hospital, so that I was able to be rolled in my chair straight in. I was again received by Sir Baker Russell & Col: Charlton R.A.M.S., the principal Medical Officer. It was a most interesting, but sad visit, as there were so many severely wounded & sick, & a good many more in bed than usual. Those who were nearly convalescent were drawn up in the corridors. Saw over 600 men in all, 26 of whom had lost limbs, the greater number arms, & one poor man, who was in bed had lost both arm & leg. I gave flowers to all those who were bedridden. They were wonderfully cheerful & uncomplaining. One poor man, who had lost a leg & was sitting in a chair, when I gave him some flowers said he wished so much to have one of my chocolate boxes, he would rather lose a limb, than not get that![26]

Queen Victoria instituted a most unusual reward in 1900: the Queen's Scarf of Honour. Eight scarves 'crocheted in Khaki-coloured Berlin wool, approximately nine inches wide and five foot long, including a four inch fringe at each end, and bears the Royal Cipher V.R.I. (Victoria Regina Et Imperatrix)' were awarded. One was presented to a senior non-commissioned officer in each of the four infantry battalions in the 2nd Brigade, chosen by a ballot of non-commissioned officers and men from their own battalion. Four were awarded to privates or troopers of the Colonial Forces who had particularly distinguished themselves: one South African, one Canadian, one Australian and one New Zealander. Although Queen Victoria was supposed

[25] Ibid.

[26] Royal Archives: VIC/MAIN/QVJ/1900, quoted in Longford, *Victoria R.I.*, p. 554.

to have crocheted these scarves entirely by herself, her eyesight was so poor that it is unsurprising that, in May 1901, the Duchess of York informed one of the recipients, Private Alfred Du Frayer, New South Wales Mounted Rifles, that she had lent her grandmother-in-law a hand. This tradition was continued by later generations: during the Second World War, Princesses Elizabeth and Margaret 'joined a local sewing circle and knitted socks and scarves for the soldiers'.[27]

Christmas Provisions for King Edward VII's Hospital for Officers, 1914

On 7 December 1914 Sir Derek Keppel, Master of the Royal Household, wrote to Sister Agnes of King Edward VII's Hospital for Officers: 'I have intended to come and see you but unfortunately have not had time to do so. It is The King's wish to send His usual Christmas Dinner for your Patients this year again. His Majesty however knows that you have many more Patients this year in your various houses, so may I ask you privately to alter the numbers, as you think necessary, on the enclosed list, so that I may be sure to send enough to go round! I may tell you, privately also, that it was The King's wish that I should consult you about this and I repeat it to you just to show what a personal interest His Majesty takes in it. What day would you like the things sent to you?'[28]

This is the list detailing what was sent for Christmas 1913:

4 Turkeys	from Baily & Son, Mount Street, W.
12 Pheasants	
9 Bottles Champagne	from the Royal Cellars
9 Bottles Port	
6 Plum Puddings	from Pastry
3 Bch Black Grapes	
3 Bch White Grapes	
18 Pears	
18 Apples	

There is no record of what was sent to the patients of King Edward VII's Hospital for Officers for their Christmas Dinner in 1914.

[27] Sarah Bradford, *Queen Elizabeth II: Her Life in our Times*, London: Viking, 2011, p. 32.
[28] Royal Archives: MRH/GV/MAIN/005/1-2.

Princess Mary's Christmas Gift, 1914

Princess Mary, only daughter of King George V and Queen Mary, was seventeen years old when war was declared. She wanted to do something to support 'our boys' and proposed to pay, out of her own personal allowance, for a gift for every soldier and sailor. This was deemed impracticable. Instead, she lent her name to Princess Mary's Sailors' and Soldiers' Fund, which was formally launched at London's Ritz Hotel on 14 October 1914. The following day a letter from the Princess was released. It caught the mood of the moment:

> I want you now to help me to send a Christmas present from the whole of the nation to every sailor afloat and every soldier at the front. I am sure that we should all be happier to feel that we had helped to send our little token of love and sympathy on Christmas morning, something that would be useful and of permanent value, and the making of which may be the means of providing employment in trades adversely affected by the war. Could there be anything more likely to hearten them in their struggle than a present received straight from home on Christmas Day? Please will you help me?

A total of £162,591 12s 5d was raised for the Fund and some 2,500,000 gifts were distributed to a broader range of categories than those envisaged by Princess Mary. These included all officers and men in the Royal Navy and the British Army; nurses; widows or parents of those killed; prisoners-of-war and internees; members of the French Mission serving with the British Expeditionary Force; and Colonial and Indian troops. Eligibility was eventually extended to every man 'wearing the King's uniform on Christmas Day 1914'. Excess funds were donated to Queen Mary's Maternity Home for the wives and infants of men serving with the Armed Forces.

The gift box itself, designed by Messrs. Adshead and Ramsay, was made of embossed brass. It was originally intended to contain an ounce of pipe tobacco, twenty cigarettes, a pipe, a tinder lighter, a Christmas card and a photograph of Princess Mary. Allowances were subsequently made for non-smokers, for the dietary requirements of Indian troops, and for nurses, resulting in a wide range of gift box contents. Such were the pressures of delivering the gift boxes on Christmas Day that these additional requirements were overruled and gifts were given without reference to either race or rank – and some of the contents were therefore omitted.

In a letter of 25 November 1914 to the *Morning Post*, the Duke of Devonshire emphasised the widespread impact of the appeal to both recipients and to British industry: 'In subscribing to Her Royal Highness's fund the public have the satisfaction of knowing that they are not only contributing to the present itself but are affording much-needed relief in industries which are suffering in the war.' Firms involved in producing the contents of the gift box included Asprey & Co. Ltd. (tinder lighters), Harrods Ltd. (pipes) and De La Rue & Co. (Christmas cards).

The gift was greatly appreciated. On Boxing Day 1914 Lieutenant-General Sir Henry (later 1st Baron) Rawlinson, General Officer Commanding IV Corps, wrote a letter – marked 'read by the King' in blue crayon – to Major Clive Wigram, Assistant Private Secretary to the King:

> I received last night a charming little packet containing pipe tobacco & cigarettes which I am told is sent me by Princess Mary. It is just what I want, for my old pipe is rapidly coming to an end, and tobacco is not too plentiful. The least I can do to shew my gratitude is to return to H.R.H. one of my Xmas Cards. Will you give it to her for me and say how much we all value her kind gift of tobacco & cigarettes?
>
> I have little news for you. Things are quite stationary at the moment here – Xmas time has brought a certain feeling of 'raprochement' [sic] between the garrisons of the trenches and yesterday there was a sort of mutual armistice in certain places to bury the dead and get in the wounded that were lying out between the two lines of trenches. This is all very well perhaps on Xmas day but tomorrow we shall begin again with the guns and continue the sniping as usual. It does not do to allow the private soldiers to become on too good terms with their enemy.[29]

Coal for the Old People of Windsor, 1921

On 3 November 1921, the Reverend C. H. Hamilton wrote to Sir Derek Keppel: 'I believe it is usual for the Vicar of Windsor to write to you about this time of the year to ask if His Majesty the King is kindly willing to give his customary gift of coal to the old people of Windsor. I have just taken up

[29] Royal Archives: PS/PSO/GV/C/Q/2552/12.

my duties as the new Vicar of Windsor, and I shall be very grateful if you will kindly ascertain what are His Majesty's wishes with regard to this matter, this year? If it is His Majesty's wish, I shall be very glad indeed to do as the Vicars have done in the past, in preparing lists of names and arranging for the distribution of the coal.'[30]

In response, the Keeper of the Privy Purse, Sir Frederick 'Fritz' Ponsonby, wrote to the Master of the Royal Household: 'Certainly the King must not economise on his charitable gifts – we have not yet got to that. Please tell the Vicar the King will give his usual gifts of coal at Christmas.'[31]

The Mobile Canteen at Sandringham, 1941

On New Year's Eve, King George VI 'went to see the Mobile Canteen, which I have started to give agricultural workers & other estate workers a hot meat meal in the middle of the day. It is run by Lady Fermoy & a band of female voluntary workers in the near neighbourhood. The food is cooked at S^{m} House, & goes out in containers in the van to the various farms & woods. It is appreciated, & supplements the peoples' rations.'[32]

[30] Royal Archives: MRH/GV/MAIN/232/1.
[31] Royal Archives: MRH/GV/MAIN/232/2.
[32] Royal Archives: GVI/PRIV/DIARY/1941.

Crisis at Christmas

The boundaries of the Christmas season have been stretched slightly, in order to take account of those events that took place shortly before or those which took place soon after. This chapter deals exclusively with family-orientated crises, such as illness, death and, exceptionally, the Abdication Crisis of 1936. The next chapter, 'Christmas and Conflict', deals with external influences, such as political turmoil, war and the threat from terrorism.

The English climate can be thoroughly depressing during the winter, when old people are most vulnerable. Despite the number of physicians on whom the Royal Family was able to call – often at short notice – it is clear that, prior to the introduction of antibiotics in the 1940s, they were extremely vulnerable, often to diseases that are now infrequent killers in the Western world, such as tuberculosis and typhoid. During the nineteenth century families were typically much larger than today. For labourers a large family was the head of the family's pension plan. Miscarriages and stillbirths were also extremely common. Fortunately, Queen Victoria suffered from neither of these problems. However, of her nine children, three died before she did, as did three of their spouses. Her eldest daughter, the Empress Frederick, died little more than six months after her mother.

Haemophilia, the so-called 'Royal disease', of which only males develop full symptoms and females act as carriers, was certainly an influence. While only one of Queen Victoria's children, Prince Leopold, Duke of Albany, died from haemophilia, two of her daughters, Princess Alice and Princess Beatrice, were carriers. The family's dynastic intermarriages then spread haemophilia to the royal families of Russia, Germany and Spain. The best-known sufferer was her great-grandson, the Tsarevich Alexei, murdered with his parents and four sisters in Ekaterinburg on 17 July 1918. Haemophilia had a particularly devastating effect on the Spanish Royal Family: King Alfonso XIII was married to Princess Beatrice's daughter, Ena, and their eldest and youngest sons were both sufferers. Queen Victoria had forty grandchildren, of whom nine died during her lifetime, mostly from disease. Two lived only very brief lives, one died in an accident and another died on active service. Crisis was a constant feature of nineteenth-century family life, even at the highest levels of society.

The Death of Queen Victoria's King Charles Spaniel, Dash, 1840

The Royal Family have always kept dogs, both for companionship and for working purposes. The corridors and rooms of Osborne House contain many sculptures and paintings of their dogs: Noble by Sir Joseph Boehm and also by Charles Burton Barber; Dot and Charnance by Otto Weber; a plaster-cast of Sharp, a collie dog, next to Queen Victoria on her spinning-wheel; and Eos by Queen Victoria. On the upper terrace there is a life-size sculpture of Eos, the Prince Consort's greyhound, black with a silver streak, named after the Greek goddess of the dawn.

During the third day of Prince Albert's visit in October 1839, his 'charming greyhound, "Eos", walked round the luncheon table, giving her paw and eating off a fork'.[1] The steps between the upper and lower terraces are flanked by a pair of greyhounds, cast in concrete with lead claws, supplied by Austin & Seeley in 1856. On 27 December 1878, the Princess of Wales wrote to the Duchess of Teck: 'Many many thanks for your *lovely* Xmas presents – the pin is quite charming so is that delightful tricoloured pencil – but as for that *darling* puggy – I really have no words to express my admiration for it – it is simply an *adorable* pug and shall *never* leave my dressing table – wherever I go – *he* will have to come and keep guard over me like a black faced angel that it is – I really am delighted with it – and never saw one like it.'[2]

On 14 January 1833, Sir John Conroy presented the Duchess of Kent with a King Charles spaniel called Dash. Dash was soon adopted by her daughter and, in a variation of 'Windsor uniform', was often dressed in scarlet jacket and blue trousers. One Christmas, much-loved Dash was given 'three india-rubber balls and two bits of gingerbread decorated with holly and candles.'[3]

After the newly crowned Queen Victoria returned to Buckingham Palace on 28 June 1838, 'an attendant standing at the foot of the stairs watched her gather her skirts and run up to her room to give *Dash* his bath'.[4] On Christmas Eve 1840, Queen Victoria wrote in her Journal: 'Albert told me that poor dear old "Dash" was dead, which grieved me so much. I was

1 Elizabeth Longford, *Victoria R.I.*, London: Weidenfeld & Nicolson, 1964, p. 133.
2 James Pope-Hennessy, *Queen Mary, 1867–1953*, London: George Allen and Unwin, 1959, p. 54.
3 Longford, *Victoria R.I.*, p. 46.
4 Ibid., p. 83.

so fond of the poor little fellow, & he was so attached to me. I had had him since the beginning of Feb: 1833.' Dash is buried in the garden of Adelaide Cottage in the Home Park at Windsor, where his marble effigy rests on a stone bearing the following inscription:[5]

> *Here lies*
> *DASH*
> *The favourite spaniel of Her Majesty Queen Victoria*
> *By whose command this memorial was erected*
> *He died on the 20th of December 1840*
> *In his 10th year*
> *His attachment was without selfishness*
> *His playfulness without malice*
> *His fidelity without deceit*
> *READER*
> *If you would live beloved and die regretted*
> *Profit by the example of*
> *DASH*

Lord Aberdeen becomes Prime Minister, 1852

In the early hours of 17 December 1852, the Earl of Derby's Tory Government was defeated by 305 to 286 votes on its budget proposals. From the Isle of Wight, Queen Victoria sent for the Earl of Aberdeen. On his way to Osborne he met Lord John Russell in Hyde Park, forming the clear impression that the latter would serve as Foreign Secretary and Leader of the House. As often happens, these loose arrangements unravelled rather swiftly, as the Queen's Journal entry for Christmas Eve makes clear:

> I heard at 12 from Ld Aberdeen, that he would come here, as he had received a letter from Ld John, containing proposals & alterations of so extensive a kind, that if persisted 'would seriously endanger the success' of L^{d} A's undertaking!
>
> This alarmed us very much, & I wrote off in a great hurry, urging the necessity of agreement & patriotism. Only a short walk in the afternoon & then began the Christmas preparations, – always a tremendous

[5] Ibid., p. 155.

> affair, but the 'crisis', spoilt half our enjoyment, by the anxiety for the ultimate result, which filled our minds . . . Christmas passes too quickly. It is so long looked forward to & anxiously prepared for, & in a moment it is past!

On 28 December 1852 the Court Circular reported that 'the Queen held a Court and Privy Council this day at the Castle'. The Queen noted that 'the Council & Audiences lasted till 5 & I was much fatigued. Ld John Russell provoked me by saying & making some injudicious remarks, respecting the poor Orléans family.'[6]

The Death of Charles, Prince of Leiningen, 1856

Queen Victoria's elder half-brother, Carl Friedrich Wilhelm Emich, Prince of Leiningen, appointed a Knight of the Garter in 1837, died on 13 November 1856. That Christmas Eve, his half-sister wrote in her Journal:

> Albert was also very busy, running backwards & forwards, & seeing that <u>all</u> was properly & prettily arranged. At 6 Mama, Amalie & my nephews arrived. Ernest gave us 2 trifles, which had belonged to & been constantly used by poor dear Charles. And then we went with them & all the Children (dear Affie being the only one missing) to the rooms with the Xmas tree & presents. We gave Mama some plate, a copy of Winterhalter's picture of dear Charles, &c. . . . In the midst of all this gaiety, poor dear Charles, whose picture was there, & whose poor sons & sorrowing mother were with us, was always recurring to my mind, making me feel the sad reality.

On New Year's Eve, Queen Victoria wrote: 'The last day in the year, always to <u>me</u> a melancholy serious thought! I have much to be thankful for, though I have also lost much, that was dear to me, – my poor dear Brother! That remains a sad blank!'[7]

[6] Royal Archives: VIC/MAIN/QVJ/1852.
[7] Royal Archives: VIC/MAIN/QVJ/1856.

The Death of the Prince Consort, 1861

On New Year's Day 1861, the Prime Minister wrote to his Sovereign:

> Viscount Palmerston presents his humble duty to your Majesty, and begs to be allowed to wish your Majesty and His Royal Highness the Prince Consort many prosperous returns of New Year's Day, with increasing happiness to your Majesty and the Royal Family, and progressive advantage to the Nation who have the good fortune to have your Majesty for their Sovereign; and to adopt the language of Pope, he would say,
>
> May day improve on day, and year on year,
> Without a pain, a trouble, or a fear.[8]

Sadly, Lord Palmerston could scarcely have been wider of the mark. The Prince Consort died on 14 December 1861, in the Blue Room at Windsor Castle.

In his memoir of Queen Victoria, the Marquis of Lorne, later 9th Duke of Argyll, husband of Princess Louise, quoted the Queen's Journal:

> Albert folded his arms and began arranging his hair just as he used to do when well and dressing. These were said to be bad signs. Strange! As though he were preparing for another and greater journey . . . About half past five I went in and sat beside his bed, which had been wheeled towards the middle of the room. 'Good little wife,' he said, and kissed me, and then gave a sort of piteous moan, or rather sigh, not of pain, but as if he felt that he was leaving me, and laid his head upon my shoulder, and I put my arm under his. But the feeling passed away again, and he seemed to wander and to doze, and yet to know all. Sometimes I could not catch what he said. Occasionally he spoke in French.
>
> Alice came in and kissed him, and he took her hand. Bertie, Helena, Louise, and Arthur came in one after the other and took his hand, and Arthur kissed it, but he was dozing and did not perceive them. Then he opened his dear eyes and asked for Sir Charles Phipps, who came in and kissed his hand. Then again his dear eyes were closed. General Grey and

[8] Arthur Christopher Benson and Reginald Baliol Brett, eds., *The Letters of Queen Victoria: A Selection from Her Majesty's Correspondence between the Years 1837 and 1861*, 3 vols., London: John Murray, 1908 (LQV I), Vol. III, p. 538.

> Sir Thomas Biddulph each came in and kissed his hand, and were dreadfully overcome. It was a terrible moment, but, thank God, I was able to command myself, and to be perfectly calm, and remained sitting by his side. So things went on, not really worse, and not better.

The Marquis of Lorne also quoted Dean Stanley, who wrote of the St George's Chapel funeral on 23 December: 'It was a profoundly mournful and impressive sight. Indeed, considering the magnitude of the event, and the persons present, all agitated by the same emotion, I do not think I have ever seen or shall ever see anything so affecting.'[9] On Christmas Eve 1861, Queen Victoria wrote to Leopold, King of the Belgians:

> My beloved Uncle,
> Though, please God! I am to see you so soon, I must write these few lines to prepare you for the trying, sad existence you will find it with your poor forlorn, desolate child – who drags on a weary, pleasureless existence! I am anxious also to repeat one thing, and that is my one firm resolve, my irrevocable decision, viz. that his wishes – his plans – about every thing, his views about every thing are to be my law! And no human power will make me swerve from what he decided and wished – and I look to you to support and help me in this. I apply this particularly as regards our children – Bertie, etc. – for whose future he had traced everything so carefully. I am also determined that no one person, may he be ever so good, ever so devoted among my servants – is to lead or guide or dictate to me. I know how he would disapprove it. And I live on with him, for him; in fact I am only outwardly separated from him, and only for a time.
>
> No one can tell you more of my feelings, and can put you more in possession of many touching facts than our excellent Dr. Jenner, who has been and is my greatest comfort, and whom I would entreat you to see and hear before you see any one else. Pray do this, for I fear much others trying to see you first and say things and wish for things which I should not consent to.
>
> Though miserably weak and utterly shattered, my spirit rises when I think any wish or plan of his is to be touched or changed, or I am to be made to do anything. I know you will help me in my utter darkness. It is but for a short time, and then I go – never, never to part! Oh! that

[9] The Marquis of Lorne (now His Grace The Duke of Argyll), *VRI: Queen Victoria: Her Life and Empire*, London: Harper & Brothers, 1901, pp. 258–9.

> blessed, blessed thought! He seems so near to me, so quite my own now, my precious darling! God bless and preserve you. Ever your wretched but devoted Child,
>
> Victoria R.
>
> What an Xmas! I won't think of it.[10]

On Boxing Day the Duchess of Wellington wrote to the Hon. Eleanor Stanley:

> This has been indeed a *sad* Christmas time for all of us. I happened to be at Windsor a fortnight before the Prince was taken ill, when the Grand Duke and Duchess Constantine were there, and of that large assembly you would have thought the Prince least likely to be taken so soon. He was in unusual spirits and apparently full of health and happiness. He must have imbibed the poison soon after that. At Cambridge he said that he had not then slept for fourteen nights. The Queen's grief, as you will easily believe, *cannot* be surpassed, but she shows a courage and an amount of fortitude that, knowing as we do how deeply she loved him and appreciated his noble and great qualities, we can scarcely understand. 'She will now live for Her Country and Her Children.' I think the Queen's sobs and tears the day the Court left Windsor were heartbreaking to hear. I hear from Osborne that the Queen's health is good and that H.M. continues to bear up with immense courage; but, as she says, all is now utter desolation. No particular Order has been issued for the Household Mourning, but I take it for granted that it will be black stuffs and crepe for six months at least.[11]

In practice, Queen Victoria withdrew from the public gaze for far longer, not opening Parliament until 6 February 1866; however, she started to write her Journal again on New Year's Day 1862:

> Have been unable to write my Journal since the day my beloved one left us, and with what a heavy broken heart I enter on a new year without him! My dreadful and overwhelming calamity gives me so much to do, that I must henceforth merely keep notes of my sad and solitary life. This day

[10] LQV I, Vol. III, pp. 605–6.

[11] Beatrice Erskine, ed., *Twenty Years at Court: From the Correspondence of the Hon. Eleanor Stanley*, London: Nisbet & Co., 1916, pp. 392–3.

> last year found us so perfectly happy, and now! Last year music woke us; little gifts, new year's wishes, brought in by maid, and then given to dearest Albert, the children waiting with their gifts in the next room – all these recollections were pouring in on my mind in an overpowering manner. Alice slept in my room, and dear baby came down early. Felt as if living in a dreadful dream. Dear Alice much affected when she got up and kissed me. Arthur gave me a nosegay, and the girls, drawings done by them for their dear father and me. Could hardly touch my breakfast.[12]

Until 1869 all the Royal servants wore crepe armbands, in mourning for Prince Albert.[13] In an almost uncanny way, Queen Victoria was following the path trodden by her maternal grandmother, Augusta, Dowager Duchess of Saxe-Coburg-Saalfeld, who was also Prince Albert's paternal grandmother. Francis, Duke of Saxe-Coburg-Saalfeld, had died at Coburg on 9 December 1806. Little more than a year later, Augusta wrote in her diary: 'Thank God! that this day of sad memories is over! This used to be such a happy evening and now I look round with eyes dimmed with tears at the loneliness surrounding me and at the vacant place never to be refilled. My thoughts turn entirely to the past, and to the beloved one who used to delight in making me and the children happy on this Christmas Eve.'[14]

Such was the reputation of General Sir Garnet Wolseley for dealing with outbreaks of rebellion, insubordination or sheer insolence in the British Empire during the last quarter of the Queen's reign that the catchphrase – when everything was organised and going as expected – was 'All's Sir Garnet!' On 27 December 1882, soon after the suppression of the Urabi Revolt in Egypt and his overwhelming victory at the Battle of Tel-el-Kebir, newly ennobled Lieutenant-General Baron Wolseley of Cairo and of Wolseley wrote to Queen Victoria, gracefully acknowledging the wide-ranging contributions of the Prince Consort to the reform of the British Army, without which many of his own triumphs might never have been achieved:

> I have just received your Majesty's most kind and gracious letter which Sir John McNeill forwarded to me. I venture to offer my best thanks for

[12] LQV I, Vol. I, p. 5.

[13] Matthew Dennison, *The Last Princess: The Devoted Life of Queen Victoria's Youngest Daughter*, London: Weidenfeld & Nicolson, 2007, p. 57.

[14] HRH Princess Beatrice, *In Napoleonic Days: Extracts from the Private Diary of Augusta, Duchess of Saxe-Coburg-Saalfeld, Queen Victoria's Maternal Grandmother 1806–21*, London: John Murray, 1941, p. 34.

> the Xmas card that accompanied it . . . I hope your Majesty will forgive my reference to the memory of a great man who is no longer with us. I would like to ask to whom it is the Army is indebted for the first autumn manoeuvres we ever had (those at Chobham)? Who was it that we have to thank for being armed with rifles instead of old muskets when we landed in the Crimea? Who was it that advocated the reduction of the punishment of flogging? the formation of an Army Reserve? Who was foremost in advising a system of military localisation very much like that we have lately introduced; in urging the necessity of the military education of our officers; in the establishment of our great Hospitals; in the improvement of our Medical Regulations?
>
> To whom are we indebted for the abolition of the absurd dress worn by the Army at Chobham; for the creation of the Victoria Cross; for the provision of good quarters for soldiers' families, and for a higher rate of pay being granted to the soldiers? Those who have read through the pages of Sir Theodore Martin's work are now aware, most people for the first time, that the Army owes more to the late Prince Consort than to any other General officer since the death of the Duke of Wellington. Surely therefore it may be said of the great Prince that he was in the highest sense a great army reformer![15]

Although initially regarded with suspicion by many members of the British aristocracy following his marriage with Queen Victoria, Prince Albert made an enormous contribution to Britain. For their nine children he was determined the 'Kensington System' must be improved. This was to ensure that the children, for whose future he had planned everything so carefully, were properly educated for the roles he envisaged that they would play on the European – if not the world – stage.

Unfortunately, his concept of a series of dynastic marriages to seal alliances was ultimately unsuccessful, as Europe was buffeted by a series of revolutions and wars. The first of these marriages was that of the Princess Royal. She married Crown Prince Frederick of Prussia, on 25 January 1858 in the Chapel Royal, St James's Palace. Her mother described it as 'like taking a poor Lamb to be sacrificed'.[16] As Emperor Frederick III he reigned for

[15] George Earle Buckle, ed., *The Letters of Queen Victoria, Second Series: A Selection from Her Majesty's Correspondence between the Years 1862 and 1885*, 3 vols., London: John Murray, 1926–8 (LQV II), Vol. III, p. 389.

[16] Longford, *Victoria R.I.*, p. 268.

just ninety-nine days in 1888, before being succeeded by their eldest son, Emperor William II. Less than ten years after the Prince Consort's death, his widow began to place the emphasis on compatibility, companionship – and even love. Thus was the rigid application of the German principle of *Ebenbürtigkeit* – or partners of equal birth or rank – abandoned, to the inestimable benefit of the British monarchy.

Prince Albert took a tremendous interest in both the arts and the sciences, culminating in the Great Exhibition of 1851 in the Crystal Palace erected in London's Hyde Park. In this endeavour he was ably assisted by a young civil servant, Henry (later Sir Henry) Cole. The proceeds of this highly successful venture – amounting to some £186,000 – were used to buy land in Kensington for the establishment of museums and cultural institutions in an area often referred to as 'Albertopolis'. They include the Victoria & Albert Museum, founded in 1852; the Science Museum, founded in 1857; and the Royal Albert Hall, which Prince Albert had planned, but which did not host its first performance until 29 March 1871.

On Boxing Day 1883, Queen Victoria wrote from Osborne to Lady Waterpark:

> You must forgive me for not having thanked you sooner for your very very kind letter, so full of kind & loving sympathy, I thank you most warmly for it & I always think of your first waiting in April when I was so utterly crushed. It is very soothing to me to feel that others do feel for me, for I do suffer much . . . Christmas & New Year's Day have been saddened to me since 61, & now I need not say what this season has become . . . One must look upwards & forwards to where we shall meet again never to part. But the conflict between not wishing to leave those one loves here, & can be of use to, & the wish to rejoin those who are not lost but gone before is very trying. I pray for strength, patience & courage, & I am sure I do feel that our Heavenly Father will not forsake me.[17]

The Royal Family knew 14 December as 'Mausoleum Day', a day on which they gathered at the Royal Mausoleum at Frogmore for a service to remember the Prince Consort. On 14 December 1895, Queen Victoria wrote in her Journal: 'This terrible anniversary returned for the 34th time. When I went to my dressing room found telegrams from Georgie &

[17] *The Diary of Lady Waterpark, Lady-in-Waiting to Queen Victoria 1865–91*, British Library ref. Add. 60750, p. 285.

Sir J. Williams, saying that dear May had been safely delivered of a son at 3 this morning. Georgie's first feeling was regret that this dear child should be born on such a sad day. I have a feeling it may be a blessing for the dear little Boy, & may be looked upon as a gift from God!'[18] Harold Nicolson wrote that 'December 14 was not the most tactful day which the future King George VI could have chosen for his advent into a world which was so soon to become embattled, angry and disillusioned'.[19]

The Illness of the Prince of Wales, 1871

On 25 November 1871, 'F. J. H.', the London correspondent of the *New York Times*, wrote an article, published on 7 December, which began:

> The somewhat alarming illness of the Prince of Wales, following close upon the illness of the Queen, and occurring in the midst of heated discussions as to the advantages and disadvantages of a monarchy, has naturally caused a good deal of uneasiness. For about a week he had been out of sorts, and feverish symptoms had been observed; but it was thought to be only an ordinary attack of influenza. On Monday last the sickness was unmistakably recognized as typhoid fever. Dr. Gull was telephoned for from London, and Sir William Jenner, the Queen's physician, who was with her Majesty at Balmoral, hurried south as fast as express engines could carry him. There can be no doubt that the attack has been a sharp one, and though the doctor's bulletins, issued twice a day, are of the most reassuring character, it cannot be assumed that all danger is over.'

Ten years earlier, the Prince Consort had died from typhoid fever. The seriousness of the situation prompted the Queen's first visit to her eldest son's estate at Sandringham. Having spent the day there on 29 November, she returned again on 8 December, after receiving Lord Granville's communication that 'there hardly seems to be hope left'.[20] According to Elizabeth Longford:

[18] Royal Archives: VIC/MAIN/QVJ/1895.

[19] Harold Nicolson, *King George the Fifth: His Life and Reign*, London: Constable & Co., p. 55.

[20] Sidney Lee, *King Edward VII: A Biography: From Birth to Accession*, London: Macmillan & Co., 1925, p. 321.

> The Queen watched her son from behind a screen, not daring to leave the house for more than half an hour each day. On 12 December she went to bed 'with the horrid feeling I may be called up'. Princess Alexandra once crawled into the bedroom on all fours lest the patient should catch sight of her. The Prince of Wales, however, in contrast to his father was attended by professional nurses and his ravings revealed a robust temperament. His pillows went flying about the room as he laughed and sang, one of them felling the Princess. 'That's right old Gull,' he roared to his doctor in high good humour – 'one more tea-spoonful'. At moments he thought he had succeeded to the throne, proposing reforms in the Household which made his attendants' hair stand on end.[21]

Prince Leopold described the harrowing circumstances in a letter to his former governor, Walter George Stirling: 'It was too dreadful to see the poor Queen sitting in the bedroom behind a screen listening to his ravings. I can't tell you what a deep impression the scene made on me.'[22]

Queen Victoria immediately sensed that, as the senior member of the family, she should take matters into her own hands: 'The arrival at Sandringham of so large a number of the family, considering too that they were by no means all on good terms with one another, made the arrangements far from easy. Then there were their Household attendants and of course the doctors. The Queen however was completely master of the situation. Not only did she guard the sick man's door as sentry to prevent a Princess from entering but she herself decided who should leave Sandringham and when they should go.'[23] This interpretation is supported by a letter that her Private Secretary wrote on 15 December: 'The Queen certainly takes things into her own hands freely. She clears the house tomorrow by sending away Alfred, Arthur, Leopold and Beatrice . . . The Duke of Cambridge stays on till Monday as the Princess particularly wishes it.'[24]

On 13 December Queen Victoria wrote in her Journal: 'This really has been the worst day of all, and coming as it has so close to the sad 14th, filled us and, I believe, the whole country with anxious forebodings and the greatest alarm. The first report early in the morning was that dear Bertie seemed very

[21] Longford, *Victoria R.I.*, p. 389.

[22] Charlotte Zeepvat, *Queen Victoria's Youngest Son: The Untold Story of Prince Leopold*, Gloucestershire: Sutton Publishing Limited, 2005, p. 93.

[23] Longford, *Victoria R.I.*, p. 389.

[24] Ponsonby, Arthur, *Henry Ponsonby, Queen Victoria's Private Secretary: His Life from his Letters*, London: Macmillan & Co., 1942, pp. 98–100.

weak, and the breathing was imperfect and feeble. The strength, however, rallied again. There had been no rest all night, from the constant delirium.' On 14 December she was cautiously optimistic: 'This dreadful anniversary, the 10th, returned again. It seems impossible to believe all that time has passed. Felt painfully having to spend the day away from Windsor, but the one great anxiety seems to absorb everything else. Instead of this date dawning upon another deathbed, which I had felt almost certain of, it brought the cheering news that dear Bertie had slept quietly at intervals, and really soundly from four to quarter to six; the respirations much easier, and food taken well.'[25]

The following day, the Prime Minister, William Gladstone, wrote to his Sovereign: 'All here are rejoiced to think that yesterday, which was so deeply marked in your Majesty's thoughts with the recollection of irreparable calamity, should have been in the midst of this new trial a day of hope and comfort. The series of telegrams which have reported gradual improvement has now grown rather a long one, and it is impossible to repress the cheerful feeling which they inspire. It still remains to desire that this feeling of hope and pleasure may not alter that temper of humble acknowledgment and trust, in which the nation has so earnestly sought by prayer for the Prince's recovery.'[26] On 21 December a bulletin announcing that the danger was past was released. Two days later, however, Queen Victoria wrote to her eldest daughter: 'His progress is terribly slow. Broken sleep – wandering (yesterday morning a great deal) and great prostration. The nerves have received a terrible shock and will take long recovering.'[27]

Any optimism was premature. On Christmas Day, she wrote in her Journal: 'At ½ p. 9 came the telegram from Sandringham. Dear Bertie had slept well till 3; pain in the leg troublesome, temperature 100, pulse 96, respirations 26, some dreaming. Did not like this report.'[28]

That day Lady Waterpark wrote in her diary: 'This was the first Christmas the Queen had spent at Windsor since the death of the Prince Consort, but she would not go to Osborne on account of the Prince of Wales's illness. He continued so ill, there were no Trees as usual or Christmas festivities. Our presents were sent to us in our rooms.'[29]

[25] Royal Archives: VIC/MAIN/QVJ/1871.

[26] Lee, *King Edward VII: A Biography: From Birth to Accession*, p. 322.

[27] Roger Fulford, ed., *Darling Child: Private Correspondence of Queen Victoria and the Crown Princess of Prussia 1871–1878*, London: Evans Brothers, 1976, p. 20.

[28] Royal Archives: VIC/MAIN/QVJ/1871.

[29] *The Diary of Lady Waterpark, Lady-in-Waiting to Queen Victoria 1865–91*, British Library ref. Add. 60750, p. 43.

On Boxing Day, for the first time in her reign, Queen Victoria published a letter to her people to thank them for the sympathy that she had received:

> The Queen is very anxious to express her deep sense of the touching sympathy of the whole nation on the occasion of the alarming illness of her dear son, the Prince of Wales. The universal feeling shown by her people during those painful terrible days, and the sympathy evinced by them with herself and her beloved daughter, the Princess of Wales, as well as the general joy at the improvement in the Prince of Wales's state, have made a deep and lasting impression on her heart which can never be effaced. It was indeed nothing new to her, for the Queen had met with the same sympathy when just ten years ago a similar illness removed from her side the mainstay of her life, the best, wisest, and kindest of husbands.[30]

However, the battle had not yet been won. The following day, the Journal continued:

> Bad telegram from Sir Wm Jenner. 'A good night till 5 o'clock, sleeping well & quietly. Then very severe spasm of breathing & of leg. Little sleep after that. Temperature the same, pulse 112, respirations 28.' This made me anxious. Telegraphed Sir Wm, enquiring if I had not better come today, instead of tomorrow, & the reply was, if not inconvenient, better today. Walked with Beatrice to the Kennels & to the Mausoleum, driving back. At 3 left Windsor with Leopold & Mary Biddulph (Fanny G. being too unwell to go), Col: Ponsonby & Mr. Collins. The 3rd weary dull journey, & undertaken with a heavy heart. Had tea in the train after Cambridge & reached Wolferton station at ½ p. 7.[31]

On New Year's Eve, the Queen, still at Sandringham, wrote in her Journal: 'Could hardly believe it was the last day in the old year, which has really been a most trying one. Ever since the beginning of August we have been in trouble of one kind or another, culminating in this dreadful illness of poor dear Bertie's. But I thank God for His great mercy, for amidst all dangers, trials, and sufferings, He has always protected us and brought us through the "fiery furnace." May I ever prove grateful for it! He was

[30] Lee, *King Edward VII: A Biography: From Birth to Accession*, p. 323.
[31] Royal Archives: VIC/MAIN/QVJ/1871.

quiet, thank God. How I pray the New Year may see him safely on the road to recovery!'

The Journal continued:

> Never before have I spent New Year's day away from home, and never did I think to spend it here, with poor Bertie so ill in bed, though, thank God! no longer in danger, at any rate not in any immediate danger. May our Heavenly Father restore him and let this heavy trial be for his good in every way! May sweet, darling Alix be preserved and blessed, and may the dear children grow up to be a blessing to their parents, to their country, and to me! Gave my photographs framed to the two excellent nurses, and Bertie's valet, etc. Writing telegrams in quantities. Then went over to Bertie, who kissed me and gave me a nosegay, which he had specially ordered, and which touched me very much, as well as his being able to wish me a happy New Year. What a blessed beginning after such dreadful anxiety![32]

Early in the New Year it was announced that the crisis had passed. There was a national day of thanksgiving on 27 February 1872, described by the Queen in a letter to Crown Princess Frederick:

> I am thankful to say that yesterday was a day of triumph – really most marvellous! Such touching affection and loyalty cannot be seen anywhere I think . . . Millions must have been out and the decorations were really beautiful – the cheering deafening. It was the first time since Bertie was a boy that he had ever been with me on a great public occasion – and such an occasion – even in former happier days – perhaps there has never been . . . 'God Bless the Prince of Wales' was always played after 'God Save the Queen' and when we were stopping at Temple Bar amid deafening cheers I took dear Bertie's hand and pressed it – people cried. Indeed he had tears in his eyes and I often felt a lump in my throat.[33]

The same day, Queen Victoria wrote to her Private Secretary: 'She is feeling very tired – but she was so deeply gratified & touched by the wonderful enthusiasm & loyalty shown that she does not much care for that. It was

[32] LQV II, Vol. II, pp. 178–81.
[33] Fulford, *Darling Child: Private Correspondence of Queen Victoria and the Crown Princess of Prussia 1871–1878*, pp. 31–3.

really a glorious sight. St. Paul's itself is a *most* dreary, dingy, melancholy & undevotional Church & the service except the last Hymn devoid of any *elevating* effect.'[34] In celebration of the Prince of Wales's recovery, Alfred, Lord Tennyson, the Poet Laureate, wrote an epilogue to the *Idylls of the King*.

As postilion, John Brown was 'in his very fullest and very handsome full dress' when, less than a week later there was an attempt on the Queen's life, as she drove into Buckingham Palace: 'You will have seen by Jane Ely's note and by the papers and the evidence what a horrid, daring thing this was! I never saw the pistol – because when I saw a strange face and heard a strange voice at my own door, where surely everyone thought I must be safe – I threw myself over Jane, – who had never seen the man. But it is entirely owing to good Brown's great presence of mind and quickness that he was seized (he held him by the throat) before he could touch me and dropped his pistol. Arthur and Leopold both saw him point it at my face!'[35]

In *The Economist*'s magazine, *Intelligent Life*, Nick Valéry wrote: 'After Prince Albert died of typhoid in 1861, a grief-stricken Queen Victoria demanded that piped water and sewage treatment be installed throughout Britain. A decade later, her son Prince Edward came close to dying of the same disease, and word about the need for flushing toilets went out across the land. From Britain, it spread to France, and thence the rest of Europe and the world.'[36]

The Death of Princess Alice, 1878

Queen Victoria's third child and second daughter, Princess Alice, Grand Duchess of Hesse, caught diphtheria from her youngest child, whom she had been nursing. She died at the New Palace in Darmstadt on 14 December 1878, the seventeenth anniversary of her father's death. She was buried at Rosenlöhe, beneath a recumbent effigy of mother and child by Sir Joseph Boehm, Queen Victoria's favourite sculptor. On the day of Princess Alice's death, her mother wrote in her Journal:

> This terrible day come round again! Slept tolerably, but woke very often, constantly seeing darling Alice before me. When I woke in the morning,

[34] Ponsonby, *Henry Ponsonby, Queen Victoria's Private Secretary: His Life from his Letters*, p. 100.
[35] Fulford, *Darling Child: Private Correspondence of Queen Victoria and the Crown Princess of Prussia 1871–1878*, p. 33.
[36] Nick Valéry, *Intelligent Life*, January/February 2012, p. 93.

was not for a moment aware of all our terrible anxiety. And then it all burst upon me. I asked for news, but nothing had come. Then got up and went, as I always do on this day, to the Blue Room, and prayed there. When dressed, I went into my sitting-room for breakfast, and met Brown coming in with two bad telegrams: I looked first at one from Louis, which I did not at first take in, saying: 'Poor Mama, poor me, my happiness gone, dear, dear Alice. God's will be done.' (I can hardly write it!) The other from Sir Wm. Jenner, saying: 'Grand Duchess became suddenly worse soon after midnight, since then could no longer take any food.'

Directly after, came another with the dreadful tidings that darling Alice sank gradually and passed away at half past 7 this morning! It was too awful! I had so hoped against hope. Went to Bertie's sitting-room. His despair was great. As I kissed him, he said, 'It is the good who are always taken.' All in the house were in great distress. Telegrams streaming in all day from all sides. Hardly able to answer them. Had already yesterday countermanded the service in the Mausoleum, for this day. That this dear, talented, distinguished, tender-hearted, noble-minded, sweet child, who behaved so admirably during her dear father's illness, and afterwards, in supporting me, and helping me in every possible way, should be called back to her father on this very anniversary, seems almost incredible, and most mysterious! To me there seems something touching in the union which this brings, their names being for ever united on this day of their birth into another better world![37]

On 18 December, Queen Victoria wrote: 'We had a touching short Service at half past two to which the whole family came. Beethoven's March from the *Eroica* was played and then the greater part of the Burial Service read and the short fine anthem by Elvey and darling Alice's favourite hymn 'Thy Will be Done'. In conclusion that fearfully sad 'Dead March in Saul' was played.'[38] The Crown Prince and Princess did not attend the funeral, 'for fear of infection'. On Boxing Day 1878, Queen Victoria wrote a letter to the nation:

The Queen is anxious to take the earliest opportunity of expressing publicly her heartfelt thanks for the universal and touching sympathy shown

[37] LQV II, Vol. II, pp. 654–5.

[38] Roger Fulford, ed., *Beloved Mama: Private Correspondence of Queen Victoria and the Crown Princess of Prussia 1878–1885*, London: Evans Brothers, 1981, p. 31.

> to her by all classes of her loyal and faithful subjects on the present occasion when it has pleased God to call from this world her dearly beloved daughter, Princess Alice, Grand Duchess of Hesse.
>
> Overwhelmed with grief at the loss of a dear child, who was a bright example of loving tenderness, courageous devotion, and self-sacrifice to duty, it is most soothing to the Queen's feelings to see how entirely her grief is shared by her people. The Queen's deeply afflicted son-in-law, the Grand Duke of Hesse, is also anxious to make known his sincere gratitude for the kind feelings expressed towards himself and his dear children in their terrible bereavement, and his gratification at the appreciation shown by the people of England of the noble and endearing qualities of her whom all now mourn.
>
> Seventeen years ago at this very time, when a similar bereavement crushed the Queen's happiness, and this beloved and lamented daughter was her great comfort and support, the nation evinced the same touching sympathy, as well as when, in December, 1871, the Prince of Wales was at the point of death.
>
> Such an exhibition of true and tender feeling will ever remain engraven on the Queen's heart, and is the more to be valued at this moment of great distress in the country, which no one more deeply deplores than the Queen herself.

The following day, she wrote to Crown Princess Frederick: 'Bertie was terribly shaken – & distressed but full of kindness & brotherly affection to you all – & most truly anxious, as I am, that this great sorrow shld. only bring the remaining 8 closer together – forgetting all small disagreements & differences – for "Love covereth a multitude of sins," & not enlarging & exagerating [sic] them. The views & interests must alas! be often very different – & we cannot expect to sympathise in one another's peculiar feelings but we shld. try to agree as much as we can & to understand one another – to bear & forbear – & this will help us over much that might divide us.'[39]

On New Year's Day the Queen wrote in her Journal: 'What a sad beginning to the New Year! What sadness, what grief on so many sides! Our darling precious Alice, one of my beloved five daughters, gone, after but six days' illness, gone for ever from this world, which is not, thank God, our permanent home! What misery in her once dear, bright, happy home! And

[39] Royal Archives: *Transcript of Extracts from Queen Victoria's Letters to the Princess Royal 1863–87*, U/32, p. 310.

my poor dear Loosy [wife of the Marquis of Lorne] far away in a distant land, in another quarter of the globe! May God preserve all my dear children, as well as all my friends, and give me strength to bear up and struggle on, in spite of all these trials, and cruel shocks and griefs!'[40]

Two days later, the Queen wrote to Lady Waterpark: 'Though I shall so soon have the pleasure of seeing you, I must write you a line to thank you warmly for the extreme kindness of your letter, which touched me deeply. If universal, & truly tender sympathy as well as the affection & admiration for my darling child would lessen the grief, I am sure it ought to do so in my case, for never was there any thing seen like the feeling in any other Country. But a sorrow & a loss like mine are great & irreparable & will be felt to the end of my days. Still it is something to feel how every one shares my grief, & feels for my poor, dear bereaved son in law, & my poor Motherless Grandchildren.'[41]

The Death of the German Emperor Frederick III, 1888

On the last day of 1887, her Golden Jubilee Year, Queen Victoria wrote a retrospect of the year in her Journal:

> It was with great regret, I parted with the old eventful one. The Jubilee time was so richly blessed, not one mishap or disturbance, not one bad day, including the last pretty little ceremony of the unveiling of my statue at Balmoral. Never, never can I forget this brilliant year, so full of the marvellous kindness, loyalty & devotion, of so many millions, which really I could hardly have expected. I felt sadly the absence of those dear ones, who would so entirely have rejoiced in this eventful time. Then, how thankful I must be for darling Beatrice coming safely through her severe confinement, & now again in the great improvement, in dear Fritz's condition. We had been in such terrible anxiety about him in November. May God help me further![42]

Crown Prince Frederick, known by the Royal Family as Fritz, had made a considerable impact on the British public during the Golden

[40] LQV II, Vol. III, p. 4. The Marquis of Lorne was Governor General of Canada 1878–83.
[41] *The Diary of Lady Waterpark, Lady-in-Waiting to Queen Victoria 1865–91*, British Library ref. Add. 60750, p. 285.
[42] Royal Archives: VIC/MAIN/QVJ/1887.

Jubilee Celebrations on 20–21 June 1887. In his memoir of Queen Victoria, the Marquis of Lorne wrote: 'The appearance of the Prince Imperial of Germany in the Jubilee procession was more like that of one of the legendary heroes embodied in the creations of Wagner than of a soldier of to-day, for nothing could exceed the splendour of his presence in a uniform wholly white, and having on his burnished steel helmet the great silver crest of an eagle with outspread wings. Every one along the route admired this beloved Prince, who, alas! at the next jubilee, ten years afterwards, had already passed "beyond these voices."'[43]

Having succeeded Emperor William I, his 91-year-old father, Emperor Frederick III died of throat cancer at Potsdam on 15 June 1888, after what James Pope-Hennessy described as a 'voiceless interlude', and was succeeded by his eldest son, Emperor William II, known to British veterans of the First World War as Kaiser Bill. Queen Victoria's Journal entry for 31 December 1888 was unusually subdued: 'The last day of this dreadful year, which has brought mourning and sorrow to so many, and such misfortunes, and ruined the happiness of my darling child. My cough being still troublesome, did not go out in the morning. Felt very tired. After luncheon, the day not having improved, thought it wiser to remain at home. A family dinner. Poor dear Vicky was very low, but promised to go to bed, and not sit up. No one of us sat up. Quietly and imperceptibly ended this sad year.'[44]

If the Emperor Frederick III had lived longer, the world might have been a different place. According to his biographer: 'Frederick William's reaction to the anti-Semitic movement was public, courageous and unequivocal. The only member of the royal family to do so and earlier than almost every other prominent non-Jew, he openly demonstrated his disgust for what he regarded as an utterly deplorable phenomenon. As early as December 1879, he attended a concert in a synagogue at the request of the leader of Berlin's Jewish community.'[45]

[43] The Marquis of Lorne (now His Grace The Duke of Argyll), *VRI: Queen Victoria: Her Life and Empire*, pp. 322–3.

[44] George Earle Buckle, ed., *The Letters of Queen Victoria, Third Series: A Selection from Her Majesty's Correspondence between the Years 1886 and 1901*, 3 vols., London: John Murray, 1930–32 (LQV III), Vol. I, p. 460.

[45] Frank Lorenz Müller, *Our Fritz: Emperor Frederick and the Political Culture of Imperial Germany*, Cambridge, Mass. and London: Harvard University Press, 2011, p. 75.

The Death of the Duke of Clarence, 1892

Prince Albert Victor Christian Edward, known as Prince Eddy, the elder surviving son of the Prince and Princess of Wales, was born at Frogmore House on 8 January 1864. For the first two decades of his life he was inseparable from his younger brother, Prince George, during the last six years of which they trained together in the Royal Navy. However, he constantly struggled to overcome what his brother's biographer referred to as 'his constitutional lethargy' [46] His immaturity is indicated by the letter that he wrote to Prince George on 15 June 1883: 'So we are at last to be separated for the first time and I can't tell you how strange it seems to be without you and how much I miss you in everything all day long.'[47] On 24 May 1890 Prince Eddy was created Duke of Clarence and Avondale. Two months later Prince George wrote to his mother from Bermuda: 'I can't make out why he should be called by both names, why not Clarence? I see a lot of the stupid jokes & puns about Clarence & Avondale. I think it is a great pity, because now his names are ridiculed the same as Albert Victor was which only does harm; the poor boy seems to be doomed to have two names.'[48]

On 6 December 1891, Queen Victoria wrote to her eldest daughter that 'the great event of Eddy's engagement with May Teck has taken place. People here are delighted and she certainly is a dear, good and clever girl, very carefully brought up, unselfish and unfrivolous in her tastes. She will be a great help to him. She is very fond of Germany too and is very *cosmopolitan*. I must say that I think it is far preferable than *eine kleine Prinzessin* with no knowledge of anything beyond small German courts etc. It would never do for Eddy.'[49]

Although Princess May was not '*eine kleine Prinzessin*' – 'a little Princess' – Emperor William II wrote to his grandmother, Queen Victoria, two days later:

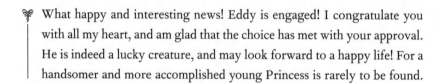

> What happy and interesting news! Eddy is engaged! I congratulate you with all my heart, and am glad that the choice has met with your approval. He is indeed a lucky creature, and may look forward to a happy life! For a handsomer and more accomplished young Princess is rarely to be found.

[46] Nicolson, *King George the Fifth: His Life and Reign*, p. 17.
[47] Ibid, p. 35.
[48] Pope-Hennessy, *Queen Mary, 1867–1953*, p. 194.
[49] Agatha Ramm, *Beloved and Darling Child: Last Letters between Queen Victoria and her Eldest Daughter 1886–1901*, Stroud: Sutton, 1990, p. 136.

> I saw much of her last year, and I must say, '*Sie gefiel mir ausnehmend gut*' [I thought her exceptionally nice]. I am sure the country at large will ring with joy, and merry will this Christmas be for you and the whole of the United Kingdom. I am very glad for Uncle Bertie; this will be a ray of light after the troubles of Sandringham and poor Georgie's illness [also from typhoid fever], who I trust is getting better now.[50]

In the light of a letter that Prince George wrote to his mother on 21 October 1886, his elder brother's engagement was a slightly surprising turn of events:

> I want to ask you something, Motherdear. Have you read that article in *Vanity Fair* of the 9th of October headed *An English Queen Consort?* If you have not, you must get it & read it. I think it is one of the best I have read & I am sure you will agree with me. Of course the first part is stuff (as you would say) but what it says is that all English people hope that dear Eddy will not marry a German but that he will marry some English woman, of course there is plenty of time to think of that. When I read it, it struck me as being so sensible & so true & the more I think it over the more I feel that it would be so much nicer if he married an English person. I think, Motherdear, that you think the same as I do, but I am afraid that both Grandmama & dear Papa wish him to marry a German, but I don't know.[51]

One can understand Grandmama's point of view: of her nine children, one married a Dane (King Edward VII), one married a Russian (Prince Alfred, Duke of Edinburgh), one married a Scot (Princess Louise), while the other six all married Germans.

Just five weeks after his engagement to Princess Mary – who was known to the Royal Family as May, after the month of her birth – the Duke of Clarence fell ill with influenza. On 8 January 1892 Prince George wrote in his diary: 'Froze hard in the night & a little snow fell. Answering telegrams for Eddy & writing letters all day.'[52] Two days later, Queen Victoria wrote in her Journal: 'Was startled and rather troubled by a telegram from Bertie, saying dear Eddy had a "very sharp attack of influenza and had now developed

[50] LQV III, Vol. II, pp. 82–3.
[51] Nicolson, *King George the Fifth: His Life and Reign*, p. 42.
[52] Pope-Hennessy, *Queen Mary, 1867–1953*, p. 222.

some pneumonia in left lung, the night restless, but strength well maintained. Laking here. Broadbent coming to-day." I telegraphed to Dr. Laking. Heard from him that Eddy had passed a more comfortable day, and that Dr. Broadbent thought "favourably of the case".'[53] Three days later, she wrote: 'Whilst I was dressing, Beatrice asked to see me, and brought a bad telegram from Dr. Broadbent to Dr. Reid to the following effect: "Condition very dangerous." How terrible! Felt I ought to fly to Sandringham, and yet I feared I should be in the way. I telegraphed to Bertie, and got the following most sad answer: "Our darling Eddy is in God's hands. Human skill seems unavailing. There could not be a question of your coming here." Can think of nothing else but dear Eddy and the terrible distress at Sandringham.'[54]

The following day she wrote:

> A never-to-be-forgotten day! Whilst I was dressing, Lenchen came in, bringing the following heart-rending telegram from poor dear Bertie: 'Our darling Eddy has been taken from us. We are broken-hearted.' Words are far too poor to express one's feeling of grief, horror, and distress! Poor, poor parents; poor May to have her whole bright future to be merely a dream! Poor me, in my old age, to see this young promising life cut short! I, who loved him so dearly, and to whom he was so devoted! God help us! This is an awful blow to the country too! Soon hundreds of telegrams of condolence came pouring in. The feeling of grief immense. Had a letter from Bertie, whom I had enquired after, saying they were all 'fairly well, but very tired and exhausted. Just had a beautiful service where our dear boy is lying. Anxious to have last sad ceremony at Windsor. Pray do not think of coming. Weather too inclement to run risks.'[55]

James Pope-Hennessy wrote that 'the sudden death of the Duke of Clarence struck England like a thunderbolt'.[56]

The 'last sad service' did indeed take place at Windsor – but not quite in the way that the Prince and Princess of Wales had hoped. On 22 January 1892, Major-General Sir Arthur Ellis, Equerry to the Prince of Wales, wrote from Windsor Castle to Sir Henry Ponsonby:

[53] LQV III, Vol. II, pp. 91–2.
[54] Royal Archives: VIC/MAIN/QVJ/1892.
[55] LQV III, Vol. II, pp. 91–2.
[56] Pope-Hennessy, *Queen Mary, 1867–1953*, p. 223.

> In every – even the saddest occurrences of life there arises a comic side – a gleam of absurdity – which helps one to bear the gloom . . . The Prince of Wales desires me to say that – the harem of Princesses was *not* locked into the further Zenana pew closet but the door got jammed, and adds that they were none of them wanted at all. No ladies were to attend, and the Princess of Wales especially requested privacy – and to avoid meeting her Osborne relations. So they all came. If Princess Beatrice was annoyed it cannot be helped and she must get over it – as she likes.
>
> We are fairly comfortable in this most conveniently built house – and most of our time is spent in a sort of a game of 'post' or hide-and-seek, looking for and searching for each other – and being hunted by servants who get lost. We all admire various little economical thrifty dodges here. In the W.C.s – NEWSPAPER squares – there was one idea of sending them to Cowell [Master of the Household] in an unpaid envelope . . . And with a cup of tea – three lumps of loose sugar on the tray!! It is admirable – and we now see why you are so rich.
>
> The avalanche of telegrams and resolutions still pour in. One day over 1700 telegrams!!! Average for five days 1000 per diem. We write till we feel scribbler's palsy coming on – and it seems to have no effect on the letters. I have appraised the Sandringham telegram bill at £2000. All the small places in New Zealand, Australia and India sending messages, all to be replied to, at so very much per word, is ghastly waste. Strange for us to be installed here and writing to you away on this side of the grave. We all clear out tomorrow – Hallelujah!'[57]

On 4 February 1892, the Prince of Wales wrote to his old friend from Oxford days, Lorina Liddell, wife of the Very Reverend Henry George Liddell, Honorary Chaplain to Queen Victoria, whose fourth daughter, Alice, was immortalised by Lewis Carroll: 'To lose our eldest son at the age of twenty-eight after only a few days' illness and on the eve of his marriage is one of those calamities that one can never really get over, and though, as time goes on, our duties and occupations will have to be followed, everything in our daily life will remind me of the gap made amongst our children.'[58]

Fortunately, May's 'bright future' was not 'merely a dream'. On 3 May 1893 at East Sheen Lodge, the home of his sister, the Duchess of Fife, the Duke of York proposed to Princess May. After the engagement was

[57] Ponsonby, *Henry Ponsonby, Queen Victoria's Private Secretary: His Life from his Letters*, pp. 359–60.
[58] Lee, *King Edward VII: A Biography: From Birth to Accession*, p. 606.

announced the following day, *The Times* published an article: 'The predominant feeling, now that a sufficient interval has elapsed since the melancholy death of the Duke of Clarence, will be that this betrothal accords with the fitness of things, and, so far from offending any legitimate sentiment, is the most appropriate and delicate medicament for a wound in its nature never wholly effaceable. There is even ground for hoping that a union rooted in painful memories may prove happy beyond the common lot.' And so it proved to be.

The Death of Queen Victoria, 1901

On 22 December 1900, Queen Victoria dictated to Thora, who was now writing the Journal for her grandmother: 'I slept a little at first, and then was rather disturbed after which I slept on again till quarter to twelve, at which I was very annoyed. I got up and had some breakfast, which I really liked, then drove out with Thora. I am rather better, but still see very badly. All my good people, my maids and Indian servants are indefatigable, and so anxious to do anything they can for me. Lenchen and Arthur and Louischen, who have come to spend Christmas here with their children, arrived, and I saw them each separately for a moment.'[59]

Christmas Day brought a tragedy for the Royal Household, with the unexpected death of seventy-four-year-old Jane Spencer, Baroness Churchill, Lady of the Bedchamber to Queen Victoria for the last forty-six years:

> Did not have a good night, was very restless, & every remedy that was tried failed in making me sleep. Then when I wished to get up, I fell asleep again, which was too provoking. Went out with Lenchen & Beatrice about 1 & the former told me Sir J. Reid wished me to know that dear Jane Churchill had had one of her bad heart attacks in the night, & that he had telegraphed for her son, as he thought very seriously of her condition. I said 'You remember, I warned & asked her son whether it was safe for her to come as she was so ill at this very time last year.' I felt anxious, & on coming home sent for Sir James, who said 'she is very ill,' so I asked if it would not be better to send at once for another lady, to which he replied 'most decidedly'.

[59] Royal Archives: VIC/MAIN/QVJ/1900.

> Later, after I had had some broth & rested a little, I took a short drive with Louischen & Thora, & we talked a great deal about dear Jane, as I was so distressed at her being so ill. Directly I returned, I again sent for Sir James, who said 'I was just coming to tell Your Majesty all was over.' She had died this morning early, in her sleep, & had just slept peacefully away. They had not dared tell me for fear of giving me a shock, so had prepared me gradually for the terrible news. I saw Harriet Phipps, who told me all about it. I naturally was much upset & very unhappy, as dear Jane was one of my most faithful & intimate friends. At 6 had a little service in the Drawing-room, performed by Mr. Ellison, who gave a very nice short address & 3 Hymns were sung, Beatrice playing the Harmonium. Then I went upstairs & rested. This has indeed been a terribly sad Christmas for us all![60]

On 27 December 1900 Princess Beatrice wrote a letter to the Empress Frederick, dictated by the Queen: 'This Christmas has been one of the saddest I ever remember, excepting '61, and you are I am sure as horrified as I am at the loss of my good beloved Jane Churchill, who died in her sleep on Christmas Day. What her loss is to me I cannot describe or even realise yet, and that it should happen here is too sad, but it is I think what she would have wished, excepting for the trouble and sorrow it has caused.'[61]

On New Year's Eve, despite 'the same unfortunate alternations of sleep & restlessness, so that I again did not get up when I wished to, which spoilt my morning & day', as if in anticipation, the Queen 'had to sign for a new Trustee to my private money, who is Louis Battenberg. Lord E. Clinton & Sir F. Edwards were witnesses.' On 13 January 1901, Queen Victoria 'had a fair night, but was a little wakeful. Got up earlier & had some milk. Lenchen came & read some papers. Out before 1, in the garden chair, Lenchen & Beatrice going with me. Rested a little, had some food, & took a short drive with Lenchen & Beatrice. Rested when I came in & at 5.30, went down to the Drawing-room, where a short service was held, by Mr. Clement Smith, who performed it so well, & it was a great comfort to me. Rested again afterwards, then did some signing & dictated to Lenchen.' Beneath that,

[60] Ibid.

[61] Ramm, *Beloved and Darling Child: Last Letters between Queen Victoria and her Eldest Daughter 1886–1901*, p. 258.

Princess Beatrice wrote, simply: ‘This is the last entry into the Queen’s Journal before her death on Jan: 22nd.’[62]

On 21 January 1901, the Duke of York wrote in his diary:

> Left Victoria by special train with Papa, William [the German Emperor], uncle Arthur & aunt Louise for Portsmouth. Crossed over in ‘Alberta’ & reached Osborne at 11.20. Thank God we found that darling Grandmama had rallied since last night & that her strength was still maintained. We found here aunts Helena, Louise, Beatrice & Marie, Baby B & Thora & the Battenberg children. At about 12.0 the doctors, Reid, Douglas Powell & Barlow allowed me to go in & see her, she looked just the same, not a bit changed, she was almost asleep & had her eyes shut, I kissed her hand, Motherdear was with me. Lunched at 1.0 in Durbar room. In afternoon, quite mild, walked with Papa, Motherdear, William [the German Emperor], aunt Louise & uncle Arthur, we first went down to Osborne pier & then to East Cowes & paid a visit to James’ convalescent home, where there were 15 soldiers back from South Africa. Had a talk to Bigge after tea. Wrote some letters. Family dinner at 8.30. Talked to Papa & Francis. Darling Grandmama rather better tonight, Motherdear saw her, she recognised her & talked to her, Papa also saw her this evening. Bed at 12.0.[63]

Sir Sidney Lee wrote ‘there was embarrassment among the Kaiser’s English relatives at his sudden and unexpected arrival. It was not a moment when they were in the mood to pay him ceremonious attention.’[64] The following day, the Duke of York wrote:

> We were all sent for to darling Grandmama’s room at 9.0. The Bishop of Winchester read some prayers & we all thought the end was coming, but she rallied in a wonderful way & became better, so we all left her. This is indeed a terribly anxious time. Very busy all the morning. I sent for May to come at once. Went for a short walk with Papa. Lunched at 1.30. At 2.30 we were all again sent for and remained with darling Grandmama for almost the whole time, until 6.30, when our beloved Queen & Grandmama, one of the greatest women that ever lived, passed peacefully away, surrounded by her sorrowing children & grandchildren. She was conscious up till 5.0

[62] Royal Archives: VIC/MAIN/QVJ/1901.

[63] Royal Archives: GV/PRIV/GVD/1901.

[64] Lee, *King Edward VII: A Biography: From Birth to Accession*, p. 801.

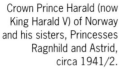

▲
The Duke and Duchess of York's Christmas card, 1934.

►
Crown Prince Harald (now King Harald V) of Norway and his sisters, Princesses Ragnhild and Astrid, circa 1941/2.

▲ The Royal Christmas card, 1940: King George VI and Queen Elizabeth in the garden of bomb-damaged Buckingham Palace, 10 September 1940.

▲ Princess Elizabeth and Princess Margaret broadcast from Windsor Castle during *Children's Hour*, to children separated from their families because of the war and the bombing of British cities, 13 October 1940.

Princess Elizabeth and Princess Margaret in *Aladdin*, Windsor Castle, December 1943.

The programme for *Aladdin*, Windsor Castle, December 1943.

The programme for *Old Mother Red Riding Boots*, Windsor Castle, December 1944

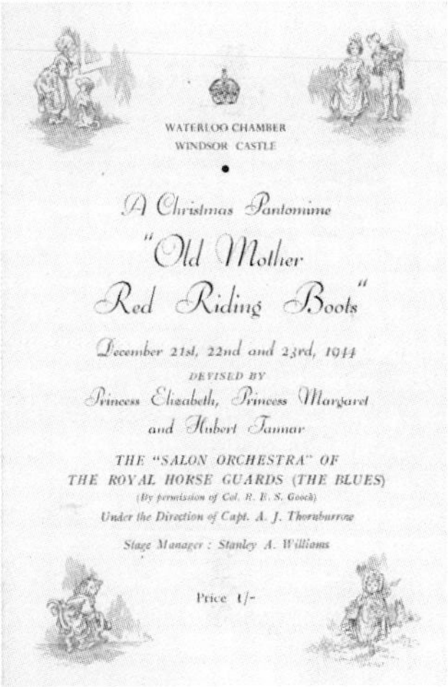

Princess Elizabeth and Princess Margaret in *Old Mother Red Riding Boots*, Windsor Castle, December 1944.

◄ The Royal Princesses' Christmas card, 1945.

► The Royal Christmas card, 1950: 'We Four', as King George VI referred to his family, in the Scottish Highlands.

▲ The Queen and The Duke of Edinburgh watch Father Christmas giving gifts to the two young daughters of the Governor General, Government House, Auckland, New Zealand, Christmas Day, 1953.

◀ Queen Elizabeth the Queen Mother's Christmas card, 1954: with Princess Margaret.

▲ Queen Elizabeth the Queen Mother's Christmas card, 1964: a winning horse.

▲ Queen Elizabeth the Queen Mother's Christmas card, 1966: leaving an aircraft of the Queen's Flight during her Australian tour.

The Prince and Princess of Wales's Christmas card, 1986.

The Prince of Wales's Christmas card, 1992.

◄ The Prince of Wales's Christmas card, 1995.

▲ The Duchess of Cornwall's Christmas card, 2005: a family group at Windsor Castle after her marriage to The Prince of Wales on 9 April 2005 – (left to right) Prince Harry, Prince William, The Prince of Wales, The Duchess of Cornwall, Laura Parker Bowles, Tom Parker Bowles.

> & called each of us by name & we took leave of her & kissed her hand, it was terribly distressing. Thank God darling May arrived in time at 5.30 to see her. I shall never forget that scene in her room, with all of us sobbing & heartbroken round her bed. After dinner we all went to her room at 10.0 & there she lay covered with flowers looking so beautiful & peaceful, the Bishop of Winchester said some prayers & we knelt all round the bed. Feel quite worn out. Bed at 12.0.

The same day, the Duchess of York wrote in her diary: 'At 10.30 I was sent for to Osborne so I went at 1.40, with Daisy, Patsy & Arthur Connaught. We got there at 5.30 only just in time to see beloved Grandmama alive for she passed away 6.30 p.m. surrounded by us all. It was too sad for words . . . The thought of England without the Queen is dreadful even to think of. God help us all.' An extraordinary era, defined for ever by a most remarkable woman, had finally come to an end.

On 23 January, the Duke of York

> left with Papa & uncle Arthur in 'Alberta' at 10.0 & reached London by special at 1.0, drove to York House. At 2.0 a meeting of all the Privy Councillors was held in the banqueting hall in St. James's Palace, first we approved of the King's proclamation (to be read tomorrow morning) & then he took the oath as King. Then Papa made a beautiful speech in which he said he wished to be called Edward VII. We then all took the Oath of Allegiance to him, I kissing his hand first & then the oath as a Privy Councillor. Saw Holzmann, about the Duchy of Cornwall, I have now succeeded Papa as the Duke of Cornwall. Both Houses of Parliament met. At 4.30 uncle Arthur & I went to the House of Lords & took the Oath. Came home at 5.0, busy answering letters & telegrams. At 8.30 Papa, Uncle Arthur, George, Christian, Lorne, & the Louis Battenbergs dined with me. After dinner Lord Clarendon (Lord Chamberlain) & Sir Spencer Ponsonby Fane came & we discussed various points connected with the funeral. Bed at 12. Very tired.[65]

Two days later, the Duke of York was back at Osborne House: 'Had a fair night & feel better, temperature still 100 so Reid would not let me get up. At 10.45 darling Grandmama was put in her coffin & carried down

[65] Royal Archives: GV/PRIV/GVD/1901.

by bluejackets of the Royal Yacht to the dining room where the coffin was placed, the room being arranged as a Chapel & 60 men of the Queen's Company of the 1st Grenadier Guards have arrived under the command of Captain Loyd, 4 of them are keeping watch in the room. May sat with me part of the day & Sir James Reid came to see me several times.'[66]

In his memoir of Queen Victoria, the Marquis of Lorne wrote that 'she had always had a dislike to the black trappings commonly used, and desired that black should be avoided as far as possible in the hangings and appurtenances used at her funeral, preferring purple and white before these, and even that black horses should be dispensed with. As in the case of the King of Italy, who went to his grave coffined in white and gold only a few short months before in Rome, so was our Queen also to be buried.'[67]

Having been invited to the unveiling of Sir Thomas Brock's Victoria Memorial, in front of Buckingham Palace, the German Emperor wrote to his first cousin, King George V, on 15 February 1911:

> Let me thank you most cordially for the very kind letter in which you invite Dona and me to be present at dear Grandmama's unveiling. You cannot imagine how overjoyed I am at the prospect of seeing you again so soon & making a nice stay with you. You are perfectly right in alluding to my devotion & reverence for my beloved Grandmother, with whom I was on such excellent terms. I shall never forget how kindly this great lady always was to me & the relations she kept up with me, though I was so far her junior, she having carried me about in her arms!
>
> Never in my life shall I forget the solemn hours at Osborne at her deathbed when she breathed her last in my arms! These sacred hours have riveted my heart firmly to your house and family, of which I am proud to feel myself a member. And the fact that for the last hours I held the sacred burden of her – the creator of the greatness of Britain – in my arms, in my mind created an invincible special link between her country and its People & me and one which I fondly nurse in my heart. This your invitation so to say sanctions these ideas of mine. You kindly refer to the fact of my being her eldest grandson: a fact I was always immensely proud of and never forgot.[68]

[66] Ibid.

[67] The Marquis of Lorne (now His Grace The Duke of Argyll), *VRI: Queen Victoria: Her Life and Empire*, p. 365.

[68] Nicolson, *King George the Fifth: His Life and Reign*, p. 182.

On 22 January 1924, King George V wrote in his diary: 'Today 23 years ago dear Grandmama died. I wonder what she would have thought of a Labour Government!'[69] Four weeks later, he wrote to his mother: 'I have been making the acquaintance of all the Ministers in turn & I must say they all seem to be very intelligent & they take things very seriously. They have different ideas to ours as they are all socialists, but they ought to be given a chance & ought to be treated fairly.'[70]

The Death of King Edward VII, 1910

Sir Sidney Lee wrote:

> The New Year found King Edward at Sandringham with the Queen and other members of the royal family, and a few days later he left to pay a visit of a week's duration with the Queen to Lord Iveagh at Elveden Hall, where he was a fellow guest with his old friends the Marquis of Soveral, Lord and Lady Arran, Lord Farquhar, the Hon. Mrs. Greville, the Hon. Mrs. George Keppel, Mr. and Mrs. James, and the Hon. Harry Stonor and Lord Carrington. The King looked really well, and seemed in great spirits, but was very anxious about the political situation, though it was understood there was to be no political talk in his presence. As was his custom he played bridge every evening and was in bed by midnight. Each morning he was out with the guns, and enjoyed the clear bracing air and the exercise.[71]

His biographer noted: 'In the early days of 1910 the King seemed to outsiders to be much in his usual health; but the doctors were nervous and anxious, they were eager to get him away from London.'[72] From the second week of March until late April 1910 King Edward VII rested at Biarritz, under doctors' orders. On the evening of his return to London, 27 April, he attended the opera at Covent Garden.

King Edward VII was an exceptionally keen and well-informed follower of the turf. According to his biographer, the King 'reckoned that the purchase of Perdita II in 1887 brought him within twenty years a quarter of

[69] Ibid., p. 384.
[70] Ibid., p. 389.
[71] Sidney Lee, *King Edward VII: A Biography: The Reign*, London: Macmillan & Co., 1927, p. 694.
[72] Ibid., p. 702.

a million'.[73] This interest was to remain with him, quite literally, to the end of his life. On 6 May 1910, the Prince of Wales wrote in his diary:

> I went over to B.P. [Buckingham Palace] at 10.15 where I regret to say I found darling Papa much worse having had a bad fainting fit. It was indeed a terrible day for us all, we hardly left him all day, he knew us & talked to us in between his attacks up till 4.30, the last thing he understood was when I told him that his horse 'Witch of the Air' had won at Kempton today & he said he was pleased. We watched by his bedside & did all we could for him, it was terrible to see him fighting for his life, but thank God he did not suffer at all.
>
> Motherdear, Toria, Louise, May, aunt Louise, Macduff & I, 4 doctors, Douglas Powell, Laking, Reid & Dawson & the two nurses, Fletcher & Harlack were in the room. The Archbishop of Canterbury said prayers we kneeling round his bed. At 11.45 beloved Papa passed peacefully away & I have lost my best friend & the best of fathers, I never had a word with him in my life. I am heartbroken & overwhelmed with grief, but God will help me in my great responsibilities & darling May will be my comfort as she has always been. May God give me strength & guidance in the heavy task which has fallen upon me. I sent telegrams to the Lord Mayor & the Prime Minister. Left darling Motherdear & Toria & drove back to M.H. [Marlborough House] with darling May. I am quite stunned by the awful blow. Bed at 1.0.[74]

Queen Alexandra acceded to her husband's request that his favourite mistress, Mrs Alice Keppel, should be allowed to visit him on his deathbed. After he lost consciousness, however, she said: 'Get that woman away.'

That evening, Queen Mary wrote simply but expressively: 'What a loss to the Nation & to us all. God help us.' The following day, King George V explained: 'May, I & the two boys drove to B.P. to see Motherdear & Toria, we went into his room & he looks so beautiful lying there, just as if he was asleep.' Having acceded to the throne at the age of fifty-nine, King Edward VII had reigned for less than ten years. An era had come to an end. On Christmas Day 1910, Queen Mary wrote in her diary: 'At 5.30 we all went up to the house to the Xmas tree, which Motherdear had kindly arranged for all of us. We missed Papa dreadfully.' On New Year's Day, the

[73] Lee, *King Edward VII: A Biography: From Birth to Accession*, pp. 582–3.
[74] Royal Archives: GV/PRIV/GVD/1910.

King wrote: 'After dinner we all went up to the house for the servants Xmas tree. Said good night to darling Motherdear, it has indeed been a sad year for us all.'[75]

The Illness of King George V, 1928

In late 1928 King George V was suffering from a respiratory illness, with a 'blood test' indicating 'acute septicaemia'.[76] An anxious Prince of Wales hastened home from East Africa and, during the three-minute drive from Victoria Station to Buckingham Palace on 11 December, was briefed on the situation by the Duke of York: 'He prepared me for the shock that my father's appearance would bring. "You will find him greatly changed," he said, "and now Dawson says an operation will be necessary in a day or two." Then he spoke admiringly of my mother. "Through all the anxiety she has never once revealed her feeling to any of us." This seemed to trouble him, for he quickly added, "She is really far too reserved; she keeps too much locked up inside of her. I fear a breakdown if anything awful happens. She has been wonderful." '[77]

The following day, Lord Dawson identified where fluid build-up was taking place and performed an operation, with a view to draining the fluid away. Harold Nicolson wrote that 'churches in England were kept open day and night for prayers of intercession'.[78] That day Queen Mary wrote in her diary: 'Drs. satisfied but it is anxious work.' Twelve days later, she wrote: 'Dull day. Good night. G. cheerier & we had a little talk but he must not talk much as it tires him. Unpacked Xmas parcels. Lots of lovely flowers arrived. At 5 all our children came to tea & sweet Lilibet, after which we went to the Throne Room where I had arranged the presents & a small Xmas tree. Katie Hamilton, Col. Paynter, Dick Molyneux & Harry Verney joined us. We missed dear George dreadfully but felt so thankful he is improving at last. Small family dinner.'[79]

In an undated letter, written that December, the Prince of Wales explained to Alan Lascelles, his Assistant Private Secretary, known to the Royal Family as 'Tommy': 'The King wasn't so well yesterday but the news

[75] Ibid.
[76] Nicolson, *King George the Fifth: His Life and Reign*, p. 430.
[77] John W. Wheeler-Bennett, *King George VI: His Life and* Reign, London: Macmillan & Co., 1958, p. 235.
[78] Nicolson, *King George the Fifth: His Life and Reign*, p. 432.
[79] Pope-Hennessy, *Queen Mary*, pp. 543–5.

seems better this evening and I hope to get away for the weekend's hunting – and now I hear your poor father has been very ill and that his heart won't last out very long. I am so sorry for your anxiety though I guess it wasn't exactly unexpected. What a worry one's family become when they get old.'[80]

On Christmas Day, Queen Mary wrote: 'Beautiful day. G. gave me a beautiful pink topaz & diamond pendant brooch when I went to see him at 9 a.m. & I was able to give him my gifts. Service at 10 & we all took the Holy Communion. Walked in the garden. Gave my presents to servants & nurses & doctors. Wrote & arranged things in the afternoon. Saw G. 2 or 3 times during the day. I gave a small dinner party to which the 4 boys, Mary & Elizabeth came, Katie Hamilton, Col. Paynter, Sir Stanley Hewitt & Gen. Trotter. We went to the Throne Room later & looked at our nice presents.'

Six days later, Queen Mary wrote in her diary: 'Very cold day, bitter wind. G. had rather a restless night. I did not go out. Sister Agnes came to tea with me. G. better in evening. All the boys & Elizabeth dined with me. Good bye to the Old Year – the last weeks have brought us much suffering – God grant the New Year may bring us peace & happiness & the restoration to health of our dear one.'[81]

The crisis had passed; however, a long period of convalescence followed, at Craigweil House, Aldwick, near Bognor in Sussex, the home of Sir Arthur du Cros. Accompanied by her nurse, the King's favourite grandchild, Princess Elizabeth, came to stay. On 13 March 1929, Queen Mary wrote: 'G. delighted to see her.' The following day, she wrote that 'I played with Lilibet in the garden making sand pies! The Archbishop of Canterbury came to see us & was so kind & sympathetic.'[82] Exceptionally, there was not a single entry in King George V's hand in his diary between Wednesday 21 November 1928 and Saturday 27 April 1929, when he wrote: 'The Neuritis in my arm being better now enables me to write a little. Sat out with May in garden but not very warm. Major Henry Segrave came down to see me & I knighted him, he having won the record for 1 mile (231 miles per hour) in a motor car & in a motor boat. A very nice young fellow of 30, who was 4 times wounded in the war.'[83] It was as a direct result of this

[80] Duff Hart-Davis, ed., *In Royal Service: The Letters and Journals of Sir Alan Lascelles 1920–36*, London: Hamish Hamilton, 1989, p. 113.

[81] Royal Archives: QM/PRIV/QMD/1928.

[82] Pope-Hennessy, *Queen Mary*, p. 546.

[83] Royal Archives: GV/PRIV/GVD/1929. Sir Henry Segrave died on 13 June 1930, as a result of an accident on Lake Windermere, during an attempt on the water speed record.

period of convalescence – following the submission of a petition from the town's people through his Private Secretary – that King George V granted the town Bognor the suffix Regis in June 1929.

The Death of King George V, 1936

More than fifteen years after his father's death, the Duke of Windsor wrote:

> A few days later I was at Sandringham for the family Christmas gathering. My brothers and their wives were already there. My father had grown thin and bent; we all shared a sense of foreboding that this might well be his last Christmas; so we tried to make it an especially happy one. In the spacious white ballroom of the Big House, where we had all had such fun in my grandfather's time, a fourth generation had begun to assert itself. Bertie's two little children, Elizabeth, who was then nine, and her sister, Margaret Rose, romped around the twenty-foot tree. Yet, in this closely-knit fabric of family ties I felt detached and lonely. My brothers were secure in their private lives; whereas I was caught up in an inner conflict and would have no peace of mind until I had resolved it. But this again was hardly the time or the place. My father died before another opportunity presented itself.[84]

On 10 January 1931, at Burrough Court, Melton Mowbray, Thelma, Lady Furness introduced the Prince of Wales to Mrs Ernest Simpson. It was not long before 'the Simpsons started to be invited regularly' to Fort Belvedere, the Prince of Wales's country house in Windsor Great Park. Anne Sebba describes 'one memorable weekend in January 1933 when Ernest was away. It was so cold that she and Thelma along with the Duke and Duchess of York all went skating on the frozen lake, the Prince having presented the two women with skates.'[85] That December 'saw the Simpsons celebrating with the Prince until 5 a.m. to see in the new year'.[86]

Twelve months later, 'the pressure from so insistent a lover was almost more than Wallis could cope with. When the Prince went to Sandringham for Christmas with his family she viewed it as "a lovely rest for us and

[84] Edward, Duke of Windsor, *A King's Story: The Memoirs of H.R.H. the Duke of Windsor K.G.*, London: Cassell & Com., 1951, pp. 259–60.

[85] Anne Sebba, *That Woman: The Life of Wallis Simpson, Duchess of Windsor*, London: Weidenfeld & Nicolson, 2011, p. 93.

[86] Ibid., pp. 95–6.

especially me".'[87] Deeply embroiled in a relationship laden with enormous personal and dynastic complications, the following Christmas was very far from 'an especially happy one' for the Prince of Wales. On Boxing Day 1935, he wrote to Wallis:

> Good night and good morning my sweetheart – as I won't be able to say either by 'phone. It's helped so much getting a few minutes talk alone at last this evening. I couldn't believe it was possible to miss this way but it's so lovely although hell while it lasts. It really is terrible here and so much the worst Xmas I've ever had to spend with the family, far worse than last year and that was bad enough. I just can't wait till seeing you Monday [30 December] and to know that boat has sailed for Canada. I'm longing for an eanum [part of their secret private language meaning 'dear little'] letter Wallis. This one has to be eanum as the mail is in a few minutes. Please don't over eat until we can again together or I'm there to say stop or you'll be quite ill I know. The pirate costume idea is good but not the idea of having to bore ourselves with others on New Year's night. Oh! to be alone for ages and ages and then – ages and ages. God bless WE sweetheart but I'm sure he does – he must.[88]

James Pope-Hennessy wrote: 'Four days before Christmas the King and Queen proceeded as usual to Sandringham by train. "Awfully cold here", Queen Mary noted on her arrival. Christmas Eve and Christmas Day were observed with the traditional Sandringham ceremonies . . . On 31 December the film *Monte Cristo*, which Queen Mary judged "excellent", was shown in the house. "The last day of the old year", she added, "which has been a most wonderful one."'[89]

In Queen Mary's diary for 1936 are two prayers asking for God's blessing. Very sadly, neither bore fruit in what must have been the most tumultuous year of Queen Mary's life, with the possible exception of 1892, when her betrothed had died of influenza. On 15 January 1936, she wrote in her diary: 'Poor George, who has not been feeling well for some days, felt worse & had to go to bed before dinner.' A day later, he 'had a cold & stayed in his room all day, not in bed all the time – Most worrying.'[90]

[87] Ibid., p. 102.
[88] Michael Bloch, ed., *Wallis & Edward: Letters 1931–37*, London: Weidenfeld & Nicolson, 1986, pp. 144–5. WE was the personal abbreviation used by Wallis and Edward.
[89] Pope-Hennessy, *Queen Mary*, p. 557. Queen Mary was referring to the Silver Jubilee Year.
[90] Ibid., p. 558.

The following day Tommy Lascelles wrote to his wife, Joan, eldest daughter of Lord Chelmsford: 'It has been a harrowing, anxious day, broken, as every death-bed and everything connected with the royal family seems to be, by occasional gleams of comedy. Anyhow, the Prince of Wales is far better prepared for a new life than he was seven years ago in Tanganyika! If the worst happens, I have no idea, of course, what my movements in the immediate future will be.'[91] That autumn, though, the King had been rather less optimistic, saying to the Prime Minister, Stanley Baldwin, that 'after I am dead the boy will ruin himself in twelve months'.[92]

Just two days later, Queen Mary confided to her diary:

> Am brokenhearted. Mild after rain. G. clearer after a fair night but weak. The Lord President of the Council, Mr. Ramsay McDonald, the Lord Chancellor, Lord Hailsham, The Home Secretary, Sir John Simon & Sir Maurice Hankey, Clerk of the Council, arrived about 11.30 to arrange about a council of state. Lord Dawson managed to get G. to say 'approved' & he was able to sign 2 little crosses as he was unable to sign his name which distressed him. The gentlemen stayed for luncheon. David & Bertie returned at 2.30 in D's airplane.[93] Walked a little. Marina arrived at 4. G. became weaker during the evening & we realised the end was approaching. We family dined alone & then went to G's room at intervals & at 5 to 12 my darling husband passed peacefully away. My children were angelic.[94]

John Reith's biographer described how the country was kept informed of developments: 'On the evening of 20 January, the BBC's domestic and Empire transmitters were brought together and the chief announcer, Stuart Hibberd, intoned the famous bulletin: 'The King's life is moving peacefully to its close.' These words had been drafted on the back of a menu card at Sandringham by the King's doctor, Lord Dawson of Penn. The broadcast was repeated at fifteen-minute intervals. Just after midnight, Reith himself read the final bulletin: 'Death came peacefully to the King at 11.55 p.m.'[95]

During that afternoon, the Archbishop of Canterbury, the Most Reverend Cosmo Gordon Lang, recorded that 'the Queen was still amazingly calm and

[91] Hart-Davis, *In Royal Service: The Letters and Journals of Sir Alan Lascelles*, pp. 194–5.
[92] Sebba, *That Woman: The Life of Wallis Simpson, Duchess of Windsor*, p. 118.
[93] It is slightly surprising that both the heir and the second in line to the throne were allowed to fly together.
[94] Royal Archives: QM/PRIV/QMD/1936.
[95] Ian McIntyre, *The Expense of Glory: A Life of John Reith*, London: HarperCollins, 1993, p. 220.

strong, the Prince of Wales full of vitality and talk, and touchingly attentive to the Queen'.[96] However, after the King's death, according to a memorandum of the same date made by Lord Wigram: 'The Prince of Wales became hysterical, cried loudly, and kept on embracing the Queen.'[97]

On 15 November 1935, Tommy Lascelles had been appointed Assistant Private Secretary to King George V. Six days after the King's death, he wrote a moving account of the service and temporary lying-in at St Mary Magdalene, Sandringham in a letter to Colonel Eric Mackenzie, Comptroller to the Governor-General of Canada:

> During his illness I never saw him at all; but went up to his room after his death, and though, like all our generation, I have seen all too many dead people, none has ever had a more peaceful face.
>
> Next evening we took him over to the little Church at the end of the garden. A dark and windy evening, with flurries of rain; there were not more than a dozen of us, including the Queen and the family; the coffin was on a little wheeled bier, flanked by a few towering Grenadiers from the King's Company; somebody had an electric torch, which was our only light; Forsyth, the King's piper, led us playing a lament I did not know.
>
> As we came round the corner of the shrubbery that screens the Church, we saw the lych-gate brilliantly lit, with Fuller, the Sandringham rector, standing beneath it in his surplice and hood. There was nobody else in sight. The guardsmen, with scarcely a sound, slung the coffin on their shoulders and laid it before the altar; and there, after a very brief service, we left it, to be watched for thirty-six hours by the men of the Sandringham Estate. I daresay that when the tumult and shouting dies, that little ceremony will remain in my mind as the most impressive of all.
>
> The departure from Sandringham was fine, too. After a short service the coffin was laid on a gun-carriage and we, with the King's white shooting-pony, walked behind it to Wolferton station on a perfect winter's morning. The road was lined with people, six and seven deep, all the way. At the top of the hill leading down to the station, a single cock pheasant rocketed across the road, very high, and immediately over the gun-carriage. All

96 Philip Ziegler, *King Edward VIII*, London: Collins, 1990, pp. 240–41.
97 Ibid., p. 241.

> the way to London people were standing bare-headed by the track, on the roads and in the middle of the fields.[98]

What had been intended as a private communication was widely circulated among friends and colleagues in Canada by Eric Mackenzie, which did not greatly please the writer.

The following day, King Edward VIII flew from Norfolk to London, the first time a British monarch had travelled in an aeroplane. Before his departure, Queen Mary wrote in her diary: 'David very brave and helpful, for he has a difficult task before him.'[99]

The Abdication Crisis, 1936

As 1919 drew to a close, the Prince of Wales was forced, against his will, since it meant additional separation from Freda Dudley-Ward just ahead of a trip to Australia, to spend three weeks with his family at Sandringham. Nevertheless, on 3 January 1920, King George V wrote to his Private Secretary: 'Yes, my sons have begun well, particularly the eldest, who has become most popular & has already made a name for himself. They will be of great assistance to me in the future.'[100] He might not have been quite so sanguine if he had known what the Prince of Wales had written to his own Private Secretary, Sir Godfrey Thomas, little more than a week earlier, on Christmas Day:

> I feel quite shy even to write after the bloody way I've been treating you lately & keeping you hanging around & never giving you long enough time to see me & settle all the millions of things that people worry you with!! I jazz around all day & merely send you down heaps & heaps of balls!!
>
> I'm so worried about it all & about YOU & everything; a sort of hopelessly lost feeling has come over me & I think I'm going kind of mad!! I'm overwhelmed with letters (I've just sent you off 2 large parcels by messenger this evening) & bloody Xmas cards & there are all the engagements etc you very rightly want a decision on & then the Admiral & hundreds

[98] Duff Hart-Davis, ed., *King's Counsellor: Abdication and War: The Diaries of Sir Alan Lascelles*, London: Weidenfeld & Nicolson, 2006, pp. 5–6.
[99] Ziegler, *King Edward VIII*, p. 244.
[100] Bigge Papers, quoted in *King George the Fifth: His Life and Reign*, p. 363.

> of big people are putting down a regular barrage of important things to settle!! . . . Please forgive all this tho' I don't ask forgiveness of the way I've treated you. I can't, as I don't deserve it. Forget me for a fortnight.[101]

It is impossible to argue that clear signs of what was to come were not already there, some sixteen years earlier. It was not long before the King himself perceived a subtle change in the fraternal balance, writing to the Duke of York soon after his marriage to Lady Elizabeth Bowes-Lyon on 26 April 1923; 'You have always been so sensible & easy to work with & you have always been ready to listen to any advice & to agree with my opinions about people & things, that I feel we have always got on very well together (very different to dear David).'[102]

Elizabeth Longford recounts how, during her Golden Jubilee Year, Queen Victoria 'insisted on modifying the Prince Consort's strict Court regulations, in order that "poor ladies" who were innocent victims in divorce cases might share her Jubilee. Before the end of the Jubilee Year she had even asked Lord Salisbury if innocent foreign divorcees might also be excluded from the ban. Her Prime Minister advised against: "It is on account of the risk of admitting American women of light character." '[103] Less than 50 years later it was just such an issue that transfixed the country and threatened the monarchy.

On 26 May 1936, Queen Mary wrote in her diary: 'Dull first then sunny. I felt very sad, my first birthday spent without my dear one, for so many years, however I kept up and was much spoilt by everybody & received numberless presents & flowers. David came at 11 to see me before the Levee. He and I gave a family luncheon which went off well & dear U. Arthur made a charming speech when he proposed my health. The band of the Welsh Guards played. When the guests had left I answered telegrams etc. Eva Dugdale came to tea. Alice S. dined with me.'

During his short reign, King Edward VIII made one visit, lasting less than two weeks, to Balmoral. Although traditionally there was an overlap of six months, while the Private Secretary of the old monarch assisted the new monarch, King Edward VIII wanted someone of his own generation – and Alec Hardinge was appointed his Private Secretary. However, he was soon

[101] Hugh Douglas, comp., *A Right Royal Christmas: An Anthology*, Stroud: Sutton, 2001, p. 130, quoted in Ziegler, *King Edward VIII*, p. 122.
[102] Wheeler-Bennett, *King George VI: His Life and Reign*, p. 154.
[103] *Victoria R.I.*, p. 497.

forced to take six months' leave after a breakdown and Lord Wigram was obliged to step back into the breach. His son later wrote of the new King:

> I saw more of him at Balmoral in 1936 when he was King. I played golf with him one day on the private course and he was rather annoyed when I beat him! During this visit Mrs. Simpson was staying with him and I was invited to parties at the Castle on more than one occasion. He definitely did have charm and he took the trouble to talk to me. He was very mean financially and always wanted to save money. Before going to Balmoral he told the Master of the Household that he only wanted to picnic in Scotland and only the absolute minimum of the travelling staff will go from London. The number was reduced to seventy-five persons! Daddy was very relieved when his six months' tour of duty as Private Secretary finished in July 1936, but he was anxious about the future.[104]

Sharing Lord Wigram's concerns, the Duchess of York wrote in some distress from Scotland to Queen Mary on 11 October 1936, shortly after the King's party had left Balmoral, explaining that 'there has also been a great sadness and sense of loss for us and all the people. It will never be quite the same for us . . . David does not seem to possess the faculty for making others feel wanted. It is very sad, and I feel that the whole difficulty is a certain person. I do not feel that I can make advances to her and ask her to our house, as I imagine would be liked, and this fact is bound to make relations a little difficult . . . Has anything transpired about Xmas? Can we all spend it together? Do suggest it to David as he loves and admires you and I am sure would arrange what you wish.'[105]

On 6 November, the Duke of York wrote to his mother: 'I have been meaning to come & see you but I wanted to see David first. He is very difficult to see & when one does he wants to talk about other matters. It is all so worrying & I feel we all live a life of conjecture; never knowing what will happen tomorrow, & then the unexpected comes.'[106]

Charles Fulford, who worked in Windsor Castle Library and lived at 1 The Cloisters, wrote: 'In December murmurs of abdication began to be heard, &, as time went on, the atmosphere here became almost electric. People in authority were all alarmed lest some patched up arrangement

[104] Neville, 2nd Baron Wigram, *Some Memoirs of My Early Life*, privately published 2002.
[105] Ziegler, *King Edward VIII*, pp. 289–90.
[106] Wheeler-Bennett, *King George VI: His Life and Reign*, pp. 282–3.

should be arrived at, knowing that as King he would not be a success, & knowing, too, what admirable alternatives there were.'[107]

There was to be no happy family Christmas – with reconciliation at its core – that year. On 9 December 1936, Queen Mary wrote in her diary: 'Rather foggy day. At 1.30 with Mary to meet David (on business) at the Royal Lodge. Back before 5. Georgie and Marina dined. Bertie arrived very late from Fort Belvedere and Mr. W. Monkton [sic] brought him & me the paper drawn up for David's abdication of this Empire because he wishes to marry Mrs. Simpson!!!! The whole affair has lasted since Nov 16th and has been very painful. It is a terrible blow to us all & particularly to poor Bertie.'[108] The following day she wrote: 'Dark gloomy day. I saw Lord Salisbury & the P.M. At 3 to Piccadilly to see Elizabeth who was in bed with a cold, too unlucky. The P.M. made his announcement in the house about David's final decision – which was received in silence & with real regret. The more one thinks of this affair the more regrettable it becomes.'[109]

The nation was split; two days later, the Archbishop of Canterbury made a controversial – and critical – broadcast, which prompted the prolific novelist, poet and satirist, Gerald Bullett, to write:

> My Lord Archbishop, what a scold you are!
> And when your man is down, how bold you are!
> Of charity how oddly scant you are!
> How Lang O Lord, how full of Cantuar!

On Christmas Eve, Queen Mary was not feeling herself: 'Arranged some of the Xmas tables with E. Opened letters & parcels. At 3 our guests arrived – Gloucesters, Alge & Alice, Cambridges & Mary, & Dick Molyneux. After tea we had the Xmas tree & presents. At dinner I nearly choked myself with my awful cough and had to go to bed early.' If anything, Christmas Day was worse: 'The cough still a nuisance I made up my mind to stay in my room (not in bed) until I felt better. A great disappointment. The family visited me at intervals & Alice kindly read to me.' On a rainy New Year's Day, 'we all wished each other a happy New Year'.[110] For the Royal

[107] The Diary of C. H. Fulford Esq – courtesy of Francis Fulford Esq.
[108] Wheeler-Bennett, *King George VI*, p. 286, note b. Walter Monckton, 1st Viscount Monckton of Brenchley, adviser to King Edward VIII, Attorney-General to the Duchy of Cornwall 1932–6, Minister of Labour and National Service 1951–5, Minister of Defence 1955–6, Paymaster-General 1956–7.
[109] Royal Archives: QM/PRIV/QMD/1936.
[110] Royal Archives: QM/PRIV/QMD/1937.

Family, the year just ended could hardly have been worse. Tommy Lascelles, newly appointed Assistant Private Secretary to King George VI, wrote to his wife from Sandringham; 'Queen Mary is nursing a cough, and don't appear much. The other Queen is delightful, and the children are admirably brought up.'[111]

Immediately after the Abdication, the Duke of Windsor went to stay at Schloss Enzesfeld in Austria, lent to him by Eugene de Rothschild. From there he wrote to Wallis Simpson on 22 December 1936:

> I just don't know how to begin to write to you when I have so much that can only be 'oohed' and said. Oh! my sweetheart the thought of the next four months' separation is an agony and just not possible to think about. I am forcing myself to pretend that I'm only away from you because I'm on a job in this country and you can't come here for business reasons! Otherwise I would have gone mad already and I've only been here ten days – ten days that have passed very slowly and with the most monotonous precision. But who cares darling how they are spent and maybe they will pass quicker later on. And now we have Christmas the nearest we have ever been to spending it together although we are further away in distance. But a boy is holding a girl so so tight Wallis . . .
>
> Oh! my beloved I am only living for the 27th April (maybe sooner who knows) and only live now for our telephone talks in the evening. WE have to thank God for that instrument just now or it really would be just too unbearable. I seem only to have talked about me till now. I know what hurt feelings you have had and that has made me so unhappy. But that was the fault of the King not of David not that it stops the hurt feelings. I could not have believed how cruel and inhuman the American newspaper business is until one has become their 'meat' as WE have . . . It's pathetic but we'll just have to write this Christmas off and make up for it by so many lovely happy ones in the future. I will go to Church in Vienna on Friday for eleven o'clock service and pray so hard that God goes on blessing WE for the rest of our lives. He has been very good to WE and is watching over US I know. I have so much more to say my sweetheart but I want you to get this for Christmas so will enclose it in a cover address to Herman and mail it now. I love you love you Wallis more and more and more and am holding you so tight.'[112]

[111] Hart-Davis, *King's Counsellor: Abdication and War: The Diaries of Sir Alan Lascelles*, pp. 6–7.
[112] Bloch, *Wallis & Edward: Letters 1931–37*, pp. 235-6.

In his diary, Tommy Lascelles confided that 'Selby, our minister in Vienna, writes that the Duke of Windsor volunteered to go to the English church on Christmas day and read the lesson. When I think of the hours we have all spent trying to get him to go to church in various parts of the British Empire, this makes me furious. And as for reading the lesson – ! There is no doubt that the family generally regarded him as potty, but his eldest brother is very nice about him, and very anxious to do what he can to help.' Fortunately, things soon settled down and he wrote to his wife on 4 January 1937: 'HM took me for a long walk this afternoon. I really like him awfully, and he talks to me, and I to him, with a naturalness that was never there with the other man.'[113] He had, after all, been the Prince of Wales's Assistant Private Secretary between 1920 and his resignation in 1928.

Charles Fulford wrote:

> While King Edward VIII reigned no one about the Court felt secure – people were being dismissed right & left from the highest to the lowest, & for no apparent reason; but now they felt at once they were safe. The new King & Queen were not so well known generally, but their domestic life was recognised as being based on the highest principles, and as Sir John Hanbury Williams, who had been intimately acquainted with the Dominions as Military Sec^{y} in Canada & S. Africa, said to me: 'The one thing that binds the Empire together is the private life of the Royal Family. That was why George V was such a success, & that is why the new King & Queen will do well.'[114]

Wallis Simpson spent Christmas Day 'at Somerset Maugham's *Villa Mauresque* at Cap Ferrat, with Sybil Colefax attempting to cheer her up'.[115] In late December, she wrote to the Duke from Villa Lou Viei, Cannes, where she was staying with her old friends, Herman and Katherine Rogers: 'Give this to whoever is doing the job. It was a large jar of the nuts we like from Honolulu so you can have them say how much you like them. I am getting rather worked up about what support we are going to get from your family for our wedding. It is so important – everyone around me realizes the importance of it re announcement etc. After all we have done nothing wrong so why be treated that way. It is not the first marriage to a commoner

[113] Hart-Davis, *King's Counsellor: Abdication and War: The Diaries of Sir Alan Lascelles*, pp. 6–7.
[114] The Diary of C. H. Fulford Esq., courtesy of Francis Fulford, Esq.
[115] Sebba, *That Woman: The Life of Wallis Simpson, Duchess of Windsor*, p. 192.

in the family. Really David the pleased expression on the Duchess of York's [sic] face is funny to see. How she is loving it all. There will be no support there. PS I've had an Xmas card from Mae West!'[116]

On 4 May 1937 – eight days before the Coronation – the Duke of Windsor and Wallis Simpson were reunited at the Château de Candé, which belonged to Charles Bedaux, a Franco-American millionaire industrialist. Following the introductory hymn, 'O Perfect Love', they were married there on 3 June 1937, Wallis having been given away by Herman Rogers. In his brief memoir, Lord Wigram concluded that 'the country was lucky that he abdicated: Mrs. Simpson had a devastating influence over him . . . I was invited to a party at the Castle and at the buffet supper the King came up to me and said: "I should like you to meet an old friend of mine, Mrs. Simpson," implying to me that I had never heard of her! We talked for about a quarter of an hour. She had a hard face but a very good figure and was beautifully dressed. She was also a clever conversationalist. I was then at Oxford and she flattered me by asking all sorts of questions about history and obviously knew very little herself. Sex was obviously her main attraction to the King.'[117] Lord Wigram told me that 'we really ought to be grateful to Mrs. Simpson for not allowing him to be our King'.

On 22 December 1937, the Duke of Windsor wrote to the new Prime Minister, Neville Chamberlain:

> When I decided to give up the throne last December, I realized that the only dignified and sensible course for me to follow, was to leave the country for a period, the length of which was naturally to be determined by a number of considerations. But I never intended, nor would I ever have agreed, to renounce my native land or my right to return to it – for all time. If my understanding of the present situation is correct, it is now proposed that my personal freedom in this respect be linked with a private family arrangement on financial matters which my brother, the present King, made with me the day before I abdicated, in such a way, that he would be permitted to break his private agreement with me if I were to exercise my right to visit my country, without first obtaining his approval under the advice of ministers.
>
> I regard such a proposal as both unfair and intolerable, as it would amount to accepting payment for remaining in exile . . . It is hardly necessary for me to repeat to you my loyalty to my brother as king; nor as a patriotic Englishman could I countenance any disruptive action in others.

[116] Bloch, *Wallis & Edward: Letters 1931–37*, p. 238.
[117] Neville, 2nd Baron Wigram, *Some Memoirs of my Early Life.*

> But I cannot refrain from saying, with the frankness you would expect of me, that the treatment which has been meted out to my wife and myself since last December, has caused us acute pain.[118]

There were aspects of the exile that the Duke and Duchess of Windsor attempted to make as English as possible. In 1938 they rented Château La Cröe, Cap d'Antibes, which had been built a decade earlier for Sir William Pomeroy Burton, Chairman of Associated Newspapers. The Duke's Private Secretary, Dina Wells Hood, described the first Christmas in their new home:

> On Christmas morning, which was fine and sunny, the Duke and Duchess attended the service at the little English church on the road to Antibes. Being the parish church of La Cröe, they made a point of supporting it both by subscriptions and by occasional attendances. Among the Christmas cheques there was always one for the local padre. After Church the whole household assembled in the big lounge. The house party came too and a few guests from the neighbourhood. The great silver and white Christmas tree standing by the terrace windows was visible from end to end of the château and its glittering branches were reflected back and forth in the tall mirrored panelling of the room. Piled round the base of the tree were heaps of small parcels in bright Christmas wrappings.
>
> La Cröe that morning had more than ever the air of a large English country house. The Christmas morning ceremony added a touch of friendly old-world feudalism to the scene. The servants filed up one after another to receive their gifts, bowing or curtseying to Their Royal Highnesses. Standing beside the great white tree, the Duke and Duchess smilingly handed out the presents. For each they had a kindly word of greeting. From butler to pantry boy, from chef to under-gardener, every servant was individually remembered. The Duchess herself had chosen and wrapped up all the gifts, not only for her guests but for each member of her staff as well. She presented me with a very lovely set of beauty preparations.'[119]

The city of Paris later offered the Windsors a town house in the Bois de Boulogne. They alternated between Paris and their country home, Le Moulin de la Tuilerie, in the town of Gif-sur-Yvette, twenty miles south-west of the city. On 17 November 1993, Diana, Lady Mosley wrote

[118] Michael Bloch, *The Duke of Windsor's War*, London: Weidenfeld & Nicolson, 1982, pp. 7–8.
[119] Dina Wells Hood, *Working for the Windsors*, London: Allen Wingate, 1957, p. 56.

to John Wieneman: 'My husband [Sir Oswald Mosley] & I nearly always had Christmas dinner with the Windsors, invited by Countess Bismarck, who had a lovely house in Paris . . . Countess Bismarck made it a lovely English Christmas for the Duke: turkey, plum pudding & a Christmas tree.'[120]

The Queen Mother and Princess Margaret in London and at Sandringham, 2001

By the end of 2001, the Queen Mother's long life was drawing slowly to a close, while her younger daughter was confined to a wheelchair, after suffering a stroke that March. Hugo Vickers wrote:

> The Queen Mother did not attend the 100th birthday parade for Princess Alice at Kensington Palace on 12 December, not because she was afraid of upstaging her but because she thought a line-up of wheelchairs would make a depressing image. At the parade Princess Alice (who could walk with help) sat between the Queen and Princess Margaret, her bridesmaids from 1935. The Queen Mother's instincts were sound. She sent flowers instead.
>
> Later that month the Queen Mother had a fall in the night, of which she made little. She did not cancel a private lunch engagement despite being in some discomfort, and no one there would ever have guessed that anything was wrong. The following day there was the Household party at St James's Palace, which she attended in a wheelchair, rising many times from this in order to speak to the various guests. And the day after that, there was the Household Christmas lunch.
>
> The next day, as the year before, the Queen Mother and Princess Margaret set off in the helicopter from Kensington Palace. Whereas Princess Margaret was muffled against the cold, Queen Elizabeth was in a purple coat, with pearls, and no scarf to protect her neck. Only when she arrived at Sandringham did the Queen Mother see the doctor and find she had a fractured pelvis.
>
> The Queen was alone at Sandringham when the helicopter landed. First came her mother in a wheelchair and then her sister, also in a wheel-chair. It heralded a worrying Christmas. Neither of them was well enough to go to the Christmas services, though the Queen Mother managed one visit to the royal stud. When the holiday was over, Princess Margaret, who was not entitled to a helicopter on her own, was taken back to London by car.[121]

[120] Courtesy of Hugo Vickers Esq.

[121] Hugo Vickers, *Elizabeth The Queen Mother*, London: Arrow Books, 2006, p. 495.

Princess Margaret died in the King Edward VII Hospital on 9 February 2002, while the Queen Mother died at Royal Lodge, Windsor Great Park on 30 March 2002.

The Illness of the Duke of Edinburgh, 2011

On the afternoon of Friday, 23 December 2011, the Duke of Edinburgh, who was suffering from chest pains, was flown by helicopter from Sandringham to Papworth Hospital, near Huntingdon. In a procedure known as angioplasty, the Duke had a stent inserted in an artery in order to relieve a blockage preventing a free flow of blood to the heart. Although the Duke remained in hospital over the Christmas period, the Queen and their four children took a twenty-minute helicopter flight to Papworth on Christmas Eve, while their six eldest grandchildren visited him on Christmas Day. According to the *Daily Telegraph*, the Prince of Wales said that his father was 'resilient' and 'very determined'. Although the Duke was able to enjoy a traditional Christmas lunch, it was the first time that he had missed family celebrations since 1956 when he was in the Southern Ocean on board HMY *Britannia* during a four-month world tour.

For Christmas 2011, the Queen and the Duke of Edinburgh invited twenty-seven members of the family to stay at Sandringham. In her Christmas Broadcast, which had been recorded on 9 December, the Queen said: 'The importance of family has, of course, come home to Prince Philip and me personally this year with the marriages of two of our grandchildren, each in their own way a celebration of the God-given love that binds a family together.' She wore her diamond and platinum 'Flame Lily' brooch, a twenty-first birthday present from the children of Southern Rhodesia. As well as showing sympathy and support for the Duke of Edinburgh, the gathering of more than 3,000 well-wishers – some three times larger than normal – outside the church of St Mary Magdalene, Sandringham on Christmas morning was attributed to the presence, for the first time, of the Duchess of Cambridge. When the Duke of Edinburgh was discharged from hospital on the morning on 27 December, Buckingham Palace released a statement: 'On departure Prince Philip thanked the staff at Papworth for the excellent care he has received during his stay. He is very much looking forward to rejoining his family.' The Duke walked to St Mary Magdalene on New Year's Day.

Christmas and Conflict during the Long Reign of Queen Victoria

The Perennial Problem of Princes

The Reverend A. H. Hore wrote that King George II had 'no quality except that of bravery (which seems to have been hereditary in the family) to recommend him to the English nation'.[1] Indeed, three of King George I's five brothers were killed in action, two while fighting the Ottoman Empire in 1690–91, during the War of the Palatine Succession, and one who drowned in the Danube while fighting the French in 1703. The bellicose tradition was continued by King George I's only son, King George II, who was the last British monarch to lead troops in action when he commanded the so-called 'Pragmatic Army' at the Battle of Dettingen, in Bavaria, on 27 June 1743, during the War of the Austrian Succession.

However, he was not the last ruler of his country to see active service. Prince William Henry, later the Duke of Clarence and subsequently King William IV, was present at the Battle of Cape St Vincent on 16 January 1780, in which seven Spanish vessels were either captured or destroyed. A week earlier, Admiral Sir George Rodney had manned a captured Spanish flagship, the sixty-four-gun *Guipuzcuana*, as an escort for the voyage back to Britain. He named her HMS *Prince William*, in honour of the Prince, who had also been present at that engagement, during which a Spanish convoy was captured off Cape Finisterre.

On 30 July 1882, Lord Granville wrote to the Duke of Cambridge about the Prince of Wales and the Egyptian Campaign: 'It is highly creditable to the pluck and spirit of the Prince to run the risks both to health and to life which the campaign offers, but it is clearly undesirable that H.R.H. should go. This is one of the penalties which attach to his high position.'[2] The following day, Sir Henry Ponsonby wrote to the Prince of Wales, on behalf of Queen Victoria:

[1] A. H. Hore, *The Church in England from William III to Victoria*, Oxford: Parker and Co., 1886, p. 275.
[2] Sidney Lee, *King Edward VII: A Biography: From Birth to Accession*, Macmillan & Co., 1925, p. 457.

> Y.R.H.'s gallant offer of joining the expedition to Egypt has greatly troubled the Queen. H.M. agreed with Y.R.H.'s desire to be of use, and warmly appreciated the gallant wish to see service. But the imperative demands of public duty compelled H.M. to point out the grave difficulties and inconveniences of such a proceeding, and having been advised by the Government as well as several leaders of the Opposition that it would be inexpedient and most unwise, considering Y.R.H.'s rank and position, to join the expedition as a spectator and impossible for Y.R.H. to be attached to it on duty, the Queen has finally and conclusively decided that it was necessary to ask Y.R.H. to abandon the idea. But H.M. was so pleased at the proposal having been made and so convinced that it would be heartily appreciated by everyone, that I think the Queen would be glad if it were made generally known.[3]

This may have struck the Prince of Wales as slightly harsh since his brother, Prince Arthur, Duke of Connaught, commanded the Guards Brigade at the Battle of Tel-el-Kebir in September 1882. On 17 November that year Queen Victoria received her victorious troops, writing in her Journal that her third son 'looked so like his beloved Father I felt quite overcome'.[4] However, the Duke of Connaught later failed in his attempts to serve in the Second Anglo-Boer War. On 29 December 1882, Queen Victoria wrote to Crown Princess Frederick: 'The end of a year is always rather tragic and the older one grows the fewer new ones one can expect to see, the more serious it becomes. But one can only trust and pray that He, who has ever protected us and ordered all for the best, will continue to guide us and help us. This past one has been – after the dreadful one of '61 – the most eventful of my life, as it took one (and almost the dearest one of all my children) into the dangers of a war and brought him out gloriously and safely. These feelings will ever, ever be engraven on my grateful heart.'[5]

Prince Albert, later the Duke of York and King George VI, was a sub-lieutenant serving in HMS *Collingwood* during the Battle of Jutland, 31 May–2 June 1916. HMS *Collingwood* was the twentieth battleship from 'the head of the line' and the Prince was commander of 'A' turret, on the forecastle deck. After the battle, Captain J. C. Lay wrote to King George V:

[3] Arthur Ponsonby, *Henry Ponsonby, Queen Victoria's Private Secretary: His Life from his Letters*, London: Macmillan & Co., 1942, p. 107.

[4] Elizabeth Longford, *Victoria R.I.*, London: Weidenfeld & Nicolson, 1964, p. 449.

[5] Roger Fulford, ed., *Beloved Mama: Private Correspondence of Queen Victoria and the Crown Princess of Prussia 1878–1885*, London: Evans Brothers, 1981, p. 130.

'Prince Albert was in bed on the sick list when we prepared for action, but got up and went to his turret, where he remained until we finally secured guns next day. Though his food that evening was of an unusual description, I am glad to tell your Majesty that he has been quite well since and looks quite well again.'[6]

In the Prince's own words: 'We opened fire at 5.37 p.m. on some German light cruisers. The "Collingwood's" second salvo hit one of them which set her on fire, and sank after two more salvoes were fired into her. We then shifted on to another light cruiser and helped to sink her as well. Our next target was a battle cruiser, we think the "Derrflinger" [sic] or "Lutzow", and one of "Collingwood's" salvoes hit her abaft the after turret, which burst into a fierce flame. After this she turned away from us and disappeared into the mist. By this time it was too dark to fire and we went to Night defence stations.'[7] Although straddled 'several times', HMS *Collingwood* remained unhit and suffered no casualties during the action. Prince Albert concluded that 'it was certainly a great experience to have been through and it shows that we are at war and that the Germans can fight if they like'.[8]

By contrast, his elder brother, the Prince of Wales, gave expression to the perennial problem of princes in his diary in August 1914. On 3 August, the day before war was declared, he wrote:

> At 11.30 the kits of the men of the service squad were inspected, followed by stables, & I got back here at 1.45 after lunch. I returned terribly depressed as of course the only topic was the war, & I haven't the remotest chance of getting out with the expeditionary force. The knowledge that I must remain in London (for some time anyhow) totally devoid of a job of any description, is becoming almost intolerable . . . After seeing the parents, I went off to the B.C. [Bath Club] at 3.00 & had another knock-up, merely to take my mind off the eternal subject; if only I could get some employment . . . Thank God the govt. have decided that France shall not be deserted. Oh!! God; the whole thing is too big to comprehend!! Oh!! that I had a job.[9]

[6] Harold Nicolson, *King George the Fifth: His Life and Reign*, London: Constable & Co., p. 278.
[7] John W. Wheeler-Bennett, *King George VI: His Life and Reign*, London: Macmillan and Co., 1958, p. 94.
[8] Nicolson, *King George the Fifth: His Life and Reign*, p. 279.
[9] Royal Archives: EDW/PRIV/DIARY/1914, quoted in Philip Ziegler, *King Edward VIII*, London: Collins, 1990, pp. 48–9.

On 12 December 1939, Captain Lord Louis Mountbatten wrote from HMS *Kelly* to Captain (later Vice-Admiral) H. T. Baillie-Grohman, captain of the veteran battleship, HMS *Ramillies*:

> I believe there is a sporting chance that my nephew, Philip of Greece, may be sent to you as a Midshipman in the New Year. He is the son of my eldest sister, who married Prince Andrew of Greece, who is the uncle of the present King. This lad's education started in France. He then went to a German Public School at his brother in law's Castle Salem in Baden and completed his education at a British Public School, Gordonstoun. I have had the most glowing accounts of him from Dartmouth and hope he will do you well if you get him.
>
> Both our King and the King of Greece have agreed that it is desirable, as far as possible, to avoid his being deliberately placed in a 'War Zone' as Greece is still legally a neutral Country. Provided the King of Greece agrees that he does not mind his young cousin running the normal risks of war, I have no doubt that the appointment will be made. Philip himself is mad keen to go as you may imagine. I need hardly stress how important it is that he should be treated as an ordinary 'snotty' unless you happen to go to a Greek port, where he would naturally be treated as a Prince of that Country by his Countrymen. I have just had a few days' leave during a refit and am off to sea again now. P.S. Very best wishes for Xmas.[10]

In early 1940, Prince Philip duly joined HMS *Ramillies* in Colombo, spending six months on convoy duty, escorting the Australian Expeditionary Force across the Indian Ocean. Greece did not enter the war until 28 October 1940, when the Italian Army invaded the country. Prince Philip was mentioned in despatches for his effective control of the searchlights of the battleship HMS *Valiant* during the Battle of Cape Matapan on 21 March 1941. The captain wrote: 'Thanks to his alertness and appreciation of the situation, we were able to sink in five minutes two eight-inch-gun Italian cruisers.'[11] Prince Philip was also awarded the Greek Cross of Valour.

In his Foreword to *Dark Seas: The Battle of Cape Matapan* (2012), the Duke of Edinburgh wrote: 'I seem to remember that I reported that I had a target in sight, and was ordered to 'open shutter'. The beam lit up a

[10] On display in the ballroom at Sandringham House in 2011 as part of an exhibition celebrating the Royal Navy career of the Duke of Edinburgh.

[11] Wheeler-Bennett, *King George VI: His Life and Reign*, p. 749.

stationary cruiser, but we were so close by then that the beam only lit up half the ship. At this point all hell broke loose, as all our 15-inch guns, plus those of the flagship and *Barham*'s started firing at the stationary cruiser, which disappeared in an explosion and a cloud of smoke. I was then ordered to 'train left' and lit up another Italian cruiser, which was given the same treatment.'

HMS *Kelly*, with Lord Louis Mountbatten still in command, was sunk off the coast of Crete by German dive-bombers on 23 May 1941. In a letter to his sister Louise, Crown Princess of Sweden, Lord Louis wrote: 'At this moment up bobbed one of our stoker petty officers, a great character and a bit of a humorist. He looked at the "pilot" and then at me and then produced a typically cheery crack, "Extraordinary how the scum always comes to the top, isn't it, sir?" '[12]

During times of desperate need members of the Royal Family have always been among the first to volunteer and to see action. Having joined the Royal Navy in 1979, Prince Andrew, now the Duke of York, was second pilot of a Sea King helicopter of 820 Squadron, flying from HMS *Invincible* during the 1982 Falklands War. He flew on anti-submarine and Exocet missile decoy missions, as well as assisting with casualty evacuation and search-and-rescue operations. Having been commissioned into the Blues and Royals in 2006, Prince Harry spent seventy-seven days as a Forward Air Controller, directing ground-attack aircraft, in Helmand Province in Afghanistan in 2007–8, before reports in a German newspaper, on an American website and in an Australian women's magazine prompted his recall on the grounds that he was a high-profile kidnap target – although he went back there in 2012.

Prince Harry's great-great-uncle, Air Commodore the Duke of Kent, was killed on 25 August 1942 when a Short S-25 Sunderland Mark III flying boat, in which he was flying to Newfoundland via Iceland, crashed into Eagle Rock near Dunbeath, Caithness in low and dense cloud conditions. In his diary, King George VI wrote: 'This news came as a great shock to me, & I had to break it to Elizabeth, & Harry & Alice who were staying with us. He was killed on Active Service. We left Balmoral in the evening for London.'[13] In the House of Commons the Prime Minister, Winston Churchill, said: 'The loss of this gallant and handsome Prince, in the prime of his life, has been a shock and a sorrow to the people of the British Empire, standing out

[12] Philip Ziegler, *Mountbatten*, London: Collins, 1990, p. 145.

[13] Wheeler-Bennett, *King George VI: His Life and Reign*, p. 548.

lamentably even in these hard days of war. To His Majesty the King it is the loss of a dearly loved brother, and it has affected him most poignantly.'[14]

The King visited the crash site on 14 September 1942, writing in his diary: 'The impact must have been terrific as the aircraft as an aircraft was unrecognisable when found. I felt I had to do this pilgrimage.'[15] There was only one survivor from the crew of fifteen. The Princess Royal went to stay at Badminton House with Queen Mary, who wrote, eight days after the crash: 'We worked very well & it did us both good – I am so glad I can take up my occupations again – Georgie wld have wished me to do so.'[16] The Duke's death had a long-lasting impact on his elder brother, who started to put his affairs in order. On 13 January 1943 the King wrote in his diary that, 'ever since George's death, these matters loom large in one's mind as one must be prepared for all eventualities'.[17]

Whether on active service or not, members of the Royal Family have inevitably been deeply involved in – and affected by – conflict at Christmas.

Rights of Navigation on the Douro/Duero, 1840

In November 1840 Spain threatened to invade Portugal as a result of a disagreement that had arisen over rights of navigation on the Douro (Duero in Spanish), a 560-mile long river, the lower one-eighth – and only navigable part – of which forms the border between the two countries. Portugal swiftly raised an army in defence of its interests. At Windsor Castle on Christmas Eve, Queen Victoria wrote in her Journal:

> Soon after 5, Lord Melbourne came. We talked of the awkward state of Spain & Portugal, the latter having refused to ratify a Treaty with Spain about the navigation of the Douro, & instead of acting in the right way, Spain has marched an army to the frontier, threatening to enter Portugal immediately, if she does not ratify. We hope by our mediation & advice, to be able to settle the matter. The Portuguese are in the wrong, Lord M. said, but the Spaniards act in a most extraordinary manner. We are bound by our Treaties, which are of very long standing, to assist Portugal, if she is attacked. However, he hopes that if we send the Fleet there, then we shall

[14] *Hansard*, 8 September 1942, Vol. 383.

[15] Wheeler-Bennett, *King George VI: His Life and Reign*, pp. 548–9.

[16] James Pope-Hennessy, *Queen Mary*, London: George Allen and Unwin, 1959, p. 608.

[17] Wheeler-Bennett, *King George VI: His Life and Reign*, p. 558.

> stop the Spaniards. But Spain being also our ally, makes things somewhat awkward for us.'

On Christmas Day, 'Lord Melbourne came to see me [and] read me a letter from Howard de Walden, saying that the Portuguese were furious at Spain's conduct, and one from Palmerston about a quarrel of the French Consul with the Emperor of Morocco about a Mohamedan servant, the former striking him a blow. As we fear the French may make this a pretext for taking Morocco, P. proposes that we should advise the Emperor of Morocco to make up with the French, which is the best way.'[18] In the event, the Portuguese–Spanish dispute was peacefully resolved through diplomatic channels on 15 January 1841. In her speech at the Opening of Parliament on 24 August 1841, the Queen said: 'Her Majesty is happy to inform you, that the differences which had arisen between Spain and Portugal, about the execution of a treaty concluded by those Powers in 1835, for regulating the navigation of the Douro, have been adjusted amicably, and with honour to both parties, by the aid of her Majesty's mediation.'[19] The Franco-Moroccan War did not break out until 1844.

The Crimean War, 1854–6

The Crimean War – in which Britain, France, the Ottoman Empire and the Kingdom of Sardinia confronted Russia – had, as its ultimate cause, the struggle for recognition of 'sovereign authority' in the Holy Land, associated with the guardianship of the Holy Places. Soon after the coup d'état that brought Napoleon III to power in 1851, his ambassador to the Sublime Porte in Constantinople insisted that the Turks acknowledge French 'sovereign authority', which derived from an agreement in 1740. The emissaries of Tsar Nicholas I argued equally forcibly that, according to treaties dating from 1757 and 1774, Russia was the protector of Orthodox Christians in the Ottoman Empire. Two years of feverish diplomatic negotiations failed to resolve the issue and a British expeditionary force set sail for the Black Sea in April 1854.

In the manner that typified her sixty-three years on the throne, Queen Victoria was devoted not only to the cause, but also to the suffering soldiery,

[18] Royal Archives: VIC/MAIN/QVJ/1840.
[19] *Hansard*, 24 August 1841.

particularly at Christmas-time. On Christmas Eve 1853, the Queen wrote in her Journal:

> Alas! as the 2 preceding years, the joy of the season was much spoilt by the anxiety respecting external & internal Politics. Took a short walk after luncheon. On coming home we found Lord Aberdeen come & saw him immediately. He said he had come to inform me of the state of the negociations [sic] with Lord Palmerston, & then read the latter's letter to him & his admirable answer, written since he got here. I annex copies of both. For what passed between us I will make use of a Memorandum by Albert, the greater part of which I will copy. Lord Aberdeen said that some of his colleagues, Sir C. Wood, the Duke of Newcastle, & Mr. Gladstone, had been very anxious that Lord Palmerston should be readmitted into the Cabinet & had had interviews with him, in which he had expressed his hope to be allowed to reconsider the step he had taken. Lady Palmerston had been most urgent with her husband on this point, saying 'this must be arranged & settled,' & working herself into a great state of excitement, to get him back again into the Govt. All the people most conversant with the H^{se} of C. stated that the Gov^{t} had no chance of going on with Lord Palmerston in the Opposition & with the present temper of the public which was greatly excited about the Oriental Question, & the disaster at Sinope.'[20]

On 30 November 1853 a Russian squadron, commanded by Admiral Nakhimov, destroyed a Turkish force that had taken shelter at Sinope in northern Anatolia.

After the British Commander-in-Chief, Field Marshal Lord Raglan, died on 29 June 1855 of a combination of dysentery and a broken heart after the failure of the British assault on the Redan, one of the linchpins of the defence of the fortress city of Sebastopol, Queen Victoria wrote to his widow:

> Words cannot convey all I feel at the irreparable loss you have sustained, and I and the country feel also, in your noble, gallant, and excellent husband, whose loyalty and devotion to his sovereign and country were unbounded. We both feel most deeply for you and your daughters, to whom this blow must be most severe and sudden. He was so strong, and

[20] Royal Archives: VIC/MAIN/QVJ/1853.

> his health had borne the bad climate, the great fatigues and anxieties, so well, ever since he left England, that, though we were much alarmed at hearing of his illness, we were full of hopes of his speedy recovery. We must bow to the will of God! But to be taken away thus, on the eve of the successful result of so much labor, so much suffering, and so much anxiety, is hard indeed! We feel, too, for the brave army, whom he was so proud of, and who will be sadly cast down at losing their gallant commander, who had led them so often to victory and glory. If sympathy can be any consolation you have it, for we all have alike to mourn, and no one more than I, who have lost a faithful and devoted servant in whom I had the greatest confidence.'[21]

Two months later, she wrote to her uncle Leopold: 'The great event has at length taken place – Sebastopol has fallen! We received the news here last night when we were sitting quietly round our table after dinner. We did what we could to celebrate it; but that was but little, for to my grief we have not one soldier, no band, nothing here to make any sort of demonstration. What we did do was in Highland fashion to light a bonfire on the top of a hill opposite the house, which had been built last year when the premature news of the fall of Sebastopol deceived every one, and which we had to leave unlit, and found here on our return!'[22]

Over the following Christmas period, Queen Victoria interested herself in anything that might help improve the conditions in which the Army lived, after so many of her soldiers had died the previous winter. On 22 December 1855 she wrote to Lord Panmure, Secretary at War:

> The Queen has received Lord Panmure's answer to her letter from Osborne, and is glad to see from it that he is quite agreed with the Queen on the subject of the Land Transport Corps. She would most strongly urge Lord Panmure to give at once carte blanche to Sir W. Codrington to organise it as he thinks best, and to make him personally responsible for it. We have only eight weeks left to the beginning of spring; a few references home and their answers would consume the whole of that time! The Army has now to carry their huts on their backs up to the Camp;

[21] The Marquis of Lorne (now His Grace The Duke of Argyll), *VRI: Queen Victoria: Her Life and Empire*, London: Harper & Brothers, 1901, pp. 235–6.
[22] George Earle Buckle, ed., *The Letters of Queen Victoria, Third Series: A Selection from Her Majesty's Correspondence between the Years 1886 and 1901*, 3 vols., London: John Murray, 1930–32 (LQV I), Vol. III, p. 180.

> if it had been fighting, it would have perished for want of them, like the last winter. If each Division, Brigade, and Battalion has not got within itself what it requires for its daily existence in the field, a movement will be quite impossible. The Queen approves the intended increase of Artillery and Sappers and Miners; but hopes that these will be taken away from the nominal and not the existing strength of the Army.'[23]

Just after the Twelfth Night in 1856 she wrote another letter to Lord Panmure, in connection with the eponymous award with which she is now most closely associated. Her very practical words of wisdom ring down the years: 'The Queen returns the drawings for the "Victoria Cross." She has marked the one she approves with an X; she thinks, however, that it might be a trifle smaller. The motto would be better "For Valour" than "For the Brave," as this would lead to the inference that only those are deemed brave who have got the Victoria Cross.'[24]

At least five individuals who were awarded the Victoria Cross were members of the Royal Household during her reign: Captain Robert James Loyd-Lindsay (later 1st Baron Wantage), then serving with the Scots Fusilier Guards, for his 'example and energy' at the Battles of the Alma and Inkerman during the Crimean War (Equerry to the Prince of Wales 1858–9); South African-born Lieutenant (later Major-General Sir) Christopher Charles Teesdale, Royal Artillery, for his gallantry at the defence of Kars, also during the Crimean War (subsequently Master of the Ceremonies and Extra Equerry to the Prince of Wales); Captain (later Major-General Sir) Howard Crauford Elphinstone, then serving with the Royal Engineers, who was awarded the VC for 'fearless conduct' during the night after the abortive assault on the Redan during the Crimean War (subsequently Tutor to both Princes Alfred and Leopold); Captain (later General Sir) Dighton Probyn, then serving with the 2nd Punjab Cavalry, Bengal Army, for his courage and steadfastness at the Battle of Agra, during the Indian Mutiny (subsequently Keeper of the Privy Purse, Secretary to the Prince of Wales and Comptroller of the Household); and Lieutenant (later Colonel) Arthur Pickard, then serving with the Royal Artillery, for 'gallant conduct during the assault on the Rangiriri Redoubt' in New Zealand on 20 November 1863 (subsequently Assistant Private Secretary to Queen Victoria 1878–80).

[23] Ibid., p. 200.
[24] Ibid., p. 203.

The Treaty of Paris, which brought the Crimean War to an end, was signed at the Congress of Paris on 30 March 1856. Queen Victoria never forgot the Crimean War, heading her journal entry for 5 November 1877 'Inkerman Day'.[25] The following year, though, she wrote: 'Remember, remember the 5th of November, gunpowder, treason, and plot.'[26]

The Neuchâtel Question, 1856–7

No sooner had the Treaty of Paris been signed than another vexatious European 'question' arose. Essentially this was an early example of sabre-rattling by Prussia, something with which Europe was to become only too familiar during the next nine decades. Having been part of Prussia since 1707, the Principality of Neuchâtel had been occupied by Emperor Napoleon I in the early nineteenth century, before returning to Prussia in 1814 and joining the Swiss Confederation the following year. In 1848 – the year of revolutions – the Principality rose against Prussian rule.

Some idea of the atmosphere of those turbulent times can be gauged from a letter that Queen Louise of the Belgians, eldest daughter of King Louis Philippe I of France, wrote to Queen Victoria from Brussels on 28 February 1848: 'What a misfortune! What an awful, overwhelming, unexpected and inexplicable catastrophe. Is it possible that we should witness such events, and that this should be the end of nearly eighteen years of courageous and successful efforts to maintain order, peace, and make France happy, what she was? I have heard, I read hourly what has happened: I cannot believe it yet; but if my beloved parents and the remainder of the family are at least safe I won't mind the rest.'[27] On 4 April 1848, Queen Victoria reassured her uncle, King Leopold, that 'I never was calmer & quieter & less nervous. Great events make me quiet & calm; it is only trifles that irritate my nerves.'[28] Nevertheless, at the end of March the Prime Minister, Lord John Russell, later 1st Earl Russell, had persuaded her to remove the Royal children 'from Buckingham Palace to what was deemed the secure haven of Osborne'.[29] King Leopold offered Claremont House, of which he was the life tenant, to King Louis Philippe, who died there on 26 August 1850.

[25] Elizabeth Longford, *Victoria R.I.*, London: Weidenfeld & Nicolson, 1964, p. 407.
[26] Ibid., p. 403.
[27] LQV I, Vol. II, p. 179.
[28] Ibid., p. 197.
[29] Lee, *King Edward VII: A Biography: From Birth to Accession*, p. 25.

On 23 September 1856 there was a rising in Neuchâtel, led by Prussian loyalists. The instigators were soon arrested and negotiations brokered by the four great powers, Great Britain, France, Russia and Prussia, ensued, with the British supporting the independence of the Principality from Prussia. On Christmas Day 1856, Queen Victoria wrote in her Journal: 'Very good news from Paris. The Bolgrad question seems really at last on the point of being settled. Also, – more hopeful about Neufchatel, & there being no war. It quite sent my spirits up.' Four days later, she followed this with another, related entry: 'Albert had seen Lord Clarendon for a long time in the afternoon, about this unfortunate Neufchatel question, which we do not quite understand, & in which I fear he has not acted quite judiciously. – Received letters this morning, from the Prince of Prussia & Fritz [her future son-in-law], the latter describing Prussia as very warlike. When I came in later, we both saw Lord Clarendon, & talked of the Army & its reductions, which annoys him as well as us, – of this eternal Bolgrad question, which is really about to be settled satisfactorily, – of the Emperor, his peculiarities, & the mistakes he had made, being so like those of Louis Philippe!'

On the last day of the year, the Queen reflected: 'Neufchatel remains an alarming element & I tremble for what may happen! – We dined alone together, a great treat to me, & talked & played afterwards. Thus ended very peacefully, poor old 56!'[30] On 26 May 1857 a treaty was signed – once again in Paris – leading to the King of Prussia's renunciation of any right of sovereignty over Neuchâtel, although he was permitted to retain the princely title. The so-called 'Bolgrad Question' was a direct consequence of the 1856 Treaty of Paris: the region in which the small city of Bolgrad – founded only in 1821 – lies, part of Bessarabia, which was ceded to Russia after the Russian–Turkish War 1806–12, had been awarded to Moldavia, which later became part of Romania. This status quo lasted until 1878. After many vicissitudes, principally during the two world wars, Bolgrad is now part of the Ukraine.

The Schleswig-Holstein Question 1863–4

In 1863 Schleswig-Holstein became a cause of friction in Europe, as it again emerged from the shadows, more than a decade after the signing of the London Protocol on 8 May 1852. Lord Palmerston is supposed to have

[30] Royal Archives: VIC/MAIN/QVJ/1856.

said that only three people had ever understood the Schleswig-Holstein Question: the Prince Consort, who was dead; a German professor, who had gone mad; and Lord Palmerston himself – but he had forgotten all about it. On Christmas Eve 1863, Queen Victoria wrote to her Prime Minister, Earl Russell:

> The news from Copenhagen and Germany are both very alarming. The time now seems at hand when some compromise must be thought of, which Lord Russell and Lord Wodehouse both mentioned to the Queen, as in all probability the likeliest way to settle this terribly complicated question; and the Queen would ask Lord Russell to give this his most serious attention, as she cannot but think that otherwise War will be unavoidable.
>
> It is no longer a question of maintaining the Treaty of '52 at all hazards, it is whether War is to be averted or not, and both parties, whether they are in the right or in the wrong, ought to give way and come to a compromise. If the Queen could feel that she had helped in staying the shedding of blood (and if once begun who knows when it will end?) she cares not for the abuse which will be heaped upon us, by those who considered they were in the right (and that Germany has right on its side the Queen must always think), but would thank God for it.[31]

On Boxing Day, Earl Russell replied: 'Lord Russell presents his humble duty to your Majesty: he quite agrees with your Majesty that there should be some compromise between Germany and Denmark. But until that compromise takes effect he thinks it will be impossible for your Majesty's Government to consent to a German occupation of Schleswig.'[32] The Second Schleswig War broke out on 1 February 1864, when Prussian forces invaded Schleswig. It ended after the Danish Government agreed terms with Prussia and Austria by signing the Treaty of Vienna on 30 October 1864.

These developments were to have a direct impact on Queen Victoria's immediate family: at Windsor Castle on 5 July 1866, her third daughter, Princess Helena, was married to Prince Christian of Schleswig-Holstein. Following two plebiscites in 1920, Northern Schleswig became the Danish county of South Jutland, while Central Schleswig, which included the port of Flensburg, seat of the last government of Nazi Germany for three weeks

[31] LQV II, Vol. I, pp. 181–2.
[32] Ibid., pp. 181–2.

in April–May 1945, remained part of Germany. Queen Alexandra, consort of King Edward VII, never forgave the Prussians for what she saw as the theft of her native land.

The Fenian Rebels, 1867

Three years later, the threat was a more local one, to the person of Queen Victoria herself, from Fenian rebels hoping to free Ireland from British rule. The Queen accepted that the Irish lower orders 'had never become reconciled to the English rule, which they hate! So different from the Scotch who are so loyal.'[33] The American-based Fenian Brotherhood acted in support of the Irish Republican Brotherhood, founded in Dublin in 1858. On 20 December 1867, Queen Victoria wrote in her Journal:

> Saw the Duke of Marlborough [Lord Lieutenant of Ireland], whom I found very nervous on account of a telegram received from Lord Monck from Canada, saying that 80 people had started in two vessels from New York, with murderous intentions against me and some members of the Government. These men intended landing in some place in the Bristol Channel. The Duke fears there may be considerable danger for the next three or four weeks, but orders have been sent to try and intercept these ships. He said he hoped I would be very cautious, that ships must watch the shore and troops be sent there. He urged on me equally not to allow our children to go about unprotected. Then held a Council at which there was a Knighthood, and a P.C. was sworn in.
>
> Saw the Duke of Marlborough once more, who had been talking with Lord C. FitzRoy and was reassured as to the measures which would be taken to ensure my safety. Saw Lord Charles later about it all, and discussed where the Guards should be lodged, etc. He is so kind, quiet and calm. Walked in the afternoon with Louise to the Swiss Cottage and then drove in the woods. It is most unpleasant to feel one's liberty now so much interfered with, and every step and turn having to be calculated. Could not help feeling nervous and upset. Prayed earnestly for help and protection in these anxious painful times.[34]

[33] Longford, *Victoria R.I.*, p. 360.
[34] LQV II, Vol. I, pp. 483–4.

That same day, she wrote in a direct manner to her Prime Minister, the Earl of Derby:

> The Queen thanks Lord Derby for his letter, but will not reply to it, as she has charged the Duke of Marlborough to write very fully to him, and to show him why she does not intend to leave Osborne. Also to explain to him how groundless his apprehensions are as to her late and distant drives after dark, which never at any time hardly take place here, and scarcely ever at Windsor, and then never without an Equerry riding in attendance. The Queen does not consider Windsor at all safe. And to London nothing will make her go, till the present state of affairs is altered. Such precautions are taken here that the Queen will be little better than a State prisoner. She may consent to this for a short time, but she could not for long.[35]

On 8 January 1868, Crown Princess Frederick wrote to her mother from Berlin:

> The Fenian movement continues to cause great sensation and concern here; people think the government has not shown energy enough quelling it at the beginning, but from what I can gather from all I read on the subject it appears to me that all measures that can be taken to stop the outrageous proceedings of these disturbers of the peace have been taken, and I admire the calm and dignified way in which the thing is taken in England. If the like evil had been on foot here – the measures taken would be such as to make the whole country suffer, I am sure, and then '*le remède serait pire que le mal*'.[36]

Three days later, Queen Victoria replied: 'Do not be alarmed about the Fenians. There has been a great deal of nonsense and foolish panic, and numberless stories which have proved sheer inventions!! One, most absurd one, frightened people so much that they took endless, useless precautions here.'[37]

[35] Ibid.

[36] Roger Fulford, ed., *Your Dear Letter: Private Correspondence of Queen Victoria and the Crown Princess of Prussia 1865–1871*, London: Evans Brothers, 1971, p. 168.

[37] Ibid., p. 169.

The Franco-Prussian War, 1870–1

The Franco-Prussian War was a grave threat to peace in Europe, pitching the two great Continental European armies against one another. As with so many European 'problems', the proximate causes can often seem rather surprising to modern eyes. After a reign marked by political instability and several civil wars, Queen Isabel II of Spain was overthrown and sent into exile by the 'Glorious Revolution' (La Gloriosa) of 1868. The coalition of moderate, liberal and republican forces that had led the revolution could not then agree on a new form of government. Parliament (the Cortes) initially rejected the idea of a republic and decided on a constitutional monarchy under a new dynasty. The search for a suitable monarch proved problematic. The throne was initially offered to Leopold of Hohenzollern-Sigmaringen, a member of the Catholic branch of the Prussian Royal House. Although hesitant, Prince Leopold accepted the Spanish offer, subject to obtaining the consent of King William I of Prussia, head of the House of Hohenzollern.

The possibility of a Hohenzollern succeeding to the Spanish throne caused understandable alarm in France, with fears of encirclement by Prussian dynastic alliances. The government of Napoleon III therefore made it clear that France was prepared to go to war to prevent such a situation arising. Unlike his Chancellor, Otto von Bismarck, who was not unwilling to provoke a war, King William I was opposed to the idea of a Hohenzollern candidacy from the outset, as the Spanish throne lacked stability and might be overthrown at any time. He therefore wrote to Leopold's father, requesting that he should persuade his son to withdraw his acceptance. Leopold's subsequent withdrawal was a significant French diplomatic victory.

Nevertheless, concerns remained and the French Ambassador, Count Vincent Benedetti, was instructed to seek an assurance from King William I that no member of any branch of the House of Hohenzollern would ever be a candidate for the Spanish throne. On 13 July 1870 the Ambassador confronted the King during his morning stroll in the Kurpark at Bad Ems, a spa town on the Lahn river, where he was taking the waters. While King William I described Benedetti as 'most importunate', Bismarck deliberately exaggerated the incident in the so-called 'Ems Telegram', the release of which led directly to the mobilisation of the Prussian Army on the emotive date of 14 July and the French declaration of war on Prussia five days later. Anticipating events, Crown Princess Frederick wrote to her mother on 18 July 1870: 'What a sad Christmas it will be! I am as well as can be expected and try very hard not to make a fool of myself, which is difficult, as my nerves are shaky.'[38]

She had no need to worry. German mobilisation was much swifter and more effective than that of the French. Within a month of crossing the border, the French Army had been comprehensively defeated in six set-piece battles on its own soil. In the German tradition, Crown Prince Frederick commanded the Prussian Army that defeated the French at the Battle of Wörth on 6 August. A telegram from King William to his wife was later lampooned in an epigram written by Coventry Patmore:

> This is to say, my dear Augusta,
> We've had another awful buster:
> Ten thousand Frenchmen sent below!
> Thank God from whom all blessings flow![39]

By 4 September 1870, Emperor Napoleon III had surrendered on the battlefield, the Second Empire had been overthrown and Marshal Bazaine and his forces were besieged in Metz, while the Siege of Paris was about to begin. That Christmas, Crown Prince Frederick commanded the 3rd Prussian Army besieging Paris. On 28 December 1870, Queen Victoria wrote to Crown Princess Frederick, referring to British officers attached to the armies as observers: 'I hear that they have begun to bombard Paris! If only it would soon end! To my despair the feeling is becoming more & more bitter here against the Prussians & unfortunately the Officers are so rude to ours (not at Head Quarters) that it increases this irritation, which is so unjust on both sides. I can't tell you how it worries me and what lances I break for them! But I am very powerless.'[40]

Two days later, Crown Princess Frederick replied:

> Many thanks for your dear letter which arrived to-day. It is so kind of you to break lances for the Germans in England; this mutual distrust is too dreadful, it must be the aim of our statesmen to dispel these feelings so unjust, unnecessary, and injurious to all that is useful. Here the feeling is getting much better . . . That the Prussian officers should be rude to the

[38] Ponsonby, Frederick, ed., *Letters of the Empress Frederick*, London: Macmillan & Co., 1930, p. 77.

[39] Basil Champneys, ed., *Memoirs and Correspondence of Coventry Patmore*, London: George Bell & Sons, 1900, p. 286.

[40] Fulford, ed., *Your Dear Letter: Private Correspondence of Queen Victoria and the Crown Princess of Prussia 1865–1871*, p. 312, note.

> English ones is bad; but I fear our dear countrymen are a little awkward and ignorant of the forms which Germans are accustomed to. I know they quite neglect to have themselves named, and this the Prussians misunderstand and take for intentional rudeness, which they then fancy is their duty to return; this is too stupid, but I know it is the case. It all comes from an imperfect knowledge of one another's national habits, for I have found those Englishmen and Germans who have lived much in both countries get on particularly well together, and be the best of friends.
>
> Prussians are really very civil, but they expect this *Vorstellen*, introducing and presenting; and if it is forgotten they are offended. I do not think half the English that go abroad have an idea of this being necessary; on the other hand the Germans do not know that it is not the custom in England and this always creates little disagreeables, and when there is so much excitable matter in the air, and feelings are so irritated, every trifle is taken at more than it is worth. Hence these eternal squabbles and misunderstandings which make me utterly wretched.[41]

She followed this with another letter on 4 January 1871: 'A thousand thanks for your dear and kind little letter for New Year's day, with the two charming little cards in it, which I have carefully put into a little book of relics.'[42] On the last day of 1870, Queen Victoria wrote of the Franco-Prussian War that 'there has perhaps never been a worse one'.[43]

During the siege of Paris, Crown Prince Frederick spent Christmas in the Palace of Versailles, as described in his war diary:

> Christmas Eve, the great day when gifts of goodwill are distributed, in an enemy's country and in the midst of war's alarms! So this time we are not to spend this chiefest festivity of German family life with our dear ones. My heart is heavy indeed, yet for this year it seems that every feeling of kindly sentiment, nay, every instinct of humanity, must be overshadowed by the grimmest horrors of war. Next after my beloved ones at home, my thoughts are above all for the unhappy widows and orphans; for indeed for thousands this Christmas will be a time of mourning. God grant that when a year hence at the home fireside we recall the many sacrifices of this War,

41 Ibid., pp. 312–13.
42 LQV II, Vol II, p. 96.
43 Longford, *Victoria R.I.*, p. 378.

its results may at any rate be such that we can say with full conviction, they have been made to secure a lasting and honourable Peace! . . .

For Christmas Eve I had organised a raffle under the Christmas tree for the eighty members of my Staff. The same was arranged in separate rooms for domestics, Staff guard, stable and escort squadrons; of course punch, pepper cakes, nuts and apples being provided as far as possible for the occasion. Every member of my Staff, as well as other invited guests, was bound each to bring with him two trifles for distribution, so that the caprice of fortune had a free scope; for instance Mr. Odo Russell won an officer's swordbelt.[44] The 160 prizes were soon disposed of amid much laughter and merriment, whilst I, to my surprise and delight, found a number of useful presents, thoughtfully chosen by wife and mother, laid out on a table specially reserved for me. In particular, a miniature pocket-revolver met with much applause among the company; purses, pincushions, riding-satchels and other little toilet requisites were not wanting.

Another raffle like that at my quarters was held for the Princes and the subordinate members of my Staff at the Hôtel des Réservoirs, from which we went on afterwards to His Majesty's, where there was a formal distribution of gifts and a supper. Every guard-house was gay with Christmas trees and their glittering lights, which were to be found even at the most distant outposts. Everything wore quite the look of Christmas-tide at home, and a spirit of gay good humour enlivened every German heart even at points where the enemy's shells were whistling by. The French could not conceal their astonishment at the doings of these northern barbarians, for even by our purchases in the shops and by meeting us about the streets they saw how friendliness and the wish to give pleasure to others animated every man among us.

Headquarters: Versailles, 25th December – Nine degrees of frost (sixteen degrees Fahrenheit) and an east wind as we went to service in the Palace chapel. It sounds like irony, amidst the miseries of war and in days that speak only of death and destruction to the foe to listen to the Christmas message of salvation: 'On earth peace and good-will toward men .' Christendom is still far from acting in the spirit of those words. The clergy have a difficult task set them to explain the contradiction involved in the strife of Christians against Christians, where each side invokes God

[44] Lord Odo William Leopold Russell, later 1st Baron Ampthill, was attached to the German Army Headquarters on a special mission in November 1870. The following October he was appointed British Ambassador in Berlin, where he spent the rest of his life, dying at Potsdam on 25 August 1884.

for its own as the only just cause, and at every success holds this to prove that the adversary has been forsaken by Heaven. I leave the solution of the problem to professed theologians, and look simply to Him who has helped us hitherto; and then I turn my thoughts to all those who are no longer with us and to those left behind who to-day can be filled only with feelings of sorrow.[45]

On Boxing Day, the Prince Consort's biographer, Theodore Martin, wrote to the Queen's newly appointed Private Secretary, Henry Ponsonby, expressing views that were widely held at the time, and which were to be put to the test twice during the next seventy years: 'What I as an Englishman complain of is this, that our statesmen did not look one inch before their noses, when this war broke out, and were not even startled by the revelations of what Germany had been about in the way of preparation for an attack on France into taking *instant* measures for strengthening our armaments both by land and sea. "United Germany" in a certain sense was all very well, but it surely required no great knowledge of Prussian hereditary policy or of human nature to know, what was likely to ensue from such immense military preponderance and such unprecedented success.'[46]

On 3 January 1871, Crown Prince Frederick wrote (in German) to Queen Victoria:

Our Christmas festival here in our headquarters at Versailles was certainly a most peculiar one. I honestly confess that I felt more inclined often to shed tears than to enjoy a festival time, for I had a longing greater than I can say to be with my wife and children, from whom I am more separated it seems with every New Year. Our honest wish to be able to greet this festival of heavenly peace with the peace that should at last be brought to the world by an end of the war with France, is blasted by the insane blindness of those who now have the power in France, and amongst these Gambetta seems to me nothing but a butcher. I cannot conceive how it is that he does not care more for the welfare of his countrymen, and how he can bear the burden of the guilt of blood that he must load upon his conscience by endless continuation of the war. It would surely be no shame to France that

[45] Alfred Richard Allinson, ed., *The War Diary of The Emperor Frederick III 1870–1871*, published by London: Stanley Paul & Co., 1927, pp. 231–4.

[46] Arthur Ponsonby, *Henry Ponsonby, Queen Victoria's Private Secretary: His Life from his Letters*, London: Macmillan & Co., 1942, p. 316.

> has fought bravely, to confess at last that she has been beaten by an Army equal to hers. No one would accuse France of cowardice, or believe that her military honour had not had justice done it . . .
>
> I cannot thank you sufficiently for the warm good wishes you have always shown for Germany, and for our Army. I am well aware that you endeavour to set in the true light the miseries of war for which the Press is doing its best to stigmatise us as 'Vandals'. You judge German affairs with the same peculiar clearness and insight that enables you to decide in all important matters with such accuracy. May God reward you richly for it, and may we again and again find through you, in your person, that support which has so often exercised a beneficial influence on the affairs of the world! So may the ground gradually be prepared upon which may arise the natural alliance that, binding England and Germany, will also embrace Austria! When these three mighty Empires stand firm together we may enjoin peace on the world, and a lasting peace may have been ensured by the present bath of blood.[47]

On New Year's Day, Queen Victoria wrote in her Journal: 'The bloody, sad, eventful year 70 has sunk in dark clouds & 71 rises as sad & gloomy, but God we pray in His mercy may soon grant us Peace. May He have mercy on the thousands of innocent lives that are being sacrificed, for no possible good to mankind!'[48]

On 18 January 1871 in the Hall of Mirrors at Versailles, at the invitation of his fellow German rulers, King William I was proclaimed German Emperor, or Kaiser. He would have much preferred to have been titled Emperor of Germany; however, Bismarck, concerned not to upset those German rulers of no fewer than twenty-five kingdoms, grand duchies, duchies, principalities and free cities, advised strongly against it.

The Queen's Reflections, 1879–80

In the manner of many diarists, Queen Victoria was in the habit of reflecting on the old year at the beginning of the new. It was in this vein that she committed her thoughts to her Journal at Osborne House on 1 January 1880:

[47] LQV II, Vol. II, pp. 104–5.
[48] Royal Archives: VIC/MAIN/QVJ/1871.

Another year past, and we begin one with heavy clouds. A poor Government, Ireland in a state of total lawlessness, and war at the Cape, of a very serious nature! I feel very anxious, and have no one to lean on. Thank God! my dear ones are all well, but many are gone, who were least expected to leave us, acquaintances, and faithful friends, my good Col. Pickard, poor Constance Westminster, and many a familiar face. God spare all I most love, for many a year, and help me on! I feel how sadly deficient I am, and how over-sensitive and irritable, and how uncontrollable my temper is, when annoyed and hurt. But I am so overdone, so vexed, and in such distress about my country, that that must be my excuse. I will daily pray for God's help to improve.[49]

The Queen chose not to mention the death on 27 March 1879 of her grandchild, Prince Waldemar, fourth son and sixth child of the Crown Prince and Princess of Prussia. On 27 December 1880, Lady Emily Russell, wife of Lord Odo Russell, wrote to Queen Victoria:

We have had the honour of seeing the Crown Princess here several times since her Imperial Highness's return from Wiesbaden, and thought her looking well, though complaining of rheumatic pains in the shoulders. We also dined along with their Imperial Highnesses the other evening, and saw the Crown Prince and Crown Princess for the first time at their Palace again since their sad loss, which naturally comes back doubly to the Princess on her sad return to the Palace here where everything reminds her so of poor dear Prince Waldemar, and of his last fatal illness, and where every day her Imperial Highness feels to miss him more and more. It is very touching to hear her talk of him and look at the empty place at the table.

One feels it is a comfort that Her Imperial Highness will have so much to think of, in the preparation for Prince William's marriage, that it will distract her thoughts a little during the first return here after all her Imperial Highness has gone through; and Prince William's engagement to Princess Victoria is a source of great happiness and comfort to both their Imperial Highnesses, who look forward with much pleasure to seeing Prince William settle, and married, to a Princess they are so fond of, and

[49] LQV II, Vol. III, p. 177.

> who has certainly won over even those who were opposed to the marriage here, where at first it was unpopular.[50]

On 27 February 1881, the future Emperor William II was married to Princess Augusta Victoria (Dona) of Schleswig-Holstein.

More Irish Problems, 1892

There was to be little perceptible improvement in the state of affairs in Ireland during Queen Victoria's long reign. On Christmas Day 1892, the Chief Secretary for Ireland, the Rt. Hon. John Morley, wrote to her from Dublin Castle:

> Mr. Morley submits his humble duty to your Majesty, and greatly regrets to have to inform your Majesty that an explosion, undoubtedly the result of criminal designs, took place at eleven o'clock last night in a small court immediately under the walls of the Castle. The explosive, which it is believed must have been dynamite or some deadly agency of that class, appears to have been placed on the pavement directly adjoining the detective offices. The theory is that the detective who has lost his life saw the object on the path, struck it with his foot, and so caused it to explode. When his comrades in the barrack rushed out to find the cause of the crash and uproar, they found him lying on the ground, so mutilated and shattered that the unfortunate man expired rather less than an hour afterwards.
>
> Every pane of glass in the windows of the adjacent rooms of the Castle, as well as of the City Hall, is broken to pieces, and so is much of the woodwork. The outrage is one of unusual daring, for the court opens from one of the most frequented streets in Dublin, had a blaze of electric light upon it at the time, and constables were constantly passing in and out. The police as yet have no clue, but are inclined to connect the crime with the similar attempt to blow up one of the rooms in the Chief Secretary's office in the course of last year. The police believe that the perpetrators must have aimed more especially at the score of detectives who have their quarters in this portion of the Castle. The constable who has been killed by this crime was fortunately unmarried, and has left no one dependent upon him. Mr. Morley deeply deplores that it should fall to him to announce this

[50] Ibid., pp. 168–9.

> disastrous incident to your Majesty, and with humble respect assures your Majesty that no effort will be spared to discover and punish these criminal disturbers of the order which now prevails in this country.'[51]

On 27 December, Queen Victoria replied: 'The Queen has received Mr. Morley's letter with much regret, and she deeply laments this occurrence of a dynamite outrage after the cessation of such outrages for the last few years. She is glad to learn that Mr. Morley will spare no effort to discover and punish the criminals, for the Queen fears the recent release of men for abetting an atrocious murder will cause an expectation that the law will not be so strictly enforced on convicts as was formerly the case.'[52]

The Jameson Raid, 1895–6

The Jameson Raid was an abortive attempt, dreamed up by Cecil Rhodes and the gold 'barons', to force British re-annexation of the Transvaal. Six hundred mounted police and volunteers, led by Dr Leander Starr Jameson, crossed the border into Transvaal on 29 December 1895, hoping to encourage a rising by mainly British migrant workers in Johannesburg, a three-day ride away. However, as they were forced to surrender just twenty miles short of their goal, the raid was a humiliating failure which simply drove the two Boer republics into closer alliance through their mutual suspicion of British motives.

On 2 January 1896, the Prince of Wales wrote to a friend: 'The accounts from the Transvaal have been a very unpleasant New Year's Card! Matters look grave and our position is quite unfortunate.'[53] The following day, the German Emperor sent a telegram to President Kruger: 'I express my sincere congratulations that, supported by your people without appealing for the help of friendly Powers, you have succeeded by your own energetic action against armed bands which invaded your country as disturbers of the peace and have thus been enabled to restore peace and safeguard the independence of the country against attacks from the outside.'[54]

[51] George Earle Buckle, ed., *The Letters of Queen Victoria, Third Series: A Selection from Her Majesty's Correspondence between the Years 1886 and 1901*, 3 vols., London: John Murray, 1930–32 (LQV III), Vol. II, p. 189.
[52] Ibid.
[53] Lee, *King Edward VII: A Biography: From Birth to Accession*, p. 720.
[54] Ibid., p. 722.

On 5 January 1896, Queen Victoria wrote to 'My dear William': 'I must now also touch upon a subject which causes me much pain and astonishment. It is the Telegram you sent to President Kruger, which is considered very unfriendly towards this country, not that you intended it as such I am sure – but I grieve to say that it has made a most unfortunate impression here.'[55]

Three days later, the German Emperor informed his grandmother that Sir Frank Lascelles, British Ambassador in Berlin, had told him that 'the raiders were "filibusters or rebels"'. In reply, the Emperor hinted that Germany 'ought to join and co-operate in keeping them from doing mischief'.[56] The die was cast. Over the next three years the two Boer republics rearmed with modern weapons, including 37,000 Mauser rifles from the Krupp factory in Germany, and a selection of modern artillery pieces, enabling them to offer effective resistance to the might of the British Army. This fiasco did Jameson's career no harm: Prime Minister of the Cape Colony 1904–8, he was granted a baronetcy in 1911. Rudyard Kipling wrote the much-anthologised poem, *If*, in tribute to Jameson's determination.

Emperor William II's *Tour d'Horizon*, 1898

On 29 December 1898, the German Emperor wrote to his grandmother from Potsdam. Although a long letter, it deserves to be quoted in full as a remarkable *tour d'horizon* of the world situation as the nineteenth century drew to a close, offering just a hint of what was to come:[57]

> Most beloved Grandmama,
> Allow me by these lines to convey to your feet my best thanks for the pretty flower-pot which graced my Xmas table, and upon which I look with feelings of gratitude for your never-ending kindness to me. Our Xmas was spent in the usual manner, with the difference that we were at the Stadtschloss in Potsdam. The children were all present, though the younger ones suffered from colds and unblowable noses. Whereas myself suffered from a sudden attack of fever and prostration, which kept me in bed for the greater part of the Xmas holidays, and came partly from being overworked.

[55] Ibid., p. 725.
[56] Ibid., p. 720.
[57] LQV III, Vol. III, p. 323.

The old year closes with a great success to your arms and policy in Africa, which will make the faces merry in British homes and the hearts of your soldiers beat higher! And well they may! For what can a soldier or sailor do better than win and fight for the country of his birth and for his Queen? I have also to thank you for all the kind messages which you sent me through Sir Frank, who transmitted them with a face happy at being able to do so and by the souvenirs of his stay at Balmoral. I am so sorry that I was not informed of the little plot you and Mama had hatched for a meeting now on our homeward voyage; had I known it beforehand, I would have braved any amount of rolling and pitching in the 'Bay' only to be able to see you!

The coming year looks queer enough! France is in a terrible plight, and the fight about Dreyfus, etc., has disclosed a fearful amount of corruption and injustice in the Government and Army circles. The longing for scandal, the perpetual, startling 'disclosures' have created a most deplorable state of excitement, which may one day ease itself in some sort of explosion towards inside or outside! Voltaire saw his countrymen were 'half apes and half tigers.' It seems to me as if they were in the act of changing from the first to the latter.

The state of Russia's finances is bad! On the brink of a collapse, one may say. First on account of the enormous amount of steadily increasing battalions, etc., which, as far as our frontiers are concerned, are nearly on war strength since fifteen years. Secondly, because there is a dreadful agricultural calamity which has been slowly developing since the last five or six years. The utterly impoverished peasants are suffering from a terrible famine, generating typhus and other diseases. Millions have been spent by private help, Red Cross, the Tsar himself without effect, so that according to my latest news the Government will have to ask for 100 millions of marks from the Emperor to fight the evil! Added to this the bills for the Siberian railway and the Navy run enormously high, so that there is cause enough for proclaiming a 'Peace Conference'! But the informations I have till now managed to extract about the so-called programme and plans are not very lucid and far from reassuring. A general agreement is to be come to, that we others are not to invent new rifles or guns or form new battalions, whereas the thickness of the armour on the British battleships is to be 'internationally' limited to a certain thickness only! I suppose for 'international' shells to be able to pierce it! Though how the Ambassadors are to find out the relation by comparison of an inch of British steel on H.M. ships to a rifle battalion in Tyrol is more than I can tell!

> Anyhow, our relations are now so clearly defined, and the necessity for respecting our mutual interests and the possibility of mutual help are gaining more and more on our subjects, that I look out with absolute confidence into the coming year! May it bring Peace or War, at all events may it bring you health and strength and success everywhere with the hand of God to shield and ward you from all evil! How nice that dear Mama could be near you! She enjoys her stay so much. With the hopes of seeing you next year in best of health, I kiss your hands, and most respectfully remain, ever your most dutiful and loving Grandson,
>
> Willy

Despite 'the great success to your arms and policy in Africa' to which the Kaiser referred – the defeat by General Sir Herbert Kitchener, later Field Marshal 1st Earl Kitchener of Khartoum, of Abdullah al-Taashi, successor to the Mahdi, at the Battle of Omdurman on 2 September 1898 – it was in Africa, and not in Europe, that the next major conflict occurred.

The Second Anglo-Boer War, 1899–1902

In 1877 Britain annexed the Transvaal. However, there was little immediate reaction from the Boers, not only because their exchequer had run out of money, but also because they hoped that the British Army would protect them from the warlike Zulus. On 17 July 1877 Queen Victoria wrote, somewhat pointedly, to Crown Princess Frederick: 'It is not our custom to annex countries (as it is in some others) unless we are obliged & forced to do so – as in the case of the Transvaal Republic.'[58] However, less than a year after the subjugation of the Zulu nation in July 1879, the Transvaalers rose in revolt, leading to the re-establishment of the South African Republic by the Convention of Pretoria. In 1886 the discovery of gold at Witwatersrand in the Transvaal hills upset the delicate balance once again. As speculators flocked to exploit these new-found riches, there was pressure on Britain to intervene on their behalf.

Sir Alfred Milner, newly appointed High Commissioner for Southern Africa and Governor of Cape Colony, swiftly formed the view that war – or at least the threat of war – was the only way to bring the Boers, under State

[58] Longford, *Victoria R.I.*, p. 411.

President 'Oom Paul' Kruger, to heel. When war was declared, the Boers held a clear advantage: with 35,000 burghers already mobilised, they faced a British army of just 13,000 troops. Despite rushing reinforcements to the Cape, the second week of December 1899 became known as 'Black Week', as the British Army suffered three successive defeats: at Stormberg, Cape Colony on 10 December; at Magersfontein, Cape Colony on 11 December; and at Colenso, Natal on 15 December. Shortly afterwards, eighty-year-old Queen Victoria famously said in an audience with Arthur Balfour, the Prime Minister's nephew: 'Please understand that there is no one depressed in *this* house; we are not interested in the possibilities of defeat; they do not exist.'[59]

On 21 December 1899, the German Emperor wrote to the Prince of Wales:

> What days of sad news and anxiety have passed over the country since we spent our delightful days at Sandringham. Many brave officers and men have fallen or are disabled after showing pluck, courage, and determined bravery! How many homes will be sad this year and how many sufferers will feel agonising pain morally and physically in these days of holy pleasure and peace! What an amount of bloodshed has been going on and is expected to be for the next months to come! Instead of the Angels' song 'Peace on Earth and Goodwill to Men' the new century will be greeted by shrieks of dying men, killed and maimed by lyddite shells and balls from Quickfirers. Truly *fin de siècle*![60]

The next day, the Empress Frederick wrote from Italy to Queen Victoria:

> I thought you would perhaps give up going to Osborne for Christmas at this critical time when business of all kinds must be so pressing. I have had an inkstand made for you; it is an attempt to produce majolica at Kronberg and I venture to hope that this piece is worthy of your acceptance, as no second will be made and the artist has taken great trouble. All my Christmas prayers and wishes and blessings I find it difficult to express . . . I am no better. Indeed the pain seems even more acute at times. No doubt the violent wind which is cold and cutting has a deal to do with it. Vicky and Adolf are here since two days. Vicky is helping me, getting the things together for South Africa for the sick and wounded and has put in

[59] Ibid., p. 554.
[60] Lee, *King Edward VII: A Biography: From Birth to Accession*, pp. 754–5.

> her contribution. I sew and knit in bed by the light of a rather sorry petroleum lamp, but, alas, one cannot effect as much as one would like.[61]

That same day, Queen Victoria wrote in her Journal: 'Saw Lord Salisbury before luncheon . . . He lamented the loss of life & the mistakes that had been made & was especially alarmed at Sir R. Buller having changed his mind so often . . . Saw Lord Roberts after tea. He knelt down & kissed my hand. I said how much I felt for him. He could only answer 'I cannot speak of that, but I can of anything else.' Field Marshal Lord Roberts's son, Frederick, had been killed at the Battle of Colenso a week earlier in an action for which he was awarded a Victoria Cross, one of just three father-and-son combinations to have been so decorated.

Queen Victoria continued:

> He said it would take a long time to do what had to be done, & thought very unfortunate mistakes had been made by the Generals. He hoped when Sir R. Buller got his reinforcements, he would be able to outflank the enemy & thus relieve Ladysmith. I asked what he meant to do himself. He thought he would concentrate his troops, & then move into the Transvaal. Spoke of the admirable attitude of the whole Empire & of all the Colonial troops being so anxious to take their part in the fighting. He is delighted to have Lord Kitchener with him, of whom he has the very highest opinion. Spoke also of dear Christle [Prince Christian Victor of Schleswig-Holstein, the Queen's grandson], who was such a friend of his poor son's. He praised him very much, & said he was an excellent soldier.

On Christmas Eve, Queen Victoria wrote in her Journal: 'This day has returned again much overclouded by anxiety & trouble & will be a very sad one for many British homes.' The same refrain was carried through to New Year's Eve: 'This is the last day of a very eventful, & in many ways sad year. I have lost many friends, amongst them one who can never be replaced, darling Marie Leiningen. Then there are the sad losses amongst my brave troops, which is a constant sorrow to me. In the midst of it all I have however to thank God for many mercies & for the splendid unity & loyalty of my Empire. – I pray God to bless & preserve all my Children,

61 Agatha Ramm, ed., *Beloved and Darling Child: Last Letters between Queen Victoria and her Eldest Daughter 1886–1901*, Stroud: Sutton, 1990, p. 242.

Grandchildren, & kind relations & friends & may there be brighter days in store for us!'[62]

On Christmas Day, General Sir Redvers Buller sent a telegram to the Queen's Private Secretary, Sir Arthur Bigge: 'Frere Camp, 25th Dec. 1899. – Please present my humble duty and thanks from all troops to the Queen. We are all well. Wounded doing very well.'[63] On 30 December, the Queen sent a telegram to Lieutenant-Colonel Robert Kekewich, who commanded the British troops besieged in Kimberley: 'Am deeply touched by your kind and loyal New Year's Greetings. I watch with admiration your determined and gallant defence, though I regret the unavoidable loss of life incurred.'[64]

On New Year's Day, the Empress Frederick wrote to her mother:

> The first words this morning and my motto for the century: 'God save the Queen'. Never was this prayer breathed more tenderly and devotedly, nor from a more grateful heart . . . My thoughts are so much with you all today, and how I should love to talk over the many subjects of deep interest and anxiety which crowd in upon one. I hope the news from South Africa is more reassuring. William wrote me a card saying he hoped peace would soon be made and this useless bloodshed put an end to. These sentiments in this form I cannot echo. Heaven knows each drop of precious British blood seems a drop too much to be shed, but to allow ourselves to be driven into giving up a struggle which was unavoidable and forced upon us at the very moment when it is most unfavourable to us, I should think most deplorable and disastrous – a mistake all round, which would only please and encourage our enemies – anxious for anything that can injure us – and dishearten and distress our friends.
>
> My opinion is that England will come out of this contest, which she was bound to undertake as part of her mission in the spread and establishment of civilisation, stronger than she went in. She will see who are her friends and who her foes, and she will also see whatever defects there may be in her armaments and reform whatever is faulty. The Empire will be welded more firmly together than ever by having faced a common danger. England will put forth her strength and, I doubt not, weather the storm.[65]

[62] Royal Archives: VIC/MAIN/QVJ/1899.
[63] LQV III, Vol. III, p. 448.
[64] Ibid., p. 451.
[65] Ponsonby, *Letters of The Empress Frederick*, pp. 464–5.

Sadly, these sentiments went unheeded by her eldest son.

That same day, Queen Victoria wrote in her Journal: 'I begin to-day a new year and a new century; full of anxiety and fear of what may be before us! May all near and dear ones be protected, above all, darling Vicky, who is far from well! I cannot help feeling thankful that, after all, dear Arthur has not gone out to this terrible war. I hope and pray dear Christle may be spared and many a tried and devoted friend. I pray that God may spare me yet a short while to my children, leaving me all my faculties and to a certain extent my eyesight! May He bless our arms and give our men strength to fulfil their arduous task!'[66]

The hopes concerning the relief of Ladysmith that the Queen had expressed in her Journal on 22 December 1899 came to fruition, as Marie Mallet recorded in her diary at Windsor Castle on 1 March 1900: 'This has been, as you say, an historical day and one to be remembered all one's life; the bells are pealing and from my window I can hear distant cheering, the good news is confirmed and Buller wired that he has been into Ladysmith and that the Boers have melted away like snow in springtime . . . I saw the beloved Queen before luncheon, beaming with joy and surrounded by loyal telegrams from all sorts of people. She was so delighted and her face had lost that look of tension it has worn through the last anxious fortnight.'[67]

Sadly, though, this was a false dawn and Christle was not to be spared, as the Queen described in her Journal on 29 October 1900:

> Went out with Evelyn M., & on coming home, Beatrice came & told me, Thora begged not to come to luncheon as a telegram had come saying that dear Christle was much worse. This I own took away all hope from me . . . Almost directly after I went upstairs, Thora came in & in a faltering voice said 'He is gone.' I could not believe it, it seemed too dreadful & heart-breaking. This dear, excellent gallant Boy, beloved by all, such a good, as well as brave & capable officer, gone! To think that he had gone through the Indian campaign, Ashanti, (where our beloved Liko was taken) the Sandaus [?] (going down in his ship) & now again in South Africa had passed through endless hardships & dangers, without being ill, or getting a scratch – to fall a victim to this horrid fever, just on the eve of his return home, – oh! it is really too piteous.

66 Royal Archives: VIC/MAIN/QVJ/1900.

67 Victor Mallet, ed., *Life with Queen Victoria: Marie Mallet's Letters from Court 1887–1901*, London: John Murray, 1968, p. 191.

> It brings back so vividly to my mind poor Liko's loss, dying of African fever, away from his dear ones. I am miserable in thinking of poor dear Lenchen, who so worshipped this son, & poor Thora, so dear, so courageous, trying to comfort me by saying so sweetly she knew 'he was happy'.[68]

That Christmas Eve, she wrote: 'We went to the Durbar Room, where the Xmas tree & present tables were arranged. I felt very melancholy as I see so very badly. I received lovely things, amongst which an enamel of dear Christle, set with little sapphires, given by Lenchen, & a lovely bracelet, in remembrance of dear Affie, given by Bertie & Alix.'[69] Alfred, Duke of Edinburgh, and reigning Duke of Saxe-Coburg and Gotha, had died on 30 July 1900. There is a splendid full-size sculpture of Prince Christian Victor outside the north gate of Windsor Castle.

Lord Kitchener sent a telegram to the Queen on Boxing Day: 'Residency, Pretoria, 26th Dec. 1900. – Your Majesty's most gracious message has been communicated to the troops. In their name I humbly beg to express our sincere hope that the New Year may prove one of great happiness to your Majesty and the Royal Family.'[70] On New Year's Eve, despite her own mounting health problems, the Queen had not forgotten the travails of her soldiers in South Africa, writing in her Journal: 'The news from S. Africa was not very good. A post of our troops had been rushed by the enemy & a gun was taken. We have however reoccupied the post.'[71] The Treaty of Vereeniging, which finally brought the Second Anglo-Boer War to a satisfactory conclusion, was not signed until 31 May 1902, more than sixteen months after Queen Victoria's death.

[68] Royal Archives: VIC/MAIN/QVJ/1900.
[69] Ibid.
[70] LQV III, Vol. III, p. 634.
[71] Royal Archives: VIC/MAIN/QVJ/1900.

Christmas and Conflict during the Twentieth Century

Shortly after the outbreak of the First World War, Thomas Hardy wrote 'In Time of "The Breaking of Nations"':

> Only a man harrowing clods
> In a slow silent walk
> With an old horse that stumbles and nods
> Half asleep as they stalk.
>
> Only a thin smoke without flame
> From the heaps of couch-grass:
> Yet this will go onward the same
> Though Dynasties pass.
>
> Yonder a maid and her wight
> Come whispering by:
> War's annals will cloud into night
> Ere their story die.

Just as Thomas Hardy foresaw, dynasties did indeed pass. By the end of the war, the three great monarchies of Central and Eastern Europe – Russia, Austria-Hungary and Germany – had fallen, on 15 March 1917, 31 October 1918 and 9 November 1918 respectively. In terms of those two historic foes, the Ottoman Empire came to an end on 1 November 1922, while the Greek monarchy suffered an interregnum between 1924 and 1935, during the Second Hellenic Republic. There was a certain inevitability about the First World War, as Harold Nicolson explained: 'By 1910 a less ignorant diagnosis of the German malady had qualified our earlier assumptions. People began to realise that here was a newly welded nation of some sixty million gifted, industrious but neurotic people; a nation which had arrived so late at the imperialist banquet that she had only been accorded a few grudging scraps; a nation elated by her seething intelligence and energy and naturally claiming her own place in the sun.'[1]

[1] Harold Nicolson, *King George the Fifth: His Life and Reign*, London: Constable & Co., 1952, p. 181.

The British Royal Family, though supported by their people, separated from the Continent by the English Channel and protected by the Royal Navy, felt somewhat insecure from the outset. According to his biographer, 'King George was not either pro-French, pro-Russian, or pro-German: he was undeviatingly pro-British. But it did not occur to him that the Germans, having become our enemies overnight, had suddenly ceased to be human; nor did he share the hysteria which, from August 1914 onwards, induced so many of his subjects to abandon their reason, their dignity, and their sense of fair play.'[2]

What befell the six sons of Prince Frederick, Landgrave of Hesse, who had married Princess Margaret of Prussia, youngest daughter of Emperor Frederick, exemplifies the terrible family rift. Though they were great-grandchildren of Queen Victoria, they naturally fought on the German side in the First World War. Prince Frederick, the eldest son, was killed in action at Kara Orman, Romania on 12 September 1916. The second son, Prince Maximilian, was mortally wounded at St Jean-Chapelle, near Bailleul in Flanders on 12 October 1914. He entrusted the locket containing his mother's picture to a British doctor, who was killed the next day. The locket eventually reached the doctor's widow, who sent it to Queen Mary, who entrusted it to the Crown Princess of Sweden, a granddaughter of Queen Victoria, who returned it to Princess Margaret. The third son, Prince Philipp, married Princess Mafalda of Savoy, the second daughter of King Victor Emmanuel III of Italy, and acted as an intermediary between Nazi Germany and Fascist Italy. After Italy surrendered to the Allies, both he and his wife were arrested. She died of wounds on 27 August 1944, after an Allied air-raid on an ammunition factory inside Buchenwald Concentration Camp. Princess Marie of Baden, wife of the fourth son, Prince Wolfgang, was also killed in an Allied air-raid, in Frankfurt-am-Main on 29 January 1944. The youngest son, Prince Christopher, was married to Princess Sophie of Greece, an elder sister of Prince Philip, Duke of Edinburgh, and died in a flying accident in the Apennines on 7 October 1943.

Prince Albert, Duke of Schleswig-Holstein, younger brother of Prince Christian Victor, or 'Christle', was a lieutenant-colonel in the 3rd Guards Uhlans of the German Army. However, he was excused from fighting against his British cousins during the First World War through a posting to the staff of the governor of Berlin. Another grandson of Queen Victoria,

[2] Ibid., p. 249.

Charles Edward, the Duke of Albany, reigning Duke of Saxe-Coburg and Gotha, KG, GCVO, was deprived of his British honours in 1917. He subsequently joined the Nazi Party and was President of the German Red Cross from 1933 to 1945.

There were casualties in the British Royal family as well. Princess Beatrice's youngest son, twenty-three-year-old Maurice, a lieutenant in the King's Royal Rifle Corps, was killed by a shell while leading an attack at Zonnebeke on 27 October 1914 during the First Battle of Ypres. On 4 January 1915 Princess Beatrice echoed the words of Rupert Brooke's poem, 'The Soldier', when writing to Sir Frederick Milner, 7th Baronet: 'All these festive days have been particularly trying . . . one cannot help one's thoughts going back to that lonely little soldier's grave in a foreign country, and to that bright young life, cut off so early.'[3] Prince Maurice of Battenberg is buried in grave 1.B in Ypres Town Cemetery.

During the ninth month of the war, the King instructed his Private Secretary to write to the Prime Minister, stressing the importance of holding the moral high ground: 'The King yields to no one in abominating the general conduct of Germans throughout this war; but none the less he deprecates the idea of reprisals and retaliation; he has always hoped that at the end of the war we shall as a Nation stand before the world as having conducted it as far as possible with humanity and like gentlemen.'[4]

In response to anti-German sentiment, the House of Windsor was proclaimed on 17 July 1917, prompting Kaiser Wilhelm II to remark that he looked forward to watching *The Merry Wives of Saxe-Coburg-Gotha*. At the same time, German princes were struck from British orders of chivalry although, in the interests of historical accuracy, their stall-plates were left in place in the various chapels. The war took an inevitable toll on the King, just as the next war was to do on his second son. On 18 November 1917, King George V tried to reassure his concerned mother: 'I am not too tired. In these days I must go about & see as many people as possible & so encourage them in their work. They appreciate it, I believe, & I am quite ready to sacrifice myself if necessary, as long as we win this war.'[5] A year later he wrote to Prince Albert: 'The great day has come & we have won the war. It has been

[3] Matthew Dennison, *The Last Princess: The Devoted Life of Queen Victoria's Youngest Daughter*, London: Weidenfeld & Nicolson, 2007, p. 247.

[4] Nicolson, *King George the Fifth: His Life and Reign*, p. 272.

[5] Ibid., p. 316.

a long time coming, but I was sure if we stuck to it, we should win & it is a great victory over one of the most perfect military machines ever created.'[6]

Christmas 1914

At Buckingham Palace on Sunday, 2 August 1914, the Prince of Wales wrote in his diary: 'I turned out at 8.00 & walked twice round the garden before breakfast at 9.15 & then wrote till church here at 11.00 when the Archbishop of Canterbury preached a sermon. Grannie & Aunt Toria came & afterwards I showed them my rooms. The greatest depression prevailed here for news arrived of a German advance on France, thro Luxembourg, with fighting in France. There was a cabinet council at 11.00 to decide whether we should help France immediately or not; the result was kept secret. The 2nd and 3rd Fleets have been mobilised, & the 1st Fleet is somewhere in the North Sea . . .'[7]

The following day, he wrote:

> War news was of a startling nature; Germany has violated Belgium's neutrality by advancing thro the land on France. This has forced the govt's hand somewhat for Sir E. Grey stated in the House, that we can no longer stand out. Papa held a 2nd council at 5.30 to issue the order for general mobilisation of the army to commence at midnight; but no expeditionary force is to be sent as yet. Redmond assured the cooperation of Ulstermen & Nationalists in the defence of Ireland, & in the colonies, imperial feeling is running very high . . . I had to come in through the garden on account of a dense crowd which was airing its patriotism in front of the Palace. The parents went out on the balcony just before dinner at 8.30 & twice again before 10.00, as fresh masses arrived. They sang & cheered the whole evening as yesterday, & when parents came out their enthusiasm was enormous. Such a relieving sign to feel that the people are backing everything up.

On the momentous 4 August 1914, King George V wrote in his diary:

> Fairly warm, showers & windy. At work all day. Saw Bigge & Bill. Had a walk in the garden. Winston Churchill came to report at 1.0 that at the

[6] John W. Wheeler-Bennett, *King George VI: His Life and Reign*, London: Macmillan and Co., 1958, p. 117.
[7] Royal Archives: EDW/PRIV/DIARY/1914.

> meeting of Cabinet this morning that we had sent ultimatum to Germany that if by midnight tonight she did not give satisfactory answer about her troops passing through Belgium, Goschen [British Ambassador to Berlin] would ask for his passports. Held a Council at 4.0. L[d] Morley & John Burns have resigned & have left the Cabinet. Aunt Helena came to tea in the garden. Motherdear, Toria & Aunt Beatrice came to see us. Worked all the evening. At 10.30 the Prime Minister telephoned to say that Goschen had been given his passports at 7.0 this evening. I held a Council at 10.45 to declare war with Germany, it is a terrible catastrophe but it is not our fault. An enormous crowd collected outside the Palace, we went on the balcony both before & after dinner. When they heard that war had been declared the excitement increased & it was a never to be forgotten sight when May & I with David went on to the balcony, the cheering was terrific. Please God it may be soon over & that he will protect dear Bertie's life. Bed at 12.0.[8]

The following day, Prince Albert, at sea in HMS *Collingwood*, wrote in his diary:

> I got up at 11.45 and kept the middle watch till 4.0. War was declared between us and Germany at 2.0 a.m. I turned in again at 4.0 till 7.15. Sir John Jellicoe took over the command from Sir George Callaghan. After divisions we went to control. I kept the afternoon watch till 4.0 p.m. Two German trawlers were captured by destroyers. Papa sent a most interesting telegram to the fleet. I put it down in words.
>
> > At this grave moment in our National History I send to you and through you (i.e. Sir John Jellicoe) to the officers and men of the fleets of which you have assumed command, the assurance of my confidence that under your direction they will revive and renew the old glories of the Royal Navy, and prove once again the sure shield of Britain and of the Empire in the hour of trial.
>
> After tea I read till dinner. I kept the 1st watch and turned in at 12.0 a.m.[9]

[8] Nicolson, *King George the Fifth: His Life and Reign*, p. 247.
[9] Wheeler-Bennett, *King George VI: His Life and Reign*, p. 76.

That same day, the Prince of Wales wrote to Prince Albert:

> Well, this is just about the mightiest calamity that has ever or will ever befall mankind . . . To think that but 17 days ago we were together with everything working peacefully in Europe, and now we are at the commencement of a most hideous and appalling war, the duration or issue of which are impossible to predict . . . 'England at war with Germany!!' that seems a sentence which would appear nowhere but in a mad novel. The Germans could never have chosen a worse moment, and serve them right too if they are absolutely crushed, as I can but think they will be. The way they have behaved will go down in history as about the worst and most infamous action of any govt!! Don't you agree? I bet you do.
>
> I am as good as heartbroken to think I am totally devoid of any job whatsoever and have not the faintest chance of being able to serve my country. I have to stay at home with the women and children, a passenger of the worst description!! Here I am in this bloody gt palace, doing absolutely nothing but attend meals . . . Surely a man of 20 has higher things to hope for? But I haven't apparently! Oh God it is becoming unbearable to live this usual life of ease and comfort at home, when you my dear old boy, and all naval and army officers, are toiling under unpleasant conditions, suffering hardships and running gt risks with your lives for the defence and honour of England . . . At such a time you will picture me here, depressed and miserable and taking no more part in this huge undertaking than Harry and George, 2 irresponsible kids who run about playing inane games in the passage. However, enough about my rotten self, for I am a most bum specimen of humanity, and so must not be considered.[10]

Just five days later, though, he wrote in his diary at Warley Barracks, Brentwood, having been posted to the King's Company of the Grenadier Guards, whose officers' mess was a 'filthy hole': 'But what does one care when living under war conditions? I am so glad to have joined up and to have escaped from the palace!!'[11]

That Christmas, the two brothers had very different experiences. Despite his fears, the Prince of Wales managed to get to France, while Prince Albert, a serving officer in the Royal Navy, was back in England and

[10] Royal Archives: GV EE 13/2, quoted in Philip Ziegler, *King Edward VIII*, London: Collins, 1990, p. 49.

[11] Ziegler, *King Edward VIII*, p. 50.

spent Christmas at York Cottage, Sandringham. At 'Head Quarters, British Army. St. Omer', the Prince of Wales wrote in his diary:

> Mayne came out with me at 7.45 but for a short way only & then I ran along the canal as far as Arcques & back, which gave me a good sweat & did me worlds of good. Then I was writing till 10.00 & motored to Bailleul with Barry to visit II Corps & wish them a happy Xmas etc. Going on to Vieux Berguin we had some lunch about 1.00, sending the car to Hazebrouck & walking to 10th Hussars H.Q. in Rue du Bois where we found Col. Barnes & Shearman at lunch!! We sat with them till past 2.00 & then walked on to Château la Motte where we played soccer for CAV Corps staff v. CAV DIV. Rotten game on a rough frozen field; they won. However it was exercise & Barry & I proceeded to Hazebrouck on foot, getting into the car at 5.00, & reaching here at 5.30. I wrote hard till a Xmas dinner at 8.15, to which several generals came; of course I was 20 years younger than any of them still the party became quite merry at the end, & we did not break up till 10.30 & I wrote for 3 hours!![12]

Crown Prince William, the eldest of five sons of Emperor William II, and therefore a great-grandson of Queen Victoria, took command of the 5th German Army in August 1914. In his war memoirs, he wrote:

> I shall never forget the first Christmas of the war. For us Germans, Holy Christmastime is, after all, the most glorious time of the year, when even the heart of the hardest of men softens at the thought of his own childhood, his home and his family. Thus I felt particularly drawn to my field-grey boys on this occasion, and I steered my car in the direction of the Argonne. I spent the afternoon in the hutments of the Württembergers with the 120th and 124th Regiments. Thick snow lay on the hilltops above this Forest of the Dead. The shells howled their monotonous and hideous melody, and from time to time the sacred silence was rent by the burst of a machine-gun's fire. And in between, one could hear the dull drone of the trench mortar shells. Nevertheless, the spirits of the men were everywhere very cheerful. Every dugout had its Christmas tree, and from all directions came the sound of rough men's voices singing our exquisite old Christmas songs.

[12] Royal Archives: EDW/PRIV/DIARY/1914.

> [Walter] Kirchhoff, the concert singer, who was attached to our Headquarters Staff for a while as orderly officer, sang his Christmas songs on that same sacred evening in the front-line trenches of the 130th Regiment. And on the following day he told me that some French soldiers who had climbed up their parapet had continued to applaud, until at last he gave them an encore. Thus, amid the bitter realities of trench warfare, with all its squalor, a Christmas song had worked a miracle and thrown up a bridge from man to man.[13]

Queen Mary set the scene for a subdued wartime Christmas at Sandringham by describing Christmas Eve: 'Arranged Xmas things. At 3 went to distribution of meat, then to Park House to see Bigge family who are staying there for Xmas. After tea we gave each other our Xmas presents in the billiard room. Rather sad without a tree or anything but one does not feel in a festive mood.'[14] Christmas Day was equally quiet, as Prince Albert described in his diary: 'I got up at 7.30 and had breakfast at 8.50. I gave the parents and Mary their presents. At 10.0 I went for a walk with the brothers & we went to see Mr. Jones. At 11.30 we went to church and I took the sacrament afterwards. Lunch was at 1.30. I changed & then went for a walk with Mary & the brothers. We went up towards Anmer, passed Captain's Close and then back by the Water Tower. After tea I wrote letters and then played billiards with Henry. Dinner was at 8.30 and I played billiards afterwards.'[15]

By New Year's Eve, the Prince of Wales had joined his family at York Cottage. He helpfully summarised 1914, from his personal perspective:

> So ends 1914 & may the New Year prove a happier one for us all, & bring with it a victorious end to this bloody War. Up to August, 1914 was a good year for me. Some capital shooting here all Jan, then a good sporting term at Oxford, followed by those wonderful three weeks in Norway with dear Aunt Maud. After Easter at Windsor I was at sea in the *Collingwood* for 10 days & then came the Summer term at Oxford followed by camp at Mytchett with the O.T.C. & 3 weeks' attachment to the 1st Life Guards when I got my 1st taste of London life in the season with dances etc. But since August I have had a bloody time doing duty in London for 3 months

[13] Crown Prince William of Germany, *My War Experiences*, London: Hurst & Blackett, 1922, pp. 122–3.
[14] Royal Archives: QM/PRIV/QMD/1914.
[15] Royal Archives: KGVI/PRIV/DIARY/1914.

> & then 6 weeks at G.H.Q. But since then I am a Grenadier which is a gt. honour.'[16]

Their Majesties' Christmas Card to the Forces, 1914

At the suggestion of General Sir William Robertson, Quartermaster General and later Chief of Staff of the British Expeditionary Force, King George V and Queen Mary sent Christmas cards to members of the British armed forces, including Empire servicemen and servicewomen, to celebrate Christmas 1914.

In the form of postcards, they bore the images of the King and Queen on the front, with a facsimile handwritten message, signed by them both, on the reverse. Three versions were produced: one for the Army, with the King in the uniform of a field marshal; one for the Royal Navy, with the King wearing the uniform of an admiral of the fleet; and a third for the wounded or sick, which was in the Army style but included a special message for the recipient's recovery. The cards were delivered in unaddressed envelopes, embossed with the Royal Arms.

The cards were produced by Downeys, the Royal photographers. The same firm packed the cards and took responsibility for their delivery, either to Royal Navy depôts, or to France and Flanders. There were 350,000 Army cards, 250,000 Navy cards and 60,000 cards for the wounded and sick. No such cards were produced for later Christmases during the First World War, as the numbers of those serving increased enormously. By the end of the war, some 5 million British men were in uniform, around one quarter of the adult male population of Great Britain and Ireland.

Christmas 1916

From the British perspective the key military initiative of 1916 was the Battle of the Somme, for which joint Anglo-French offensive great hopes were harboured. King George V spent 1 July, the first day of the battle, at the Royal Pavilion in Aldershot. In his diary, he wrote:

> We motored to Hankley Common where French & Hunter met me & I inspected the 4th Canadian Division under Genl Watson (Canadian

[16] Royal Archives: EDW/PRIV/DIARY/1914.

> Dominion Day) 15,000 on parade, a fine lot of men. On our way there we visited the wounded at Waverley Abbey, M^{r} and Mrs Anderson's private house which they have turned into a hospital, most comfortable & well arranged. Ld French & Jack Dawnay came to stay. Cust relieved Godfrey. Walked in the grounds with May. This morning the 4th Army & the French on our right each side of the river Somme near Albert advanced on a front of 20 miles after a terrible bombardment, so far, the progress is good. The Royal Engineers' band played at dinner.

Two days later, he recorded that 'the fighting in France is progressing, but our casualties are heavy, 1,300 officers & 41,000 men'.[17] Very sadly, he was misinformed. On the first day alone, the British Army suffered 57,470 casualties: 21,392 killed, died of wounds or missing, 35,493 wounded and 585 prisoners-of-war. The King visited the Somme front on 14 August 1916. The Battle of the Somme degenerated into an appalling battle of attrition and one of the objectives for 1 July, Beaumont Hamel, was not captured until 13 November 1916.

Like so many other families, the British Royal Family was often forced to endure long periods of separation and uncertainty during the First World War. On Christmas Eve 1916, Queen Mary wrote to Prince Albert, who was still serving with the Royal Navy:

> I am thinking of you so much today, when in former & happier times we have always been together to celebrate the occasion in a festive way. Alas, this year it is again not possible to spend a really joyful Xmas, so we must just make the best of it. After a busy week of Xmas shopping & the sending off of endless presents & souvenirs we culminated today in a large family luncheon to those remaining in Town, Grannie & A^{t} Toria not coming owing to their colds still being so bad – however we are to go there to tea. About 4. today we gave each other our Xmas presents in the room next the Indian Rm where I arranged tables & a small tree. We missed you & David very much indeed. 6.45 just returned from Marl. Hse where Grannie gave us such nice presents, also things for you & David which I shall hope to take to the Cottage for you both. David does not return now till Jan: 2 – so I suppose he won't join us at Cottage till the 4th or so. We don't know yet when we shall go down. Forgive more as I am in a hurry.[18]

[17] Royal Archives: GV/PRIV/GVD/1916.

[18] Royal Archives: GVI/PRIV/RF/11/247.

That same day, the King wrote in his diary: 'Rained & snowed in the night. Service at 10.0 & had the Holy Communion afterwards. Walked in the garden with Seymour. After luncheon we went with the 3 children to King George's Hospital & we gave each of the 1600 patients a book for Xmas, we each did a floor (5 floors). All very well arranged. Worked with Wigram.'[19]

On Christmas Day, the Prince of Wales was serving in France with HQ 14th Corps, in camp near Méaulte:

> Turning out at 9.00 I shoved off in a car with Joey before 10.00 & we followed Fatty & Gathorne round by Maricourt to 17th Div. H.Q. & on via Bernapay xrds & Montauban to H.A. H.Q. & then thro. Carnoy & past Plateau to Camp 15 to attend 2nd G. Gds. church parade as it was Xmas day. Rawlinson & G. Fielding also attend & the service was held in the church army hut at 11.30 & lasted about ¾ hr & we had W. Gds. band!! I stayed behind afterwards & lunched with old Bill at Bn. H.Q. after we had been round to see the Coys. at dinners tho. the only extras they got were beer & plum pudding!! However it was something for them to be out of the line poor devils & they'll get their proper Xmas dinners when they get back to the rest area next month!! We had a v. cheery lunch & I got rather tight alas & stayed till 4.00 as some of the others came in afterwards & played the gramophone. Wonderful fellows!! I walked back here across country & it was a bloody awful wallow thro. the mud too & raining into the bargain & I did not get in till 5.30 with an awful 'head'!![20]

Christmas 1939

On 24 September 1939, King George VI wrote to Queen Mary: 'I am keeping a War Diary now & have got it up to date.'[21] In his War Diary, King George VI wrote:

> On Friday Sept. 1st at 6.0 a.m. Hitler gave the order to march into Poland. This was the end of all our peaceful efforts at negotiation with Hitler, & we sent our Ultimatum on Saturday to the effect that if the German Troops had not been recalled from Poland by 11.0 a.m. on Sunday a state of War

19 Royal Archives: GV/PRIV/GVD/1916.

20 Royal Archives: EDW/PRIV/DIARY/1916.

21 Wheeler-Bennett, *King George VI: His Life and Reign*, p. 404.

> would exist between us & Germany. There was no reply. The die was cast. We were at War with Hitler & his regime, & all that it stands for.
>
> Sunday September 3rd As 11 o'clock struck that fateful morning I had a certain feeling of relief that those 10 anxious days of intensive negotiations with Germany over Poland, which at moments looked favourable, with Mussolini working for peace as well, were over. Hitler would not & could not draw back from the edge of the Abyss to which he had led us. Despite our protestations that the Polish Question could have been settled without force, Hitler had taken the plunge, with the knowledge that the whole might of the British Empire would be against him to help Poland, our ally. France is our ally. Italy has declared herself neutral for the present.[22]

Eleven days later, after 'E & I visited the Port of London Authority in the forenoon', came the first major personal crisis of a war that was to drain away the King's energy. As he recorded: 'I saw David on our return. I had not seen him since he left England on Dec 11th 1936. We talked for about an hour. There were no recriminations on either side. I told him I was glad the business matter was amicably settled & he agreed. I found him the same as I had always known him. He looked very well & had lost the deep lines under his eyes. He was very glad to be back in England, he told me he had already seen Winston Churchill this morning. I expected that he had as he was very confident about himself, & had quite forgotten what he had done to the country in 1936.'

The next day, 'Mama came to lunch. She was very interested in what I told her about David, but had no intention of seeing him if she could avoid it. I was able to reassure her on this point. I saw the P.M. this evening. He thanked me for putting him wise as to the line of argument to go on. He told me he had definitely put him off going to Wales as to the matter of his & her reception there, but had suggested that he might be attached to one of the Home Commands for the moment. I told the P.M. I did not like the idea at all, & that the sooner he went to France the better for all concerned. He is not wanted here.'[23]

It is important to record that the wounds eventually healed, at least to some extent, with Queen Mary writing in her diary on 5 October 1945:

[22] Ibid., p. 405.

[23] Royal Archives: GVI/PRIV/DIARY/1939, quoted in Wheeler-Bennett, *King George VI: His Life and Reign*, p. 417.

'Lovely day. Lunched with Bertie who arrived this morning from Balmoral. At 4 David arrived by plane from Paris on a visit to me – I had not seen him for nearly 9 years! it was a great joy meeting again, he looked very well – Bertie came to dinner to meet him.'[24]

Between 4 and 10 December, King George VI visited the British Expeditionary Force (BEF) in France, writing in his diary: 'I motored to Dover with Harry, & crossed the Channel in the 'Codrington' (Com^{d} Swinley) to Boulogne. We had a rough crossing but no-one was seasick . . . During the 2 hour motor drive to Arras Gort [commander of the BEF] told me all about H-B's [Leslie (later 1st Baron) Hore-Belisha, Secretary of State for War] visit to him, & how angry Gort was that he had made those untrue remarks to the War Cabinet, & he resented them as H-B had seen the troops & had not troubled to see the defences. H-B's remark that Gamelin had told him the French built concrete pill boxes in 3 days, when Gamelin had said 3 weeks, was the last straw. It appears that my visit is a timely one . . . French Generals Billotte & Blanchard on each side of me. Very hard work speaking French.'

The King's description of his visit continued: 'Général Georges, who commands the northern group of French Armies, in which the B.E.F. is serving, & is Gort's C in C, came to dine. . . Gort likes him, & can talk to him easily. A great improvement on the last war's generals . . . We then went for an hour into the Hackenberg Fort, one of the biggest forts on the Maginot Line proper. It is built inside a hill, with 80 ft of earth above the steel & concrete of which it is built. It took 5 years to build, & has guns & mortars of all dimensions in it. An underground battleship rather describes it.' On his return to Buckingham Palace on Sunday, 10 December, the King wrote: 'I was very glad to be back, as the days had been strenuous ones, but the whole visit did me a great deal of good. I was in the fresh air most of the daylight hours, & away from papers. I spent all the rest of the day trying to read a week's papers, & signing the ordinary routine papers, also of a week's standing. I did enjoy my hot bath before dinner.'[25]

The following day, during his third visit to the front, the Duke of Windsor visited the Second French Army – and was rather less impressed with the Maginot Line. In his report, submitted five days later, he wrote: 'I gained the general impression that the MAGINOT LINE is an effective barrier, but cannot be looked upon as impregnable. Most of the FRENCH

[24] James Pope-Hennessy, *Queen Mary*, London: George Allen and Unwin, 1959, p. 614.
[25] Royal Archives: GVI/PRIV/DIARY/1939.

officers with whom I discussed the strength of it seemed to consider that it was so strong that a rear position was hardly necessary. They have, nevertheless, reconnoitred a rear line some 10 to 12 kilometres in rear, and state that they are doing a little work on it. I saw no evidence of this work, but this was probably because I generally passed through this line in the dark. When I passed it in daylight, I saw no signs even of field defences . . . The MAGINOT LINE does not seem to be an insuperable barrier . . . At present, once the crust is broken there is nothing to stop exploitation by armoured forces . . . After that, there will be nothing but a few demolitions and troops in the open to stop an advance to PARIS. It is perhaps fortunate that the Germans did not attack through Luxembourg and Belgium in November.'

On 27 December 1939, Queen Elizabeth wrote to Queen Mary from Sandringham:

> We all missed you very much at Xmas, and we wondered so much how your festivities were going. It was very nice for us having Alice here, and also David & Rachel & their 2 children [the Hon. David (later Sir David) Bowes-Lyon, Queen Elizabeth's younger brother, and his wife and family], but it was sad not being all together for our annual meeting of the Family. The three officers of the Guard dined on Xmas Day, also the Fullers, and Lilibet dined down too. We had crackers & hats, & I gave a thought to your dear little black bonnet! It is very cold. Yesterday when we were out shooting 3 large bombers came over very low, & the children were thrilled because they thought that they saw black Swastikas on the wings. However, I think they proved to be our own aircraft.[26]

The first major tragedy of the war was the sinking of the battleship *Royal Oak* on 14 October 1939. Less than a year earlier, the *Royal Oak* had been entrusted with the task of carrying the body of Queen Maud of Norway, formerly Princess Maud of Wales, who had died in London, back to Oslo for burial. Recently returned from a gruelling sortie in the North Sea, the *Royal Oak* was torpedoed by the German submarine *U-47* within the supposedly impenetrable base at Scapa Flow in the Orkney Islands, with the loss of 833 of her complement of 1,234. More than 100 of the dead were Boy Seamen, below the age of eighteen. According to Marion Crawford, the Princesses' governess, known to the family as 'Crawfie': 'One night over the wireless

[26] Queen Elizabeth to Queen Mary, 27 December 1939 – Royal Archives: QM/PRIV/CC12/116, quoted in William Shawcross, *Queen Elizabeth the Queen Mother*, London: Macmillan, 2009, p. 503.

we suddenly got the horrible news that brought us slap up against reality. A grave voice regretfully announced the sinking of the battleship *Royal Oak*. We were continually studying *Jane's Fighting Ships* and the little girls took a personal interest in every one of them. Lilibet jumped horrified from her chair, her eyes blazing with anger. I can still hear her little voice: "Crawfie, it can't be! All those nice sailors."'[27] She later said, wistfully: 'I kept thinking of those sailors, Crawfie, and what Christmas must have been like in their homes.'[28]

On New Year's Day 1940, the King wrote: 'I went to London in the evening. I held a Privy Council to sign a Proclamation calling up the men between the ages 23–28. This makes it easier for the Minister of Labour to work out who are to remain in Industry. These classes will be called up during the year, & will affect nearly 2,000,000 men. Later I went by train on the G.W. Ry. & spent the night in the train.' On 2 January, King George VI

> got out at Newbury Racecourse & was met by Bulgy Thorne, who commands the 48th Division. One of his Brigades was formed up on the racecourse. A very cold morning & it took place at 9.30 a.m. Then I motored in Berkshire & Wiltshire all day seeing the various units of the Division. I stopped at Tottenham House, the Marquess of Ailesbury's home in the Savernake Forest. His family has an old custom. Whenever the reigning Sovereign enters the Hall, the Marquess has the right to blow 2 blasts on the Horn. The Horn consists of a small elephant tusk hollowed out, which has metal bands showing hunting scenes on it. Ailesbury blew the Horn very well. George III was the last Sovereign who had heard it. He often stayed there on his way to Weymouth. The 48th Divn is a Territorial one, & is the first to go out as a Divn. I go into the train at Hungerford, & after 5 hours in a very cold train I arrived at Wolferton.[29]

Christmas 1940: An Evocative Royal Christmas Card Connects with the People

If there was one event that, more than any other, is perceived to have bound the Sovereign to his people during the Second World War, it was the bombing of Buckingham Palace in September 1940. At a time when 'the Blitz'

[27] Marion Crawford, *The Little Princesses*, London: Cassell & Co., 1950, p. 62.
[28] Ibid, p. 66.
[29] Royal Archives: GVI/PRIV/DIARY/1939/40.

by Hermann Goering's Luftwaffe was meting out such terrible damage to London and other major British cities, the Royal Family shared the trials and tribulations of the population at large. Although Buckingham Palace and its grounds were struck by bombs nine times during the war, it is the two earliest attacks, at the height of the Battle of Britain, which echo down the years. The Royal Family's Christmas card for 1940 was an evocative image of the King and Queen standing amidst the ruins of part of Buckingham Palace in mid-September that year.

During the war, the King and Queen generally slept at Windsor Castle, while spending their days at Buckingham Palace. On 11 September 1940, Tommy Lascelles described the first attack in a letter to his wife: 'Our bomb was a delayed-action one, which fell up against the swimming pool in that excrescence just to the left of my office window – beyond the garden entrance from which the King and Queen always emerge for the Garden Party. It fell on Monday night, and went off at 1.30 a.m. on Tuesday; it blew the north end of the bath out, and Their Majesties' sitting room. So we are all living rather hugger-mugger in the back rooms; but I think all will be straight again tomorrow. Their Majesties were photographed among the ruins, and early this morning I conducted a party of about forty journalists round them.'[30]

That same day, the King wrote to his mother that 'we have seen some of the awful havoc which has been done in East London, & have talked to the people who are quite marvellous in the face of adversity. So cheerful about it all, & some have had very narrow escapes.'[31] Just two days after that, the King and Queen were to enjoy their own 'very narrow escape', as the King described in his War Diary:

> We went to London & found an Air Raid in progress. The day was very cloudy & it was raining hard. We were both upstairs with Alec Hardinge talking in my little sitting room overlooking the quadrangle; (I cannot use my ordinary one owing to the broken windows). All of a sudden we heard an aircraft making a zooming noise above us, saw 2 bombs falling past the opposite side of the Palace, & then heard 2 resounding crashes as the bombs fell in the quadrangle about 30 yds away. We looked at each other, & then we were out into the passage as fast as we could get there.

[30] Duff Hart-Davis, ed., *King's Counsellor: Abdication and War: The Diaries of Sir Alan Lascelles*, London: Weidenfeld & Nicolson, 2006, pp. 15–16.

[31] Shawcross, *Queen Elizabeth the Queen Mother*, p. 522.

> The whole thing happened in a matter of seconds. We all wondered why we weren't dead. Two great craters had appeared in the courtyard. The one nearest the Palace had burst a fire hydrant & water was pouring through the broken windows in the passage. 6 bombs had been dropped.
>
> The aircraft was seen coming straight down the Mall below the clouds having dived through the clouds & had dropped 2 bombs in the forecourt, 2 in the quadrangle, 1 in the Chapel & the other in the garden. The Chapel is wrecked, & the bomb also wrecked the plumber's workshop below in which 4 men were working. 3 of them were injured & the fourth shocked. Looking at the wreckage how they escaped death is a wonder to me.

In fact, one of them, sixty-five-year-old Alfred John Davies of 8 Ranmere Street, Wandsworth, died of his injuries in neighbouring St George's Hospital a week later. The King's account continued:

> E & I went all round the basement talking to the servants who were all safe, & quite calm through it all. None of the windows on our side of the Palace were broken. We were told that the bomb in the forecourt was a delay action (D.A.) bomb so we gave orders for all the east windows to be opened in case it exploded, & we remained in our shelter & had lunch there.
>
> There is no doubt that it was a direct attack on Buckingham Palace. Luckily the Palace is very narrow, & the bombs fell in the open spaces. The Chapel sticks out into the garden. It was a ghastly experience, & I don't want it to be repeated. It certainly teaches one to 'take cover' on all future occasions, but one must be careful not to become 'dugout minded'. Admiral Sir E. Evans, one of the London Regional Commissioners, was with us as we were going to visit the damage in East & West Ham in the forenoon. But this we did in the afternoon when the 'All Clear' went. I slept well & hope for no ill effects of the experience of 'having been bombed'.[32]

Queen Elizabeth described the attack in a letter to Queen Mary:

> I hardly know how to begin to tell you of the horrible attack on Buckingham Palace this morning. Bertie & I arrived there at about ¼ to 11, and he & I went up to our poor windowless rooms to collect a few odds and ends . . .

[32] Royal Archives: GVI/PRIV/DIARY/1940, quoted in *King George VI: His Life and Reign*, pp. 468–9.

> It is curious how one's instincts work at these moments of great danger, as quite without thinking, the urge was to get away from the windows. Everybody remained wonderfully calm and we went down to the shelter . . . I was so pleased with the behaviour of our servants. They were really magnificent. I went along to the kitchen which, as you will remember, has a glass roof. I found the chef bustling about, and when I asked him if he was alright, he replied cheerfully that there had been *un petit quelque chose dans le coin, un petit bruit*, with a broad smile. The *petit quelque chose* was the bomb on the Chapel just next door! He was perfectly unmoved, and took the opportunity to tell me of his unshakeable conviction that France will rise again![33]

It is hard to argue with this passage, from the King's official biography: 'A magnificent piece of bombing, Ma'am, if you'll pardon my saying so, was the comment of one of the police constables, an old soldier, on duty at the Palace to the Queen, immediately after the raid.'[34] This incident was kept secret, even from Winston Churchill, who wrote in his memoirs: 'I must confess that at that time neither I nor any of my colleagues were aware of the fact . . . Had the windows been closed instead of open, the whole of the glass would have splintered into the faces of the King and Queen, causing terrible injuries. So little did they make of it that even I who saw them and their entourage so frequently only realised long afterwards . . . what actually happened.'[35]

The Queen later said: 'I'm glad we've been bombed. It makes me feel I can look the East End in the face.'[36] In fact, things may not have been quite so straightforward, as Max Hastings observed: 'Edward R. Murrow, the American broadcaster, told his CBS radio audience on 15 September that there was no great outpouring of public sentiment following news that bombs had fallen on Buckingham Palace; Londoners shrugged that the king and queen were merely experiencing the common plight of millions: "This war has no relation with the last one, so far as symbols and civilians are concerned. You must understand that a world is dying, that old values, the old prejudices, and the old bases of power and prestige are going."'[37]

33 Shawcross, *Queen Elizabeth the Queen Mother*, pp. 522–3.
34 Wheeler-Bennett, *King George VI: His Life and Reign*, pp. 468–9.
35 Winston Churchill, *Their Finest Hour*, London: Cassell & Co.,1949, p. 334.
36 Betty Spencer Shew, *Queen Elizabeth the Queen Mother*, London: Hodder & Stoughton, 1954, p. 76.
37 Max Hastings, *All Hell Let Loose*, London: HarperPress 2011, pp. 101–2.

The following weekend, the King wrote in his War Diary:

> During the forenoon 2 Hurricanes came & 'dive bombed' the Castle so as to give the guard on the Round Tower practice & to show them what happened. I was dressing & when it began I instinctively ducked behind the dressing table. Yesterday's experience was still too clear in my mind to avoid doing so. We went to the Mews to see the places for the winter accomodation [sic] of the Windsor Castle Defence Force Company. At the moment they are in tents. They will occupy the stalls & loose boxes, & some of the horses will go to Ascot.
>
> Sunday was uneventful here, but B.P. had 2 'dud' bombs, one which went through E's Empire Room & landed near the bath in the bathroom next to the Regency Room, & the other fell in the garden to which was attached part of the bomb dropping gear. An aircraft was hit over St. George's Hospital & these bombs probably came off it. Some incendiary bombs also fell in the garden but went out. The R.A.F. had a wonderful day. 185 German aircraft to 25 with 13 pilots safe.

That Christmas, the Princesses joined the children of the King's tenants in a Nativity Play in St George's Hall, Windsor Castle. In a letter to Queen Mary, 'Crawfie' wrote that Princess Elizabeth 'looked like Edward V in her Coronation Crown and tunic of pink and gold'.[38] Princess Margaret sang 'Gentle Jesus' at the crib. On 21 December, their proud father wrote: 'Saturday the children took part in a Xmas Nativity Play with the school children of the Park School. Margaret as the 'child' played her part remarkably well & was not shy. I wept through most of it. It is such a wonderful story.'[39] Charles Fulford wrote that 'Princess Margaret acted the part of a little child who saw the scene of the Nativity in a dream; & when she sang a little hymn, kneeling and unaccompanied, the Queen had to resort to her handkerchief, & the Dean said that he was not ashamed to admit that he wept copiously, and I felt near it myself, it was extraordinarily moving. The dresses were beautiful, & Princess Elizabeth looked magnificent as one of the 3 Orient Kings in red & gold brocade.'[40]

[38] Marion Crawford to Queen Mary, 23 February 1941 – Lambeth Palace Library, Lang Papers 318, ff. 67–9.

[39] Royal Archives: GVI/PRIV/DIARY/1940, quoted in Wheeler-Bennett, *King George VI: His Life and Reign*, p. 741.

[40] Diary of C. H. Fulford Esq. – courtesy of Francis Fulford, Esq.

After Christmas the Royal Family went to Norfolk – but not to Sandringham House itself – as the King explained in his diary on 27 December:

> We left Windsor at 10.0 a.m. & motored to Sandringham in time for lunch. We are staying at Appleton so as not to attract the enemy's attention to the place. The house has been entirely furnished from Sandringham House & it is very warm & comfortable. I did my best to let this house before the war after Uncle Charles of Norway gave it back to me after Aunt Maud's death. But now in these days it has come in very usefully, & it has made it possible for us to live in Norfolk. I have built a concrete air raid shelter just outside and connected with the house in case we shall need it. It is well camouflaged by trees. I hope we shall be able to have a little rest & change here as I know I need it.[41]

Shortly after the marriage on 22 July 1896 of his youngest daughter, Princess Maud, to Prince Carl of Denmark, later King Haakon VII of Norway, the Prince of Wales wrote to his brother-in-law, Crown Prince Frederik of Denmark: 'I have given Maud and Charles a small house, their own country retreat – about one mile from here – they will always have a pied-à-terre when they come over to England. I know they will appreciate this very much.' Queen Maud was born on 26 November 1869 and visited Appleton most years in order to celebrate her birthday and also to spend Christmas with the Royal Family. Ironically, though, the building of that concrete air-raid shelter was the ultimate downfall of Appleton House. It was both startlingly unattractive and dominant and also far too expensive and difficult to remove. Appleton House was allowed to decay until it was finally demolished in July 1984.

The traditional shoot took place on New Year's Eve 1940, as the King recorded: 'We shot Commodore Beat & had a very enjoyable day. It is a very good partridge & wild pheasant year (it would be) & I am very lucky to be able to be here to take advantage of it. I feel it is all wrong my being away from London & from my work, but I do feel that I need a change for my health, both mentally & bodily. This is the last day of 1940 & I do not regret its end. So much has happened during the year that is awful. Let us hope 1941 will see us nearer the end of the war. I have written daily entries so as to finish the book by the end of 1940.'[42]

[41] Royal Archives: GVI/PRIV/DIARY/1940.

[42] Ibid.

Fortunately, though, there was just enough room for the King's 'Retrospect of 1940', a process of evaluation and assessment he committed to his War Diary just once, at the end of this tumultuous year:

> Looking back on 1940 the 1st half year consisted of a series of disasters for us. Scandinavia & Iron Ore, no Staff talks with Holland & Belgium, invasion of Denmark & Norway & evacuation, invasion of Holland, Belgium, & France, evacuation from Dunkirk of B.E.F. (an epic for history), collapse of France. This all happened between January & June. Italy's entry. Winston coming in as P.M. & labour serving with him in his government stopped the political rot. Poor Neville Chamberlain, whose resignation as P.M. was hard for me to accept, & whose untimely death robbed me of an adviser & friend.
>
> Our feverish preparations to repel an invasion with no armaments, which did not materialise. Then the Blitzkrieg by the German Air Force by day & night against aerodromes & London which we countered magnificently. Civilian defence services & morale of people splendid. Industrial rearmaments in aircraft & guns despite bombing of Midland towns & cities. Reinforcements to Middle East of men & material via the Cape made Libyan campaign possible & the success it deserved to be. Italy's invasion of Greece & the latter's successful campaign in Albania. The Navy's part in keeping open our trade routes, altho' the loss of merchant shipping has been severe despite our Convoy system. The magnetic mine, then the acoustic mine have both been mastered to a degree.
>
> The 2nd six months have certainly shown the world what we can stand, & the U.S.A. in re-electing President Roosevelt for a 3rd Term on the theme of Aid for Britain in the way of armaments has been responded to by the American people. I hope this theme will be put into practical effect very soon. Hitler has not had everything his own way. He must be worried over his diplomatic actions with Spain & Russia, which have not borne fruit so far.[43]

On 7 January 1941, the Queen wrote to Queen Mary:

> We are all feeling much better for our quiet stay at dear little Appleton – Mabel Butcher & Marrington worked absolute <u>miracles</u> over carpets

[43] Royal Archives: GVI/PRIV/DIARY/1940, quoted in Shawcross, *Queen Elizabeth the Queen Mother*, p. 531.

& lights, and every room has a carpet which fits perfectly, and even the furniture fits! The drawing room here has the new armchairs & sofas from the Hall at S, the radio, & the piano from the drawing room at S. It makes a very comfortable living room, and as I have my writing table in Bertie's room, the lady can use the drawing room all the morning for writing. The children are looking quite different already. I am afraid that Windsor is not really a very good place for them, the noise of guns is heavy, and then of course there have been so many bombs dropped all around, & some so close. It is very difficult to know what is the best thing to do with them.

The weather has been very bad here, and snow lies everywhere. Bertie has shot every day possible, and looks much refreshed. All the people seem very well, and on Saturday the Women's Institute's tea party takes place! How I wish that you & Mary were to be there to sing & laugh. I believe there are to be patriotic *tableaux* this year. I wonder who will be Britannia! We went to see the Newfoundland soldiers who are living in the beautiful new Church School. They seem quite happy, but it is sad to see them there instead of the children.

It seems almost unbelievable that one can spend days here so like the good old pre-war ones. It is a real refreshment, and our visit to Sheffield seems less of a burden in consequence. Our Xmas at Windsor was rather tragic, because Lilibet & I both felt terribly ill for 2 days. It was a sort of internal flu – which Bertie had too, and made everything a great effort. It was disappointing too, because George & Marina came for 3 nights, & we retired to bed once before dinner, & also poor Alexandra developed German measles, so that we were rather parted! I am anxiously watching the children for signs of the first spots! I am very sad at losing Dorothy Halifax [The Viscountess Halifax accompanied her husband, who served as Foreign Secretary 1938–40, to Washington when he was appointed Ambassador to the United States], who is a real pillar of strength to me, but feel sure that the Americans will like & admire them both, as we do. I am still enraged beyond words over the futile and wicked destruction of the City of London. The Guildhall one can never forgive, and I am beginning to really hate the German mentality – the cruelty and arrogance of it.[44]

[44] Royal Archives: QM/PRIV/CC12/147, quoted in Shawcross, *Queen Elizabeth the Queen Mother*, p. 531.

The Queen duly attended the Sandringham Women's Institute party, writing to the Duke of Kent on 14 January 1941:

> I am still so disappointed and miserable about Xmas, for I really felt so ill and unwell, & fear that we produced no 'festive spirit' at all. You were both so angelic & understanding over everything, and it was a refreshment to see you both here. We had a marvellous fortnight at A . . . Poor Sandringham looked so forlorn, surrounded completely by waves of barbed wire, & (hush please) but Bertie has done away with all those very large & ugly clumps of shrubs & trees, so that it looks a little naked & uncherished.
>
> Everything goes on much the same, & 'Annie' was in grand form. I went to the Women's Institute party, and this year we had very patriotic *tableaux*! If only you could see them. Dear Mrs. Way, as Neptune, glaring furiously through a tangle of grey hair & seaweed, & Miss Burroughs (the Verger's daughter) as Britannia were HEAVEN. The words were spoken by the Fullers' cook, who was draped in the Union Jack, and it was all perfect.[45]

On 7 February 1941, the Queen wrote to her niece, Elizabeth Elphinstone: 'It became quite a joke in the end . . . I am still just as frightened of bombs, & guns going off, as I was at the beginning. I turn bright red, and my heart hammers – in fact I'm a beastly coward, but I do believe that a lot of people are, so I don't mind! Well, darling, I must stop . . . Tinkety tonk old fruit, & down with the Nazis.'[46]

Unsurprisingly, the King and Queen's Christmas card that year is quite unlike other Royal Christmas cards. The official collection of Royal Christmas cards from the reign of King George VI in the Royal Archives has no copy of this card. Ironically, the page for 1940 is empty, apart from the following annotation: 'No copy. (Tuck's records destroyed in air raid.)'[47]

[45] Royal Archives: QEQM/OUT/MISC, quoted in Shawcross, *Queen Elizabeth the Queen Mother*, p. 532.
[46] Royal Archives: QEQM/OUT/ELPHINSTONE, quoted in Shawcross, *Queen Elizabeth the Queen Mother*, p. 532.
[47] Royal Archives: PS/PSO/GVI/PS/MAIN/01610.

Christmas in the Bahamas, 1941 and 1943

On 18 August 1940, following the fall of France, the Duke of Windsor was appointed Governor of the Bahamas, which he described as 'a third-class British colony'.[48] On 16 December 1941, just nine days after the surprise Japanese attack on Pearl Harbor, the Duchess wrote to her Aunt Bessie, Mrs D. Buchanan Merryman:

> What can I say about all that has happened, except that I am glad that we are going to be in the war, which is better than being on the outside. This place is going to be isolated – no boat and only a sea-plane now and again – and everything will be very curtailed. Anyway, from the start of this war it has been a question of the complete re-adjustment of our lives. I think it is wise of them to play at war in Washington – especially with *you* as air-raid warden! . . . I can't believe however that the East Coast is apt to be attacked. The Russian news is good and the Germans seem to be running there as well as in Africa. Xmas will be dull and sad. I have 2 children's parties – Xmas eve Nassuvians and Xmas day English evacuees.[49]

On 23 December 1941, Sir Alec Hardinge, the King's Private Secretary, wrote:

> I enclose herewith a telegram for the Prime Minister. I shall be much obliged if you will send it in cipher so that it reaches him on Christmas morning:
>
> The Prime Minister
> Private and Personal
>
> The Queen and I send our warmest Christmas wishes to the President and Mrs. Roosevelt as well as to yourself and the members of your delegation.
>
> You, and the vital work in which you are all engaged, are much in my thoughts and I pray that the success of your conversations may bring us nearer to happiness in the New Year.
>
> George R. I.
>
> 25th December 1941[50]

[48] Michael Bloch, *The Duke of Windsor's War*, London: Weidenfeld & Nicolson, 1982, p. 364.
[49] Ibid., p. 226.
[50] Royal Archives: PS/PSO/GVI/C/152/20 and PS/PSO/GVI/C/152/21.

On 29 November 1943 the Duchess of Windsor wrote from Government House, Nassau, to Major John F. Tolle, Quartermaster Corps, who was based in Miami and was responsible for supplies in the Bahamas:

> Regarding the Christmas arrangements, we have decided to have an 'At Home' instead of the seated dinner which we felt we could not undertake this year due to the increase in the number of troops here. We will give sandwiches, snacks etc. and I am writing to ask you if I could have six turkeys and six hams, enough candy, nuts and raisins for 1,000 people, also one hoop of cheese. I would be grateful if you have any other suggestions for this party, while will be from 5:00 to 7:30 p.m. and will be in the form of a buffet.[51]

Although the Governorship was a five-year appointment, it actually ended on 30 April 1945, the day that Hitler committed suicide. The Windsors sailed from Nassau three days later.

Christmas Pantomime, Windsor Castle, 1942

Sleeping Beauty, the second of a series of Windsor Castle Christmas pantomimes, was written and produced by H. I. Tannar, Headmaster of the Royal School at Windsor. It took place on 12 December 1942 in the Waterloo Chamber and was observed closely by Charles Fulford:

> My seat was next to the centre aisle up which Their Majesties passed to their seats in the middle of the front row; & as I made my bow the Queen smiled & said 'Good afternoon, Mr. Fulford'. The Pantomime, the 'Sleeping Beauty', was first class, beautiful scenery, & dresses & very amusing. The Princesses took part in all the principal dances, & their dancing alone is worth all the money, they are so graceful.
>
> Princess Elizabeth as the Prince [Salvador] was delightful, & in the 2nd act, dressed in white satin with a white wig, was quite lovely. Princess Margaret as the principal fairy [Thistledown] had a rather bigger part & acts so well. They both use their hands & gestures well & their diction is admirable. There was one little scene in which the little Duke of Kent & Princess Alexandra with the most entrancing little daughter of Lord Gage

[51] Courtesy of Mrs Sophie Dupré.

> & 2 other tiny children sang Nursery rhymes, after which they came down in front & sat on stools at the feet of the King & Queen & the Princesses Helena Victoria & Marie Louise.[52]

Dinner and Dancing, Windsor Castle, 1943

In 1943, for the first time since his brief trip to France to see the British Expeditionary Force in December 1939, the King was able to visit his servicemen in the field, something that had long been on his mind. On 12 June 1943 he flew to Algiers, travelling incognito as 'General Lyon'. During the next two weeks he covered some 6,700 miles, mostly by air. On 19 June 1943, he boarded the cruiser, HMS *Aurora*, for a one-day visit to Malta, the heroic island to which he had awarded the George Cross on 15 April the previous year.

King George VI often grouped together days – or even weeks – in his diary. For the period covering 23–26 December 1943, he wrote:

> E. joined me in London & we gave the servants their Xmas presents. We went to Windsor for tea. Friday we were busy with Xmas cards & more present giving in the afternoon . . . Let's hope next Xmas will see the end of the War. The P.M. is better & hopes to go to Marrakesh to convalesce on Sunday. He has announced the appointments of Alex, C in C, Allied Armies in Italy, of Monty, C in C, British Group of Armies for 'Overlord'. F.D.R. announced Eisenhower's appt as Supreme Allied Com^{dr} for 'Overlord'. Jumbo Wilson succeeds Eisenhower in the Med^{n}. Spaatz is relieving Eaker in the U.S. Air Force here, which is a pity, as Eaker has done very well. Tito has declared against the Monarchy in Yugoslavia & has disowned the Yugoslav govt in Cairo.'[53]

In his diary, Tommy Lascelles described Christmas at Windsor Castle:

> Sunday 26 December – Carols in St. George's. They did some of the old familiars – 'Wenceslas' and 'The First Noel', as well as the incomparable 'In dulce jubilo' and 'The Holly and the Ivy' – which last is the most beautiful of the lot. Dinner at the Castle; Caroline on one side of the King, with whom she seemed to hit it off well enough. Philip of Greece and

[52] Diary of C. H. Fulford Esq. – courtesy of Francis Fulford, Esq.
[53] Royal Archives: GVI/PRIV/DIARY/1943.

> young Milford Haven also there. After dinner and some charades, they rolled back the carpet in the crimson drawing-room, turned on the gramophone and frisked and capered away till near 1 a.m. The King was wearing his tuxedo made of Inverness tartan, which is a source of much pleasure to him.[54]

Thirteen-year-old Princess Margaret had a rather different perspective: 'Philip came!' she wrote. The two young guests – Prince Philip and David, 3rd Marquess of Milford Haven – 'went mad and we danced and danced . . . the best night of all.'[55] Princess Elizabeth wrote to Crawfie, 'we had a very gay time with a film, dinner parties, and dancing to the gramophone'.[56] David Milford Haven was best man at the marriage of Princess Elizabeth and Prince Philip on 20 November 1947.

In her biography of Queen Elizabeth II, Sarah Bradford wrote: 'Philip had been at Windsor for Christmas 1943, when he was in the audience for the Christmas pantomime, *Aladdin*, with Princess Elizabeth in the title role, wearing the classic "principal boy" costume of jacket, revealing stockinged legs, and with Princess Margaret as her beloved Roxanna.'[57]

Charles Fulford wrote:

> Princess Margaret & 2 other girls sang 'Three little maids' from the 'Mikado' quite up to Savoy style. There were several topical allusions directed against the Master of the Household, Privy Purse, & the Crown Equerry, & much badinage at the expense of Kelly's dilatoriness in painting the State portraits. One tiny boy came on clad only in an inadequate leopard skin, which slipped off as the curtain fell & he appeared with an entirely undraped posterior presented to the King who was nearly reduced to hysterics.
>
> There was a very impressive finale in which the Princesses recited an epilogue, hoping that in the coming year we should be able to welcome home all the forces overseas. The King stopped as he came out with the Duchess of Kent (the Queen having a slight cold was not present) & asked me if I could hear all right. "Yes, Sir, very well indeed; it was a very fine show," at which he said "Yes, better than last year, don't you think?"

54 Hart-Davis, *King's Counsellor: Abdication and War: The Diaries of Sir Alan Lascelles*, p. 189. When created Duke of York in 1920, Prince Albert was also created Earl of Inverness.

55 Sarah Bradford, *Elizabeth: A Biography of Her Majesty the Queen*, London: Heinemann, 1996, p. 103.

56 Sarah Bradford, *Queen Elizabeth II: Her Life in our Times*, London: Viking, 2011, p. 52.

57 Ibid.

> Princess Alexandra had a small part & having done her bit came & sat at her mother's feet.[58]

The New Year period was once again spent at Appleton House, as the King recorded in his diary: 'We had two very good days shooting at Commodore & Anmer, where we got 1200 pheasants. These are my best days here & the weather was fine & cold . . . The P.M. is definitely of the opinion that any date in May is permissible for 'Overlord' & it could take place in the first week of June which is the right moon period for it.'[59] Operation Overlord, the Allied invasion of Normandy, took place in June, although adverse weather conditions forced a twenty-four-hour delay from 5 to 6 June 1944.

From 13 to 16 January 1944, General Sir Alan Brooke, Chief of the Imperial General Staff, was invited to stay with the Royal Family in Norfolk:

> We found however Sandringham empty, as the King is using a smaller house close by which the late King had given the Queen of Norway. At the gate we were stopped by a policeman who after examining our identities turned on a series of little magic blue lights on either side of the avenue up to the house. On arrival there I was met by Piers Legh [Equerry to the King], who took me round to the drawing room. There I found the Queen alone with the two princesses. She said she had some tea for me, which she rang for and then poured out for me. The older of the two princesses also came along to assist in entertaining me, whilst the younger one remained on the sofa reading *Punches* and emitting ripples of giggles and laughter at the jokes.
>
> The King came in a little later and also sat at the small table whilst I drank my tea. After tea the King asked me to come to his study and I had about an hour with him, discussing the war, various appointments, the Prime Minister, the new medals etc. In every subject he displays the greatest interest and is evidently taking the greatest trouble to keep himself abreast of everything.[60]

[58] Diary of C. H. Fulford, Esq. – op. cit.

[59] Royal Archives: GVI/PRIV/DIARY/1943.

[60] Alex Danchev and Daniel Todman, eds., *War Diaries 1939–45: Field Marshal Lord Alanbrooke*, London: Weidenfeld & Nicolson, 2001, pp. 511–12.

Christmas Pantomime, Windsor Castle, 1944

On 16 June 1944, only ten days after the start of Operation Overlord, the King spent a very busy day in the Normandy beachhead, having boarded the cruiser, HMS *Arethusa*, in Portsmouth. Conscious that 'the troops rather feared that their campaign had been put in the shade by the Press ever since the landing in Normandy', King George VI visited his armies in Italy from 23 July to 3 August 1944. On 26 July, while the King was in Italy, the Queen wrote to Queen Mary that, 'he feels so much not being more in the fighting-line'. Between 11 and 16 October 1944 he was able to visit 21st Army Group in the Low Countries, as a guest of General Sir Bernard Montgomery, later Field Marshal 1st Viscount Montgomery of Alamein. Much to his regret, the King was never able to visit his servicemen and servicewomen in the Far East.

Sarah Bradford wrote:

> at Christmas there was always a pantomime in which the Princesses took part, scripted by a local schoolmaster with a supporting cast of local schoolchildren. Sometimes even the Guardsmen appeared on stage with the King directing operations. Pantomime posters were put up in the empty frames from which the ancestral portraits had been removed for safe-keeping with ludicrous effects: Mother Goose appearing in a vast heavy gilt frame labelled Henrietta Maria, or Dick Whittington and his cat as Charles I. A friend and contemporary of [Princess] Elizabeth's who lived near the Castle described life there as having 'a happy family atmosphere'; contrasting it with her own family relationships which were difficult, she said, 'it was really what a family should be . . . they were very, very, devoted'.[61]

The pantomime for Christmas 1944, the last of the Second World War, was *Old Mother Red Riding Boots*, which implies that it was a bold mixture of all the best bits of all the best pantomimes. The programme was devised by the two Princesses – then aged eighteen and fourteen – with the assistance of Herbert Tannar. Princess Elizabeth took the part of Lady Christina Sherwood, while Princess Margaret appeared as The Honourable Lucinda Fairfax. The production, which took place in the Waterloo Chamber, also benefited from scenery designed by the Academy Award-winning art

[61] Bradford, *Elizabeth: A Biography of Her Majesty the Queen*, p. 100.

director, Vincent Korda; from the participation of the Salon Orchestra of the Royal Horse Guards (The Blues), under the direction of Captain J. A. Thornburrow; and from the involvement of sound technicians from the BBC. The two Princesses – and the Chorus – sang 'Swinging on a Star', which had won the 'Best Original Song' Oscar that year for the film *Going My Way*.

In the Royal Archives there is a file that details the tremendous amount of work involved in staging *Old Mother Red Riding Boots*, one of the aims of which was to raise money for charity.[62] Responsibility for the production rested with Stanley Williams, Superintendent of the Castle, who wrote to Claude Whatham on 15 November 1940: 'After commissioning you to design the scenery for the Princesses Pantomime I have now had an offer from Sir Alexander Korda, of Metro-Goulwyn-Mayer [sic], to lend us his Chief Designer. In the circumstances, would you mind very much standing down for this gentleman, who, I understand, proposes to do a more elaborate scheme. At the same time, I should be very grateful if you and your friend would assist us with these designs.'[63]

The Queen could scarcely control her enthusiasm during the rehearsals in a letter of 18 December to her close friend, Sir Osbert Sitwell: 'Windsor is ringing with words like lights, cut it, grease paint, Mother Hubbard, finale, opening chorus, etc.'[64] The production took place on four consecutive nights – 20–23 December 1944 – and the first night, for which tickets cost just one shilling, was reserved for employees of the Royal Household and their families. Tickets on the following three nights were sold at three different prices: 2/6, 5s and 7/6. Quite apart from the participants listed above, it would appear that little expense was spared in ensuring that the players looked wonderful, even during wartime. L. & H. Nathan Ltd, Court Costumiers & Theatrical Dress Makers, of 12 Panton Street, Haymarket, SW1, provided costumes and accessories, including Pompadour dresses for the Princesses and numerous other items ranging from a donkey costume to wigs and masks, at a total cost of £46 18s 6d.

The itemised expenses for *Old Mother Red Riding Boots* were as follows:

[62] Royal Archives: MRH/SUPTWC/CSP.

[63] Ibid.

[64] Queen Elizabeth to Sir Osbert Sitwell, 18 December 1944 – Sitwell Papers – quoted in Shawcross, *Queen Elizabeth the Queen Mother*, p. 589.

Debtor	Service provided	Amount
Strand Electric and Engineering Co.	Lighting and electrical services	£17 7s 2d
L. & H. Nathan	Hire of costumes	£46 18s 6d
Oxley & Son	Printing of programmes and tickets	£13 4s 10d
Winsor & Newton Ltd	Paint for scenery and wall decorations	£6 6s 10d
Albert Arnold Ltd	Repairs to musical instrument (double bass)	£18 18s 0d
Herbert Tannar	Music and private expenses	£5 15s 5d
Captain J. A. Thornburrow	Travelling expenses for orchestra	£7 4s 0d
Mr. Claude Whatham	Travelling expenses	£2 0s 0d
Expenses	In respect of entertaining Mr. V. Korda and his staff &c.	£10 1s 3d
Cash balance to Wool Fund		£303 19s 0d
Total		£431 15s 0d

Against these expenses must be offset ticket sales:

20 December – £12 7s 0d
21 December – £107 10s 0d
22 December – £112 15s 0d
23 December – £116 5s 0d

With £71 10s 0d from the sale of programmes and donations of £11 8s 0d, the sum of £293 19s 0d was raised for the Wool Fund, which was used to buy yarn, from which were knitted garments for servicemen and women.

How was *Old Mother Red Riding Boots* received? The King was pleased and proud, but typically restrained, writing in his diary: 'We got to Windsor for lunch; the fog was less. We went to the Pantomime in which Lilibet & Margaret acted on Thurs. & Sat. Better than ever & they both did their parts very well & enjoyed them.'[65] Quite understandably, non-family members might beg to differ. Tommy Lascelles could have been Arts Critic for *The Slough and Windsor Observer*: 'Saturday 23 December – The fog cleared on Thursday, and we got down to Windsor in time for luncheon, John driving me in our car. We all went to the Princesses' pantomime. It was too long, and

[65] Royal Archives: KGVI/PRIV/DIARY/1944, quoted in Shawcross, *Queen Elizabeth the Queen Mother*, p. 589.

the funny parts were not funny, but it was redeemed by a really charming and amusing ballet, a seaside scene in the nineties – rather like a Boudin picture. Princess Elizabeth, in clothes of the period, was, as the King remarked, extraordinarily like the photographs of Queen Mary at the same age.'[66]

However, in his diary Charles Fulford wrote:

> It was a brilliant production as far as scenery & dresses went, & the whole show went with a rattle. Princess Elizabeth looked quite charming in her various costumes, this time as a lady & not a Principal Boy as in former years. She and Princess Margaret with Cyril Woods, who is a messenger in the Office of Supply, carried the whole show on their shoulders, & their singing & dancing was, as always, delightful. One of the best scenes was the Ballet, in which Princess Margaret was most enchanting dancing a solo dance clad in a Victorian costume with frilly pantaloons. The King wished me Good afternoon as they came out.'[67]

Greek Entanglements, Christmas 1944

However, there was a far more serious side to the war that year, even if it was drawing slowly to a close. On 28 December, the Queen wrote to Queen Mary:

> We had a quiet but very busy Xmas Day, with a few people to dine, and we danced a reel after dinner, which was very energetic, wasn't it? Poor old Thora is here – it is so sad to see her so tottery, but I think that the few days have done her good, also Louie who has an anxious time and really cherishes Thora in a most touching way. We are hoping to get to A for a visit on Saturday if Winston gets back, but of course Bertie will not feel able to go unless he is safely home. I do hope that some good will come of the visit to Athens, tho' one feels that occupation of a country by the Germans, leaves a terrible legacy of anarchy & cruelty & a weakening of moral forces – Indeed the Nazis are the forces of Evil. May the coming year see the end of this ghastly struggle & the return to law & order in Europe is my fervent prayer, & with every loving wish for 1945.[68]

[66] Hart-Davis, *King's Counsellor: Abdication and War: The Diaries of Sir Alan Lascelles*, pp. 279–80.
[67] Diary of C. H. Fulford, Esq., courtesy of Francis Fulford, Esq.
[68] Royal Archives: QM/PRIV/CC13/114, quoted in Shawcross, *Queen Elizabeth the Queen Mother*, p. 589.

By way of explanation of the Prime Minister's visit to Athens, Tommy Lascelles wrote in his diary on 23 December:

> The Greek skein (on the political side) is more tangled than ever; the Greeks are all sending each other contradictory telegrams verging on falsehood, and it is not altogether apparent that King George [of Greece] himself is being entirely truthful.

Just a day later, he wrote:

> John Martin told me, for my ear alone, that the Prime Minister is plotting to fly out to Athens – and worse, that he might take Eden with him. They certainly should not both go; and for Winston to go may be magnificent, but it certainly ain't war – nor would his arrival necessarily bring peace to that distracted country. They would all promise to do what he told them, and then, as soon as he had left for home, do something entirely different.
>
> Later. Winston telephoned to me at 5.35 p.m., saying that he proposed starting for Athens, with A.E. [Anthony Eden], this evening, Charles Portal [Marshal of the Royal Air Force, Chief of the Air Staff] having guaranteed them a spell of exceptionally good flying weather. He had obviously made up his mind, and, equally obviously, nothing that I or even the King could say was going to shake him (it is rare than one gets a chance of saying anything when Winston has the telephone, plus the bit, between his teeth). So there was little I could do save to promise to put the proposition, for his approval, before the King. This I did at once; he took it with sang-froid, and at once rang up Winston himself.[69]

The King wrote: 'On Sunday evening the P.M. told me he was going to fly to Athens to hold a conference of all the Greek political parties including E.A.M.–E.L.A.S. He would take Eden with him & try to find a solution to the problem. He was worried about it & asked my permission to go. He would only be there for a few days. I had to change my plans for going to Sandringham. It was very cold & foggy over Christmas.'[70] Despite these developments, the Royal Family made the most of things on Christmas Day, as Tommy Lascelles described: 'Joan, John, Caroline and I dined at the Castle; 15 couples, and they danced to the gramophone till 1 a.m.'[71]

[69] Hart-Davis, *King's Counsellor: Abdication and War: The Diaries of Sir Alan Lascelles*, pp. 279–80.
[70] Royal Archives: KGVI/PRIV/DIARY/1944.
[71] Hart-Davis, *King's Counsellor: Abdication and War: The Diaries of Sir Alan Lascelles*, p. 280.

At Peace: Christmas 1945

On 7 May 1945 King George VI wrote in his diary: 'The Press had worked everybody up that VE Day would be today as the news was already known. The P.M. wanted to announce it but Prest. Truman & Ml. Stalin want it to be announced tomorrow at 3.0 p.m. as arranged. The time fixed for Unconditional Surrender is Midnight May 8th. This came to me as a terrible anti-climax, having made my broadcast speech for record purposes with cinema photography & with no broadcast at 9.0 p.m. today!!' The next day, however, when the Royal Family finally appeared on the balcony at Buckingham Palace, was uplifting: 'We went out 8 times altogether during the afternoon and evening. We were given a great reception.'[72] The Royal Christmas card that year was a photograph of the Royal Family acknowledging the crowds from the balcony at Buckingham Palace on V.E.-Day, Tuesday May 8th 1945.

Despite the end of the war, the world's problems were far from at an end. Indeed, many unanticipated challenges had arisen as a direct result of the comprehensive defeats of both Germany and Japan, most notably the ambitions of the Soviet Union in both Europe and the Far East. The King's diary entry for Christmas week 1945 echoes his concerns: 'The Foreign Ministers' Conference in Moscow ended on the 27th . . . Atomic energy is to be controlled by a Commission of the United Nations Organisation which is to be set up. The Far East Commission is settled for Japan. The Balkan question of Roumanian & Bulgarian govts suggests a broadening of them by two more members of democratic parties. China & Korea were also discussed. Mr. Bevin has done well. Mr. Byrnes (U.S.A.) gave a lot away as usual. M. Molotov gave away nothing.'[73]

On 31 December his Private Secretary wrote: 'Thick fog all day. So ends 1945, which, as I wrote to the King today, may prove to have been the most exacting year of his whole reign. It has been a tough year for me too. But we beat the Boche.'[74] In many respects, the 'thick fog' was to last for more than forty years, until the fall of the Berlin Wall on 9 November 1989 and the collapse of the Soviet Union two years later. Thus the caution that the King expressed in his Christmas Broadcast that year was fully justified by subsequent events.

72 Wheeler-Bennett, *King George VI: His Life and Reign*, p. 625.
73 Royal Archives: GVI/PRIV/DIARY/1945.
74 Lascelles, *King's Counsellor: Abdication and War: The Diaries of Sir Alan Lascelles*, p. 377.

Christmas and Communication

The first occasion on which a British monarch made a broadcast was on 23 April 1924. King George V, introduced by his eldest son, opened the British Empire Exhibition at Wembley, before the Bishop of London, the Right Reverend Arthur Winnington-Ingram, said a prayer. This live radio broadcast was made at the initiative of John Reith (later 1st Baron Reith), Managing Director of the British Broadcasting Company Ltd (BBC) as it was then known. It was the first time that a large number of his subjects would have heard the King's voice and, as such, it was an important milestone. That evening the King wrote in his diary: 'Everything went off most successfully.'[1] In Harold Nicolson's opinion: 'His was a wonderful voice – strong, emphatic, vibrant, with undertones of sentiment, devoid of all condescension, artifice or pose. The effect was wide and deep.'[2]

King George V's Christmas Broadcasts 1932–5

Eight years later, Sir John Reith proposed another innovation: a live Christmas broadcast by the King, to his subjects around the world. On 11 December 1931, the Statute of Westminster recognised that the Dominions were sovereign countries, united by a common Head of State, thereby marking the effective legislative independence of these countries, and forming the basis for the continuing relationship between the Commonwealth and the Crown. Reith felt a Christmas broadcast would be an appropriate way to inaugurate the BBC's Empire Service, now the World Service. In his diary, King George V wrote: 'Sunday Xmas Day. Sandringham. Norfolk Fog early then the sun came out. We went to church at 11.30 & stopped for the Holy Communion. Walked for a little in the sun. At 3.35 I broadcasted a short message of 251 words to the whole empire from Francis' room.'[3]

[1] John W. Wheeler-Bennett, *King George VI: His Life and Reign*, London: Macmillan and Co., 1958, p. 207.

[2] Harold Nicolson, *King George the Fifth: His Life and Reign*, London: Constable and Co., 1952, p. 526.

[3] Royal Archives: GV/PRIV/GVD/1932.

One of his biographers wrote:

> Those '251 words' had been chosen and arranged with infinite care, and the King himself had weighed and scrutinised every one of them. The homely simplicity and kindliness of his latest addresses to the Country and Empire had been widely appreciated, and had strangely moved all who heard them since the day on which he had returned thanks to the Empire for its sympathy in his illness. He knew himself now to be regarded as the Father of the great Family of Nations which the Statute of Westminster bound only more closely together under his leadership when it severed certain less personal ties. It was as a father of a family and the Father of the larger Family of Nations that he spoke each year those Christmas messages and he chose ideas, and words to clothe them, which suited the occasion, the conditions, and the character of the man who would speak them. The very simplicity of thought and the chosen words gave them the King's authentic signature. He was a simple, natural, frank and friendly man and his favourite words were like himself.
>
> Shortly before the time fixed, he walked along the corridor to a little room which Lord Knollys had once used as an office, tucked away in a corner beside the private stairs and looking on to the front drive. This little ground-floor room, which the King himself never entered in the normal course, best satisfied the requirements of broadcasting. It was furnished simply enough as an office and the King sat before a small walnut table to deliver his message.[4]

Tom Fleming wrote: 'The King agreed to do some voice tests to choose a position for the small table which would hold the microphones in front of his favourite wicker armchair. (Just before the actual broadcast, it seems, he sat down too heavily, went through the seat of the chair, and exclaimed – with regal restraint – "God bless my soul!")'[5]

Apart from a warning about the dangers of ambient noise, such as rustling papers, 'the King was given no other lessons in the art of broadcasting. He was reminded of the light signals (flashing red to stand-by; permanent red meaning "on the air") by a little card specially printed and placed by the cue-light case. (He preferred to be cued by hand – often a tap on the

[4] John Gore, *King George V: A Personal Memoir* London: John Murray, 1941, pp. 422–3.

[5] Tom Fleming, intro., *Voices out of the Air: The Royal Christmas Broadcasts 1932–81*, London: Heinemann, 1981, p. 7.

shoulder.) He was very nervous about broadcasting, and had taken immense trouble with his choice of simple, easy language.'[6]

The words had been carefully selected with the assistance of his friend, Rudyard Kipling, and the broadcast was preceded by an hour-long programme of Christmas greetings from around the Empire and Commonwealth:

> Through one of the marvels of modern Science, I am enabled, this Christmas Day, to speak to all my peoples throughout the Empire. I take it as a good omen that Wireless should have reached its present perfection at a time when the Empire has been linked in closer union. For it offers us immense possibilities to make that union closer still. It may be that our future will lay upon us more than one stern test. Our past will have taught us to meet it unshaken. For the present, the work to which we are all equally bound is to arrive at a reasoned tranquillity within our borders; to regain prosperity without self-seeking; and to carry with us those whom the burden of past years has disheartened or overborne.
>
> My life's aim has been to serve as I might, towards those ends. Your loyalty, your confidence in me has been my abundant reward. I speak now from my home and from my heart to you all. To men and women so cut off by the snows, the desert, or the sea, that only voices out of the air can reach them; to those cut off from fuller life by blindness, sickness, or infirmity; and to those who are celebrating this day with their children and grandchildren. To all – to each – I wish a Happy Christmas. God Bless You![7]

In his diary, the King wrote: 'After tea we had the Xmas tree for the people here in the ball room & gave over 600 presents. This has been a difficult year, but God has helped us to overcome some of our troubles. The National Gov^t^ is a strong one & is backed up by the country. I am an optimist. Good bye 1932.'[8]

The King's 1932 Christmas Broadcast is estimated to have reached a worldwide audience of some 20 million people, although the Prince of Wales chose to play golf, rather than listen to his father. The microphones at Sandringham were connected through Post Office land-lines to the Control Room at Broadcasting House. From there, connection was made to BBC

[6] Ibid., p. 9.
[7] Office of His Majesty's Private Secretary, comp., *Speeches and Replies to Addresses by His Majesty King George V: May 1910–January 1936.*
[8] Royal Archives: GV/PRIV/GVD/1932.

transmitters in the Home Service, and to six short-wave transmitters at the Empire Broadcasting Station at Daventry.[9] On Christmas Day 1932, Major Alec Hardinge, the King's Assistant Private Secretary, wrote to Sir John Reith: 'The King wishes me to convey to you his congratulations on the singular success which attended the inauguration of the Empire Broadcast this afternoon. His Majesty can well imagine how complicated the organisation of such a programme must have been, and the results were, in his opinion, extraordinarily good. As regards the King's own broadcast, His Majesty has learnt from different parts of the country that it was received most distinctly, and you will doubtless, in due course, let His Majesty have reports of the reception in different parts of the Empire.'[10]

A popular event – which eventually came to define the festive season – King George V broadcast to the Empire every Christmas during the rest of his life. Despite the undoubted effect of his sonorous tones, he did not relish the task, writing in his diary on Christmas Day 1934: 'At 3.30 I broadcasted my message to the Empire, very glad when it was over.'[11]

That year's Christmas Broadcast was introduced by Walter Walton Handy, a sixty-five-year-old shepherd from Ilmington in Warwickshire. His words were pre-recorded by the BBC in the library of Ilmington Manor, owned by Spenser Flower of the brewing family. Bolstered by a pint of *Flower's*, Walton Handy, who briefly found fame as 'the Cotswold Shepherd', said:

> Where I stand used to be the old Tithe barn, my Grandad and my great-Grandad used to thresh the corn. I was born two hundred yards from here, and I a' been a Shepherd all my life and I taken many places where old Cotswold sheep. My Dad worked for ten shillings a week and brought up eleven of us and all alive and well today. I'm the only one left in the village and I've a brother in New Zeyland and if by chance he's listening to I today I wish he'd write to I, for I hadn't heard from him for many years, perhaps he might remember the old verse my Dad used to say to me:
>
> Do your best for one another,
> Make a life of pleasant ease,
> Help a worn and weary brother,
> Pulling hard against the strain.

[9] www.royal.gov.uk.
[10] Fleming, *Voices out of the Air: The Royal Christmas Broadcasts 1932–81*, p. 10.
[11] Royal Archives: GV/PRIV/GVD/1934.

> We used to have some merry Christmases in those days. Our Christmas pudding was a suet long roll in which our mother used to push the plums in, and Christmas was a great time for the old Mummers and also for the Dancers. My wife 's Dad used to play the old Tabor and pipe. I could tell ye much more of our ould Christmas customs but my time is up, so goodbye and a merry Christmas from an old Shepherd. In the name of Ilmington a Merry Christmas to you all and in the name of the Empire, God Bless our Gracious King.'[12]

Walton Handy's words were complemented by bell-ringing from the village church and by carols from the Ilmington Singers. On 16 February 1935, the *Evesham Journal and Four Shires Advertiser* reported:

> In the course of his talk which was heard by millions, Handy asked his brother, Josh, who went to New Zealand 22 years ago to write to him if he was listening. This week the answer came. Brother Josh's letter was posted at Auckland on December 30th and the writer tells of the thrill he experienced when he heard his brother Walton's voice from over 14,000 miles away. 'We had been talking about you,' says the letter, 'as we knew from the papers that Ilmington was going to broadcast in the Empire programme, and were sitting round the radio listening. When you began to speak I shouted, "That sounds like our Walt." My wife ridiculed the idea, but as you went on my surmise was correct. The reception was good and it was wonderful to hear you over 14,000 miles away after an absence of 22 years.'

The following year, King George V gave his last broadcast to the Empire, noting in his diary: 'At 3.30 I broadcasted my message to the Empire, it took 5 minutes.' Sadly, from the manner of his delivery, 'many of his listening public deduced a marked decline in his state of health'.[13] In his final broadcast, the King referred not only to the great success of his Silver Jubilee Year but also, and presciently, to the 'anxieties' that 'surround us':

> I wish you all, my dear friends, a happy Christmas. I have been deeply touched by the greetings which in the last few minutes have reached me from all parts of the Empire. Let me in response send to each of you a

[12] http://freepages.genealogy.rootsweb.ancestry.com.

[13] Wheeler-Bennett, *King George VI: His Life and Reign*, p. 264.

greeting from myself. My words will be very simple but spoken from the heart on this family festival of Christmas.

The year that is passing – the twenty-fifth since my Accession – has been to me most memorable. It called forth a spontaneous offering of loyalty – and may I say of love – which the Queen and I can never forget. How could I fail to note in all the rejoicing not merely respect for the Throne, but a warm and generous remembrance of the man himself who, may God help him, has been placed upon it.

It is this personal link between me and my people which I value more than I can say. It binds us together in all our common joys and sorrows, as when this year you showed your happiness in the marriage of my son, and your sympathy in the death of my beloved sister. I feel this link now as I speak to you. For I am thinking not so much of the Empire itself as of the individual men, women, and children who live within it, whether they are dwelling here at home or in some distant outpost of the Empire.

In Europe and many parts of the world anxieties surround us. It is good to think that our own family of peoples is at peace in itself and united in one desire to be at peace with other nations – the friend of all, the enemy of none. May the spirit of good will and mutual helpfulness grow and spread. Then it will bring not only the blessing of peace but a solution of the economic troubles that still beset us.

To those who are suffering or in distress whether in this country or any part of the Empire, I offer my deepest sympathy. But I would also give a Christmas message of hope and cheer. United by the bonds of willing service, let us prove ourselves both strong to endure and resolute to overcome.

Once again as I close I send to you all, and not the least to the children who may be listening to me, my truest Christmas wishes, and those of my dear wife, my children, and grandchildren who are with me to-day. I add a heartfelt prayer that, wherever you are, God may bless and keep you always.[14]

King George VI's Christmas Broadcasts, 1937–51

The reign of King Edward VIII lasted less than a year and did not encompass the Christmas festival. King George VI, as is now well known from

[14] Fleming, *Voices out of the Air: The Royal Christmas Broadcasts 1932–81*, pp. 17–18.

the popular 2010 film *The King's Speech*, did not relish public speaking. As his biographer wrote: 'In the peace of Sandringham, beloved of his father and himself, the King could take stock of the stupendous events which had occurred during the twelve months since his father's death. A year earlier the peoples of the British Commonwealth and Empire had listened to King George V's last Christmas broadcast, and many had judged from it of the Sovereign's impaired state of health. This Christmas there was to be no Royal broadcast. The new Monarch was not yet ready to assume that part of his father's great heritage. The happenings had been too momentous, too overwhelming, for him to address his peoples thus familiarly.'[15]

On New Year's Day, however, *The Times* printed 'The King's Message':

> SERVICE TO THE EMPIRE
>
> MUTUAL TRUST AND AFFECTION
>
> The King has issued the following New Year message 'to the Peoples of the British Empire':–
>
> On this, the first New Year's Day of my Reign, I send to all the Peoples of the Empire my warmest wishes for their welfare and happiness.
>
> In succeeding to the Throne, I follow a father who had won for himself an abiding place in the hearts of his peoples, and a brother whose brilliant qualities gave promise of another historic Reign, a Reign cut short in circumstances upon which, from their very sadness, none of us would wish to dwell.
>
> DEDICATION TO SERVICE
>
> I realize to the full the responsibilities of my noble heritage. I shoulder them with all the more confidence in the knowledge that the Queen and my mother Queen Mary are at my side. Throughout my life it will be my constant endeavour to strengthen that foundation of mutual trust and affection on which the relations between the Sovereign and the Peoples of the British Empire so happily rest. I ask your help towards the fulfilment of this purpose, and I know that I do not ask in vain.
>
> To repeat the words used by my dear father at the time of his Silver Jubilee, my wife and I dedicate ourselves for all time to your service, and

[15] Wheeler-Bennett, *King George VI: His Life and Reign*, p. 297.

> we pray that God may give us guidance and strength to follow the path that lies before us.
>
> George R.I.
> 1st January 1937

Tom Fleming wrote: 'On Christmas Day 1937, King George VI had decided that, although he had no intention of following his father's example and making it an annual occurrence, he particularly wanted to say thank-you on behalf of The Queen and himself to all his subjects at the end of a very special year, in which the nation and the Empire had taken the new Royal family to their hearts.'[16] His biographer wrote of Christmas 1938: 'There was no Christmas broadcast. With his deep dislike of the microphone, the King had no intention of continuing his father's annual custom of addressing his peoples at this season, and was only persuaded to do so later under the compulsion of public duty.'[17]

The following year, however, it was evident that Christmas broadcasts should resume. In his diary, the King makes clear his lack of enthusiasm for the task: 'We went to church in the forenoon. Gave the presents to the children, & later to the servants. I broadcast a message to the Empire at the end of the B.B.C. Round the Empire Programme. This is always an ordeal for me, & I don't begin to enjoy Christmas until after it is over.'[18]

Nevertheless, having resolved that while the war lasted, he would not wear civilian clothes, King George VI, in the uniform of an Admiral of the Fleet, sat in front of two microphones at Sandringham and addressed the Empire:[19]

> The festival which we know as Christmas is above all the festival of peace and of the home. Among all free peoples the love of peace is profound, for this alone gives security to the home. But true peace is in the hearts of men, and it is the tragedy of this time that there are powerful countries whose whole direction and policy are based on aggression and the suppression of all that we hold dear for mankind.
>
> It is this that has stirred our peoples and given them a unity unknown in any previous war. We feel in our hearts that we are fighting against

[16] Fleming, *Voices out of the Air: The Royal Broadcasts 1932–81*, p. 21.
[17] Wheeler-Bennett, *King George VI: His Life and Reign*, p. 361.
[18] Ibid., p. 429.
[19] William Shawcross, *Elizabeth: A Biography of Her Majesty the Queen*, London: Macmillan, 2009, p. 88.

wickedness, and this conviction will give us strength from day to day to persevere until victory is assured. At home we are, as it were, taking the strain for what may lie ahead of us, resolved and confident. We look with pride and thankfulness on the never-failing courage and devotion of the Royal Navy, upon which, throughout the last four months, has burst the storm of ruthless and unceasing war.

And when I speak of our Navy today, I mean all the men of our Empire, who go down to the sea in ships, the Mercantile Marine, the mine-sweepers, the trawlers and drifters, from the senior officers to the last boy who has joined up. To every one in this great Fleet I send a message of gratitude and greeting, from myself as from all my peoples. The same message I send to the gallant Air Force which, in co-operation with the Navy, is our sure shield of defence. They are daily adding laurels to those that their fathers won.

I would send a special word of greeting to the Armies of the Empire, to those who have come from afar, and in particular to the British Expeditionary Force. Their task is hard. They are waiting, and waiting is a trial of nerve and discipline. But I know that when the moment comes for action they will prove themselves worthy of the highest traditions of their great Service. And to all who are preparing themselves to serve their country, on sea or land or in the air, I send my greeting at this time. The men and women of this far-flung Empire working in their several vocations, with the one same purpose, all are members of the great Family of Nations which is prepared to sacrifice everything that freedom of spirit may be saved to the world.

Such is the spirit of the Empire; of the great Dominions, of India, of every Colony, large or small. From all alike have come offers of help, for which the Mother Country can never be sufficiently grateful. Such unity in aim and in effort has never been seen in the world before. I believe from my heart that the cause which binds together my peoples and our gallant and faithful Allies is the cause of Christian civilization. On no other basis can a true civilization be built. Let us remember this through the dark times ahead of us and when we are making the peace for which all men pray.

A new year is at hand. We cannot tell what it will bring. If it brings peace, how thankful we shall all be. If it brings continued struggle we shall remain undaunted. In the meantime I feel that we may all find a message of encouragement in the lines which, in my closing words, I would like to say to you:

> I said to the man
> who stood at the gate of the year,
> 'Give me a light that I may tread safely
> into the unknown.'
>
> And he replied,
> 'Go out into the darkness
> and put your hand into the hand of God.
> That shall be to you
> better than light
> and safer than a known way!'
>
> May that Almighty Hand guide and uphold us all.[20]

This address was to have a greater impact than any other Royal Christmas Broadcast. Not only was it perfectly attuned to the moment – the 'Phoney War' or 'Sitzkrieg' as it was ironically known; the prevailing uncertainty; the unfailing resolve; and the sense of an Empire with a common cause – but the BBC was besieged with enquiries about the poem. However, the King did not know the author's name, having quoted from the last part of a longer poem, sent to him on a Christmas card. The author – who had heard the broadcast but not immediately recognised her own words – was Minnie Louise Haskins, a Sunday school teacher and later a lecturer in Social Sciences at the London School of Economics, who had written the poem in 1908.

One result of the broadcast was the first public publication of a collection of Minnie Louise Haskins's poetry.[21] Another was that J. Arthur Rank used 'The Gate of the Year' in *The Mortal Storm*. A re-working of an earlier Rank picture called *Turn of the Tide*, the film ends with a family listening to a broadcast in which a recording of the King's Christmas Broadcast was used. Yet a third was that Queen Elizabeth had the words of the poem engraved on brass plaques, which are affixed to the gates of the King George VI Memorial Chapel at Windsor Castle, where he is buried. The Queen Mother's remains now lie there as well, while the poem was read at her State Funeral on 9 April 2002.

King George VI's diary entry for Christmas Eve 1940 ends: 'I was busy with Xmas presents & with Logue over my broadcast. But I went to bed

[20] *King George VI to his Peoples 1936–51: Selected Broadcasts and Speeches*, London: John Murray, 1952, pp. 19–21.

[21] Minnie Haskins, *The Gate of the Year*, London: Hodder & Stoughton, 1940.

early with a temperature & a chill. Such a pleasant outlook for Xmas day.'[22] Fortunately, neither the King's health nor his broadcast were quite as bad as he had feared.

Of Christmas Day, the King wrote:

> I had a fairly good night & woke up feeling better & refreshed. I had no temperature. John Weir came to see me & found nothing very wrong so I got up for church. I made my broadcast to the Empire at 3.0 p.m. I stressed the point of separation of families owing to the war. The children separated from their parents. I also stressed the fact of a new unity here at home. All classes of the people had joined together now in helping to win the war, & that this spirit of fellowship which is growing in war must continue after the war is won. I feel this so strongly. The Labour Party has joined the National Govt for the war, & it is up to the people to see that Bevin & his type don't use their power now for their own ends later. Life will not be easy after the war & we shall all have to stick together to rebuild our towns and cities & make a new start in life.[23]

These are some of the words the King spoke:

> Time and time again these last few months I have seen for myself the battered towns and cities of England and I have seen the British people facing their ordeal. I can say to them that they may be justly proud of their race and nation. On every side I have seen a new and splendid spirit of good fellowship springing up in adversity, a real desire to share burdens and resources alike. Out of all this suffering there is growing a harmony which we must carry forward into the days to come when we have endured to the end and ours is the victory. Then when Christmas Days are happy again and good will has come back to the world we must hold fast to the spirit which binds us all together now. We shall need this spirit in each of our lives as men and women, and shall need it even more among the nations of the world. We must go on thinking less of ourselves and more for one another; for so, and so only, can we hope to make the world a better place and life a worthier thing.[24]

[22] Royal Archives: KGVI/PRIV/DIARY/1940.
[23] Ibid.
[24] *King George VI to his Peoples 1936–51: Selected Broadcasts and Speeches*, London: John Murray, 1952, pp. 26–7.

Between 10 and 17 December 1940, the Duke of Windsor visited Miami and met President Roosevelt, the first of a dozen meetings that took place during the war. On New Year's Eve, the President wrote that 'it was indeed good to see you again after all these years and when an airbase is finally decided upon, you and I will have to make an 'inspection trip' to see it'. The Duke of Windsor broadcast a Christmas message to America, 'a piece which demanded some tact,' according to Michael Bloch.[25]

The Duke's message was reported in the Boxing Day edition of *The New York Times*;

> Great Britain has again become entangled in the strifes and quarrels of the Old World, where the teachings of the church and the message of Christmas have not been heeded, and where the leaders of great peoples have stirred up in the peaceful masses feelings of hatred which fundamentally they neither feel nor understand. Yet on the continent of America, with which we in the Bahamas are so closely associated, there are two peoples that for decades have lived peacefully side by side, with a frontier several thousand miles long, unguarded by a single fort or a single soldier, because they have the same comprehension of the scheme of life which has been evolved in perfect harmony by the New World. However, this is no time for retrospection, for as members of the British Commonwealth of Nations we in this colony are engaged in Britain's conflict, at the same time confident in the strength and character of our race and that their endurance and tenacity will bring this tragic war to a successful conclusion.

On 30 December 1940, *The Milwaukee Sentinel* reported the Duke of Windsor had spoken 'most sympathetically and unaffectedly without pose or pretense'.

Despite the 'ordeal' undergone by the King, there is ample evidence that his wartime Christmas Broadcasts had a tremendous impact on the morale of those serving on the front line and of those working on the home front. On Christmas Day 1941, Cyril Coates was a writer in SS *Stratheden*, sailing from Suez to Halifax via Durban. In his diary, he wrote:

> I got up this morning with a pleasant holiday-like feeling as though something quite nice and out of the ordinary was going to happen. Of course,

[25] Michael Bloch, *The Duke of Windsor's War*, London: Weidenfeld & Nicolson, 1982, pp. 174–8.

> apart from the fact of more liquor than usual flowing around the ship, it has been just exactly the same as any other day, with the usual routine duties being performed . . . I listened to the King's speech which came over at 11.20 am ship's time. A good speech – well delivered. King George the VI always seems to have difficulty in getting a speech across, but today I thought was a marked improvement.[26]

Nineteen-year-old sound engineer John Longden manned the BBC's control desk for the broadcast heard by Cyril Coates. According to his obituary in the *Daily Telegraph*, he was 'firmly told that on no account was he to speak to His Majesty. "He was very nervous and kept straightening his tie," Longden recalled. "It became increasingly difficult not to speak to him, because he kept pacing around, and eventually he asked me: 'How's it going?' I was so nervous I could only reply slowly."'[27]

On Christmas Day 1942, following the successful conclusion to the Battle of El Alamein, when church bells rang in England for the first time since the start of the war, Captain Myles Hildyard, who had just rejoined the Sherwood Rangers after a stint as Divisional Intelligence Officer, wrote to his parents: 'I am sitting on my bed waiting for the King's speech, writing on your *Old England* by Mottram. I have only looked at the pictures. They are delightful and new to me. Your parcel arrived yesterday and I put it by my bed to open in the morning.'[28]

Far away from the deserts of North Africa, Nella Last, a housewife from Barrow-in-Furness, Lancashire, was working in a canteen. The Abdication Crisis of 1936, and the revelation that the monarchy still held a tight grip on the public imagination, prompted anthropologist Tom Harrisson, poet Charles Madge, and film-maker and surrealist Humphrey Jennings to found Mass Observation, a social research group with the goal of recording 'everyday life in Britain'. Volunteer contributors were encouraged to record their lives – as well as those of their friends, neighbours and work colleagues – in exhaustive detail, by submitting regular diary entries to the offices of Mass Observation. When war broke out, Nella Last offered her services and began a diary that eventually extended to more than 2 million words.

On Friday, 25 December 1942, she wrote:

[26] Imperial War Museum Documents Collection.

[27] *Daily Telegraph*, 24 November 2011.

[28] Myles Hildyard, *It is Bliss Here: Letters Home 1939–1945*, London: Bloomsbury Publishing, 2005, p. 204.

It was a riot, and the laughter, coupled with the Christmas drinks the boys had had, seemed to set them all off. There is one 'mother's darling', who often comes in, so polite, so aloof and superior; when, after the King's speech, the National Anthem was played, he astonished us all by standing up and, in a beautiful Welsh tenor voice, singing the Red Flag. Then he sat down and promptly went to sleep! Boys surged in and out, and I said to one lot, 'Dear me, boys, you cannot have had a very good dinner to be eating again so soon,' and one of them said, 'We don't really want it, but this canteen is the only place to go, and you have to eat in a canteen, haven't you?' I said, 'Not a bit of it, it's your club – have a cup of tea and join in the fun over there.'[29]

On the night of 11/12 August 1942, Eric Newby took part in Operation Whynot, a Special Boat Service raid on the airfield at Gela, Sicily. The whole raiding party was captured. On 9 September the following year, despite a broken ankle, he took advantage of the confusion surrounding the Italian Armistice to escape from the prison hospital at Fontanellato, near Parma, assisted by Wanda Skof and her father. That Christmas he was still on the run in the Apennines with a fellow escapee:

On Christmas Day, after a great lunch, we were taken to the house of an engineer who was in charge of the hydro-electric works on the mountain and there, at three o'clock, to the accompaniment of awful whistlings and other atmospherics, we heard the laboured but sincere-sounding voice of the King speaking from Sandringham.

'Some of you may hear me in your aircraft, in the jungles of the Pacific or on the Italian Peaks,' he said. 'Wherever you may be your thoughts will be in distant places and your hearts with those you love.' And although it was almost certainly not intended for people like us, the effect of what he said was too much in conjunction with all the food we had eaten and the wine we had drunk, and the people in the room witnessed the awful spectacle, something which they are unlikely ever to see again, of two Englishmen with tears running down their cheeks. And late that evening I received a little strip of paper with only two words on it – Baci [Italian for kisses], Wanda. It was the best Christmas I had ever had.[30]

[29] Richard Broad and Suzie Fleming, eds., *Nella Last's War*, London: Profile Books, 2006, pp. 225–6.
[30] Eric Newby, *Love and War in the Apennines* London: Hodder and Stoughton, 1971, p. 216.

Just four days later, Eric Newby was recaptured and spent the rest of the war as a prisoner-of-war. After the war he returned to Italy to find Wanda. They were married at the church of Santa Croce in Florence in April 1946.

In his diary entry covering Christmas 1943, King George VI wrote: 'Saturday, Xmas Day, I did my usual broadcast. The 5th War Xmas one. It is difficult to put the same theme in a new way each year.'[31] However, the King managed it very skilfully, saying:

> Since I last spoke to you many things have changed. But the spirit of our people has not changed. As we were not downcast by defeat, we are not unduly exalted by victory. While we have bright visions of the future we have no easy dreams of the days that lie close at hand. We know that much hard working and hard fighting, and perhaps harder working and harder fighting than ever before, are necessary for victory. We shall not rest from our task until it is nobly ended. Meanwhile within these islands, we have tried to be worthy of our fathers; we have tried to carry into the dawn the steadfastness and courage vouchsafed to us when we stood alone in the darkness.[32]

The King worked extremely well with new themes. At 9 p.m. on 6 June 1944 – D-Day – he echoed the words of Field Marshal Sir Douglas Haig's Special Order of the Day, 11 April 1918: 'Four years ago, our Nation and Empire stood alone against an overwhelming enemy, with our backs to the wall.' He continued:

> Tested as never before in history, in God's providence we survived the test; the spirit of the people, resolute, dedicated, burned like a bright flame, lit surely from those Unseen Fires which nothing can quench. Now once more a supreme test has to be faced . . . At this historic moment surely not one of us is too busy, too young or too old to play a part in a nation-wide, a world-wide, vigil of prayer as the great crusade sets forth. If from every place of worship, from home and factory, from men and women of all ages and many races and occupations, our intercessions rise, then, please God, both now and in a future not remote the predictions of an ancient Psalm may be fulfilled: "The Lord will give strength unto His people: the Lord will give His people the blessing of peace."[33]

[31] Royal Archives: GVI/PRIV/DIARY/1943.

[32] *King George VI to his Peoples 1936–51: Selected Broadcasts and Speeches*, p. 36.

[33] Wheeler-Bennett, *King George VI: His Life and Reign*, p. 607.

While he may not have found the selection of subject matter easy, the King at least found that, with experience and the passage of time, the delivery of a radio broadcast came steadily more easily to him. On Christmas Day 1944, he wrote in his diary: 'We had our annual rush to get cards off, giving the servants here their presents, & the preparations of my broadcast which went well on Christmas Day. I did not have Logue with me. I knew I did not need his help.'[34] In his diary, Tommy Lascelles wrote: 'The King delivered the broadcast excellently, with only one bad pause, on the hard G in "God"; time, 7½ minutes.'[35]

That same day, during a brief lull in the Battle of the Bulge, Major Neville Wigram, 2nd Battalion, the Grenadier Guards, wrote to his father, Lord Wigram, now Keeper of the Privy Purse and Deputy Governor of Windsor Castle, as he had twice a week since childhood: 'I have just been listening to the King's excellent speech and the National Anthem has just been sung. I hope all his hopes for the future come true as soon as possible. I need not tell you where my thoughts are at this moment. I think I can picture you sitting in the drawing room at NT [Norman Tower, Windsor Castle] (your last Christmas there) and now Mummy or you are saying, "Who's going to come out for a walk?" How I wish I was with you all but we must try and make better arrangements next year!'[36]

On 21 December 1945, Tommy Lascelles wrote in his diary: 'Christmas dispersal: Their Majesties to Sandringham (first Xmas there since 1939), and I to Windsor.' Six days later he added: 'A peaceful and cheerful Xmas, the first I've had for years which has not been punctuated by telephone calls and telegrams. The King spoke well on Xmas day – eleven minutes, and no serious hitch.'[37] For his part the King wrote simply: 'We had 5 days shooting in fairly good weather. I made my Christmas broadcast on Christmas Day.'[38]

On Christmas Day 1945, King George VI said:

> For six years past I have spoken at Christmas to an Empire at war. During all those long years of sorrow and danger, of weariness and strife, you and I have been upheld by a vision of a world at peace. And now that vision has

[34] Royal Archives GVI/PRIV/DIARY/1944, quoted in Shawcross, *Queen Elizabeth the Queen Mother*, p. 589.

[35] Duff Hart-Davis, *King's Counsellor: Abdication and War: The Diaries of Sir Alan Lascelles*, London: Weidenfeld & Nicolson, 2006, p. 280.

[36] By kind permission of Lord Wigram.

[37] Hart-Davis, *King's Counsellor: Abdication and War: The Diaries of Sir Alan Lascelles*, p. 376.

[38] Royal Archives GVI/PRIV/DIARY/1945.

become a reality. By gigantic efforts and sacrifices a great work has been done, a great evil has been cast from the earth, and no peoples have done more to cast it out than you to whom I speak. With my whole heart I pray to God, by whose grace victory has been won, that this Christmas may bring to my peoples all the world over every joy they have dreamed of in the dark days that are gone.

This Christmas is a real homecoming to us all, a return to a world in which the homely and friendly things of life can again be ours. To win victory, much that was of great price has been given up, much has been ravaged or destroyed by the hand of war. But the things that have been saved are beyond price. In these homelands of the British peoples, which we have saved from destruction, we still possess the things that made life precious; and we shall find them strengthened and deepened by fires of battle. Faith in these things held us in brotherhood through all our trials and has carried us to victory. Perhaps a better understanding of that brotherhood is the most precious of all the gains that remain with us after all these hard years. Together all our peoples round the globe have met every danger and triumphed over it; and we are together still. Most of all are we together as one world-wide family, in the joy of Christmas.

I think of men and women of every race within the Empire returning from their long service to their own families, to their own homes, and to the ways of peace. I think of the children, freed from unnatural fears and a blacked-out world, celebrating this Christmas in the light and happiness of the family circle once more reunited.

There will be the vacant places of those who will never return, brave souls who gave their all to win peace for us. We remember them with pride and with unfading love, praying that a greater peace than ours may now be theirs. There are those of you, still to be numbered in millions, who are spending a Christmas far from your homes, engaged in east and west in the long and difficult task of restoring to shattered countries the means and manners of civilized life. But many anxieties have been lifted from you and from your folk at home; and the coming of peace brings you nearer to your heart's desire.

There is not yet for us the abundance of peace. We all have to make a little go a long way. But Christmas comes with its message of hope and fellowship to all men of good will, and warms our hearts to kindliness and comradeship. We cannot, on this day, forget how much is still to be done before the blessings of peace are brought to all the world. In the liberated countries millions will spend this Christmas under terribly hard conditions, with only the bare necessities of life. The nations of the world are not yet a united family. So let our sympathy for others move us to humble gratitude that God has given to our Commonwealth and Empire a wonderful spirit of unity and understanding.

To the younger of you I would say a special word. You have grown up in a world at war, in which your fine spirit of service has been devoted to a single purpose – the overthrow and destruction of our enemies. You have known the world only as a world of strife and fear. Bring now all that fine spirit to make it one of joyous adventure, a home where men and women can live in mutual trust and walk together as friends. Do not judge life by what you have seen of it in the grimness and waste of war, nor yet by the confusion of the first years of peace. Have faith in life at its best and bring to it your courage, your hopes, and your sense of humour.

For merriment is the birthright of the young. But we can all keep it in our hearts as life goes on if we hold fast by the spirit that refuses to admit defeat; by the faith that never falters; by the hope that cannot be quenched. Let us have no fear of the future, but think of it as opportunity and adventure. The same dauntless resolve, which you have shown so abundantly in the years of danger, that the power of darkness shall not prevail, must now be turned to a happier purpose, to making the light shine more brightly everywhere. The light of joy can be most surely kindled by the fireside, where most of you are listening.

Home life, as we all remember as Christians, is life at its best. There, in the trust and love of parents and children, brothers and sisters, we learn how men and nations too may live together in unity and peace. So to every one of you who are gathered now in your homes or holding the thought of home in your hearts, I say – a merry Christmas and God bless you all.[39]

During the late summer and early autumn of 1951 King George VI underwent a series of increasingly intrusive tests in order to ascertain the nature of his illness. There followed a prolonged period of convalescence. As a result, that year's Christmas Broadcast was, for the first time, recorded 'piece by piece as his strength allowed'.[40] The explanation given by Buckingham Palace was: 'The King's voice has not yet regained its normal

[39] *King George VI to his Peoples 1936–51*, pp. 55–7.
[40] Wheeler-Bennett, *King George VI: His Life and Reign*, p. 802.

strength and is still liable to be a little uncertain.'[41] In his final broadcast, the King typically thanked those who had treated him and offered him solace during a very difficult period: 'For not only by the grace of God and through the faithful skill of my doctors, surgeons and nurses have I come through my illness, but I have learned once again that it is in bad times that we value most highly the support and sympathy of our friends. From my peoples in these islands and in the British Commonwealth and Empire – as well as from many other countries – this support and sympathy has reached me, and I thank you now from my heart. I trust that you yourselves realize how greatly your prayers and good wishes have helped and are helping me in my recovery.'[42]

According to his biographer,

> February 5 [1952] was a day of perfect weather, dry and cold and sunny. King George had never been in better form. It was a 'Keeper's Day', a day of rural sport, and the King shot hares with his usual accuracy. He was as carefree and happy as those about him had ever known him to be. At the end of the day he sent a word of congratulation to each of the keepers, and that evening, with his customary precision, he planned the next day's sport. At dinner he was relaxed and contented. He retired to his room at 10.30 and was occupied with his personal affairs until about midnight, when a watchman in the garden observed him affixing the latch of his bedroom window, to which a new fastening had lately been attached. Then he went to bed and peacefully to sleep. Very early on the morning of February 6 his heart stopped beating.[43]

The same day, Queen Elizabeth wrote to Queen Mary: 'I was sent a message that his servant couldn't wake him. I flew to his room, & thought that he was in a deep sleep, he looked so peaceful – and then I realised what had happened.'[44]

[41] *The Times*, 22 December 1951.
[42] *King George VI to His Peoples 1936–51*, p. 101.
[43] Wheeler-Bennett, *King George VI: His Life and Reign*, p. 803.
[44] Queen Elizabeth to Queen Mary, 6 February 1952 – Royal Archives: QM/PRIV/CC14/44, quoted in Shawcross, *Queen Elizabeth the Queen Mother*, p. 653.

Queen Elizabeth II's Christmas Broadcasts, 1952–2011

On Christmas Day 1952, Queen Elizabeth II broadcast her first Christmas Message to the Commonwealth, from her study at Sandringham. A BBC report noted that she used the same desk and chair that both her father and grandfather had used.

Each Christmas, at this time, my beloved father broadcast a message to his people in all parts of the world. Today I am doing this to you, who are now my people. As he used to do, I am speaking to you from my own home, where I am spending Christmas with my family; and let me say at once how I hope that your children are enjoying themselves as much as mine are on a day which is especially the children's festival, kept in honour of the Child born at Bethlehem nearly two thousand years ago.

Most of you to whom I am speaking will be in your own homes, but I have a special thought for those who are serving their country in distant lands far from their families. Wherever you are, either at home or away, in snow or in sunshine, I give you my affectionate greetings, with every good wish for Christmas and the New Year.

At Christmas our thoughts are always full of our homes and our families. This is the day when members of the same family try to come together, or if separated by distance or events meet in spirit and affection by exchanging greetings. But we belong, you and I, to a far larger family. We belong, all of us, to the British Commonwealth and Empire, that immense union of nations, with their homes set in all the four corners of the earth. Like our own families, it can be a great power for good – a force which I believe can be of immeasurable benefit to all humanity.

My father, and my grandfather before him, worked all their lives to unite our peoples ever more closely, and to maintain its ideals which were so near to their hearts. I shall strive to carry on their work. Already you have given me strength to do so. For, since my accession ten months ago, your loyalty and affection have been an immense support and encouragement. I want to take this Christmas Day, my first opportunity, to thank you with all my heart.

Many grave problems and difficulties confront us all, but with a new faith in the old and splendid beliefs given us by our forefathers, and the strength to venture beyond the safeties of the past, I know we shall be worthy of our duty. Above all, we must keep alive that courageous spirit

> of adventure that is the finest quality of youth; and by youth I do not just mean those who are young in years; I mean too all those who are young in heart, no matter how old they may be. That spirit still flourishes in this old country and in all the younger countries of our Commonwealth.
>
> On this broad foundation let us set out to build a truer knowledge of ourselves and our fellow men, to work for tolerance and understanding among the nations and to use the tremendous forces of science and learning for the betterment of man's lot upon this earth. If we can do these three things with courage, with generosity and with humility, then surely we shall achieve that 'Peace on earth, Goodwill toward men' which is the eternal message of Christmas, and the desire of us all.
>
> At my Coronation next June, I shall dedicate myself anew to your service. I shall do so in the presence of a great congregation, drawn from every part of the Commonwealth and Empire, while millions outside Westminster Abbey will hear the promises and the prayers being offered up within its walls, and see much of the ancient ceremony in which Kings and Queens before me have taken part through century upon century.
>
> You will be keeping it as a holiday; but I want to ask you all, whatever your religion may be, to pray for me on that day – to pray that God may give me wisdom and strength to carry out the solemn promises I shall be making, and that I may faithfully serve Him and you, all the days of my life. May God bless and guide you all through the coming year.[45]

On Christmas Eve 1952, Queen Mary wrote in her diary: 'Lovely day. Very busy. We had the present giving after tea in the Ball Room as usual. Lovely gifts, children enchanted with presents. I stayed down till nearly 7. Rather tired.' The following day, she added, approvingly: 'Beautiful day. Got up early. Very busy with letters, etc. At 12 kind Mr. Anderson came & administered the Holy Communion to me & to Constance Gaskell in my room, just a short service. Listened to Lilibet's excellent broadcast in afternoon. First rate. Went down to tea & went to Xmas room later, stayed till about 7. The children enchanting as usual. We missed the Gloucesters & their 2 children as unfortunately Richard caught German measles a few days ago, such a pity.'[46]

[45] Office of the Private Secretary to Her Majesty Queen Elizabeth II, comp., *Speeches and Replies to Addresses by Her Majesty Queen Elizabeth II: February 1952–December 1960.*
[46] Royal Archives: QM/PRIV/QMD/1952.

Hugo Vickers wrote that:

> Queen Elizabeth stayed at Sandringham with the Queen and the immediate Royal Family. Prince Paul of Yugoslavia, who had attended the King's funeral the year before, sent her some chocolates. She wrote [on 5 January 1953]: 'The extraordinary thing is, that they are all good! I have never had a box of chocolates before which didn't have a pink flavoured with bath-salts, or nougat made with iron filings & sand, and it is so exciting to know that yours are all delicious.' Her sense of humour was returning. Christmas at Sandringham without the King had its own sadness. This was accentuated by the realisation that Queen Mary was fading fast. She only got up in the late afternoon and stayed mostly in her room.'[47]

Queen Mary died at Marlborough House on 24 March 1953, having seen her eldest granddaughter succeed to the throne, after the abdication of her eldest son and the early death of her second son.

After the Coronation, the Queen and the Duke of Edinburgh embarked on a world tour. By Christmas 1953, they had reached New Zealand and the Queen gave her Christmas Broadcast from Government House in Auckland. The day before, she gave an address to children at Auckland Domain:

> It gives me great pleasure to be here to-day, to hear your voices and to see so many happy faces. My husband and I, while we have been travelling half way round the world, have been looking forward very much to our first meeting with the children and young people of New Zealand. For we all belong to one great family. Your welcome to-day has warmed our hearts because it has reminded us that, even after this long journey, we are still at home.
>
> I am sure that you are all very proud that you are New Zealanders. You are the future citizens of your country and before many years it will be your task – and your privilege – to make your city and your country even greater than they are to-day. My husband and I thank you for your splendid welcome and we wish you a very Happy Christmas and New Year.[48]

[47] Hugo Vickers, *Elizabeth The Queen Mother*, London: Arrow Books, 2006, pp. 318–9.

[48] Office of the Private Secretary to Her Majesty Queen Elizabeth II, *Speeches and Replies to Addresses by Her Majesty Queen Elizabeth II: February 1952–December 1960*, p. 25.

In the absence of the Queen and the Duke of Edinburgh, the Queen Mother presided over Christmas at Sandringham. She wrote to the Queen on 28 December that the children had enjoyed themselves 'galloping down the passage' to see the tree and gasping at it with '"oh's" & "ah's" & isn't it BEAUTIFUL'.[49]

In a recent biography, Sarah Bradford wrote:

> The palace seemed to be opening up to the people: at Christmas 1957 the Queen made her first televised Christmas broadcast. Prince Philip wrote the final draft of her speech, which the monarch delivered with more directness than usual. Harold Nicolson wrote that the Queen came across 'with a vigour unknown in pre-Altrincham days'. She faced down her critics as 'unthinking people . . . [who] carelessly throw away ageless ideals as if they were old and outworn machinery'. She went on: 'we need the kind of courage that can withstand the corruption of the cynics so that we can show the world that we're not afraid of the future . . . In the old days the monarch led his soldiers on to the battlefield. I cannot lead you in battle, I do not give you laws or administer justice but I can do something else – I can give you my heart and my devotion to these old islands and to all the peoples of our brotherhood of nations.'
>
> The novelty of seeing the Queen performing the annual electronic ritual, instead of just hearing her, united the nation on Christmas afternoon: the 3 p.m. broadcast was seen by 16.5 million people, producing the largest amount of press cuttings since the Coronation. In private she suffered almost as much from nerves as her father had, writing to a friend that the broadcast had ruined the family Christmas.[50]

The Queen has made a Christmas Broadcast every year of her reign except for 1969. In that year the documentary programme, *Royal Family*, was televised over the holiday. In her 1983 Christmas Broadcast, the Queen said:

> In the year I was born, radio communication was barely out of its infancy; there was no television; civil aviation had hardly started and space satellites were still in the realm of science fiction. When my Grandfather visited India in 1911, it took three weeks by sea to get there. Last month I flew back from Delhi to London in a matter of hours. It took King George V three

[49] Royal Archives: QEII/PRIV/RF, quoted in Shawcross, *Queen Elizabeth the Queen Mother*, p. 690.

[50] Sarah Bradford, *Queen Elizabeth II: Her Life in our Times*, London: Viking, 2011, pp. 110–11.

> months to make the round trip. In two-thirds of that time Prince Philip and I were able to visit Jamaica, Mexico, the United States and Canada in the winter, followed by Sweden in the summer, and ending up in the autumn with Kenya, Bangladesh and finally India for the Commonwealth Heads of Government Meeting in New Delhi. Travel and communication have entered a completely new dimension.

On the other hand, she was also quick to warn that 'this mastery of technology may blind us to the more fundamental needs of people. Electronics cannot create comradeship; computers cannot generate compassion; satellites cannot transmit tolerance.'[51]

The Christmas Broadcast has been pre-recorded since 1960 so that tapes could be sent round the world to Commonwealth countries, enabling transmission at locally convenient times. Another break with tradition came in 1989. The Queen delivered part of that year's Christmas broadcast from the Royal Albert Hall. The privately invited audience heard her speech before the general public. Surrounded by children from the Commonwealth waving their countries' flags, the Queen addressed the 'Joy to the World' Christmas concert on 19 December. In 2011, Queen Elizabeth II said: 'The Commonwealth is a family of 53 nations, all with a common bond, shared beliefs, mutual values and goals.' Over the years, the Queen has become so proficient in television broadcasting that, as Andrew Marr explained on 20 February 2012 in the documentary *The Diamond Queen*, she is known as 'one-take Windsor'.

[51] www.royal.gov.uk.

Bibliography

Principal Manuscript Sources

The Royal Archives: *The Diary of Queen Charlotte* – by kind permission of Her Majesty Queen Elizabeth II.

The Royal Archives: *Queen Victoria's Journal* (QVJ) – by kind permission of Her Majesty Queen Elizabeth II.

The Royal Archives: *The Diary of Prince George of Wales, later The Duke of York, later The Prince of Wales, subsequently King George V* (GV/PRIV/GVD) – by kind permission of Her Majesty Queen Elizabeth II.

The Royal Archives: *The Diary of Queen Mary* (QM/PRIV/QMD) – by kind permission of Her Majesty Queen Elizabeth II.

The Royal Archives: *The Diary of Prince Edward of York, later The Prince of Wales, subsequently King Edward VIII* (EDW/PRIV/DIARY) – by kind permission of Her Majesty Queen Elizabeth II.

The Royal Archives: *The Diary of Prince Albert of York, later The Duke of York, subsequently King George VI* (GVI/PRIV/DIARY) – by kind permission of Her Majesty Queen Elizabeth II.

The Diary of Lady Waterpark, Lady-in-Waiting to Queen Victoria 1865–91, British Library ref. Add. 60750.

The Private Journal of Lady Wigram 1926–27 – courtesy of Lord Wigram.

The Diary of C. H. Fulford Esq. 1935–1945 – courtesy of Francis Fulford Esq.

Published Sources

Abbey, Charles J. and Overton, John H., *The English Church in the Eighteenth Century*, London: Longmans, Green and Co., 1878.

Allinson, Alfred Richard, ed., *The War Diary of the Emperor Frederick III 1870–1871*, London: Stanley Paul & Co., 1927.

Anon., *Anecdotes, Personal Traits, and Characteristic Sketches of Victoria the First, from her Birth, and Brought down to the Period of Her Majesty's Marriage with His Royal Highness Prince Albert of Saxe-Coburg*, London: William Bennett, 1840.

Ashton, John, *A righte Merrie Christmasse!!!*, London: Leadenhall Press Ltd., 1894.

Aspinall, Arthur, ed., *The Letters of George IV, 1812–1830*, 3 vols., Cambridge: Cambridge University Press, 1938.

Aspinall, Arthur, ed., *Letters of the Princess Charlotte 1811–17*, London: Home and Van Thal, 1949.

Aspinall, Arthur, ed., *The Correspondence of George, Prince of Wales, 1770–1812*, 8 vols., London: Cassell & Co., 1963–71.

Beatrice, HRH Princess, *In Napoleonic Days: Extracts from the Private Diary of Augusta, Duchess of Saxe-Coburg-Saalfeld, Queen Victoria's Maternal Grandmother 1806–21*, London: John Murray, 1941.

Benson, Arthur Christopher and Brett, Reginald Baliol, eds., *The Letters of Queen Victoria: A Selection from Her Majesty's Correspondence between the Years 1837 and 1861*, 3 vols., London: John Murray, 1908 (LQV I).

Bloch, Michael, *The Duke of Windsor's War*, London: Weidenfeld & Nicolson, 1982.

Bloch, Michael, ed., *Wallis & Edward: Letters 1931–37*, London: Weidenfeld & Nicolson, 1986.

Bloomfield, Georgiana, *Reminiscences of Court and Diplomatic Life*, Vol. I, London: Kegan Paul, Trench, 1883.

Bradford, Sarah, *Elizabeth: A Biography of Her Majesty the Queen*, London: Heinemann, 1996.

Bradford, Sarah, *Queen Elizabeth II: Her Life in our Times*, London: Viking, 2011.

Bray, William, ed., *The Diary of John Evelyn*, New York and London: M. Walter Dunne, New York & London, 1901.

Brett, Reginald Baliol, ed., *The Girlhood of Queen Victoria: A Selection from Her Majesty's Diaries between the Years 1832 and 1840*, London: John Murray, 1912 (GQV).

Broughton, Mrs Vernon Delves, ed., *Court and Private Life in the Time of Queen Charlotte: Being the Journals of Mrs. Papendiek, Assistant Keeper of the Wardrobe and Reader to Her Majesty*, 2 vols., London: Richard Bentley & Son, 1887.

Brown, Michèle, *Royal Christmas Book*, London: Windward, 1985.

Buckle, George Earle, ed., *The Letters of Queen Victoria, Second Series: A Selection from Her Majesty's Correspondence between the Years 1862 and 1885*, 3 vols., London: John Murray, 1926–8 (LQV II).

Buckle, George Earle, ed., *The Letters of Queen Victoria, Third Series: A Selection from Her Majesty's Correspondence between the Years 1886 and 1901*, 3 vols., London: John Murray, 1930–2 (LQV III).

Cathcart, Helen, *Sandringham: The Story of a Royal Home*, London: W. H. Allen, 1964.

Chambers, James, *Charlotte and Leopold*, London: Old Street Publishing, 2007.

Champneys, Basil, ed., *Memoirs and Correspondence of Coventry Patmore*, London: George Bell & Sons, 1900.

Chibnall, Marjorie, ed. and trans., *The Ecclesiastical History of Orderic Vitalis*, Vol. II, Oxford: Clarendon Press, 1968.

Churchill, Winston, *Their Finest Hour*, London: Cassell & Co., 1949.

Cooke, Clement Kinloch, *A Memoir of Her Royal Highness Princess Mary Adelaide, Duchess of Teck*, London: John Murray, 1900.

Craig, Elizabeth, *Court Favourites*, London: Andre Deutsch, 1953.

Crawford, Marion, *The Little Princesses*, London: Cassell & Co., 1950.

Danchev, Alex and Todman, Daniel, eds., *War Diaries 1939–45: Field Marshal Lord Alanbrooke*, London: Weidenfeld & Nicolson, 2001.

Dasent, Arthur Irwin, *John Thadeus Delane Editor of 'The Times'*, Vol. II, London: John Murray, 1908.

Deloney, Thomas, *Strange Histories or, Songs and Sonnets, of Kinges, Princes, Dukes, Lords, Ladyes, Knights, and Gentlemen*, London: R. B. for William Barley, 1612.

Dennison, Matthew, *The Last Princess: The Devoted Life of Queen Victoria's Youngest Daughter*, London: Weidenfeld & Nicolson, 2007.

Douglas, Hugh, comp., *A Right Royal Christmas: An Anthology*, Stroud: Sutton, 2001.

Erskine, Beatrice, ed., *Twenty Years at Court: From the Correspondence of the Hon. Eleanor Stanley*, London: Nisbet & Co., 1916.

Fleming, Tom, intro., *Voices out of the Air: The Royal Christmas Broadcasts 1932–1981*, London: Heinemann, 1981.

Fulford, Roger, ed., *Dearest Child: Private Correspondence of Queen Victoria and the Crown Princess of Prussia 1858–1861*, London: Evans Brothers, 1964.

Fulford, Roger, ed., *Dearest Mama: Letters between Queen Victoria and the Crown Princess of Prussia 1861–1864*, London: Evans Brothers, 1968.

Fulford, Roger, ed., *Your Dear Letter: Private Correspondence of Queen Victoria and the Crown Princess of Prussia 1865–1871*, London: Evans Brothers, 1971.

Fulford, Roger, ed., *Darling Child: Private Correspondence of Queen Victoria and the Crown Princess of Prussia 1871–1878*, London: Evans Brothers, 1976.

Fulford, Roger, ed., *Beloved Mama: Private Correspondence of Queen Victoria and the German Crown Princess of Prussia 1878–1885*, London: Evans Brothers, 1981.

King George VI to his Peoples 1936–51: Selected Broadcasts and Speeches, London: John Murray, 1952.

Gore, John Francis, *King George V: A Personal Memoir*, London: John Murray, 1941.

Hart-Davis, Duff, ed., *In Royal Service: The Letters and Journals of Sir Alan Lascelles 1920–1936*, London: Hamish Hamilton, 1989.

Hart-Davis, Duff, ed., *King's Counsellor: Abdication and War: The Diaries of Sir Alan Lascelles*, London: Weidenfeld & Nicolson, 2006.

Haskins, Minnie, *The Gate of the Year*, London: Hodder & Stoughton, 1940.

Hastings, Max, *All Hell Let Loose*, London: HarperPress, 2011.

Hildyard, Myles, *It is Bliss Here: Letters Home 1939–1945*, London: Bloomsbury, 2005.

Hood, Dina Wells, *Working for the Windsors*, London: Allan Wingate, 1957.

Hore, A. H., *The Church in England from William III to Victoria*, Oxford: Parker and Co., 1886.

Jaffé, Deborah, *Victoria: Her Life, her People, her Empire*, London: Carlton, 2000.

Lacey, Robert, *Majesty*, London: Hutchinson, 1977.

Lambton, Lucinda, *The Queen's Dolls' House*, London: Royal Collection Enterprises, 2010.

Latham, Robert, ed., *The Shorter Pepys*, Berkeley: University of California Press, 1985.

Lee, Sidney, *King Edward VII: A Biography: From Birth to Accession*, London: Macmillan & Co., 1925.

Lee, Sidney, *King Edward VII: A Biography: The Reign*, London: Macmillan & Co., 1927.

Longford, Elizabeth, *Victoria R.I.*, London: Weidenfeld & Nicolson, 1964.

Lorne, Marquis of (now His Grace The Duke of Argyll), *VRI: Queen Victoria: Her Life and Empire*, London: Harper & Brothers, 1901.

Ludwig, Emil, *Kaiser Wilhelm II*, trans. E. C. Mayne, London and New York: G. P. Putnam's Sons, 1926.

Lutyens, Mary, ed., *Lady Lytton's Court Diary, 1895–1899*, London: Rupert Hart-Davis, 1961.

Marie Louise, HH Princess, *My Memories of Six Reigns*, London: Evans Brothers, 1956.

Martin, Theodore, *The Life of His Royal Highness the Prince Consort*, 5 vols., London: Smith, Elder, 1875–80.

Mallet, Victor, ed., *Life with Queen Victoria: Marie Mallet's Letters from Court 1887–1901*, London: John Murray, 1968.

McIntyre, Ian, *The Expense of Glory: A Life of John Reith*, London: HarperCollins, 1993.

Müller, Frank Lorenz, *Our Fritz: Emperor Frederick III and the Political Culture of Imperial Germany*, Cambridge, Mass. and London: Harvard University Press, 2011.

Murray, Amelia, *Recollections from 1803–37: With a Conclusion in 1868*, London: Longmans, Green and Co., 1868.

Newby, Eric, *Love and War in the Apennines*, London: Hodder and Stoughton, 1971.

Nicolson, Harold, *King George the Fifth: His Life and Reign*, London: Constable and Co., 1952.

Paxman, Jeremy, *The Victorians*, London: BBC Books, 2009.

Percy, Algernon, *A Bearskin's Crimea: Colonel Henry Percy VC and his Brother Officers*, Barnsley: Leo Cooper, 2005.

Plowden, Alison, *The Young Victoria*, London: Weidenfeld & Nicolson, 1981.

Ponsonby, Arthur, *Henry Ponsonby, Queen Victoria's Private Secretary: His Life from his Letters*, London: Macmillan & Co., 1942.

Ponsonby, Frederick, ed., *Letters of the Empress Frederick*, London: Macmillan & Co., 1930.

Ponsonby, Frederick, *Recollections of Three Reigns*, London: Eyre & Spottiswoode, 1957.

Pope-Hennessy, James, *London Fabric*, London: B. T. Batsford, 1939.

Pope-Hennessy, James, *Queen Mary, 1867–1953*, London: George Allen and Unwin, 1959.

Pope-Hennessy, James, ed., *Queen Victoria at Windsor and Balmoral: Letters from her Grand-daughter Princess Victoria of Prussia, June 1889*, London: George Allen and Unwin, 1959.

Ramm, Agatha, ed., *Beloved and Darling Child: Last Letters between Queen Victoria and her Eldest Daughter 1886–1901*, Stroud: Sutton, 1990.

Reeve, Henry, ed., *The Greville Memoirs: A Journal of the Reign of Queen Victoria from 1837 to 1852*, Vol. II, London: Longmans, Green & Co., 1885.

Russell, William Howard, *The Prince of Wales' Tour: A Diary in India*, London: Sampson Low, Marston, Searle & Rivington, 1877.

Rutherford, Jessica, *A Prince's Passion: The Life of the Royal Pavilion*, Brighton: The Royal Pavilion, 2003.

Sandys, William, *Christmas-tide, its History, Festivities and Carols, with their Music*, London: John Russell Smith, 1852.

Scott, Percy, *Fifty Years in the Royal Navy*, London: John Murray, 1919.

Sebba, Anne, *That Woman: The Life of Wallis Simpson, Duchess of Windsor*, London: Weidenfeld & Nicolson, 2011.

Shawcross, William, *Queen Elizabeth the Queen Mother*, London: Macmillan, 2009.

Shew, Betty Spencer, *Queen Elizabeth the Queen Mother*, London: Hodder & Stoughton, 1954.

Sitwell, Osbert, *Queen Mary and Others*, London: Michael Joseph, 1974.

Strachey, Lytton, *Queen Victoria*, London: Chatto & Windus, 1921.

Thomson, Katherine, *Memoirs of the Court of Henry the Eighth*, 2 vols., London: Longman & Co., 1826.

Turner, Michael, *Osborne House*, London: English Heritage, 1989.

Vickers, Hugo, *Elizabeth The Queen Mother*, London: Arrow Books, 2006.

Victoria, HM Queen, *Leaves from the Journal of our Life in the Highlands from 1848 to 1861*, ed. Arthur Helps, London: Smith, Elder, 1868.

Warner, Marina, *Queen Victoria's Sketchbook*, London: Macmillan, 1979.

Watkins, John, *Memoirs of Her Most Excellent Majesty Sophia-Charlotte, Queen of Great Britain, from Authentic Documents*, London: Henry Colburn, London, 1819.

Wheeler-Bennett, John W., *King George VI: His Life and Reign*, London: Macmillan & Co., 1958.

Wigram, George Neville Clive, 2nd Baron, *Some Memoirs of my Early Life*, privately published, 2002.

William, Crown Prince of Germany, *My War Experiences*, London: Hurst & Blackett, 1922.

Wilson, Philip Whitwell, *The Greville Diary*, 2 vols., London: Heinemann, 1927.

Windsor, HRH Duke of, *A King's Story: The Memoirs of H.R.H. the Duke of Windsor K.G.*, London: Cassell & Co., 1951.

Wyndham, Maud Mary, ed., *Correspondence of Sarah Spencer, Lady Lyttelton, 1787–1870*, London: John Murray, 1912.

Zeepvat, Charlotte, *Queen Victoria's Youngest Son: The Untold Story of Prince Leopold*, Gloucestershire: Sutton Publishing Limited, 2005.

Ziegler, Philip, *King Edward VIII*, London: Collins, 1990.

Index

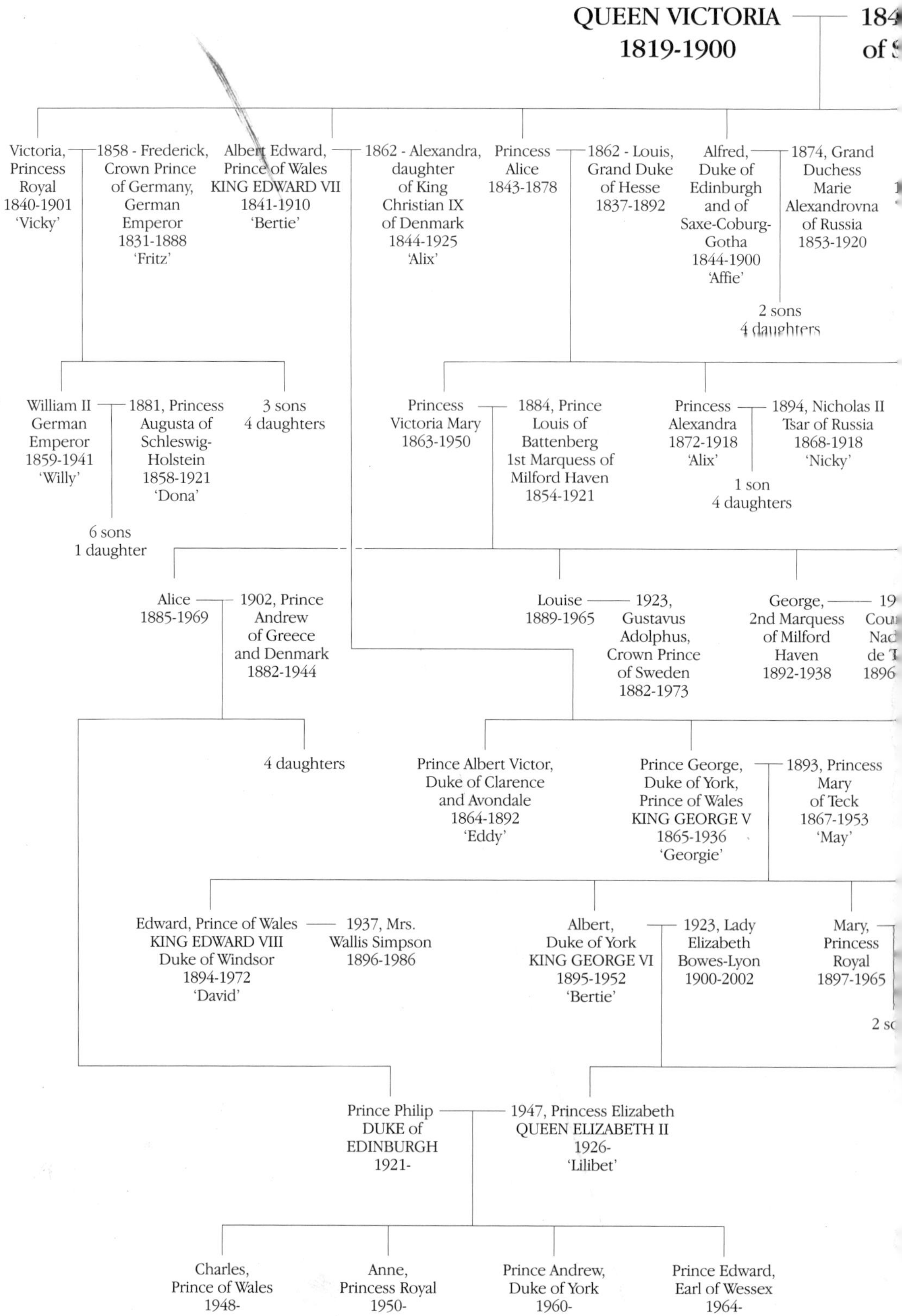
QUEEN VICTORIA 1819-1900
184
of S
Victoria, Princess Royal 1840-1901 'Vicky'
1858 - Frederick, Crown Prince of Germany, German Emperor 1831-1888 'Fritz'
Albert Edward, Prince of Wales KING EDWARD VII 1841-1910 'Bertie'
1862 - Alexandra, daughter of King Christian IX of Denmark 1844-1925 'Alix'
Princess Alice 1843-1878
1862 - Louis, Grand Duke of Hesse 1837-1892
Alfred, Duke of Edinburgh and of Saxe-Coburg-Gotha 1844-1900 'Affie'
1874, Grand Duchess Marie Alexandrovna of Russia 1853-1920
2 sons 4 daughters
William II German Emperor 1859-1941 'Willy'
1881, Princess Augusta of Schleswig-Holstein 1858-1921 'Dona'
3 sons 4 daughters
6 sons 1 daughter
Princess Victoria Mary 1863-1950
1884, Prince Louis of Battenberg 1st Marquess of Milford Haven 1854-1921
Princess Alexandra 1872-1918 'Alix'
1894, Nicholas II Tsar of Russia 1868-1918 'Nicky'
1 son 4 daughters
Alice 1885-1969
1902, Prince Andrew of Greece and Denmark 1882-1944
Louise 1889-1965
1923, Gustavus Adolphus, Crown Prince of Sweden 1882-1973
George, 2nd Marquess of Milford Haven 1892-1938
4 daughters
Prince Albert Victor, Duke of Clarence and Avondale 1864-1892 'Eddy'
Prince George, Duke of York, Prince of Wales KING GEORGE V 1865-1936 'Georgie'
1893, Princess Mary of Teck 1867-1953 'May'
Edward, Prince of Wales KING EDWARD VIII Duke of Windsor 1894-1972 'David'
1937, Mrs. Wallis Simpson 1896-1986
Albert, Duke of York KING GEORGE VI 1895-1952 'Bertie'
1923, Lady Elizabeth Bowes-Lyon 1900-2002
Mary, Princess Royal 1897-1965
Prince Philip DUKE of EDINBURGH 1921-
1947, Princess Elizabeth QUEEN ELIZABETH II 1926- 'Lilibet'
Charles, Prince of Wales 1948-
Anne, Princess Royal 1950-
Prince Andrew, Duke of York 1960-
Prince Edward, Earl of Wessex 1964-